The iMac Way
Your Guide to the Digital Universe

Hans Hansen and Brad Miser

The iMac Way
Your Guide to the Digital Universe
Copyright© 2002 by Que

International Standard Book Number: 0-7897-2052-3

Library of Congress Catalog Card Number: 99-65690

Printed in the United States of America

First Printing: July 2001

04   03   02   01   4   3   2   1

Trademarks

Warning and Disclaimer

II

Acquisitions Editors
Karen Whitehouse
Heather Kane

Book Packager
Justak Literary Services

Managing Editor
Thomas F. Hayes

Indexer
Sharon Hilgenberg

Technical Editor
Mario Murphy

User Reviewer
Brown Partington

Interior Designer
Katie Linder

Cover Designer
Anne Jones

Page Layout
Jay Hilgenberg
Katie Linder

Contents at a Glance

Table of Contents

Part I: Digital Audio

Contents continued

Contents continued

Contents continued

Contents continued

Part III: Digital Graphics

Contents continued

Contents continued

Part IV: Digital and Beyond

Contents continued

Contents continued

Contents continued

Contents continued

About the Authors

Hans Hansen is the author of five books on using Macintosh computers, including *Zen and the Art of Resource Editing* and *The Tao of AppleScript.* For ten years he was a contributor to the Berkeley Macintosh Users Group and editor-in-chief of the prestigious *BMUG Newsletter.* Hans is a founder and the chief technology officer of Octavo, a digital imaging company specializing in high-resolution electronic access to rare books and manuscripts for libraries and institutions around the world (www.octavo.com).

Hans enjoys writing about and playing with his multitude of Macs and other technological wonders, as well as hiking along the Pacific coast, cooking organic meals, drinking good wine and stout, driving his SAAB, and otherwise getting away from the digital universe. Hans is a photographer and digital image composer, as well as a typesetter and book designer, who lives and works in Oakland, California. If you'd like to know more about Hans, or better yet, tell him about yourself, you can visit his iMac on the Internet. Just surf on over to www.hanshansen.com, or email him at imacway@hanshansen.com.

Brad Miser has been living the Macintosh Way ever since he first glimpsed the mighty Macintosh SE (say, "that's a nice machine, but the screen is so small"). In the years since, Brad has written extensively about all things Macintosh. Brad loves to help people get the most out of their Macs, and has even been known to occasionally provide help where none is desired. He hopes that his books help people make the most of the best personal computer on earth.

When he is not "making pages," Brad also loves movies as well as any sort of gadget, which has resulted in a deep-seated fascination with digital video and a great appreciation for iMovie. By day, Brad is an engineer (who likes to write?—you must be kidding) who develops technical documentation, online help systems, and other "stuff" for Mezzia, Inc. (www.mezzia.com). He has also been a proposal specialist for Rolls-Royce, a development editor for Pearson Education, and a test officer for the U.S. Army.

In addition to *The iMac Way,* Brad has written many other Mac books including *Special Edition Using Mac OS X, The Mac OS X Guide, The Mac OS 9 Guide, The Complete Idiot's Guide to iMovie 2, The Complete Idiot's Guide to the iBook, The Complete Idiot's Guide to the iMac,* and *Using Mac OS 8.5.*

Brad would love to hear from you about your experiences with this book (the good, the bad, and the ugly). You can write to him at bradmmiser@home.com.

Acknowledgments

From Hans Hansen

I'm not alone in my love of making stuff with my iMac, nor in bringing you this book. Brad, whom I first worked with many years ago on *The Tao of AppleScript,* has written the section of chapters in this book about digital video (Chapters 5-10). Making movies and using iMovie is something to which Brad brings much excitement and a great ability to express himself in easy-to-follow prose. Brad has written many books about using the Mac, including his latest on using Mac OS X.

For this book I also owe much appreciation to its editor Marta Justak, who has pulled all the parts of it together into a cohesive and well-presented whole. And to Karen Whitehouse, who managed the delicate business of bring this book to you.

I hope you enjoy this book and find your own path through the digital universe, the iMac way.

From Brad Miser

I'd like to thank the following people on *The iMac Way* project team:

Hans Hansen, my co-author, who created the original vision for this book and who graciously allowed me to share in it. Great work, Hans!

Marta Justak of Justak Literary Services, my agent and the packager of this book, who brought me into this project and managed, developed, and produced the book from start to finish. Thanks Marta, you have done it again!

Karen Whitehouse and Heather Banner Kane, my Pearson acquisitions editors, who assembled a top-notch project team and were kind enough to include me on it. Karen and Heather, I very much appreciate your confidence in me.

Don Mayer, CEO and founder; Hapy Mayer, CFO and co-owner; and especially, Dawn D'Angelillo, VP of marketing of Small Dog Electronics for providing the hardware and software that I needed to write my part of this book. Small Dog is a great Mac-friendly retailer; check them out at www.smalldog.com or call them at 802-496-7171. Also check out the ad on the inside back cover of this book for a special discount when you buy something from Small Dog—only for readers of *The iMac Way*. Thanks to Small Dog for being an important part of this effort.

And now for a few people who weren't on the project team, but who were essential to me personally:

Amy Miser, for supporting me while I took on this project and being understanding about my need to do it; living with an author isn't always lots of fun. Amy, I promise, no more books—until the next one!

Jill, Emily, and Grace Miser, for helping me "on location" while shooting the clips for this book and providing valuable play breaks while I was pounding keys. Girls, you brought lots of smiles to my face in some stressful times.

Suresh Murthy and Scott McCorkle of Mezzia, Inc., for providing the schedule flexibility and encouragement that I needed to be able to complete my part of this book on schedule. Guys, I would never have believed that there was any place as great to work as Mezzia if I wasn't living it myself! It's amazing!

From both of us, thanks to the following:

Katie Linder, for the interior design of the book. Katie, you made this book a pleasure to look at!

Jay Hilgenberg and Katie Linder, for laying the book out. Jay and Katie, you did a great job on this book; it looks super!

Sharon Hilgenberg, for lending her wonderful indexing skills to this project. One of the most important parts of a computer book is the index; Sharon's index to this one can't be beat. Thanks!

Anne Jones, for developing the book's cover. Anne, it is too bad that you can't judge a book by its cover, because if you could, everyone would see that this book is top-notch.

Brown Partington, for reviewing the material from the user's perspective and providing meaningful comments that helped us improve the book. Nice job Brown—and keep pushing the limits of your iMac!

Tell Us What You Think!

As the reader of this book, *you* are our most important critic and commentator. We value your opinion and want to know what we're doing right, what we could do better, what areas you'd like to see us publish in, and any other words of wisdom you're willing to pass our way.

As a publisher for Que, I welcome your comments. You can fax, email, or write me directly to let me know what you did or didn't like about this book—as well as what we can do to make our books stronger.

Please note that I cannot help you with technical problems related to the topic of this book, and that due to the high volume of mail I receive, I might not be able to reply to every message.

When you write, please be sure to include this book's title and author as well as your name and phone or fax number. I will carefully review your comments and share them with the author and editors who worked on the book.

Fax: 317-581-4666

E-mail: feedback@quepublishing.com

Mail: Publisher
                Robb Linsky
                Que
                201 West 103rd Street
                Indianapolis, IN 46290 USA

Unfettered at last, a digital monk,
I pass the old analogue barrier.
Mine is a traceless virtual life.
Of those mountains, which shall be my home?

(All Zen Poems by Hans Hansen)

Introduction

Your iMac is an amazing machine. This machine can process endless streams of zeros and ones at speeds unimagined even just a couple years ago. With all this power, your iMac can convert images, sounds, and movies into binary data representations for transmission, manipulation, or storage, and then back into images, sounds, and movies. Incredible!

Your iMac is an amazing tool. With this tool you can direct the streams of zeros and ones to different places, collecting them and organizing them. You can tweak them with filters and algorithms to alter them in new and unique ways. You can even compose original data streams, using only your imagination. Astounding!

Your iMac is an amazing work of art. This work of art has been designed by human hands to perfect proportions. Every stream of zeros and ones is contained within space and time. Every component from its mouse and keyboard to its display, to its speakers, is in harmony with the demands of life, the universe, and everything. Beautiful!

So what *amazing* things will you do with your iMac? Will you let it run, unleashing the machine on your digital media? Will you use it, leveraging its potential as a digital tool to create? Will you admire it, letting its existence inspire and confound you?

Whatever you choose to do with your iMac, this book will attempt to encourage you, support you, and entertain you along the way. This is the iMac way; this is exploring the digital universe.

> ### HOW *AMAZING* IS YOUR iMAC, REALLY?
>
> Pretty darned amazing. Your iMac can run circles around most personal computers—fast, colorful, easy-to-use, audio-rich, multi-dimensional circles. The iMac isn't a dumbed-down Mac, compromised and cheap, only good for Internet Web browsing and email. The iMac is the real thing, a full Macintosh with all the trimmings; it is distinguished only by its all-in-one, consumer-friendly design. A design that has taken the computer industry by storm—in its first year, the iMac was consistently the best selling personal computer. That's pretty amazing.

What Is the Digital Universe?

If you hadn't already figured it out, this book has a theme: digital, digital, digital. Now I know that some of you out there think you know what digital is, but if you stop and think about it, you come up a bit vague. Let me take a moment to provide some background.

Digital is zeros and ones; a.k.a., false and true, off and on, not and is, black and white, evil and good, yang and yin, etc. *Digital* refers to systems that represent things. They might be Arabic numerals, little red lights, fingers on your hands or toes on your feet (digits). There might be ten of them, there might be a billion of them, there might just be two of them—there cannot be one of them—one thing can only represent one thing, not more than one thing. In the case of transistor-based technology similar to that used in your iMac, the machine uses a digital system of zeros and ones, binary numbers, to represent things. Because digital systems are inherently mathematical, with enough zeros and ones, you can represent just about anything ever devised (curious existentialistic fact that is too deep to analyze here, *see: the meaning of life, the universe, and everything*). And so today we pretty much refer to any binary media data and processing almost exclusively as "digital."

Digital technology: digital cellular phones, digital TV, digital music players, digital cameras, personal computers, hand calculators, etc.; these all use digits to represent precise and finite structures, whether they are of numbers, text, geometry, audio, or imagery. These devices are designed to reproduce and manipulate these structures in lots of cool ways. In fact, there are many hundreds of types of digital structures (digital media formats) and not all devices recognize the same digital structures, but they do all use zeros and ones.

BITS, NYBBLES, BYTES, CHAWMPS, AND GAWBLES

Beware techspeak! Just as Eskimos have over 40 different words for snow, the digerati have lots of words for different kinds of binary units. Some are more formalized than others: bit, byte, kilobyte, megabyte, gigabyte, terabyte, petabyte. Here's a quick rundown on the values of each of these:

Bit	1 or 0, the most basic unit
Nybble	4 bits (equals one hexadecimal digit)
Byte	8 bits (equals a value of 0 to 255)
Chawmp	16 bits (in a 32-bit architecture)
Gawble	32 bits (in a 32-bit architecture)
K	short for kilobyte (KB), equals 1,024 bytes, approximately one thousand bytes equals 1,024 characters of text
meg	short for megabyte (MB), equals 1,048,576 bytes, approximately one million bytes, about the length of this book's text
gig	short for gigabyte (GB), equals 1,073,741,824 bytes, approximately one billion bytes, about the length of an encyclopedia's text

continued...

tera	short for terabyte (TB), equals 1,099,511,627,776 bytes, approximately one trillion bytes, theoretically about the contents of a library of books
peta	short for petabyte (PB), equals 1,125,899,906,842,624 bytes, approximately one million billion bytes, theoretically about the number of words ever written
exa	short for exabyte (EB), equals 1,152,921,504, 606,846,976 bytes, approximately one billion billion bytes, theoretically about the number of words ever printed

Exploring the Digital Universe

If you have an iMac, you're in the right place, and that's really all you need to know to use this book. Simply jump right in, anywhere. This book is designed with you in mind—I know who *you* are. You're smart enough to own an iMac, you're interested enough to be reading this, and you're ambitious enough to be curious about exploring the digital universe. With this basic understanding, you can trust me to guide you to the information you need, when you need it. That's how to use this book.

If you want to know a bit more about the construction of this book, you'll find that it is organized into four sections: digital audio, digital video, digital graphics, digital and beyond. Within each of these sections arc chapters focused on one part or another of working with these media. They begin with using and interacting with the media, and proceed with how to capture that media type, how to edit and manipulate it, how to refine and produce your creations, and finally how to publish it by using a CD or the Internet. At the end of each section is a chapter introducing advanced tools used by professionals, which you might aspire to try.

Using an iMac can be a spiritual experience. You might not believe it, but if you manage to create something that surprises you—something you didn't know you could do—then you will understand what I'm talking about. If this seems daunting, please don't be distressed, it will come naturally to you in time. To help you recognize and enjoy the spiritual side of your iMac, you'll find that this book can be lighthearted and hopefully entertaining. So consider yourself warned: Each chapter begins with a short *Zen* poem, which I've composed entirely for my own amusement, if not for yours.

> ### ZEN AND THE ART OF COMPUTER BOOKS
>
> OK. Those of us who write, edit, and publish computer books know that you reader folks don't tend to patiently read them straight through from cover to cover. You like to browse around, picking up ideas here and there—maybe if I'm really lucky you'll go as far as to read a whole page before getting antsy and turning away to your iMac to try something. Because we recognize this not so surprising fact, we go out of our way to entertain you with lots of little bits and pieces tossed in and about (such as this right here). Like nuts in a candy bar, or potholes in the road, or stars in the sky, hopefully these make your experience special.

Which iMac Do I Need to Have?

All iMacs are not equal. You probably noticed this when you bought yours. Some were more expensive than others, some were different colors than others, and some even looked different from others you'd seen your friends use. The fact is that, unless you have the newest, most expensive iMac, you're not going to be able to just sit down and do everything in this book. However, even if you have the oldest iMac or the most basic iMac, you'll be able to do a lot of what is in this book. And for much of what you can't do, you can buy additional equipment to be able to do it, or go over to a friend's house and use their iMac, or save your money and upgrade.

If you're really concerned about what you can do with your particular iMac, you can locate it in the following information. For the purposes of this book, every iMac is capable of digital audio, as well as collecting audio from CDs, so if this is your main interest, you're covered. iMacs that are capable of digital video capturing and editing are described as DV models and have FireWire interface ports. Some DV models also include DVD-ROM drives, which can play DVD movies. iMacs that are capable of recording CDs are currently the most advanced, but of course external CD-R drives are available.

> ## MAC OS 8, 9, OR X?
>
> Which Mac OS you are using may affect what things you are capable of doing, or at least what they look like compared to what you'll see in this book. All iMacs are capable of running the latest versions of the Mac OS, and so I suggest that you upgrade to at least Mac OS 9 or the new Mac OS X.
>
> As with any Mac OS upgrade, check to make such that any applications that you depend upon are compatible with the newest Mac OS, or have updated versions available. This book has been written covering iMacs installed with Mac OS 9.1, as well as Mac OS X (version 10.0).

Different Thinking iMacs

So far Apple has made five different significant iMac revisions, in two distinct generations, each with varying levels of capability. If you'd like to know more about which iMac you have, take a look through this list and see what you find.

First Generation *(available August 1998)*

The original iMac was introduced August 15, 1998, in a unique turquoise color called Bondi Blue (named for a beach in Australia where the water and sand create a vivid turquoise-blue translucent color). All first generation models are recognizable by their tray-loading CD-ROM drive and door on the side over the interface ports. The original Bondi Blue iMacs had a special Infrared interface (IrDA) on the front next to the headphone jacks.

Common Name	Colors	CPU	Speed	Features
iMac	Bondi Blue	G3	233MHz	CD-ROM, IrDA

First Generation, revised *(available January 1999)*

The revised iMacs of the first generation are recognizable by their fruit-flavored colors of Blueberry, Strawberry, Lime, Grape, and Tangerine, the tray-loading CD-ROM drive and door on the side over the interface ports. In July, 1999, this model was speed-bumped to 333MHz.

Common Name	Colors	CPU	Cpeed	Veatures
iMac	Fruit Flavors	G3	266MHz	CD-ROM
iMac (revised July 1999)	Fruit Flavors	G3	333MHz	CD-ROM

Second Generation *(available October 1999)*

The second-generation iMac was introduced in October 1999, about one year after the original. This generation introduced a whole new enclosure design with slot-loading CD drives and an advanced built-in sound system designed by Harman/Kardon. Also three variations of the iMac were introduced. A low-end model iMac with roughly the same features of previous iMacs, only it is available in the color Blueberry. A mid-range model called iMac DV adding digital video capabilities in the form of FireWire interfaces and **DVD-ROM** drives, available in all five fruit-flavored colors: Blueberry, Strawberry, Lime, Grape, Tangerine. A high-end version with an even faster processor, more **RAM**, and a larger hard drive called the *Special Edition* was introduced, but only available in a very transparent Graphite color.

Common Name	Colors	CPU	Xpeed	Features
iMac	Blueberry	G3	333 MHz	CD-ROM
iMac DV	Fruit Flavors	G3	400 MHz	DVD-ROM, FireWire
iMac DV Special Edition	Graphite	G3	450 MHz	DVD-ROM, FireWire

Second Generation, revised *(available July 2000)*

Introduced in the summer of 2000 along with a new extended keyboard and optical mouse, the revised second generation iMacs are recognizable by their new colors of Indigo, Ruby, Sage, and Snow—all based on the more transparent design of the Graphite special edition iMac (except Snow, which is a more opaque all-white design). These models were bumped up in speed, had a new mid-range model called DV+, which featured a DVD-ROM drive, and the special edition models were only available in the colors Snow and Graphite.

Common Name	Colors	CPU	Speed	Features
iMac	Indigo	G3	350 MHz	CD-ROM
iMac DV	Indigo, Ruby	G3	400 MHz	CD-ROM, FireWire
iMac DV+	Indigo, Ruby, Sage	G3	450 MHz	DVD-ROM, FireWire
iMac DV Special Edition	Graphite, Snow	G3	500 MHz	DVD-ROM, FireWire

Second Generation, further revised (*available February 2001*)

Introduced in early 2001, this further revision of the second generation focuses on CD burning and iTunes with the introduction of wild-looking new color pattern designs. These patterns are printed directly into the plastic shell of the iMac giving them a very interesting and unique appearance. Similar to the previous models, these iMacs feature slot-loading CD-R drives and the simplification of the iMac line-up by the removal of the DV indication—all these models include FireWire interfaces, while none of them are any longer available with DVD-ROM drives. These models were further speed-bumped to 400MHz, 500MHz, and 600MHz.

Common Name	Colors	CPU	Speed	Features
iMac	Indigo	G3	400 MHz	CD, FireWire
iMac	Indigo, Flower Power, Blue Dalmatian	G3	500 MHz	CD-R, FireWire
iMac	Graphite, Flower Power, Blue Dalmatian	G3	600 MHz	CD-R, FireWire

Part I

Digital Audio

Music is evolving. Your iMac is an amazing digital audio machine: with its powerful G3 (or G4) processor you can compress digital audio, transforming it in a myriad of ways and making it extremely portable, its large hard drives make it possible to collect huge libraries of music in one place, its CD and available CD-R drives let you read and write your own CDs.

Your iMac is an amazing digital audio tool: sophisticated software allows you to edit and manipulate digital audio in the same way that professionals do, you can sequence and mix original music compositions with your iMac whether it is your first ditty or your latest concerto.

Your iMac is an amazing digital audio work of art: D/A converters in your iMac allow for high-quality recording and reproduction of audio so that you can capture audio from external sources and play back audio via built-in speakers, connected headphones, or use a line-out to an external amplifier, even while displaying psychedelic visuals. So whether you want to collect and listen to popular music, digitize your own audio sources, edit sound waves to create special effects, or even produce professional recording, the iMac is an amazing computer to use.

In this section we'll explore digital audio, the iMac way:

> Chapter 1: Collecting Music

> Chapter 2: Editing Digital Audio

> Chapter 3: Burning Your Own CDs

> Chapter 4: Advanced Digital Audi0

Why, it's but the motion of fingers and mice!
And here I've been seeking it far and wide.
Awakened at last, I find the display
Above the keys, the river surging high.

Chapter One

Collecting Music

Do you like music? Most people do. People listen to music while they work, play, eat, sleep, exercise—in fact, while they're doing almost anything. With the digital age, there is a far wider selection of music than ever before, and all of that is available at the click of a mouse—no more warbling cassette tapes, no more skipping CDs, no more advertisement filled commercial radio.

The iMac can be the center of your musical universe. You can compress copies of all your CDs so that you don't have to shuffle those reflective discs around when you want to listen to something different. You can even have your own playlists for different listening moods.

In this chapter we're going to look at:

> Using Apple's audio application iTunes

> Creating your own MP3 files from your CDs

> Managing your music collection by creating playlists

> Tuning into streaming audio on the Internet

> Spacing out visually while listening to your music

Listening to Music with iTunes

This year Apple created and released its own MP3 music application called *iTunes*, which is specially designed to work with a Mac. With this software you can listen to a CD, *rip* the CD into your iMac, storing it on your hard drive as compressed MP3 files, organize and select tracks of music to play, search out music by name or the name of its artist or album, open up MP3 streams live from the Internet, and even select music and burn it onto a CD. iTunes also has a cool visual mode that displays abstract patterns and colors based on the sound waves of audio being played. In this book we are working with iTunes 1.1, but Apple will surely be upgrading and extending the features of iTunes for many years to come.

Figure 1.1 iTunes is a great application for listening to music and organizing collections.

COMPUTER SOUND

Sound has been a part of computers since their beginning. Early personal computers made sound by attenuating a simple clicking into buzzing and humming, achieving a distinct computer instrumentation able to control pitch but not volume (frequency not amplitude). Today, computers make sound that is far more realistic by using D/A (digital to analog) conversion processors—circuitry to convert digital sound data into an amplifiable analog audio signal.

iTunes comes free with every Mac available today. If you purchased your iMac before iTunes was released, you can download it for free from Apple's Web site at `http://www.apple.com/itunes`. If you don't have it already, I suggest you go get a copy and play with it before you go any further here. There are many MP3 playing applications available out there, but iTunes is one of the best. Some will argue that it doesn't have every advanced feature of other applications, but iTunes is easier to use, more stable, cleaner sounding, and smoother performing than any others.

TURNING UP THE VOLUME

iTunes has a volume control, but this doesn't affect the maximum volume setting on your iMac; instead, you need to adjust the iMac's system volume. You can do this either by using the Sound control panel, or if you have the latest generation iMac which includes an optical mouse and a full size keyboard, you have special keys you can use to adjust the volume up or down, or mute the sound altogether. There is also a key to eject a CD. You'll know the keys are working because a visual indicator of the sound level will appear at the bottom of the screen and your iMac will beep each time you press a volume key.

LISTENING TO YOUR IMAC

If you have a second-generation iMac with a slot-loading CD drive, you have a wondrous, high-quality sound system built in that is hard to replicate even in stand-alone speakers. This system produces good range and a crisp sound, but because it is made of just

continued…

two midsize drivers, it is a bit weak in the bass. For this problem, Harman/Kardon has available a $100 add-on subwoofer called the iSub that is designed specifically to extend the range and power of the built-in speakers. The iSub is a USB device that you simply plug in and it works.

If, however, you have a first-generation iMac, which has just okay speakers that are a bit flat and weak, you can use the sound output jack on the interface panel on the side of your iMac to plug in external speakers. Perhaps the best external speakers to use with an iMac are the Harmon/Kardon SoundSticks, which are similar in quality to the built-in, second-generation iMac's speakers with the iSub.

No matter which iMac you have, you can always use headphones—a good quality pair of headphones can produce a clearer sound than most external speakers, and they won't bother other people who maybe nearby. The iMac has been designed for family use, so it includes a pair of headphone jacks on the front below the display. When you plug something into the sound output jack or a headphone jack, the sound to the built-in speakers will be muted.

Using iTunes

You'll find iTunes to be straightforward and easy to use. Simply stick in a CD that you want to listen to, and it will appear in iTunes' source list. If you are connected to the Internet, iTunes will automatically go to an online resource called CDDB (Compact Disc Database) and look up the name of the album and its tracks. This information is not a part of the standard audio CD format; only an identifier number is encoded on audio CDs, which is used when looking up the disc's information. After the CD is displayed in the Source list, you can select it (if it isn't already automatically selected) and view the contents of the CD.

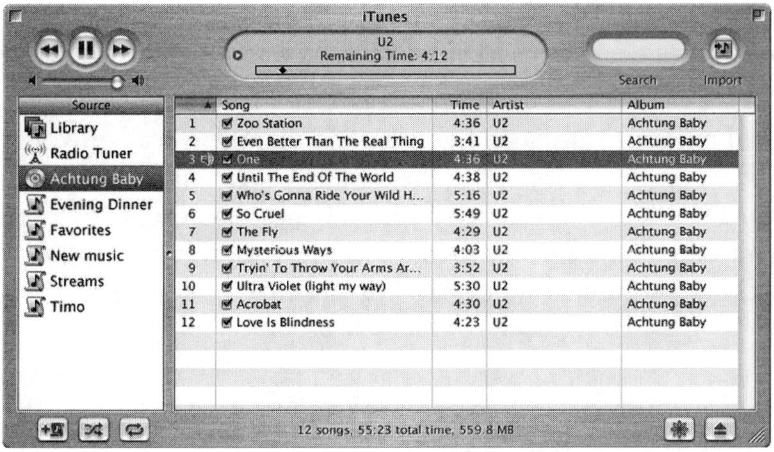
iTunes
U2
Remaining Time: 4:12
Search
Import
Source
Library
Radio Tuner
Achtung Baby
Evening Dinner
Favorites
New music
Streams
Timo
Song
Time
Artist
Album
1 Zoo Station 4:36 U2 Achtung Baby
2 Even Better Than The Real Thing 3:41 U2 Achtung Baby
3 One 4:36 U2 Achtung Baby
4 Until The End Of The World 4:38 U2 Achtung Baby
5 Who's Gonna Ride Your Wild H... 5:16 U2 Achtung Baby
6 So Cruel 5:49 U2 Achtung Baby
7 The Fly 4:29 U2 Achtung Baby
8 Mysterious Ways 4:03 U2 Achtung Baby
9 Tryin' To Throw Your Arms Ar... 3:52 U2 Achtung Baby
10 Ultra Violet (light my way) 5:30 U2 Achtung Baby
11 Acrobat 4:30 U2 Achtung Baby
12 Love Is Blindness 4:23 U2 Achtung Baby
12 songs, 55:23 total time, 559.8 MB

Figure 1.2 You can use iTunes to listen to a CD simply by inserting it in your iMac and then selecting it from the Source list.

To play a CD or any music selection within iTunes, you use the play controls at the top left of the iTunes window. If you want to play a specific track within a CD, you can simply double-click on it to play it.

Selecting Sources

There are many possible sources to choose from when using iTunes. At the top of your Source list is the Library; this is your collection of music stored on your iMac. Below the Library is the Radio Tuner, which contains a list of Internet-broadcast MP3 streams that you can listen to live in a similar manner to traditional radio stations. You may not have any other sources listed on your iTunes Source list, but if you stick in a CD, it will appear here, and if you connect a portable MP3 music player (via USB), it will also appear in the Source list. You can also add custom playlists to your Source list. When you select a source, its contents will appear. The display of the contents will function differently, depending on what type of source it is.

Browsing the Library

When the Library is selected, you will see a listing of all the MP3 files on your iMac that have been added to iTunes (it will ask you if it should automatically search out and add all the music on your iMac when you launch iTunes the first time). If you have MP3 files on your iMac that you want to add to iTunes, you can simply drag them into the iTunes window—once iTunes knows about a file it remembers it—all music added to any playlist becomes part of the Library.

Figure 1.3 Browsing the Library, you can select artists and albums to view and listen to.

At the top-right of the iTunes window, there is a round button that changes function, depending upon the current selection. When you are viewing the Library, this button allows you to toggle the display of artist and album above the contents listing. When you first select the library, it will show you "All" the items in the library, as well as display the number of items, their playtime length, and the byte-size being used on your hard drive to store them.

Figure 1.4 Searching for music by name, artist, or album is as easy as typing a few characters in the Search field.

You can use the artist and album listing to narrow the content listing to display just the tracks that are related to your selection. For example, you might select an Artist such as U2; then iTunes will narrow the album listing to those by U2, as well as the track listing to songs by U2. To broaden your list back to everything, simply scroll to the top of your list and select the top item "All."

You can also reduce the list of displayed tracks by using the search field at the top of the iTunes window and typing a string of text to help you locate your music quickly. iTunes will display a listing of any music that matches within its track name, album, or artist.

Resizing the iTunes Window

The iTunes window may look very fixed in shape and proportion with its brushed titanium appearance, but it is very flexible. You can resize the window by dragging the lower-right corner. You can adjust the width or the source list, as well as the artist and album frames (when browsing the library), and you can change the width and contents of any of the columns in the contents listing.

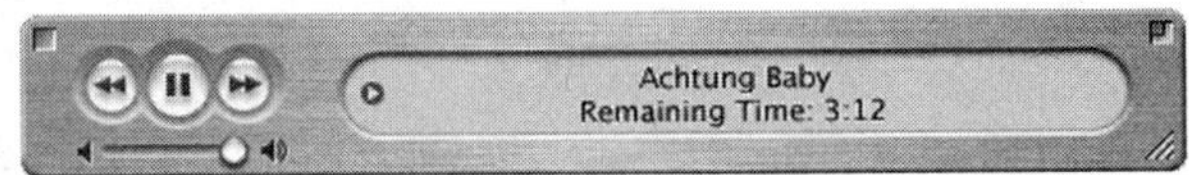

Figure 1.5 Use the zoom control to reduce the iTunes window to this small display.

Figure 1.6 Resizing the window to its smallest width will reduce the display to just the play controls.

Clicking the zoom box in the upper-right corner of the iTunes window will shrink the window down to a small version with only the play controls and the current selection display. The width of this little window can be adjusted to squeeze it way down further to just the play controls. This is great when you are using iTunes to listen to music while working in other applications; you can keep the iTunes window small and visible so that you can quickly reach its controls and monitor what you are listening to.

Ripping Your Own MP3s

The power of MP3 software such as iTunes comes when you *rip* your CDs onto your iMac's hard drive where you can listen to them anytime you like, as well as copy them to other devices, such as a portable MP3 player or burned onto a CD. "Ripping" a CD means to "read and encode" it from the digital audio format on an audio CD to a compressed digital audio format that can be stored on your iMac. Ripping doesn't mean to rip-off, or steal, the music. iTunes refers to the reading and encoding process as importing, which is technically accurate.

When you import the contents of a CD, each track (or just the tracks you select) is read from the disc, and its data is reformatted into a newer, much more compact format called *MP3*. Each track is then stored in its own file on your iMac's hard drive in a Music folder. iTunes automatically organizes the files into folders for the artists and album, as well as automatically naming the files based on the track names.

WHAT IS MP3?

Based upon the MPEG digital motion picture compression schemes, MP3 is short for MPEG I Layer 3. It is a digital audio compression algorithm that achieves a compression factor of about 12 while preserving sound quality. It does this by optimizing the compression according to the range of sound that people can actually hear. MP3 is currently the most powerful algorithm in a series of audio encoding standards, developed under sponsorship of the Motion Picture Experts Group and formalized by the International Organization for Standardization (ISO). MP3 files (filename extension ".MP3") can be downloaded from many Web sites and can be played by using software available for most operating systems. MP3 files are usually downloaded completely before playing, but streaming MP3 data is also possible.

Importing Music from a CD

It is very easy to import the music of a CD into MP3 files on your iMac. Simply insert the CD into your iMac, select the CD from the source list, and click the Import button at the top-right of the iTunes window. Then it's just a matter of waiting.

iTunes will automatically convert the digital audio into MP3 files and store them on your hard drive, as well as adding them to the Library. It will take some time to read each track and process the data, displaying a progress bar and an estimate of the encoding speed. iTunes will automatically play the music as it is encoded. The speed of the importing will be reduced if you do other things on your iMac such as use other software or listen to different music from the same CD you are encoding.

Figure 1.7 While encoding a CD's tracks, iTunes displays a progress bar and checks off completed tracks in the listing.

If you are interested in importing a collection of CDs, perhaps dozens or hundreds, you can set iTunes to automatically Import the contents of a CD when it is inserted and then automatically eject it when it is done. To specify this action, choose Preferences from the bottom of iTunes' Edit menu and then use the CD Insert pop-up menu to specify the action you'd like iTunes to take when a CD is inserted. Keep in mind that each full CD of music you add will average about 60 megs of space on your hard drive—every 10 CDs about 600 megs, and every 100 CDs about 6 gigs—of course, the space requirements can vary depending on the length of the music and the quality of encoding that you choose.

MP3 Encoding Options

The MP3 digital audio format is flexible in its encoding methods, offering the possibility of smaller files of lower quality and larger files of higher quality. In general, at better quality settings, MP3 will reduce the size of audio data (as compared to the raw format of digital audio on a CD) to one-tenth its size. iTunes allows you to modify the MP3 encoding settings (as well as choose other encoding formats) from the Advanced settings within its Preferences.

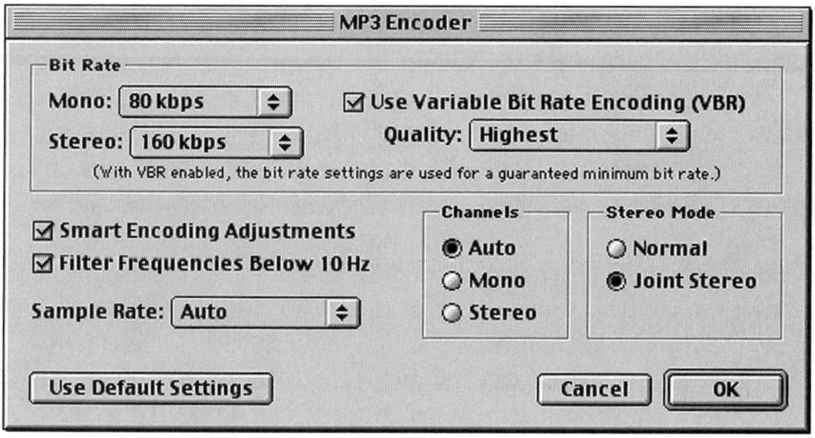

Figure 1.8 Here you can see the advanced customization settings for MP3 encoding.

The configuration menu offers three standard settings: Good Quality, Better Quality, and High Quality, as well as custom configuration. Which one you choose will depend on your needs and concerns for quality reproduction. If you are listening to music on your iMac, you have little need to be concerned about saving hard drive space and probably want higher quality audio reproduction. However, if you use a portable MP3 player with a very limited memory capacity, then you'll want to use a more aggressive encoding to make files that you use with it smaller, sacrificing some level of quality.

DIGITAL AUDIO COMPRESSION

Working with digital sound has been limited for many years because it requires over 10 megs of data for each minute of CD-quality digital sound data. This is why the Compact Disc that holds about 740 megs of music data has been so successful—it is an easy way to transport such large amounts of data. However, this is all raw, uncompressed audio data and recently great strides have been made to compress digital audio while maintaining reasonable quality. In fact, the average MP3 file is compressing CD-quality audio to about $\frac{1}{12}$ of its raw size (a full audio CD can be compressed to around 62 megs) while still maintaining nearly the same quality audio.

continued...

To make sound data smaller, there are two realms of techniques: those that don't affect the sound directly and those that alter the sound, reducing it to only what is perceivable. The first techniques use methods such as compression of silence to simplify the digital representation of blank bits or constant tones into reduced descriptions, as well as by joining channels when possible (when stereo sounds are equal they are mono). The second techniques use methods that are based on careful scientific observation of human hearing to throw away sound data that cannot be easily perceived. This includes understanding how hearing is sensitive in different frequency ranges; humans can hear between 20Hz and 20,000Hz, but are most clearly sensitive between 2,000Hz and 4,000 Hz, so more data is devoted to sounds in this range. There is also an effect of sound masking, where sounds in some frequencies cover over sounds in other frequencies and so those masked sounds can be rendered less perfectly with less data or eliminated altogether. Another method called temporal masking is related to detail within sounds; for example, quieter sounds cannot be heard if they follow a louder sound for a short period of time, and so can be eliminated.

All these techniques and others can be applied together to significantly reduce the bulk of audio data while maintaining the perception that it is unaltered. Most software for encoding compressed audio data provides options for you to determine how strongly to filter the audio data with these techniques so that the quality of the sound can vary depending on the choices of the user and may not sound quite as perfect as the original uncompressed data. Audio that is highly compressed may sound a bit flat or fuzzy, but this might sound perfectly acceptable if the source is spoken text rather than a symphonic orchestra.

MP3 Tags

In addition to the audio data itself, the MP3 format includes special information tags that catalog the music in MP3 files. Each file can have a variety of tags that keep track of the music's title, artist, album, year of publication, track number, as well as miscellaneous notes, relative volume levels, and encoding options. When you import music using iTunes, it looks up the appropriate information for a CD from the Internet and automatically tags the files it creates with as much information as it can find.

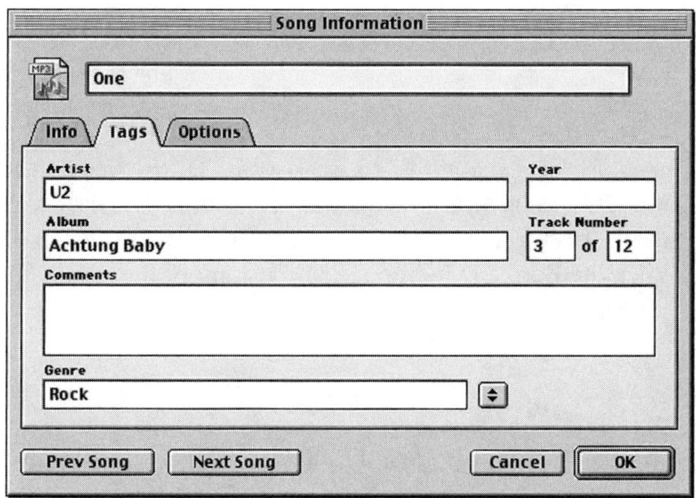

Figure 1.9 iTunes lets you view and edit the MP3 tags of a track.

You can view and edit the MP3 tags for a selection using iTunes by choosing Get Info from the File menu or by pressing ⌘-I. The Get Info window will display fixed information about the MP3 file, the editable tags, and options specific to iTunes. iTunes also provides buttons at the bottom of the Get Info window to display the previous or next tracks if you want to see or edit them in series. If you select multiple tracks before choosing Get Info, you will be presented with a special window for editing them all at once as a batch.

Creating Your Own Playlists

The real power of iTunes is unleashed by its ability to build a playlist and by its playback modes. Because having a really large collection of music on your iMac is like having your own jukebox or radio station, iTunes uses the power of a computer to provide advanced means for organizing and playing music from your collection. You can use its playlist features to build a list of music to play, choosing your favorite music for different special occasions or listening moods. Or you might compose a playlist to organize a CD to burn, assigning tracks that go together in an order you define. You can combine playlists with the shuffle and repeat playback modes to set your iMac on autopilot, navigating your collection like a robotic DJ.

CREATING YOUR OWN CDs

iTunes also has the ability to work with CD-R drives to write your own CDs from MP3 files in your collection. Simply make a playlist with tracks on it that you want to write, and when you're ready, click the Burn CD button at the top-right of the iTunes window.

Creating a Playlist

To create your own playlist, simply click the New Playlist button at the bottom left of the iTunes window or type ⌘-N. An untitled playlist will be added to your source list. Its name will be highlighted for you to retype your preferred name for your playlist; give it a name which describes it, such as "Music to work by" or "Romantic evening" or "Birthday party." After you have named it, you can begin to add music to it.

Switch to the Library or another source from which you'd like to select music for your playlist. After you have located a track, an album, or another playlist, simply drag it to the playlist title in the Source list to copy it to your playlist. After you have added items to your playlist, you can view your playlist by selecting it from the Source list. Items in a playlist can be organized into a specific order or playback sequence simply by dragging them up or down the list to insert them in a new location. You can also display a playlist in its own iTunes window by double-clicking on its name in the Sources list, handy when you are organizing several playlists at the same time or want to see the contents of a playlist while you are building it.

	Song	Time	Artist	Album	Track #
1	Let's Stay Together	3:17	Green, Al	Pulp Fiction	4 of 16
2	Soundtrack	4:04	A3	The Sopranos	1 of 14
3	Macy's Day Parade	3:34	Green Day	Warning	12 of 12
4	Bitter Sweet Symphony	5:58	Verve	Urban Hymns	1 of 13
5	Telling Stories	3:57	Tracy Chapman	Telling Stories	1 of 11
6	Orbital –	4:30	The Saint	Urbal Beats	10 of 16
7	Gotta Serve Somebody	5:19	Bob Dylan	The Sopranos	4 of 14
8	Thank You	3:38	Dido	No Angel	6 of 12
9	put your lights on	4:45	Santana(featuring …	Super Natural	3 of 13
10	Holding Back The Years	4:29	Simply Red	Greatest Hits	1 of 15
11	Everybody Wants to Rule the …	4:11	Tears For Fears	Songs From The Bi…	3 of 8
12	ELVIS ATE AMERICA	3:00	Passengers	Passengers: Origin…	11 of 14
13	Desert Rose (with Cheb Miami)	4:45	Sting	Brand New Day	2 of 10

CD for My Car — Warning, Remaining Time: 2:42 — Search — Burn CD — 13 songs, 55:27 total time, 72.8 MB

Figure 1.10 Your playlists can contain any music on your iMac; you also use a playlist to organize a CD to burn.

MANAGING PORTABLE PLAYERS

If you have a portable MP3 player that you can connect to your iMac, you can use iTunes to manage its memory and copy music onto it (see iTunes documentation to see which brands and models of players are supported). When the player is connected, it will be displayed in the Source list alongside your Library and playlists. Viewing it will show you what it currently contains. Copy music to it by dragging tracks to its playlist, resequence items by dragging them up and down the playlist, and remove items by selecting them and pressing Delete.

Shuffle and Repeat Playback

iTunes has options for randomizing or repeating the playback sequence of tracks in a playlist (or selection in the Library). To randomize the playback order, simply click the shuffle button in the lower right of any iTunes window—this is the button with the two crossing intertwined arrows. The shuffle mode is great from large collections; simply select "All" artists and albums while browsing the library, and iTunes will randomly select a track to play from your whole library and keep playing randomly selected tracks until it has played every track once.

iTunes has two repeat options that you can turn on if you want to repeat a selection over and over. You can specify Repeat One, which will play a single track over and over, or you can specify Repeat All, which will repeat all the songs in a playlist or selection over and over. When you combine the Repeat All function with the Shuffle play mode, iTunes will randomly play all the selected music in random order forever until you stop it—great for parties.

Tuning in Streaming Internet "Radio"

Just as you can have MP3 files on your iMac to listen to, there are MP3 streams available on the Internet that you can tune into. These streams can be anything their creators want to broadcast. You'll find individuals playing selections from their music collections, commercial radio stations and college radio stations streaming their FM broadcasts, and even live online talk shows. Streaming broadcasts can serve thousands of listeners or just one listener; they can be anywhere in the world. In fact, it is even possible for you to broadcast your own stream right from your iMac with the right software.

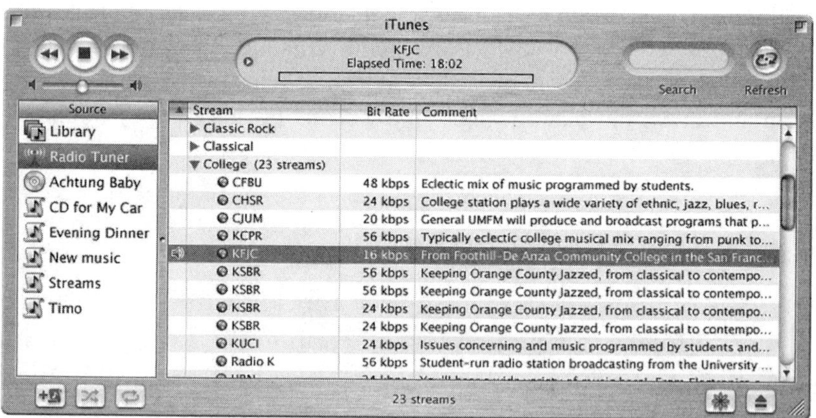

Figure 1.11 There are hundreds of streams to choose from within the Radio Tuner.

iTunes provides a Source feature for selecting Internet radio streams. Select Radio Tuner from the Source list, and you will be presented with a list of stream categories. You can reveal the contents of a category by clicking once on the small triangle control next to the category name. When you first open a category, iTunes will go out on the Internet to a service it uses and look up the current contents of that category, displaying it a few seconds later. You can then select and play any of the streams listed.

> ### OTHER BROADCASTS
>
> There are many thousands of streaming MP3 broadcasts available, far beyond what is listed within the Radio Tuner source in iTunes. You can locate and open additional streams from online services such as broadcast.com and 365.com. These services will also host your own broadcasts if you like.
>
> If you know the URL of a stream you want to access, you can use iTunes' Open Stream command at the top of the Advanced menu or by type ⌘-U.

Streaming MP3 Bit-rates

In the listing of streams, in addition to the name of the stream, you will see its bit rate and some notes describing it. The bit rate is of interest because this will affect the quality as well as your ability to tune in a broadcast. If you are using a dial-up 56 K modem connection to the Internet, you will be forced to choose lower bit-rate streams, as those with bit rates of 56 K and higher will not work for you. If you have a very high bandwidth connection to the Internet, you can choose any bit rate, especially higher ones with better quality. When you first play an MP3 stream, iTunes will cache a few seconds of it so that as the stream is briefly interrupted (as things can be on the Internet), it can continue to play. If a stream is interrupted or unable to transmit enough data through your connection, it will stop or not work at all.

Spacing Out with Your iMac

Sometimes, you just need to space out, and iTunes can help you. It has a special mode that you can turn on by clicking the button with the "flower" icon on it at the lower-left of the iTunes window, switching the window display to a richly animated psychedelic pattern of colors and waveform geometry based on the music being played at the same time. The display slowly rotates through patterns and colors; a more powerful iMac will be able to display higher resolution and animate more smoothly. When iTunes changes tracks to a new song, it will display its title, artist, and album information in the lower-left corner, kind of like a music video.

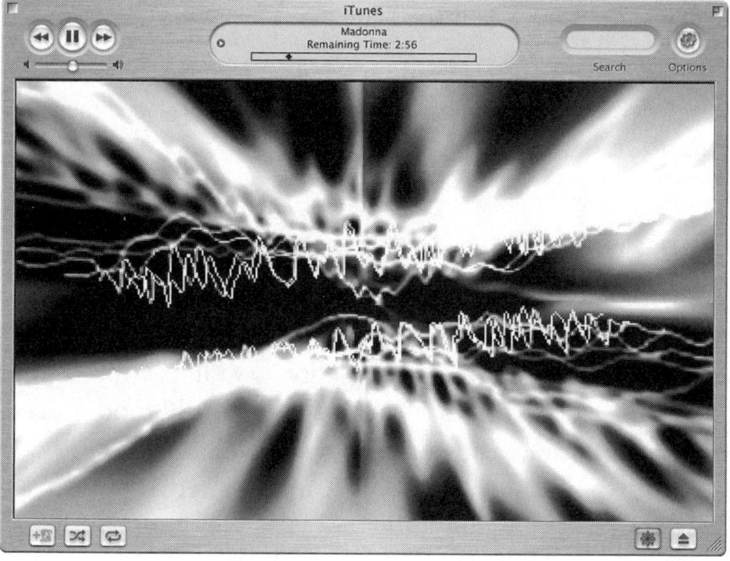

Figure 1.12 The visual display mode of iTunes is a great way to present your iMac at parties.

There are a variety of options for the visual display, affecting its size, animation quality, and even hidden controls and the ability to display images. You can adjust how big the visual area is within the window by selecting a size from the Visual menu, or you can specify full screen mode, which will take the entire screen and display the visual effects turning your iMac into a very expensive but very cool lava lamp. Within the iTunes window, when the visual mode is in effect (but not full screen), the round button in the top-right provides access to options that affect the quality of the display resolution and frame rate. At any time while watching the visual effects, you can press Shift-? to display help shortcuts. The Q and W, A and S, and Z and X keys also can be used to switch the display effects, rotating through preset filters, geometry, and colors.

> **PROJECT YOUR VISUALS**
>
> If you have a second-generation DV iMac, you have the ability to connect it to an external monitor or video projector. Imagine using your iMac to drive a huge projected display with iTunes playing music and providing colorful visual effects. It's neat!

16-bits,
44.1 kilohertz—
for the listener,
a beep.

Chapter Two

Editing Digital Audio

Editing audio is great fun. What you hear is probably the most real-istically reproducible sense, and the right use of audio can convince you that something that is unreal is real—thus, the importance of audio soundtracks for animation and special effects in movies. Manipulating audio gives you a sense of altering reality, whether you are cleaning up a recording, editing out something bother-some, or adding depth and dimension to an otherwise flat record-ing. With audio editing you can enhance your iMovies, adjust the beeps and blips made by your iMac, remix your favorite trance album, or just fool around.

You'll discover that there are many great outlets for audio creativity in an iMac. Using software designed to manipulate digital sound, you can clip, copy and paste, mix together, and filter sounds to cre-ate your own engineered audio experiences. You can create your own high-quality engineered music, or you can simply enhance the Mac OS user interface with your own appearance soundtracks and alert beeps.

In this chapter we're going to look at:

- ➤ Creating, viewing, and saving new audio files

- ➤ Converting and recording sound clips

- ➤ Editing sound clips by selecting, copying, and inserting

- ➤ Filtering and processing sound waves for special effect

Working with Digital Audio

Before you can work with digital audio, you need software that allows you to open and edit audio data. This is different from listening to an audio CD or playing an MP3 file; here we want to be able to "see" the audio and work with it. A good digital audio editing application for the casual sound enthusiast is Sound Studio by Felt Tip Software. This simple and elegant application is available as shareware for $35 (it is free to use for 14 days) from `www.felttip.com`, and it is available for both Mac OS 9 and natively for Mac OS X. Sound Studio displays audio with waveforms and allows selecting, copying and pasting, importing and exporting different sound formats, and basic sound filtering. Download a copy and give it a try.

> ### The Physics of Sound
>
> To understand digital sound, it is helpful to first be clear on how the physics of sound work by compressing air into waves that your ears can feel. Those waves can be loud or soft in volume, and they can be high or low in pitch. The volume of a sound is its amplitude; the louder a sound is, the larger its wave is and the greater the change in air pressure. The pitch of a sound is its frequency; the higher pitch a sound is, the closer its waves are together. A loud, low-pitched rumbling has a larger amplitude and a lower frequency, while a soft, high-pitched whistling has a smaller amplitude and a higher frequency. Indeed, sound is all about time; without the passage of time to allow a change in air pressure to occur, there could be no sound.

Recording a Sound

When you first launch your sound editing software, you need something to work with to see how the software functions. I suggest you simply record something—your iMac has a built-in microphone. Begin by choosing New from the File Menu, give your sound a name, and then select 44.1kHz, 16 bits, and Stereo, if they aren't already selected. A new window will appear for you to record into.

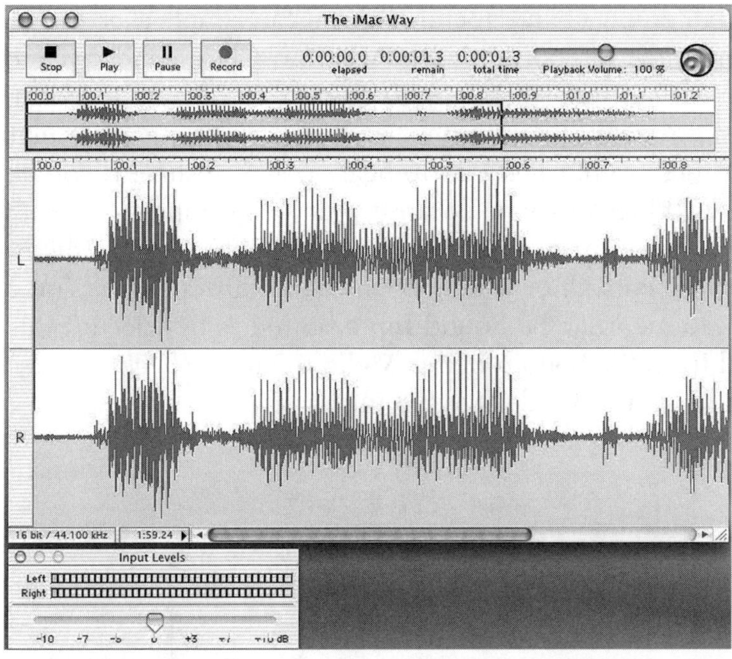

Figure 2.1 Felt Tip Sound Studio is an elegant digital audio editing application available on the Internet at `www.felttip.com`.

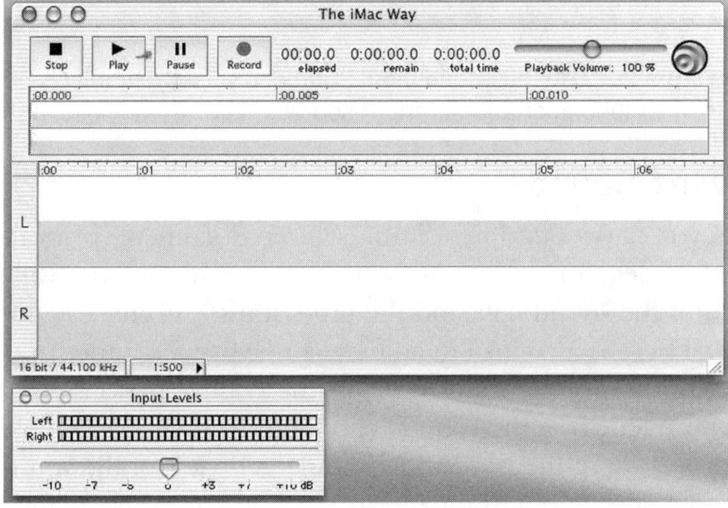

Figure 2.2 Here is an empty new Sound Studio document, ready for recording.

With an empty sound document, you can simply click the record button in the top portion of the window. Click it and say something to your iMac; then click Stop to end the recording. The digitized sound wave will appear in the window. You now have something to experiment with. Click Play to hear your recording. If you don't hear anything, it may be because your sound input is not set to the iMac's built-in microphone (or it could be that the volume isn't turned up enough or you didn't speak loudly enough). You can check to see what the Sound Input Source is by selecting this command from the bottom of the Audio menu or checking your Sound Control panel (Mac OS 9).

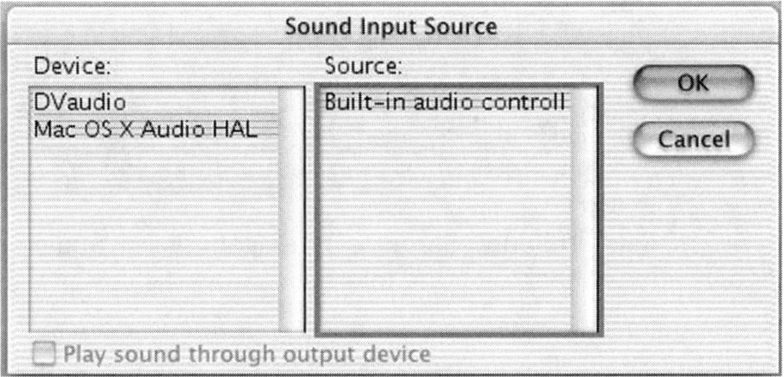

Figure 2.3 Use the Sound Input Source to select your iMac's built-in microphone or another input source.

Viewing Sound

Once you have sound in a Sound Studio document, you will see a variety of details about it. At the top of the window, you will see the length of the sound data and the time of the current selection point. There is a control to adjust the playback volume. In the upper portion of the window below the control buttons is a view of the entire length of the sound "clip" with its time marked out. The lower portion of the window is an enlarged view of the sound, which you can zoom in on and increase in size by enlarging the size of the window. When you select a portion of the sound clip from the upper reference, that portion of the clip will be displayed in the lower portion of the window.

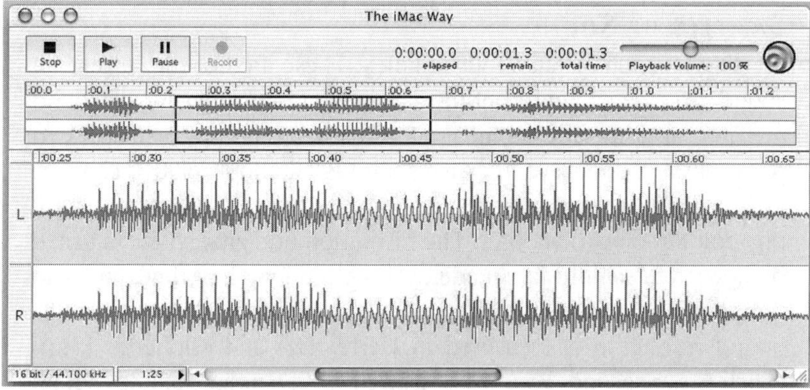

Figure 2.4 This is your view of the sound data. The upper portion displays the entire length of the sound clip, while the lower portion only displays a zoomed-in portion.

At the bottom of the window in the left corner is a display of the sound data bit depth and sample rate, as well as an indication of the level of zoom of the data in the window. You can click on the zoom level to reveal a pop-up menu to change the ratio of the data in the window, allowing you to zoom in or out. The easiest way to navigate your sound clip is to use the upper sound clip reference to click and drag out a selection to view in the lower part of the window. As you zoom in, you'll see more and more clearly a representation of the actual sound's waveform, indicating its relative amplitude and frequency.

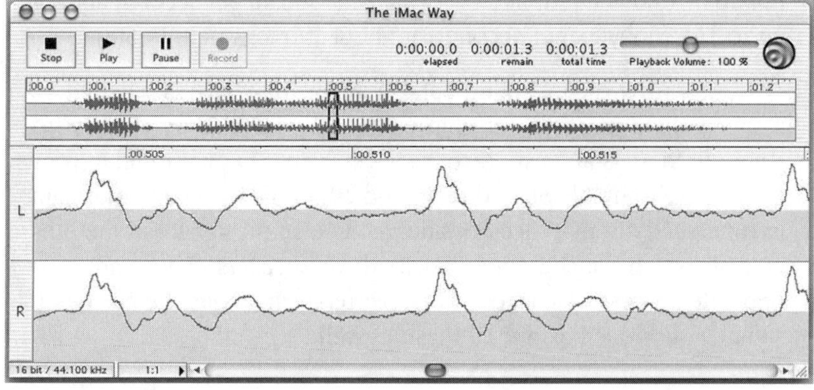

Figure 2.5 When you zoom in on a minute section of your sound clip, you'll see the waveform being generated by its data.

SAMPLES OF SOUND

Digital sound is all about samples. These are like the "pixels" of sound data, each representing a value for the intensity of sound pressure at a specific moment. It actually requires two samples to represent a sound wave because sound is all about relative changes in air pressure, and it requires two samples to represent change from one point in time to another. The resolution of digital sound is based on how often samples are made over a given length of time, and also determines the maximum frequency possible to capture digitally. Sound resolution is measured in Hertz (Hz, and Kilohertz, kHz), which is per second. Your iMac, as well as CD audio, samples sound at 44.1kHz, which is 44,100 times each second. With this number of samples, it is possible to represent a maximum frequency of half that resolution, devoting at least two samples to create the highest sound wave, in this case 22,050Hz. Anything higher is clipped off. (This method of digitizing audio is known as Pulse Code Modulation or PCM.)

This maximum amount wasn't arbitrarily engineered; it just happens that human hearing generally has a range of 20Hz to 20,000Hz, so 22,050Hz is enough to digitally represent the human-audible range of sound waves. At each of the 1/44,100 of a second samples, a value is assigned using 16-bits, providing a value between 0 and 32,767, for the amplitude (volume) of the sound wave. This provides a great deal of "head room" for both very soft and very loud sounds. Furthermore, this is all done twice for separate left and right stereo sound channels, so CD quality audio is 44,100 samples multiplied by 16 bits multiplied by 2 channels of data per second, adding up to 172 kilobytes per second (or about 10 megs per minute).

Converting digital sound data to an analog signal is handled by a special kind of computer chip called a *D/A converter (Digital to Analog)*; there is at least one of these in every CD player and in your iMac as well. Simply put: you feed a digital waveform stream of data into one end of this processor and get an electric signal out the other end, which can be amplified to drive speakers. There are also opposite processors called A/D converters, which digitize an analog signal; your iMac has one of these as well.

Saving Your Sound Clip

If you like what you've recorded, you can save it as a file to your iMac's hard drive (or you can discard it by closing it without saving). Choosing Save from the File menu will present you with a save panel. The name you gave your sound when you created it will automatically be filled in, or you can rename it now before saving. The Save panel includes a Format pop-up menu where you can choose to save your sound clip as a native Sound Studio document or in another digital audio data format: AIFF, Sound Designer II, System 7 Sound, Windows WAVE. If you'd like to listen to your sound with other applications, or even convert it using another application (perhaps iTunes), try the audio industry standard AIFF.

Figure 2.6 When saving your sound clip, you can choose from a variety of standard sound data formats.

Converting Digital Audio

Besides recording sound with a microphone right into your iMac, you can convert digital audio data from other sources, such as a CD or an MP3 file. To give you the widest range of options for importing from different data formats, Sound Studio uses the help of QuickTime. Choose the Import with QuickTime command from the File menu and then select an audio data file, such as an MP3 converted from a CD by iTunes.

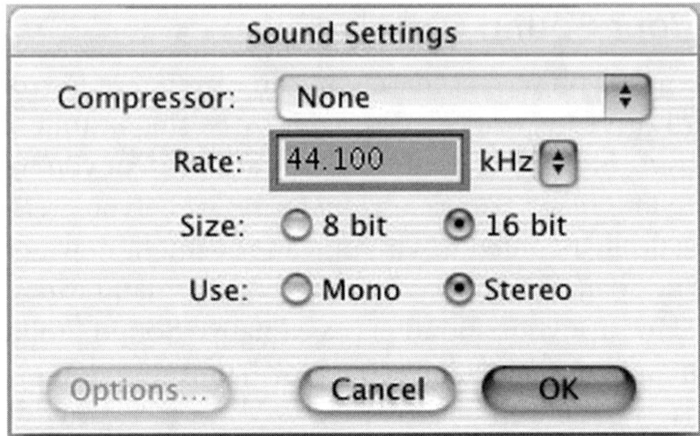

Figure 2.7 When importing, you can choose the settings for the sound.

After you have selected a digital audio file to import, you will be presented with options for how you'd like to convert it. For the highest quality conversion, try this setting: Compressor of None, Rate of 44.100 kHz, Size of 16 bit, and Stereo. For a larger file it may take a couple minutes to import the file. When it is done, you will see a window, and the sound clip reference in the upper portion of the window will begin to fill in with the sound waveform.

If you want to import sound from a CD, you may have to use another application such as iTunes to read the data from the disc. For the highest quality conversion, set up iTunes to convert the audio data to AIFF with the same quality settings used in Sound Studio.

Recording Analog Sources

You can record live presentations, make weird sound effects by banging stuff together, re-record old vinyl albums or tapes, and do anything that produces sound. If you want to produce your own recordings, with better quality than the example we began with (recording by speaking into the built-in microphone in your iMac), you'll want to use the Sound Input mini-jack. By connecting an external microphone, or the output of a recording device such as a tape player, you can use your iMac to digitize audio with very high quality (it is also possible to use other digital input sources, such as USB or FireWire, if you have audio equipment that supports these interfaces).

Once you have connected your external sound device, you need to select the Sound Input. When using Sound Studio, choose the Sound Input Source command from the bottom of the Audio menu.

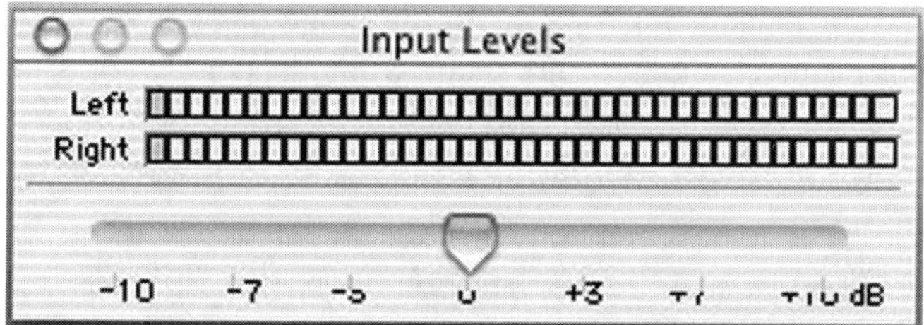

Figure 2.8 Use the Input Levels to check and adjust the volume of your audio input.

With the Sound input selected, create a new document. Sound Studio by default displays an Input Levels meter, which you can use to adjust the volume of your source, even while you are not recording. If you are using a microphone, test the level by speaking into it and adjust the volume (either in Sound Studio or on the microphone if it has a volume control) until the level peaks in the yellow. If you are using a playback device, start it playing and adjust its volume accordingly.

After you have set your levels, your iMac is ready to record. Simply click the Record button when you are ready to begin, and click Stop to end. Keep in mind that recording sound can take up lots of hard drive space, so if you are making a long recording, be prepared.

> ### GOOD RECORDING
>
> Good sound always begins at the source and in most cases this is a microphone (unless you are artificially synthesizing sounds). A good quality microphone, just like a good camera, can be an amazing thing. Your iMac has many great high-quality components, but the microphone is not exactly among them. It is very functional, of course, but if you are recording audio to be listened to and enjoyed, you'll need an external microphone. Clarity and range will increase dramatically with cost. A truly cheap microphone costing less than $50 will work, but it may capture sound with lots of noise and sound harsh. An expensive microphone in the range of $100 to $150 dollars will be much quieter and sound a bit deeper. A good microphone costing $300 to $1,000 will be a solid performer both producing consistent and quality results, and also becoming a lasting long-term investment.
>
> Of course, having a good microphone isn't the only thing needed for recording good sound. How you use the microphone also counts a great deal. The environment where a recording is made obviously can have an effect on the recording; assuming that the environment is quiet, an open space may sound very dead, but a space that is too small can echo and sound confined. But these factors can be either compensated by, or overshadowed by, how a microphone is positioned. So listen carefully and try different things. Keep in mind that the goal is usually a clear, undistorted recording. If you have the ability to mix your own audio, you can get much better results by recording each instrument or part individually with a mono microphone.

Editing Digital Audio

Once you have audio to work with in your iMac, the fun begins—editing and manipulating sound clips can be very powerful and lots of fun. You can select parts of your recording and copy and paste them to rearrange their order, or clean them up. You can also select different parts of your sound clip and apply filters and effects that change the sound waves themselves.

Before you begin editing sounds, you should try to create the best environment you can for being able to hear them. This begins with a quite room and good speakers. If you have a second generation iMac, you have a great sound system built-in, and it can be improved substantially with the iSub to extend its low-end range and allow the tweeters to concentrate their effort on the mid-range and high-end. If you're trying to get the very best possible results, you'll want to hook up your iMac to an external sound system with high-quality studio speakers.

In general, when reproducing sound while editing, processing, or mixing, you want to use equipment that matches the quality of the equipment that will be used by your audience. So if your listeners will be using an iMac (or less than the quality of an iMac), you are already set. Usually, you don't want to use headphones to work with sound, as it is very unnatural and tends to have louder mid-range and high-end than is experienced with speakers. Also, you should turn off equipment that may be adding to background noise while you are working with your audio because it will distract your ear or "color" the sound you are hearing.

Selecting Sounds

The first step to editing, is selecting. Begin by zooming in on a section of your recording by using the sound clip reference in the upper part of the Sound Studio document window. Then you can click and drag across the sound waves in the lower portions of the window to highlight them. Clicking and dragging between the left and right channels of a stereo sound clip will select both channels, while clicking and dragging from above the left channel, or below the right channel, will select just that channel. Clicking the Play button will play what you've selected, or you can simply press the Spacebar.

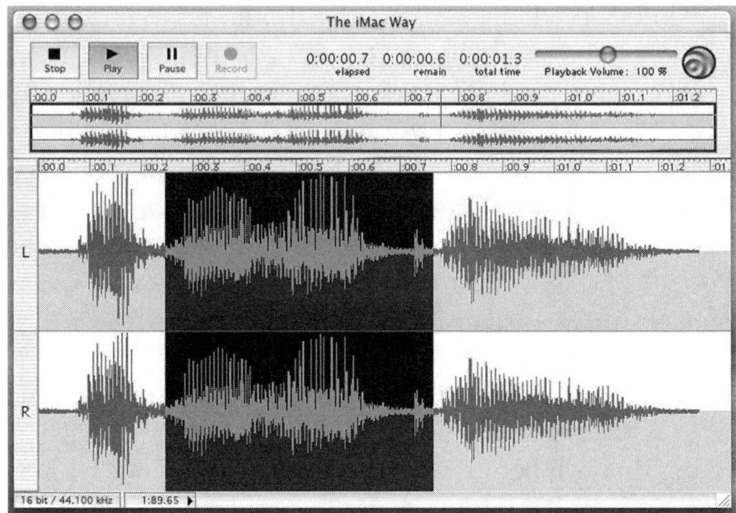

Figure 2.9 Click and drag across the waveform display to select a portion of your sound clip.

If you watch the display while playing, you'll see a cursor indicating the progress of the playback. This will help you recognize what the sounds you hear look like, and as you recognize their shapes, you can adjust your selection to focus in on what you want to select to work with. You'll see that quiet parts of your sound clip are thin and light, and noisy parts are wide and dark. You can, with a bit of practice, learn to recognize the patterns of speech or other sounds you are working with by their waveforms.

Clipping Sounds

The simplest editing technique is to clip out parts of the audio to remove them or move them by using cut, copy, and paste commands. By carefully controlling playback, you can locate the beginning and end of a section of audio that you'd like to copy or remove. You can then select its waveform and play just the selection you want to hear if you selected it correctly. You can then copy it or remove it by cutting or deleting. If you copy or cut a selection of audio, you can paste it somewhere else; just point and click to set the audio insert cursor where you want the audio snippet to go, and then paste it.

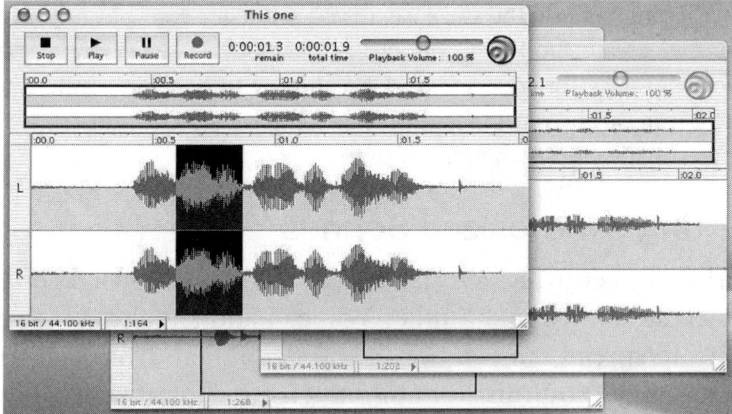

Figure 2.10 Copying and pasting sound is as easy as selecting it in the waveform viewer.

Sound Studio lets you have many audio documents open at the same time, so if you have a very complex bit of editing to do with lots of separate clips, you might want to build an entirely new document by copying pieces from other recordings and pasting them together in a new window. If you find that one clip doesn't play smoothly into another, you might use filters to help blend or fade them into each other.

CONSIDERING YOUR EDITS

When you are ready to begin working with a sound or selection of audio recordings, the first step is to edit them and then sequence them together. This means to trim out blank parts, remove unwanted parts, or otherwise cut, copy, and paste whole sections of the recording. You can then easily use these parts later when you process and mix them.

Begin by listening to your source and take notes about how it needs to be edited before further processing takes place. Listen for wind noise, keys, animals, air conditioners, echoes, as well as pops and clicks. Next, go ahead and begin editing the source (or a copy of it) to remove parts you don't want, or to trim the beginnings and ends so that they are clean and sharp. If you want to clear gaps of unwanted noise, you can select them and fill them with silence.

continued...

> Editing is also the stage where you sequence your pieces together and create the timing of your production. Try to create a comfortable pace for your audio; don't allow it to become frantic when you trim out bits in the middle, nor let it get slow by not removing parts that would be better left out.

Inserting Synthesized Sounds

In addition to copying and pasting sound, you can insert sound waves created by Sound Studio. You can add snippets of silence, perhaps to spread out two noises and keep them from being too close together. You can add noise to create natural wind or waterfall effects or to blend with other sounds. You can add lengths of a perfect tone, or even combinations of tonal waves to create a frequency modulated synthesis.

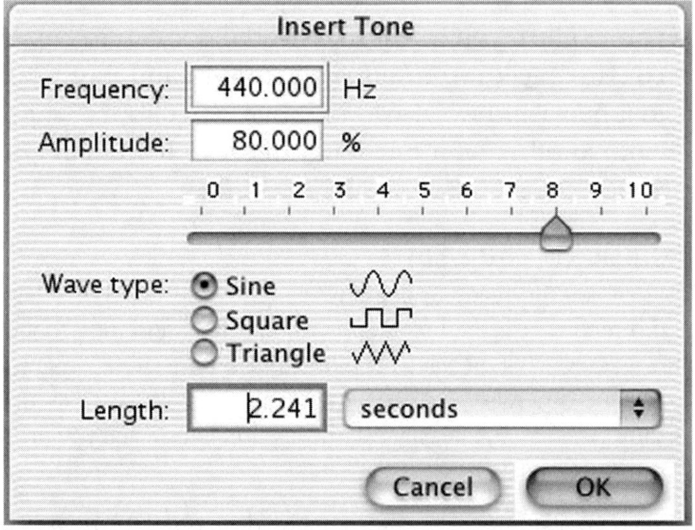

Figure 2.11 Use the Insert Tone command to add or create a perfectly synthesized tone.

To add a synthesized sound (or silence), first select a point in your sound clip where you'd like it inserted. Then use one of the commands in the Insert menu. Select the type of sound wave to insert and the length of sound to synthesize.

Filtering Sounds

While cutting and pasting snippets of audio can lead to creative effects and be kind of fun, filters unleash a whole new level of audio manipulation. Rather than simply using the sound waves as they are recorded and presented, filters allow you to change the sound itself, manipulating the sound waveforms to affect the amplitude and frequency of the sound. With filters you can do simple manipulations such as amplifying the selection of audio or reversing it to play backwards. Some filters are much more complex, creating echo effects or cleaning the selected audio to smooth its range, remove pops and clicks, and trim out levels of noise. Sound Studio has about a dozen audio filters you can use to affect your sound clips.

Figure 2.12 Sound Studio's Filter menu gives you many ways to manipulate your sound clips.

Let's take a quick look at a couple of the more common audio filters. Keep in mind that a filter will literally change the waveform's amplitude and frequency, so overmodulation and clipping are easily possible if you use an effect with too high a setting (or repeatedly). Also, you will probably want to save an unaltered copy of your audio document before making wild changes to it—you never know what you might get.

Amplify

An Amplify filter increases the amplitude, or volume, of a sound wave by the percentage you specify. This can be very useful if you have a section of audio that is too quiet compared to audio around it; by selecting the quiet part and using an Amplify filter to increase its volume, you can level out the sound. Of course, you might also use an Amplify filter to add emphasis to a section of audio. This sort of filter has a hard opening and closing, which means that if you want to gently ramp up or down the amplification, you'll need to use different methods.

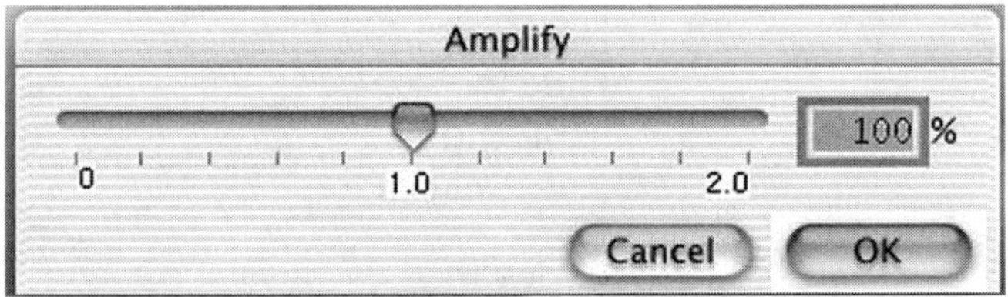

Figure 2.13 Use an Amplify filter to increase the modulation of sound waves to make them louder.

Echo

Probably the most abused filters are those that create Echo effects. They can be very dramatic when applied to a selection of audio, so people tend to get carried away playing with them (and by all means have fun if you can). But an Echo filter is also a very practical effect that when applied with subtlety can open up a deadsounding section of audio and make it sound more natural and roomy. An Echo filter allows you to specify the amount of delay between the source and the repeating (looping) audio and the strength at which each successive repeat is overlaid.

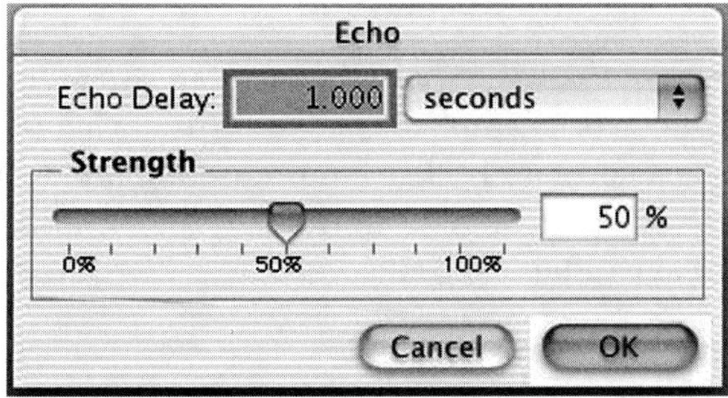

Figure 2.14 An Echo filter can create a more dynamic environment, adding a little depth to a recording or creating a huge canyon-like effect.

Fade In, Out, and Special

The Fade filters are a useful set of filters. These are used to ramp up or down the volume of a selection, perhaps good for the beginning or the ending of a sound clip. Over a short period of time, they can be used to simply soften the start or finish of a sharp noise, preventing cracking and popping.

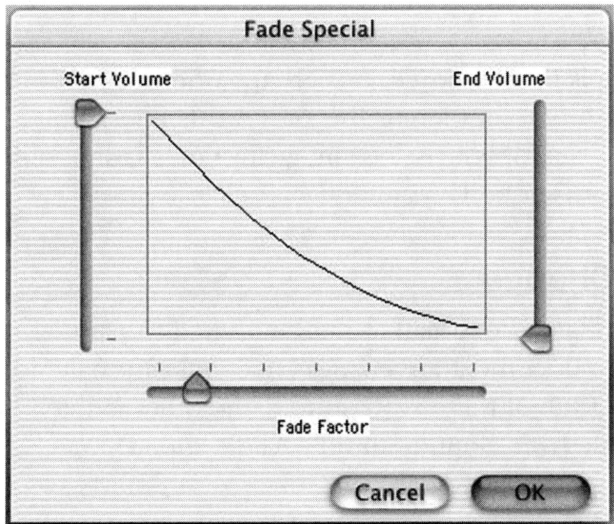

Figure 2.15 The Fade Special filter is useful to create longer and gentler fades (which are nonlinear).

Noise Gate

Some filters are designed to help deal with noisy sound clips. The Noise Gate filter, for example, is useful for reducing pops and clicks, as well as constant background noise like wind. As with many filters, this one is quite powerful and different settings can have dramatically different results.

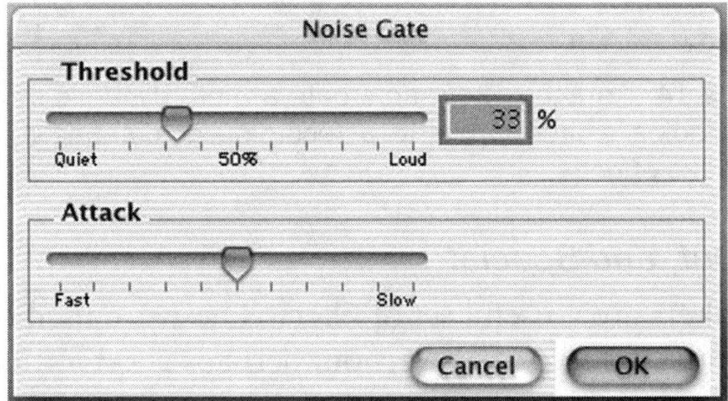

Figure 2.16 Use the Noise Gate filter to trim background noise from your sound clips.

Backwards

When you get really bored, or perhaps when you're looking for something different, there is the Backwards filter. This filter reverses the playback of your selection, giving you that nostalgic Beatles, Hendrix, or Beastie Boys effect.

Global Changes

Beyond edits and effects that can be limited to parts or selections of an audio document are changes that you can make to an entire audio file. One of these is Resample, the other is Pitch Shift; both are available from Sound Studio's Audio menu.

Resample

To change the data rate of a sound file, if it is too high or at an unusual data rate, or if it is a mono sound and you'd like it to be stereo (even the other way around), you can use the Resample command to convert the audio data to a new setting.

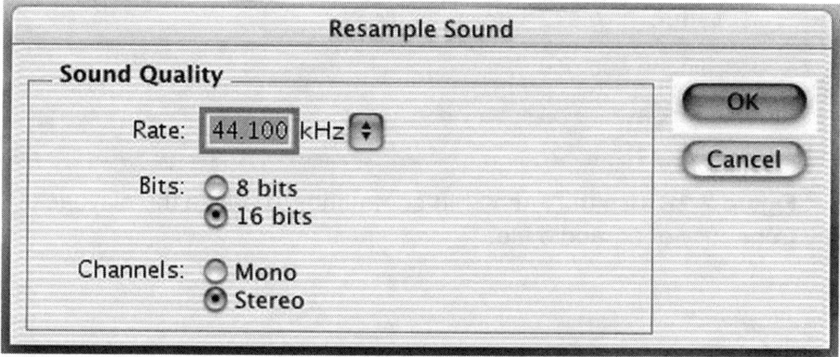

Figure 2.17 Use the Resample command to change the data rate of an audio file.

When you resample data of any kind, including sound data, you are interpreting it into a different resolution. This can be done smoothly without noticeable loss of clarity, or it can dramatically affect the quality, making it sound awful, particularly if you repeatedly resample the same data.

Pitch Shift

Similar to resampling data, you can use Sound Studio to change the pitch of a sound file. In this case rather than changing the data rate, you are instead specifying a new time frame to play back the same amount of data, which has the effect of increasing or decreasing the sound frequencies within the recording. Increasing the pitch makes everything sound higher and faster; decreasing the pitch makes it sound lower and slower.

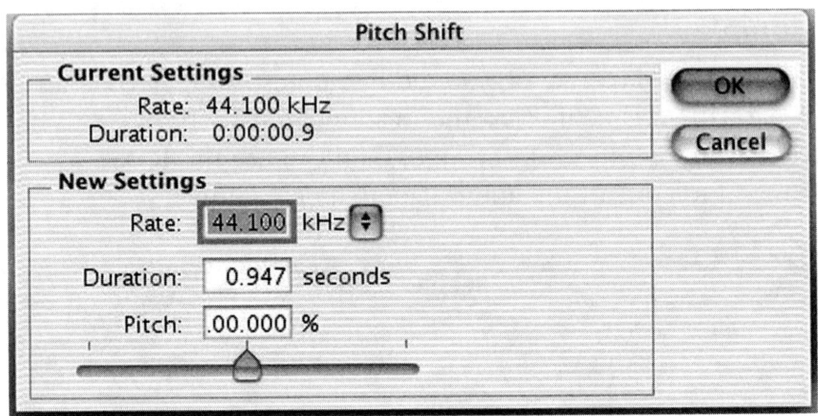

Figure 2.18 Use the Pitch Shift command to change the playback frequency of an audio file.

Reflecting the surface
of the thundering sky,
I stick in a disc—
What a downpour!

Chapter Three

Burning Your Own CDs

The latest generation of iMacs have a built-in CD-RW drive, which allows them to not only play CDs and read CD-ROMs, but also to record CDs on either burn once recordable CD media or the newer, rewritable CD media. If you don't have the latest iMac, you can easily get a CD recorder and plug it in via FireWire or USB. Not only is Apple providing great computers with CD recorders, but they also have created great software for making CDs. You can either make your own audio CDs using iTunes, or make your own data CD-ROMs right on your desktop just by inserting a blank disc and dragging files and folders onto it. If you have need of advanced CD formats, such as ISO 9660 or Video CD, you can use professional CD mastering software such as Roxio Toast. So, while the floppy disk might be dead, the compact disc is more powerful than ever.

In this chapter we're going to look at:

> Making an audio CD using iTunes and MP3 files

> Making a data CD-ROM in the Finder with Disc Burner

> Mastering a CD by using advanced, third-party software

Exploring Compact Disc Technology

So what is a CD, technically? It is a storage device that can hold up to 650 megs of data, or 74 minutes of music. This data is stored as a long and continuous stream of bits (ones and zeros), less than the width of a hair and over several miles long, all coiled up into a spiral of engraved pits in a thin metal foil. This stream of pits begins at the inside of the disc and spins outward until it ends at the edge (the opposite direction of an old vinyl record).

The data stream can be read by focusing a laser on the surface of the disc and following the track of the spiral. When the light of the laser is reflected back by the surface of the disc to a photodiode, it is read as a true bit (on, or one), and if there is no light reflected because it has gone past the surface into a pit, then it is read as a false bit (off, or zero). Within the data stream on a CD is the data comprising either the audio or the files on a ROM, as well as time-codes that tell the player or drive where in the data stream it is.

As the data stream is read, the drive spinning the disc must speed and slow at the rate of rotation in order to maintain a constant and even speed as the data is read near the inside or toward the outside of the disc (also known as CLV, Constant Linear Velocity). This speed varies from 200 to 500 revolutions per minute, and it is controlled by the timecodes embedded within the data stream. The normal constant rate of reading the data stream off a CD is 150 K per second—this is a base-end normal speed for an audio CD. A CD-ROM drive rated as 2x (two-times), 4x, 8x, or 24x means that the drive is capable of reading the data stream off a CD that many times faster than the base speed—24x is a drive that can read 3.6 megs of data off a CD in one second.

The pits that comprise the data stream on a CD are made in differ-ent ways, depending on the type of CD it is.

Manufactured CDs

A manufactured CD, such as an audio CD or software **CD-ROM**, which you might buy from a store, is made by stamping out thin pieces of metal foil and adhering them on the top-side of a plastic disc—the carrier that gives the CD its shape and thickness. The foil is covered with a coating of clear varnish over it to protect the foil; then the label is silk-screen printed on top of that.

The average manufactured CD costs about 25 to 33 cents per unit for a minimum of several thousand units. Larger runs can be even less expensive. This doesn't include packaging costs for a jewel case or printed inserts.

Recordable CDs

A recordable CD that you can make at home with a CD-R drive hooked up to your iMac is a bit different. In this case, rather than stamping a foil, the drive permanently burns opaque spots into a heat-sensitive layer of dye in special recordable CD media, using a laser in a similar manner to that in which it reads data. These opaque spots function the same as the pits in a manufactured CD, resulting in a disc that can work in a normal CD player or CD-ROM drive.

The average CD-R media costs about 50 to 70 cents when you buy it in packages of ten discs.

Rewritable CDs

A third type of CD is a rewritable CD, the latest technology. A CD-RW disc is similar to a CD-R disc, but more complex and much more expensive. It can cost as much as six times as much. It also has a special, heat-sensitive layer that is made opaque by heating with a laser beam, but in this case that layer is surrounded by other chemical layers, which allow the writing effect to be erasable rather than permanent, making the disc reusable again and again. Most drives you can buy today are both CD-R and CD-RW capable. In many cases, it is still more cost effective to use CD-R media to give away to friends, or throw away if its contents are outdated, than to use the much more costly rewritable CD media.

The average CD-RW media costs 2 to 4 dollars per unit.

Making an Audio CD Using iTunes

What a difference a decade makes. Ten years ago the compact disc was still a new and mysterious reflective circle of plastic and metal. Today, everyone uses them—kids are growing up in a world with these shiny discs everywhere. And now you (and the kids) can make your own CDs, too.

		Song	Time	Artist	Album	Track #
1	☑	Music	3:27	Madonna	Music	1 of 10
2	☑	Everybody Wants to Rule the ...	4:11	Tears For Fears	Songs From The Bi...	3 of 8
3	☑	Macy's Day Parade	3:34	Green Day	Warning	12 of 12
4	☑	A Love Before Time (Mandarin)	3:41	Yo-Yo Ma, Tan Du...	Crouching Tiger, H...	15 of 15
5	☑	Gotta Serve Somebody	5:19	Bob Dylan	The Sopranos	4 of 14
6	☑	Thank You	3:38	Dido	No Angel	6 of 12
7	☑	Desert Rose (with Cheb Miami)	4:45	Sting	Brand New Day	2 of 10
8	☑	Orbital -	4:30	The Saint	Urbal Beats	10 of 16
9	☑	Let's Stay Together	3:17	Green, Al	Pulp Fiction	4 of 16
10	☑	Bitter Sweet Symphony	5:58	Verve	Urban Hymns	1 of 13
11	☑	Telling Stories	3:57	Tracy Chapman	Telling Stories	1 of 11
12	☑	Don't Tell Me	4:40	Madonna	Music	7 of 10
13	☑	ELVIS ATE AMERICA	3:00	Passengers	Passengers: Origin...	11 of 14
14	☑	Soundtrack	4:04	A3	The Sopranos	1 of 14
15	☑	put your lights on	4:45	Santana(featuring ...	Super Natural	3 of 13
16	☑	Holding Back The Years	4:29	Simply Red	Greatest Hits	1 of 15

Figure 3.1 Using iTunes is the easiest way to make your own audio CD.

The easiest way to make an audio CD is to use iTunes, Apple's MP3 player. It is quite easy—just launch iTunes, make a new playlist, drag some music to it (not more than 74 minutes worth!), click the Burn Disc button, and slip a blank disc into your iMac. We'll look at these steps in more detail, but if you're feeling adventurous just go give it a try.

CD RECORDERS

If your iMac didn't come with a built-in CD-R drive, you'll need to buy one in order to make your own CDs. There are a variety of models available with different features, but mostly the differences are related to the speed at which they can record data onto a disc and the interface with which they connect to your iMac, using USB or FireWire. Be sure to get one that specifically states that it supports the iMac. Before you buy, look on the Internet for advice about different models and suppliers. There are quite a lot to choose from and some are much better than others. You should expect to pay somewhere around $300 for a good drive.

USB OR FireWire INTERFACE

If your iMac supports FireWire (this would be any second generation iMac DV model), you will probably want a CD-R drive that uses a FireWire connection. FireWire is much faster than USB and more reliable for working with storage peripherals. A FireWire drive may be slightly more costly than a USB CD-R drive, but the difference is well worth it.

If your iMac doesn't have FireWire, only USB, then you don't have any choice—but it's okay because there are several good CD-R drives for USB. When using a CD-R drive with USB, you need to realize that because USB is a slower type of peripheral connection that you may not be able to write CDs at the full speed of your CD recorder. You will probably find that you can only get reliable recording rates at the drive's 2x speed, even if the drive supports 4x recording.

RECORDING SPEED

Just as CD-ROM drives can read the CD data stream at different speeds (2x, 4x, 8x, 24x, 32x), recorders can write data to CD-R media at different multiples of the base rate. Most common recorders can write at 1x, 2x, and 4x speeds. You may not always be able to record at the top 4x speed, as your data throughput may be limited, but not all CD-R media is sensitive enough to work at higher speeds. In fact, the latest generation of CD recorders can do 8x,

continued...

12x, or even 16x recording, but this only works with CD-R media that is designed for these speeds, and may be a bit more costly.

The speed consideration of a CD recorder is of secondary concern to the interface because you may be limited by USB, a significant bottleneck on data throughput; only FireWire drives will be able to use faster 4x, 8x, or 12x recorders. If you do have a DV iMac with FireWire, buy as fast a drive as you can afford; you'll appreciate the speed every time you use it.

Make a Playlist to Organize Your CD

The first step in making an audio CD is to define the music you want to hear. Using iTunes, you must create a playlist and add the music you want written to your CD. Click the new Playlist button at the bottom of the iTunes window and give your new playlist a name so that you know what it is (perhaps as in my example, "CD for My Car"). Then switch the source to the Library and browse your collection to find tracks to add. You can drag a whole album by grabbing its name in the Browsing list and dragging it to your playlist in the Source list. Or you can add specific tracks by dragging them to your playlist.

You can view your CD playlist by clicking its name in the Source listing. You will see all the tracks you have added in the order in which you added them. Rearranging the order of the tracks is as easy as grabbing them and dragging them up or down the list to insert them somewhere else. Remove a track from your playlist by selecting it and pressing Delete.

At the bottom of the iTunes window, you will see a total for the length of the audio within the playlist. Since an audio CD only can hold 74 minutes of music, keep the total below this amount.

Figure 3.2 in the iTunes window shows the following playlist:

	Song	Time	Artist	Album	Track #
1	☑ Music	3:27	Madonna	Music	1 of 10
2	☑ Everybody Wants to Rule the …	4:11	Tears For Fears	Songs From The Bi…	3 of 8
3	☑ Macy's Day Parade	3:34	Green Day	Warning	12 of 12
4	☑ A Love Before Time (Mandarin)	3:41	Yo-Yo Ma, Tan Du…	Crouching Tiger, H…	15 of 15
5	☑ Gotta Serve Somebody	5:19	Bob Dylan	The Sopranos	4 of 14
6	☑ Thank You	3:38	Dido	No Angel	6 of 12
7	☑ Desert Rose (with Cheb Miami)	4:45	Sting	Brand New Day	2 of 10
8	☑ Orbital –	4:30	The Saint	Urbal Beats	10 of 16
9	☑ Let's Stay Together	3:17	Green, Al	Pulp Fiction	4 of 16
10	☑ Bitter Sweet Symphony	5:58	Verve	Urban Hymns	1 of 13
11	☑ Telling Stories	3:57	Tracy Chapman	Telling Stories	1 of 11
12	☑ Don't Tell Me	4:40	Madonna	Music	7 of 10
13	☑ ELVIS ATE AMERICA	3:00	Passengers	Passengers: Origin…	11 of 14
14	☑ Soundtrack	4:04	A3	The Sopranos	1 of 14
15	☑ put your lights on	4:45	Santana(featuring …	Super Natural	3 of 13
16	☑ Holding Back The Years	4:29	Simply Red	Greatest Hits	1 of 15

16 songs, 1:07:15 total time, 86.6 MB

Figure 3.2 To make a CD, you need to create a playlist to its contents.

Burn Your Music

After you have defined your playlist, you're ready to burn your disc. With your playlist selected in the Source listing, the button at the upper-right of the iTunes window will change to Burn Disc. Click this button once to reveal the glowing yellow and black button underneath, and then again to begin the burning process. iTunes will ask you to insert a blank disk. Insert one in your CD-R drive. iTunes will automatically begin when it detects the blank disc.

The burning process begins by preparing the music data to be written. If you have selected MP3 files from your music collection, iTunes will have to convert them to the data format used on an audio CD (this format is AIFF), invisibly caching the data on your hard drive. When it has finished preparing the data, it will write the disc, which will take as long as the length of the music you have selected in your playlist divided by the "x" speed of your CD-R drive (a full 74-minute disc will take about 9 minutes to record in an 8x drive).

Figure 3.3 Before iTunes can write the audio data to the disc, it must prepare the data.

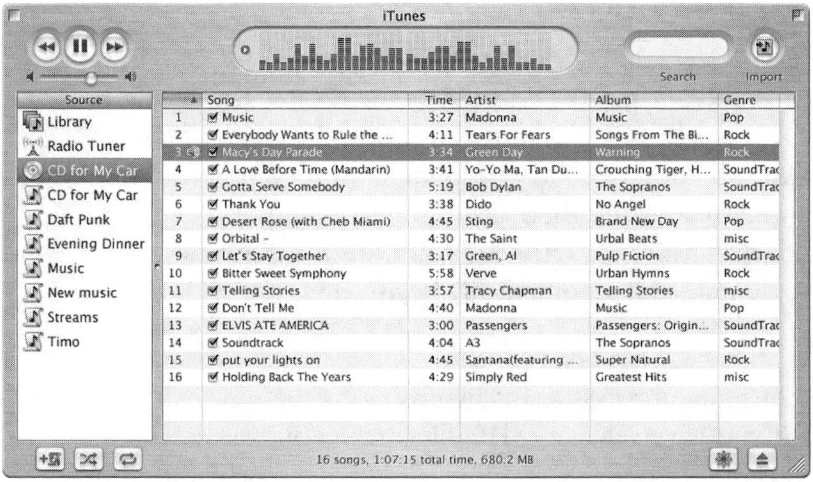

Figure 3.4 When your disc is finished burning, iTunes will display it in the Source listing.

When iTunes is finished, it will make a little "bling" sound and mount the disc on your iMac, just as any audio CD, selecting it in the Source listing. You can now enjoy your audio CD. You can play it right there in iTunes, or you can eject the disc and take it away.

> **CHOOSING BLANK MEDIA**
>
> Obviously, before you can record a disc you must have a blank unrecorded piece of CD-R media in the recorder. There are many types and brands of media available, and the quality of many CD-R media is very poor, causing data loss and audio skips and blips. Media with green or blue color dyes underneath is generally not as good as media that uses a "clear" dye. For the best results use media labeled as "silver" or "gold," which has a silver or gold reflecting surface underneath, such as discs made by the Matsui brand. These have the longest data shelf life, and they will almost always write without failing.

iTunes CD Burning Options

iTunes is all pretty automatic with few configurable options; however, it does have a couple of options. In the Preferences, under the Advanced tab, is a section for CD Burning. Within this section, you can see the CD burner that iTunes has selected to use, an option for the Burn Speed, and an option for Gap Between Tracks.

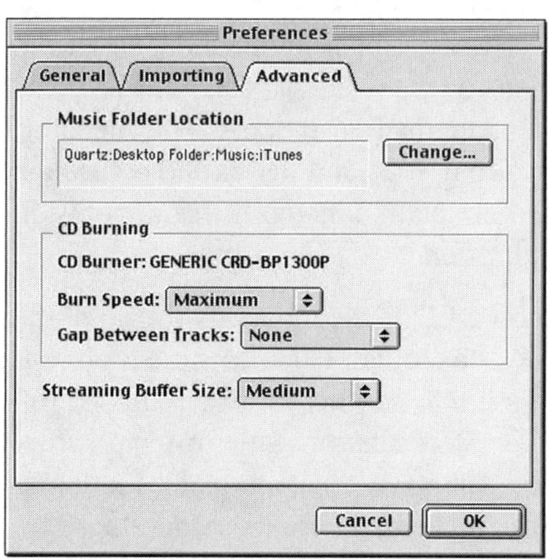

Figure 3.5 The iTunes Preferences has a section for CD Burning options.

If you are encountering errors writing to your CD media, you may want to reduce the Burn Speed setting to something slower. If you are using a USB CD recorder, try 2x or even 1x. If you can't burn a CD even at 1x without errors, then something else is wrong, either with the quality of your media or the connection to the CD recorder.

The Gap Between Tracks option enables you to set the length of time that is inserted between audio tracks being burned on your CD. The default setting is "2 seconds," which will add a two-second blank space between audio tracks. This space is useful for very old CD players to be able to skip from track to track, but most players don't need it. If a selection of music you are burning will be disrupted by the gaps, you can eliminate them (common on some classical music, for example, where there is no pause between one piece of music and another).

THE CD AUDIO FORMAT AND AIFF

The CD Audio format is kind of an unusual digital format because it doesn't have a file structure, such as data that you use on a computer; instead, it is a digital stream that just begins and goes on without any data other than that for playing back sound. No track numbers, titles, artist or album information, just sound data. The data does have timecodes that are a part of the sectors that the data is formatted in, rather than an independent encoding. But digital sound has come a long way, and newer audio CDs may have extra information added on them in methods that are outside the original data format specification.

While audio on a CD is a continuous stream of data, when you want to move that data around, either to store it on your iMac's hard drive or to encode it into another format, you need to use an interchange file that can store (permanently or temporarily) all kinds of digital audio data. The most common audio file format is AIFF, or Audio Interchange File Format, which was developed by Apple many years ago and is used throughout the computer industry. An AIFF file can contain uncompressed audio data just like an audio CD, as well as compressed data and music notation formats, such as MIDI. When iTunes prepares MP3 files for burning to CD, it is encoding the audio into AIFF files.

Writing a Data CD-ROM with Disc Burner

In the past, you needed special software for writing data to CDs, the most popular of which is called *Toast*. With this software, you'd select a disc format, specify the data to be written, and then burn the disc. While recording a CD, you couldn't do anything else with your computer, because it might interrupt the writing and ruin your CD. But in another sensible Apple moment, you can now make CDs right in the Finder on your desktop, fill them up by dragging files over, and burn the disc all at once when you're ready to eject it—in the background. A real breakthrough, to be sure.

In order to make a CD-ROM on your desktop, you'll need to be running Mac OS 9.1 with the latest version of the Disc Burn software installed (Mac OS X support may be available when you read this). You can update your Mac OS by downloading the Disc Burn software from the Apple Web site (`www.apple.com`). You'll also need a supported CD recorder, such as one that is built in to your new model iMac, or an external third-party model supported by the software.

Mounting a Blank Disc

To use the Disc Burn software, simply insert a blank CD into your iMac. Your iMac will read the disc, recognize that it is empty, and then ask you how you want to use it, displaying a dialog box with different format options.

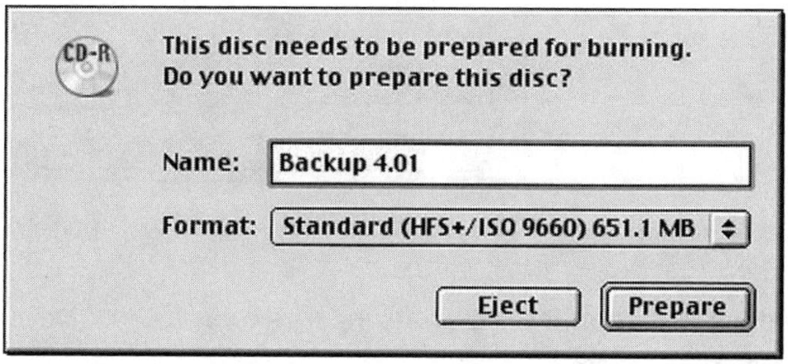

Figure 3.6 When you insert a blank CD on a supported drive, you will be asked how you want to prepare the disc.

You can give your CD a name and select one of three formats: Standard, iTunes, and MP3. To make a CD with data from your hard drive that can then be read by other computers, use the Standard format. Click Prepare to mount the disc on the desktop. This doesn't actually begin writing anything to the disc, so you don't have to worry about the media being used yet.

If you select the iTunes format, iTunes will be opened, and you can set up an audio CD and burn it as usual. If you select MP3, the disc will mount off the desktop, and you can drag over MP3 files to make a disc that can be played in special MP3 CD players.

Fill Up Your CD

After you have a blank CD mounted on your desktop, you can begin to fill it up. Simply drag files and folders to it like you do to copy stuff to any mounted storage volume. You can store anything relatively permanently on a CD. You can use a CD-R to back up important data or to archive data that you want to keep a copy of, but need to get off your iMac to make more space for new files and applications. You can also make a CD to transfer files to another computer or to send them to a service.

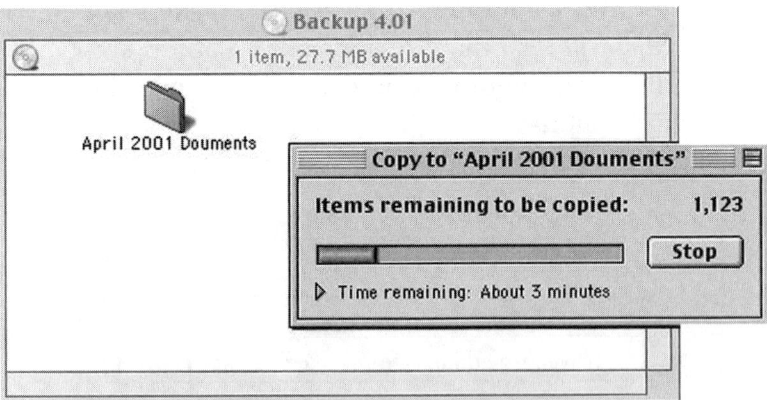

Figure 3.7 Fill up your CD by dragging files over to it just like copying files to any disk.

You can make a CD-ROM of any files on your iMac. This means that you can create a storage volume on a CD that will behave very much like a hard drive volume. The CD will mount on your desktop. It can have files and folders. It even can have a name and an icon. But there is one key difference—it is not changeable. Once you create a CD-ROM, however you organize it, the content and structure of windows and icons is permanent. You can no longer drag stuff onto it. You can't move stuff around within it. You can't change names of items or anything about them. You can't even permanently move the position of any windows from the disc from wherever they are set to open—the next time you put in the disc, they'll be right where they were recorded. Because of all this, you need to think about these things when you set up the CD, *before* you burn it.

Burn It

Anything that you add to the CD is actually copied to an invisible storage disk image until you are ready to burn it permanently onto the disk. When your disc is full or otherwise ready to be written, simply choose Burn CD-R from the Special menu, or you can drag it to the Trash, or you can press ⌘-Y to put it away. When you attempt to eject the blank CD, the system will ask if you want to burn it and eject, or if you want to discard it (which will eject it without writing the data you've copied over to it).

Figure 3.8 It can take a while for your CD to be prepared, burned, and verified.

After you have started your disc burning, the data will be prepared, the disc will be written, and then the data written on the disc will be verified—double-checking its data by comparing it to the original. You should always verify any data that is valuable and that you hope to have permanently saved on the disc. If you encounter errors in verification, it is likely that the media that you are using is of poor quality or your CD recorder is writing at too high a rate.

You should be aware when you are burning a disc that the process of recording a CD is not interruptible under any circumstances. If your iMac suffers a power disruption or otherwise causes a CD to be interrupted while being recorded, the disc won't work, and it will have to be discarded. Also, if the data cannot get from your iMac to the CD recorder in time to be written, it will also fail.

Re-burning a Disc CD-RW

Most new CD recorders support a new more advanced CD media called CD-RW or CD Rewritable. These more expensive discs are CDs that can be erased and used again, which are useful if you find yourself throwing away a lot of CD-R discs because you don't need the data written to them anymore. If not, you may want to stick with regular CD-R discs because they are so much less expensive.

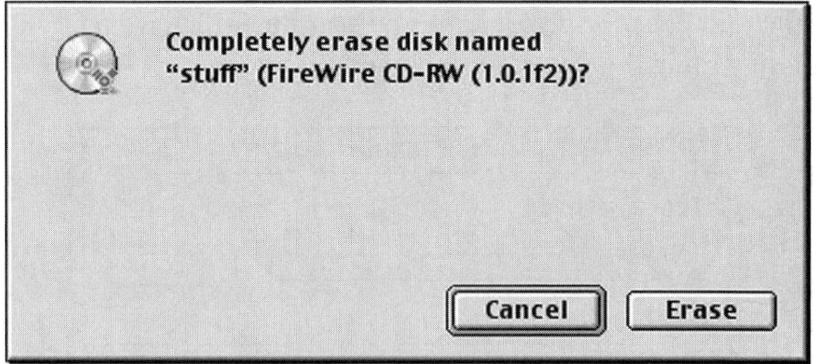

Figure 3.9 Select a CD-RW disc on your desktop and choose Erase Disk from the Special menu.

It can take a while to erase a CD-RW disc. While some CD mastering software only erases the disc's file directory, handling the rest of the erasing as it is writing the disc (essentially writing over the data), the Disc Burn support in the Finder will erase the whole disc, writing every bit on the disk to a blank state (zeroing it out). This takes as long to do as writing a full amount of data to the disc.

The CD Data Format

The stream of data on CDs can hold many different types of data, and there are many industry standard formats. These formats all follow the basic principles of the original audio CD design. The recordable portion of a CD consists of at least three parts: a lead-in block that holds directory information and is located on the inner 4 mm of the surface of the disc, a program block that holds the body of the audio or data of the CD and can be as wide as 33 mm of the disc surface, and a lead-out block that marks the end of the CD, using an additional 1 mm of the disc surface.

Within the program block is the data stream, which is recorded onto and read from the CD in chunks called *sectors*, each sector holding exactly 2,352 bytes (a byte is 8-bits, or eight ones or zeros). A sector of data is used in different ways for different formats. An audio CD uses the entire sector to hold digital audio. A data CD-ROM sets aside several bytes within each sector to record error detection and correction information, and may be further broken in to filing-system blocks of 512, 1,024, or 2,048 bytes. When you choose to use a particular CD format, your mastering software is aware of these details and records the data you specify into the appropriate format automatically.

With your iMac you can create four basic types of CDs: standard digital audio, Mac OS HFS, ISO, and Mac OS HFS/ISO hybrid. There are additional CD types you can create, but they are well outside the scope of this book; they include CD-i, Video CD, and Enhanced Music CDs. There is also a special ability for CD-ROMs called *multiple-session*, which are a method of writing several separate data streams on the same disc.

Standard Audio

The CDs you are probably most familiar with are audio CDs, known by their official title, compact disc digital audio. These CDs can be read in just about any CD player, including your home, car, or portable CD players, as well as the CD/DVD-ROM on your iMac or any other computer.

Mac HFS

A Mac HFS CD is one that uses the standard Macintosh file system, which includes the ability to use long filenames and Macintosh resource forks, similar to the ability to store a Macintosh application without destroying it. Mac HFS CDs are not mountable on non-Macintosh computers.

ISO 9660

ISO 9660 is the international standardized file system used for CDs on non-Macintosh systems. Your iMac can mount an ISO CD, but generally it cannot use the contents of it. The reason for this is because it is likely that the software on an ISO CD will need to be run in a Microsoft Windows environment. File names on an ISO CD must also conform to length limitations of 8 characters for the name and a period and 3 characters for the file type. It is also typical for these file names to be in all uppercase letters. Like this: README.TXT

Mac OS HFS/ISO Hybrid

If you're interested in creating a CD that can be natively used both on a Mac and a Windows PC, you can use the Mac OS HFS/ISO format. This type of CD has information for both Mac HFS and ISO 9660 file systems. This can allow for Macintosh files, with their long file names, and PC files to coexist on the same disc. It also includes the ability for the data of a single file to have two different file names and be shared for both systems.

Mastering a CD Using Roxio Toast

You may find that using iTunes to make audio CDs doesn't suit
your needs and neither does using Disc Burner within the Finder.
If you want to make CDs in a special format, or with more control
over options, then you'll need a professional CD mastering application.
For many years the most widely used and respected mastering
software has been Toast, formerly from Adaptec and now under
the brand Roxio.

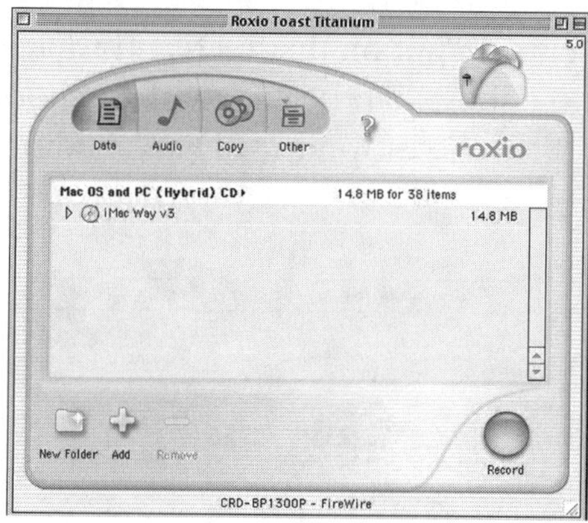

Figure 3.10 Roxio Toast is an advanced CD mastering software,
which can author CDs in just about any format ever invented.

Toast is great software, and it makes mastering CDs easy. It works
with many types of data, including individually specified files from
different sources, or with whole hard drive volumes and disc image
files. It supports many CD formats, including Mac OS HFS, cross
platform ISO 9660, Mac/ISO hybrid, audio CD, CD-I, Video CD,
Enhanced Music CD, and multitrack CD-ROM XA, and even in
the latest version DVD data formats. And most importantly, Toast
supports a huge variety of CD recorders made by all manufactures,
and with different interfaces such as USB, FireWire, SCSI, ATA,
PCMCIA. You can't go wrong using Toast. The latest version adds
burning CDs in the background as well as a new simpler interface
and compatibility with Apple's CD burning software (iTunes and
Disc Burner).

Toast works a bit differently than making CD-ROMs in the Finder (like Disc Burner). With Toast the data you are writing is not automatically copied into a temporary disk image to write from; instead, you have to gather and organize the data you want written to the CD yourself. This gives you great flexibility in what kind of data you are working with and how it is stored.

Setting Up Toast to Master a Disc

When you first run Toast, it will present you with a window in which you specify the format of the CD you want to create, what data you want to select to put on that CD, and what settings or options there are to choose. To begin, you first choose from the modes at the top of the Toast window: Data, Audio, Copy, or Other.

Figure 3.11 Begin by selecting a format type for your CD, in this case an audio CD.

The Data format mode allows you to set up a variety of CD-ROM data type discs, specifying the files, folders, or disks to use as the source and their options. The Audio format mode allows you to set up an audio CD, selecting AIFF or MP3 audio files and defining their order and options. The Other mode gives you access to many additional CD formats, including Video CD, MP3 Disc, DVD, Disc Image, Mac Volume, ISO 9660, Custom Hybrid, CD-I, Enhanced Music CD, Multitrack CD-ROM XA, and Device Copy.

Toast also has a mode called Copy. This mode is kind of neat as it allows you to somewhat automatically duplicate a CD accurately without having to copy all its data off to your hard drive and then set up a new disc to record it.

Figure 3.12 If you want to make a perfect duplicate of a disc, use Toast's copy mode.

The Toast window also displays the currently active CD recorder at the bottom edge—yours should be listed. If not, you can choose Recorder Info from the Recorder menu and click Rescan. If it doesn't appear, you'll need to troubleshoot your connection. Make sure that it is a mechanism supported by Toast, and that you have the necessary drivers loaded in the system for the drive (or you may have a conflict with iTunes and Disc Burner).

In the lower right corner of the mastering window is a Record button to begin writing the CD. When you click the Record button, you will be presented with further options on how to record the disc.

> ### MULTI-SESSION DISCS
>
> Typically, a CD is recorded all at one time and cannot be interrupted in the process. It must begin with the lead-in block and end with a lead-out block—all for one continuous data stream. This is the idea of disc-at-once.
>
> However, newer CD-ROM drives and formats have evolved, which allow for multiple data streams on a CD. These are called *multi-session discs*. Each session is recorded all at once and begins and ends with lead-in and lead-out blocks. You can have as many sessions on a CD as there is space for, and each session's lead-in and lead-out blocks use up several additional megs of data. The benefit of multi-session discs is that when you only have a small amount of data to record you can later add more data to the same piece of CD-R media without having to waste its remaining space. Multi-session discs aren't compatible with all CD data formats x 2 and on Mac OS HFS CDs, each session will be considered a separate volume when the CD is mounted on the desktop.

Burning a Disc with Toast

Ready to burn your disc? All the data selected? Are the options for the CD format specified? Click the Record button. Toast will present you with a dialog box of writing options. This is the last step.

Before you burn a disc, you can specify the speed at which you want to write the disc. If you want to run the write as a simulation to further test that everything is working properly, you can check the option for Simulation Mode.

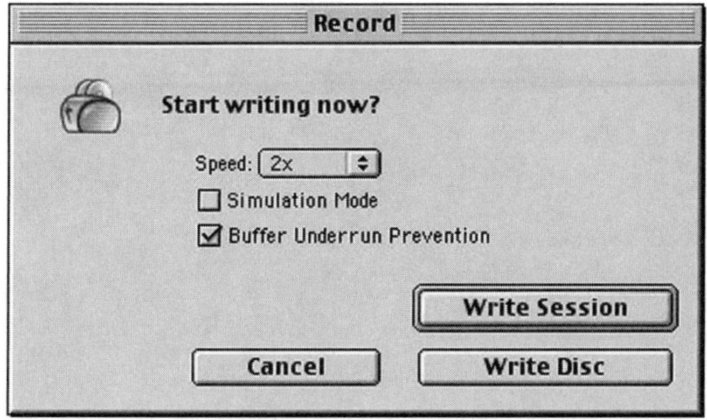

Figure 3.13 Toast has a couple of options before you burn your disc.

You can now write the disc by choosing whether you want to write an entire disc—using all of it even if the data will be much smaller than the full capacity of the media—or if you want to write a session allowing you to come back later and record another data stream (only for multiple-session compatible formats and players). All iMac CD-ROM drives support multiple-session discs so there is probably no reason not to go ahead and write your data stream as a multiple-session compatible data stream (writing an entire disc can never have an additional session added, even if you are only writing a small portion of the media's capacity).

Click Write Session or Write Disc to burn your CD. Once the writing process has begun, there is no canceling it or interrupting it. Toast will show you the relative progress of the recording session and the time remaining until it is completed.

If there are any problems along the way, Toast will stop and present you with its best explanation of what has happened, which will likely be quite cryptic. The data stream being written in that session will be unusable (other successful sessions of a multiple-session disc will still work). If it is possible, Toast will try to recover the remaining portion of the disc for additional sessions by writing a lead-out block. If you get an error, try checking all your settings and the physical connections, and then run a simulation to see if your adjustments help solve the difficulty.

Figure 3.14 Toast allows you to burn in the background on your iMac, but if it gets interrupted, the disc will fail.

If all is well, Toast will make a distinctive "bing" sound when it finishes and ask you if you'd like to verify the disc or Eject. I recommend verifying anything of importance.

Figure 3.15 When the disc is done writing, Toast will ask you if you want to verify it or eject it.

If you don't respond in a few seconds (perhaps you step away while your CD is recording), Toast will go ahead and begin verifying the disc by reading every sector and comparing it with the original data. If it finds any discrepancies, it will let you know immediately. Any errors at this point in the recording process usually only happen for one reason—bad media. It may be simply that the media isn't working well at the speed the recorder is working at, 4x is too fast for the most inexpensive media. Again, I recommend "silver" type media, which tends to be the most reliable. You can interrupt the verification process at any time, and it is possible to re-verify or later verify data if nothing is changed about the original source.

When the verification is complete, Toast will "bing" again and let you know that it has successfully completed recording the disc. You can click Eject to take your CD! You now have a CD you've made yourself. Try it out, put it in your iMac, and see how it mounts and displays the data you selected.

The old master loaded the tray
And turned up the volume,
Revealing the Source itself.
Look where discs hide the sound.

Chapter Four

Advanced Digital Audio

If you want to go beyond listening to music with iTunes, playing with sound waves, and burning your own CDs, the iMac has a wealth of professional audio applications from which to choose. You might want to be a DJ and organize and present music for clubs and events. You might want to be a foley artist (someone who makes sound effects for action in the movies that doesn't get recorded on location, including footsteps, water pouring, etc.), recording home-made sound effects to dub into your iMovies. You might want to be a musician and self-publish your own songs on CD or on the Internet. In the past, the equipment to do these things was expensive and bulky, but today you can do these things at home with your iMac.

The iMac has much to offer the digital audio professional. In fact, Macs are widely used in music recording, sound mixing, and studio engineering. They have high-quality, built-in audio circuitry and use standard, audio data formats. Macs have a friendly, easy-to-use interface that appeals to the creative professional. They have good inputs and outputs for connecting external audio equipment. Apple and the Mac have a long history of audio involvement, which means that software for working with audio on the Mac is quite advanced. In this chapter we're going to introduce some of the programs and tools you can use to produce professional quality audio with your iMac.

In this chapter we're going to look at:

- Making your own music with interactive synthesizers

- Engineering with sequencing and mixing tools

- Publishing audio electronically using streaming Internet broadcasting

Making Music

Most people don't want to produce or engineer audio; they want to make music. And just like some artists like to use illustration software to draw pictures, rather than a real pen or brush, many musicians like to use their computers to orchestrate their songs, rather than hire a band and use real instruments. Making music on your iMac can range from homebrewed electronic drum and bass to highly evolved classical orchestrations. The more complex the music, the more time and experience required to produce it. Let's look at four software applications designed for different levels of music creation: Mixman, Rebirth, Reason, and ProTools.

> **LEARNING MORE ABOUT AUDIO ENGINEERING**
>
> There are many great resources for learning more about working with sound on the Mac. In fact, Macs are used within the most sophisticated sound studios and labs so there are thousands of people who are knowledgeable about music and studio work with Macs. There are lots of places to go to learn more about digital audio and sound engineering, and many of the best are actually local DJ enthusiast shops in college towns and their Web sites.

Interactive Music

The easiest way to put together some quick good sounding tunes without much experience as a musician is to use software that provides all the basics at a click of a button using pre-made rhythms and loops. For example, software such as Mixman Studio Pro (www.mixman.com) provides drumbeats, melodies, vocal samples, and many other sampled and looped snippets of music that you can turn into your own recording just by clicking to turn them on and off at your own intervals—the timing is kept in sync automatically. You can even use this software to record your own samples and mix your recordings. The Pro version of these applications provides advanced features for mixing multiple tracks, panning and spatial filtering, as well as tweaking the pitch and reverb.

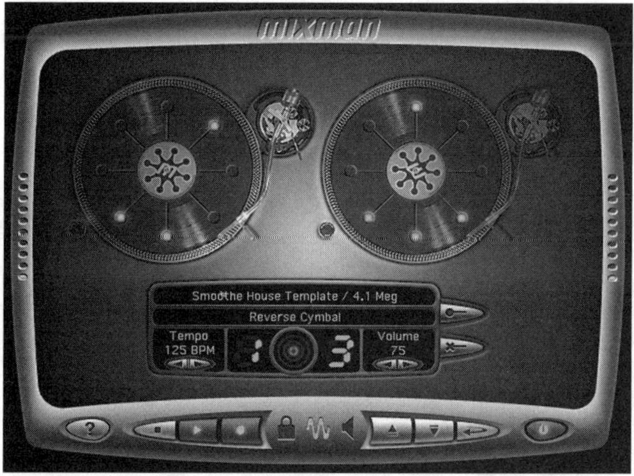

Figure 4.1 A demo version of Mixman Studio is available from `www.mixman.com`.

This type of plug-and-play music creation is a great way to begin experimenting with computer based music. Mixman also has available dozens of add-on sound sets, many licensed from mainstream artists, with which you can add and remix on your own, having the ultimate home DJ kit.

SAMPLES, SAMPLING, LOOPS

You'll notice that many of these digital audio applications make realistic sounds by using samples—short, recorded snippets that contain the basic unit of an instrument: a note, a voice, or an effect. When samples are made of other recordings and retain a distinctive sound from them, this is called *sampling*, and is often done in DJ remixing of music. Looping samples is a way to create repeating rhythms and effects.

Drum Machines

When it comes to creating original drum and bass, your iMac can dig deep and smoke. With the use of software such as Rebirth, a Roland drum machine emulator, you can fabricate intricate basslines, compose rhythm sets, synthesize melodies, and mix and sequence them all together. The quality of this emulator is right up there with the real thing and indeed many professional musicians use Rebirth to add drum and base to their recordings as well as live performances.

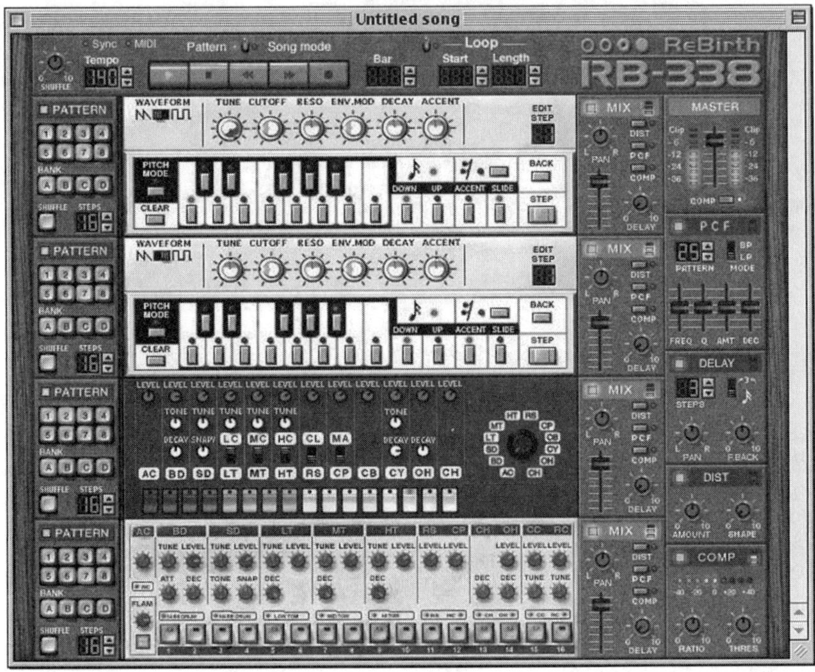

Figure 4.2 A demo version of Rebirth is available from Propellerhead Software (www.propellerheads.se).

Using Rebirth is quite complex, but the documentation is good, and there are many online tutorials and guides available. The basic principals involve setting particular sounds to occur along beats of 16, which can be repeated (looped) or switched to different beat sets or patterns. You can then sequence various patterns on separate synthesizers to build out the length of your song. You can also adjust the volume level and pitch, reverb, and other functions to modify the synthesizer's output. You can record all your interactions and modification in real-time as a performance and when you play them back, the knobs, sliders, and buttons will move by themselves. Many Rebirth projects are available as samples and finished music that you can download and modify.

> ### 808 AND BEYOND
>
> The sounds of the classic drum machines and bassline synths Roland TB-303, TR-808, and TR-909 form the backbone in every techno musician and DJ's work. Unfortunately, owning any of these machines still remains a dream for most of us. They stopped manufacturing those awkward, beautiful, great sounding boxes over 15 years ago. The handful of these artifacts still in existence are collector's items and would cost you an arm and a leg. Instead, you can use a software-based emulator, which is based on carefully engineered samples under license, and can produce close, if not identical, output.

Synthesizers

A synthesizer is an electronic musical instrument that creates natural or unnatural sounds artificially using complex algorithms and processing. The most elaborate electronic music has been done in studios filled with racks of hardware synthesizers, each wired into various filters and sequencers, in turn hooked up to keyboards and drum pads. Now you can find many popular synthesizer features emulated in the same fashion as a traditional drum machine, the latest and greatest is Reason, a very advanced and fully customizable software synth studio. There is almost no limit to the musical capabilities of modern synthesizers; you can create techno beats, grungy guitars, or even symphonic pianos.

If you think using a traditional drum machine such as those in the Rebirth emulation application is difficult, Reason, which emulates racks full of these devices, is many times more complex—but along with that complexity comes a level of creative potential that is unmatched by simple preprogrammed interactive applications.

When you have a rack of devices, they need to be patched together. While this is handled automatically, at the press of the Tab key, Reason flips the rack around for you to see and manually rewire patch cables by clicking and dragging. By adding interfaces to your virtual rack, you can even connect external "real" hardware.

Figure 4.3 A demo version of Reason is available from Propellerhead Software (www.propellerheads.se).

What Is MIDI?

Musical Instrument Digital Interface (MIDI) is a protocol allowing note and control information to be communicated from keyboards to sound modules and to be recorded on sequencers. MIDI is not a sound format, but rather a format for organizing musical notes—think of it as sheet music for a computer. MIDI can do more, even be a protocol for different music devices to interact with each other. But MIDI doesn't contain any digital sound itself; instead, a MIDI device must be used to create the sound from instructions in a MIDI file. Your iMac can play MIDI music files by using QuickTime, which just happens to include MIDI capabilities.

Figure 4.4 Click and drag virtual patch cables to build your own custom rack.

Studio Engineering

The line between making music and studio engineering is a bit fuzzy in the electronic world where recording a track is one click away from *sequencing* in some loops and mixing it down to a master. However, the techniques and tools of sound engineering are a bit different from those used to make the sounds in the beginning. Any recording or live source designed for presentation goes through some kind of engineering, either to simply adjust its levels or to add effects by reprocessing it. More elaborate recordings are broken down into many pieces and carefully timed and sequenced. Of course, all you need is an iMac. Let's look at what you can do with your music once you've recorded it.

Sequencing

Sequencing is a very modern technique for engineering audio and music. Just about everything you hear from a produced source, such as commercial music, radio spots, or even television and movie soundtracks, has been through some sort of sequencing. The more elaborate professional digital audio editing applications have the abil-

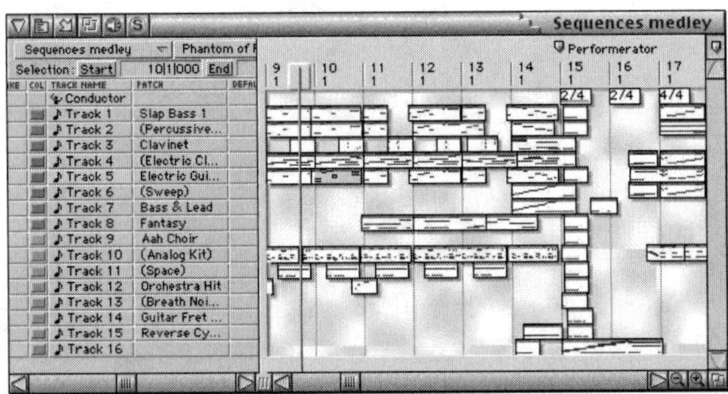

Figure 4.5 Sequencing audio can be very elaborate and powerful.

ity to design a recording from many pieces, overlaying and mixing them, as well as repeating and structuring them—this is called *sequencing*. You can use different types of audio, such as sampled voice or sampled rhythms, and combine them with **MIDI** tracks to build a very complex piece of music.

A typical sequencing interface displays a listing of tracks, one each for each instrument or audio sample, and a scrolling timeline in which to organize them. By dragging around elements, you can change the sequence in which different parts are played or overlap them to play simultaneously. You can play back your sequence as you are editing it so that you can quickly hear the results of your changes.

A professional application that is actually available for free (because the company which produces it makes their money from selling audio hardware for professional studios) is ProTools FREE from

Digidesign at `www.digidesign.com` (or `www.protools.com`).
You may find that this software is very complex and difficult to use;
however, it does come with extensive manuals and tutorials.
ProTools has advanced digitizing, mixing, and sequencing controls.
Using it, you can record and play up to 8 tracks of digital audio,
record and play up to 48 MIDI tracks, use non-linear, random-
access editing and mix automation, process audio with up to 5
RTAS plug-ins per track, use up to 5 inserts and 5 sends per track,
route up to 16 busses, work with 16-bit or 24-bit sessions.

For the most sophisticated sound recording, mixing, editing, and
orchestration, Digital Performer from Mark of the Unicorn is an
extremely feature-full professional digital audio application available
commercially for about $795; for more information see
`www.motu.com`. Digital Performer is an integrated digital audio
and MIDI sequencing production tool. It provides a comprehensive
recording, playback, and editing environment for a large variety of
audio applications. It allows you to simultaneously record and play
back multiple tracks of digital audio and MIDI data in an integrated, creative environment. Digital Performer's multitrack sequencer
design, combined with nondestructive digital audio editing capabilities, provides unprecedented flexibility and control over the music
that you make. Digital Performer literally replaces racks full of
recording gear. You get the capabilities of a multitrack digital
recording system—automated 32-bit digital mixer, reverb, effects,
EQ, and compression.

GOOD ENGINEERING

Once you have your source edited and your parts sequenced, you
can add effects to smooth out your material or to accent it with special filters. You can add fades at the beginning or end of a selection
to soften it out. You can add slight echoes to make it feel more
expansive. You can filter out hiss and noise. You can change the pitch
and speed. The options for processing are almost limitless, thanks to
digital audio.

continued...

Making good sound is like making a good photograph, you want a clear reproduction with good contrasts and without noise, but you also want a level of atmosphere and wide range. Keep in mind that when you are working with audio, you are working with performance—something that happens dynamically in time. Having a good ear is helpful, but considering natural issues of timing and rhythm is ultimately more important. Trying different things to experiment with sound is essential. Subtle effects can have the most impact on the quality of your audio creations.

Mixing

When you have multiple sound tracks that you'd like to combine together, whether they will be literally combined into a single audio recording, or whether some tracks will be discrete (such as stereo left and right), you need to be able to adjust their levels individually to emphasize different aspects of each at different times—this is called *mixing*. Most applications that have this ability create a traditional mixing board interface where the levels of individual tracks are adjusted with sliders and knobs.

Figure 4.6 A mixing board is useful if you're a DJ or a recording engineer.

Mixing is different than sequencing in that you are creating the balance and levels of each track of audio on the fly as it is played back in order to make a performance. The software records (remembers) your adjustments so that you can repeat the performance or modify it. When you are finished, you have a distilled stereo mix of your digital audio.

> ### GETTING THE LEVELS RIGHT
>
> The final stage in making good audio is mixing, where the levels and balance are adjusted for pleasing and interesting listening. You may be simply amplifying and equalizing the volume to bring out quiet sections or tone down loud sections. Or you may be adjusting the volume of competing tracks, such as drums, bass, piano, and voice, to bring forward each at times when they are leading the music. You may also be adjusting the balance between channels of stereo, so that drums appear to one side, a piano to the other, and voice in the middle.
>
> Indeed, mixing is a very artistic process. You can dramatically and subtly change the mood and effectiveness of your audio by mixing it differently. It may be helpful when you are mixing to have a goal for the type of environment and experience you are trying to convey, such as a natural live recording in a real place (such as a jazz club), leaving a level of light noise and perhaps a lot of stereo spread and strength, or a very clean studio recording where each instrument is blended very closely and sharply.

Notation

An additional and powerful feature of using digital audio tools to create music is their ability to automatically draw up traditional music notation that can be printed and read. This can only be done from music that is being synthesized by the computer (or through a **MIDI** interface) where the computer is tracking and programming each note of the orchestration.

The notation interface can be used directly to create and edit music, either being entered with the iMac's keyboard and mouse, or by using a **MIDI** music keyboard to capture notes as they are played. You can play back the music from this interface as well, to immediately hear the results of your composition.

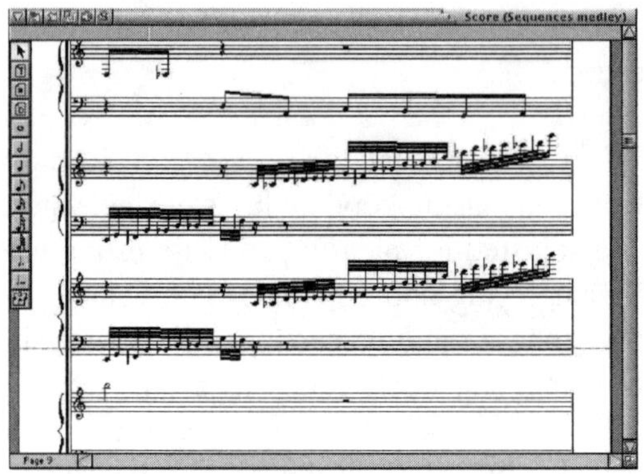

Figure 4.7 Music notation can be generated automatically and edited by using digital tools.

Publishing Your Creations

If you're a musician, the Internet can be a great place for you to get exposure for your music. You can create a home page for you or your band. You can post samples of your work as downloadable MP3 files. You can embed QuickTime samples of your music that can be played right in a visitor's Web browser. The most ambitious thing you can do to put sound on the Internet is to use **MP3** streaming to create and broadcast your own virtual radio station. Of course, you don't have to be a musician, you can share any kind of audio performance.

Embedded QuickTime

Perhaps the easiest way to add music to a Web site is to embed it in the same way that you embed a QuickTime movie. To do this you'll need to first convert your audio file to a QuickTime file. This is easy if you have purchased the upgrade to the Pro version of QuickTime, which allows you to import files using QuickTime Player. Use the Import command, and you can select almost any digital audio format file (including MP3) and open it. It will open as a new unsaved file. You can play the file at this point, and even edit it by copying and pasting portions of it. When you are ready to save the file, use the Save As command and select the option for Make Movie Self-contained. You now will have a QuickTime format file that you can use on your iMac or post as part of a Web site.

To embed a QuickTime movie file (in this case just an audio track), you use the <EMBED> tag in your HTML, which links to the QuickTime file and uses the QuickTime browser plug-in to display a QuickTime controller within your Web page.

MP3 Downloadable

Probably the simplest way to share your audio is to make it a downloadable file. Begin by creating an MP3 file or similar self-contained and easy-to-play back digital audio file of your audio. You can then upload this file to a directory on your Web site, or even use your iTools iDisk. Then you can simply put a link to the file's URL on a Web page so that people can download it and listen to it, using their own MP3 players.

If you create a downloadable audio file, be sure to encode it with information about the audio, such as your name and the name of the audio track. This way someone who has it on his computer will be able to come back and remember what the file is and who it came from.

Streaming

One way to have a lot of fun with audio and the Internet is to use MP3 streaming software and a broadcasting server to create your own live digital audio radio station. All you need is your iMac, a good fast and stable Internet connection, an MP3 streaming software application, and a streaming server or an account with a broadcast provider. Once established, any MP3 you play will be broadcast out onto the Internet where anyone can listen with MP3 software that supports listening to MP3 streams. And using a fast computer like your iMac, you can even digitize audio on the fly and broadcast it live, right from a microphone or other audio input.

To get an idea of what streaming MP3 broadcasting can be like, you can go to any of various sites on the Internet and "tune in" to an MP3 stream of your choice. One popular site is `live365.com`, which has thousands of streams to choose from and will host your own broadcasts for free. You can use iTunes to listen to streaming MP3, but you will need other software to broadcast.

There are three ways you can create your own MP3 streaming broadcast. You can upload MP3 music files to a host account where the data is stored and played by a remote server automatically. You can relay a live stream from your iMac to a broadcasting server service. Or if you are capable, you can run your own stream server and serve directly to listeners. This last option is very complicated and not something you'll likely be able to do yourself. However, the second method, using a broadcasting service, is very easy.

To create your own MP3 stream, first set up an account with a streaming service such as `live365.com`. From them, you will get an IP address and port number that are specific for you and point to your broadcast. Use an MP3 player that supports broadcasting, such as SoundJam MP, and enter your broadcast account's IP address and port number, as well as your account password, into the Stream Broadcast settings. That's it. Now everything you play with your MP3 player will be broadcast simultaneously to the broadcasting server for anyone to listen to. You can provide additional information for your stream, such as the genre of music you are playing or other keywords which people can search for to find your stream. And you can, of course, provide a link from your Web site directly to the URL for your stream, which people can link to and begin listening to immediately.

Figure 4.8 A service such as `live365.com` can be used to set up your own Internet radio.

RULES OF BROADCASTING

There is one thing to keep in mind when broadcasting music on the Internet—copyright. I'm not a lawyer so don't take this as advice, merely something to consider, because there are many laws and rules to follow when you are working with copyrighted audio. Generally, if you have created the audio yourself, you can do whatever you want with it. But if it is someone else's, then there are restrictions that include having permission to use the audio and to be able to share it with others. If you are providing a downloadable (or embedded download) file, you must own or have permission and a release to provide it.

However, if you are using MP3 streaming to broadcast it, then you may be able to follow similar rules and restrictions that radio

continued...

stations and other broadcasters follow. These are in brief: your program must not be part of an "interactive service," meaning that you cannot perform sound recordings within one hour of a request by a listener or at a time designated by the listener; in any three-hour period, you should not intentionally program more than three songs (and not more than two songs in a row) from the same recording; you should not intentionally program more than four songs (and not more than three songs in a row) from the same recording artist or anthology/box set; continuous looped programs may not be less than three hours long; rebroadcasts of programs may be performed at scheduled times as follows: programs of less than one-hour: no more than three times in a two-week period; programs longer than one hour: no more than four times in any two-week period; you should not publish advance program guides or use other means to pre-announce when particular sound recordings will be played; you should only broadcast sound recordings that are authorized for performance in the United States; you should pass through (and not disable or remove) identification or technological protection information included in the sound recording (if any).

All this actually provides you with the possibility to create the equivalent of your own radio station to have fun with. Of course, you have to have the time and the Internet bandwidth to spare.

Digital Video

In addition to entertaining and enlightening us, movies also enable us to capture moments in time that will never come again. In effect, movies can be a time machine that we can use to enhance the experiences we enjoy in our own memories and to enjoy the memories of others.

Movies are also a means for us to express our own creativity and to communicate our own ideas to other people—preferably in an entertaining and enjoyable way.

Digital Video (DV) technology enables you to capture high-quality footage *and* then transform that raw footage into a *movie* that people will actually enjoy watching. With DV on the iMac, you can express yourself in ways that are limited only by your own imagination. Your movies can have plots, transitions, sound effects, music, special effects, and more. And you can distribute and watch your movies in many ways, such as videotape or on the Web.

In this section, we'll explore digital video, the iMac way:

- ➤ Chapter 5: Creating Digital Video Masterpieces
- ➤ Chapter 6: Creating a Video Track
- ➤ Chapter 7: Adding Transitions, Titles, and Special Effects
- ➤ Chapter 8: Creating Sound Tracks
- ➤ Chapter 9: Finishing, Distributing, and Watching Digital Video
- ➤ Chapter 10: Advanced Digital Video

Visual freedom at last,
No more dependencies:
iMovie in the iMac,
Smoke behind the rocket

Chapter Five

Creating Digital Video Masterpieces

While digital video (DV) technology and your iMac enable you to create digital movies, there is more to do than just hitting the record button and hacking away in iMovie if you want to create *good* digital movies. You need to have some idea about the fundamentals of making movies, whether in the analog or digital world. You also need to build a DV toolkit and understand how to use the tools that are in it. Finally, you have to plan your movie and then shoot it. Only then will you be ready to use DV editing tools to metamorphize all of the bits and bytes into a digital movie that is worthy of your audience.

In this chapter, we're going to look at:

- ➤ Discovering movie-making fundamentals
- ➤ Finding the path to digital movie nirvana
- ➤ Learning about which DV tools you should have and use
- ➤ Planning your movie
- ➤ Planning a shoot and then shooting the plan

Making Good Movies Is Not an Accident

Movies don't just happen. They are the result of lots of hard work by a lot of people. There are literally thousands of tasks that need to be accomplished, and even more decisions that have to be made. And all of this has to be guided by the director's vision of what the movie should eventually be. There are three fundamental phases of movie making.

> **Planning**—During the planning phase, every aspect of the movie is developed and planned. The major tasks include writing a script or screenplay, developing the storyboards, identifying the resources you will need, and so on. The tasks that are required to make the movie are also planned. Shot lists are made, location shoots are scheduled, cast and crew members are chosen, and on it goes.

> **Production**—This is the part that most of us think about when we visualize the movie-making process. During this phase, the cameras roll and the video clips (from which the movie is eventually made) are captured.

> **Post-production**—During post-production, the clips are laid into a track to form the basic movie. Special effects and music are added. The movie is edited and re-edited until it meets the creator's vision for what it should be. Only after the post-production process does the collection of clips actually become a movie.

If you're like many people, your image of movie-making probably focuses mostly on the production phase. However, this is really a misconception.

Hollywood moviemakers spend much more of their time and effort in the planning and post-production processes than they do in the production phase. A major movie usually takes about two years from project go-ahead to delivery to your local theater. Shooting the movie usually lasts for only two or three months out of those two years. The planning process often requires nine months or more, and post-production consumes the rest of the schedule.

This happens for a couple of reasons. One is that shooting a film is *really* expensive. Having the cast and crew working fulltime costs lots of money. Paying for sound stages is also costly, and it's even more expensive to take the production on the road to shoot on location. This is strong incentive to keep shooting time to a minimum. Another reason that shooting time is kept to a minimum is that before scenes can be filmed, these scenes must be defined in detail so that the cast and crew knows what to do. This requires that scenes be set up so that the characters do interesting things, and the scenes that are shot can actually be used to make a movie.

Although you probably aren't going to be creating any movies on the scale of Hollywood movies, the basic principles you use should be the same—albeit scaled down quite a bit. You should spend a good amount of effort planning your movie before you ever take your camcorder in hand to begin filming. After you capture your clips, you should spend even more time creating a movie from those clips.

THE IMPORTANCE OF PLANNING

DV technology is geared towards the production and post-production phases of the process. For example, you can use iMovie to build and edit your movie. Because this book is about the iMac way (and not about movie making in general), most of this section of the book is devoted to using DV tools to create a movie from your clips (in other words, post-production). If you really want to make great movies, you should learn more about classic movie planning tools so that you can devote an appropriate amount of effort to the "front-end" of the process. You'll find many Web sites devoted to movie making, and there are also lots of books on the topic.

Following the iMac Way to Great Digital Video

With your trusty iMac and a few other tools, you can create movies that you and other people will actually *enjoy* watching. Whether you mainly want to create home movies as a way to document your life or create entertaining movies that have plots, characters, and other Hollywood-type elements, DV helps you do it.

> ### DIGITAL VERSUS ANALOG
>
> And the winner is...digital by a mile. Digital technology has overwhelmed analog in almost every area of life. Why is this? Because digital technology almost always provides better quality with greater speed, smaller size, less cost, and easier operation than does analog technology. DV is a prime example of this. While DV is fairly easy to edit and modify (especially when using iMovie), editing video that is on videotape is almost impossible for non-professionals.

Creating a DV movie, just like any other creative activity, is done through a series of steps or tasks. Done well, each step contributes something positive to the end result. You can skip some steps if you don't need them to make the process match the complexity of your movie.

The major steps to create a DV movie are the following:

- ➤ Build an iMac DV studio
- ➤ Plan your movie
- ➤ Plan your video shoot
- ➤ Shoot the video clips
- ➤ Create the video track
- ➤ Create the sound tracks
- ➤ Finish, distribute, and watch the movie

You'll learn something about each of these steps in this section of the book. The first four items on the list are covered in this chapter. The last three items are covered in subsequent chapters.

Building an iMac Digital Video Studio

There is a basic set of hardware and software that you must have to work with DV; there are also other tools that you might want to explore when you are ready to take the "next step." The basic tools are covered in this section while some advanced tools are covered in Chapter 10, "Advanced Digital Video."

There are four items without which you are pretty much dead in the DV water. The good news is that you probably already have at least three of them (including the most expensive one).

> An iMac

> A copy of iMovie

> A digital video camera

> QuickTime (specifically, QuickTime Pro)

iMac

Because you are reading *The iMac Way*, you probably already have an iMac (not much of a stretch, is it?). There have been a variety of models of iMacs over the past several years—the good news is that many iMac models are suitable for DV work.

---

iMAC DV

Unlike many names that Apple has used for various Mac models over the years, iMac DV models do have a meaningful name. The "DV" indicates that the iMac has FireWire ports, which you need to be able to connect a digital video camera to it. Many modern iMacs also include a CD-RW drive.

Figure 5.1 iMac DV models, such as this DV/400, are ideal for creating your own DV movies.

To be suitable for DV work, your iMac should have the following:

> **FireWire ports**—You need to be able to connect a digital video camera to your iMovie through FireWire. You might also want to add an external FireWire hard drive to your system to help you store all of the DV data that you will accumulate.

Is Your iMac Cold?

If your iMac doesn't have FireWire, you aren't totally left out of the game. You can use iMovie to edit any video that you get from sources other than a digital video camera. You can also add a digitizer to your system that will enable you to capture video clips. The quality or ease of use isn't nearly what you can obtain with a digital video camera, but it will work.

> **Plenty of RAM**—DV work is processor and memory intensive. Your iMac should have at least 128 MB of RAM.

➤ **Lots of disk space**—DV files are *huge*. You need to have several hundred MB of free disk space to create a short DV movie. For movies longer than a few minutes, you will need GBs of free storage space.

You will likely need more disk space as you create iMovie movies. However, you can't add another internal disk drive to your iMac. To gain more space to store your DV projects, you have three options. One is to clear space off your iMac's hard drive so that you have enough free space. Another is to add an external FireWire hard drive to your system. The third is to replace your iMac's hard drive with one that has more capacity (don't try this one unless you really know what you are doing).

ADDING A FIREWIRE HARD DRIVE

The easiest way to increase the working space that you have available is to add a FireWire hard drive to your system (assuming that your iMac has FireWire ports of course). Make sure that you get a relatively fast drive, such as one that is rated for at least 7200 RPM. An excellent example of such a drive is the LaCie 7200 RPM 60 GB FireWire external hard drive.

An excellent source for this drive is Small Dog Electronics. At the time of this writing, Small Dog offers this drive for about $339. You can visit Small Dog at `www.smalldog.com` or call them at 802-496-7171.

Because you have bought this book, you are eligible for a special discount on a purchase from Small Dog. See the ad on the inside back cover of this book for details.

While it isn't a requirement for DV work, having a CD-RW drive can be useful for DV work. You can store completed movies on CD-R discs, and you can move pieces of your DV projects onto discs to remove them from your iMac's internal drive when you are done working with them.

Any iMac can support a CD-RW drive. If your iMac doesn't have
an internal CD-RW drive, you can add an external USB or
FireWire drive. A FireWire drive is the better choice because it is
a bit faster, but either will work just fine. For example, the
EZQuest CD-RW FireWire drive, currently costing around $299,
enables you to store data on CD-R and CD-RW discs.

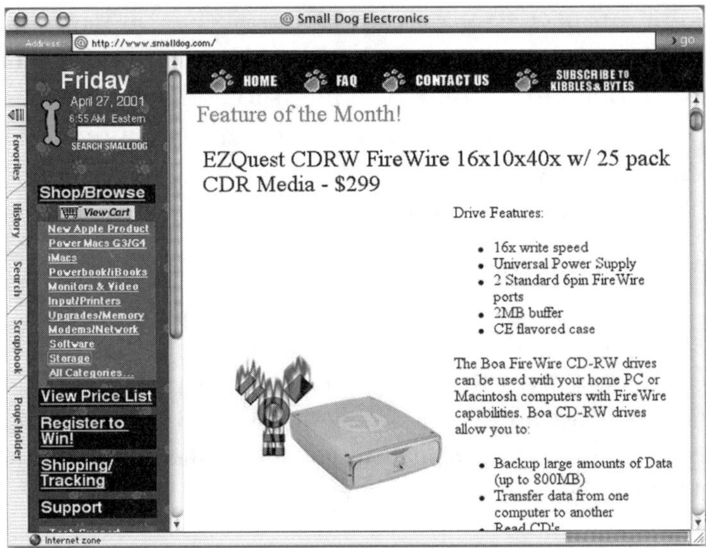

Figure 5.2 A drive such as this EZQuest CD-RW drive is a good
addition to your DV toolkit.

iMovie

Apple's iMovie is an excellent video editing application that
enables "the rest of us" to become our own movie studio. iMovie
features powerful video production features and yet is relatively
easy to use (thus separating it from all other video editing applications). You'll get started with iMovie in Chapter 6, "Creating a
Video Track." And, of course, you'll use iMovie heavily throughout the rest of this section of the book.

Digital Video Camera

A DV camera enables you to capture your own video and easily import clips into iMovie via FireWire.

This section assumes that you have added or will add a DV camera to your toolkit. If you don't have a DV camera yet, read on to figure out which one is right for you. If you already have a DV camera, you can skim through much of this section (reading the sections on features might help you understand your camera a bit better).

The Sometimes Baffling World of DV Cameras

Obtaining a DV camera can be a baffling, and sometimes intimidating, process. There are lots of brands, and each offers many models with dozens of different features. This adds up to more choices than you might want to deal with.

> ### THE TWO IMMUTABLE LAWS OF BUYING ELECTRONICS
>
> When you deal with electronic devices of any kind, including computers and cameras, there are a couple of things that you need to accept if you are going to be happy with anything you buy over the long term. The first is that a new and better model will always be available soon after you get yours. The second is that the newer and better model will cost no more, and probably less, than the model you just bought. This is progress; and in the world of electronics, progress happens so fast that you can easily become dissatisfied with a purchase made only a month or two ago. You'll be happier if you just accept this phenomenon and don't worry about it. Do the best you can when you buy a new device, and try not to think about it anymore. If you keep thinking about it, you will either be continually frustrated with your purchases, or you won't ever buy anything because you will always be waiting for that next model to come out.

However, you can quickly reduce the dozens of choices you have down to just a few.

> **BUYING THROUGH ELIMINATION**
>
> The easiest method is to buy through elimination. The goal is to limit the many options you have down to just a couple so that you can choose between them without going stark-raving mad. As you determine each of four major factors, you eliminate all the cameras that don't meet your criteria. After a few of these factors, you have a "short list" from which to select a camera to buy.

The good news is that very few of the options that you have are "bad." All of the DV cameras that are being sold offer some features and benefits. Individual models might be "better" than others, but more than likely, whichever model you choose should work for you.

As you begin to learn about cameras, you might feel overwhelmed by the sheer number of models and features that you encounter. Here's a little secret: Most of these features make no difference in your selection of a particular model. Only a few features really matter, and you can use these key features to reduce the number of options that you have to three or fewer.

iMovie Compatibility

Compatibility with iMovie should be one of the most important factors that you consider when you choose a DV camera. What does iMovie compatibility mean? Basically, it means that you have the easiest time and get the best results using that camera with iMovie. This is because you can control the camera from within iMovie—this makes transferring clips from the camera into iMovie a snap.

This factor is quite easy to figure out because Apple maintains a list of iMovie-compatible cameras on the iMovie Web page. To see this list, go to `www.apple.com/imovie/shoot.html`. You will have the best results if the camera that you choose is on this list.

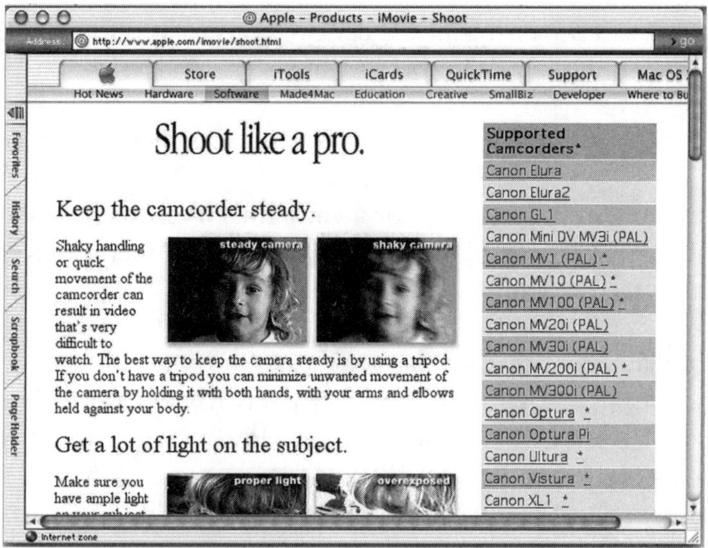

Figure 5.3 If a DV camera is on the Support Camcorders list on this Web site, it is a possible choice for DV work on your iMac.

Format

There are lots of video camera formats; the good news is that you need to consider only two: Digital8 and MiniDV. The difference between them is, as you probably surmised, size. Digital8 cameras use a digital tape that is the same physical size as an 8mm tape. MiniDV tapes are considerably smaller, and MiniDV cameras tend to be considerably smaller, as well. Because of the size benefits and the fact that it has become the standard for DV camcorders, I recommend that you consider only cameras that use the MiniDV format.

FIREWIRE BY ANY OTHER NAME STILL ROCKS

FireWire is what makes a DV camera so incredibly cool. FireWire is a standard, so you don't have to worry about FireWire cameras being hard to find. But, you should be aware that FireWire is Apple's brand name for this technology. The brand independent name for FireWire is IEEE 1394. Sony has its own name for this technology; it

continued...

> calls IEEE 1394 devices i.LINK devices. Whether you see IEEE 1394 or i.LINK, think FireWire, because they all mean the same thing.

Cost

How much you have to pay for a camera is likely to be one of the first things that you think about. And it might indeed be the most important factor of all.

Set a budget for your camera purchase. And make it a really firm number because if you don't, you're likely to experience feature-creep, which leads to price-creep. For almost every model you choose, there is another model that does more and does it better that costs just "a little bit" more. When you decide to move up, the same thing happens. And so it continues, until you are up to the most expensive camera there is.

To quickly find out how much specific models cost, make a note of some of the models you see on the supported cameras list. Go to your favorite retail Web site—mine is www.smalldog.com.

Figure 5.4 You can use a Web retail site to quickly determine which cameras you can afford.

Search for the models that you noted and see how much they cost. Look for models whose cost is close to your budget.

Sources of Information for DV Cameras

Just by considering the three factors described in the previous sections, you should be able to reduce your camera options from dozens to a short list of just two to three models. With this number of choices, it becomes possible to compare specific models to decide which is the best fit for you.

Now that you have your short list, you must begin to figure out the features that the models on your list offer. Using the Web, this is not very difficult.

There are three basic sources of detailed product information. One is the manufacturer's Web site. A second is a retail site. The third is a product review site. Each of these has pros and cons, and you should look at each for each model of camera you're considering.

To see what its manufacturer claims about a model, use the link provided on the iMovie compatibility list to jump to the manufacturer's site for that model. These pages usually provide lots of detailed information about specific camera models.

In addition to providing price information, retail Web sites offer you detailed information about the products that they sell, including cameras. You can actually purchase the camera at the retail site—sometimes at a discount—so it serves a dual purpose for you.

You can also find information about specific camera models on Web sites that offer product reviews. Sources of product reviews include magazine sites, video professional sites, and even individuals' sites. Reviews for the particular models that you are considering can be a bit tough to find; but after you've found them, they can be sources of additional and sometimes more detailed information that can really help you select your future camera. One example of such a site is at `home.cnet.com`.

> **FIND THE SOLUTION WITH SHERLOCK**
> Using Sherlock to search for a specific model can also result in lots of good information.

Other Factors to Consider

Now that you know how to get lots of information on each model that you are considering, what factors are really important? Even though that all depends on your preferences, there are a handful of major factors that you should consider. These include the following:

- ➤ **Size, Shape, and Comfort**—How often you shoot video with a camera is usually a matter of how convenient it is to carry and use. Fortunately, MiniDV cameras are very small; in fact, a few are almost pocketsize! Make sure that the camera you get is small enough that you're willing to haul it with you (you can't shoot video if you don't have the camera with you!).

- ➤ **Viewfinder**—Two basic options are available to you for the viewfinder. One is the traditional viewfinder that you look though with one eye pressed against it. The other is a flip-out LCD screen that shows you what you are recording and that can be used for playback. These come in various sizes, with bigger ones being easier to see with the trade-off being the camera's size, weight, and power use. Most DV cameras have both types of viewfinders, so the main factor to consider is the size of the LCD screen.

- ➤ **Magnification**—The power of the lens determines how close you must be in order to shoot something. Two values are quoted for DV cameras. One value is for optical zoom, and the other is for digital zoom. Optical zoom uses the physical lenses to achieve magnification; digital zoom uses digital enhancements to make the image larger. Optical zoom provides higher quality, but both are useful. For both values, bigger numbers are better (for example, a 20X optical zoom is better than a 10X optical zoom).

If it comes down to a choice, larger optical magnification is more important than a larger digital magnification is. Optical magnification actually improves the image, whereas digital magnification uses the same amount of data to generate the image. For example, a 20x optical zoom with a 75x digital zoom is probably preferable to a 15x optical zoom with a 250x digital zoom.

➤ **Lighting Options**—Some models have built-in lights to use when you shoot in low-light conditions. Others feature shoes into which you can plug external lights, such as those used for high-quality still cameras. Some models are designed to use the same lights as their 35mm film-based still image cousins.

➤ **Input and Output Ports**—In addition to the FireWire port, other ports are available to get information into or out of the camera. These include a headphone jack so that you can connect and use a higher-quality or focusable microphone, additional audio/video input/output ports, and so on.

A PORT YOU MUST HAVE

Make sure that the model you get has a port that enables you to record from an external source. This is usually called A/V port. Often, this is the same port that is used to export video from the camera (the same jack is used to record from a source as is used to export the video into your iMac via FireWire). This feature enables you to use an analog source to capture clips for your movies (in effect, such camcorders function as digitizers). For example, you can record from a VCR and then use FireWire to transfer that footage into iMovie so that you can use it in your movies. This is easy to do, and the quality is very good (better than with many dedicated digitizing devices). Even better is a model that enables you to pass-through a signal so that you don't even have to record it with your DV camera because the signal passes through the DV camera into your Mac (via FireWire).

After you have created a short list and evaluated the features that the models on that list offer, one model is likely to emerge as the best mix of the various factors for your purposes. (If your research doesn't reveal any significant differences, it probably doesn't really matter which you choose, does it?)

With your selected model in mind, all that remains to do is to make the buy. Visit your favorite site (my favorite one is `www.smalldog.com`) and lay your money down.

QuickTime Pro

QuickTime is Apple's name for its technology that Macintosh and other computers use to display time-synchronized data. That sounds rather technical, but it isn't really. *Time-synchronized data* is any information that consists of multiple parts that have to work together "in synch." The simplest example of this sort of data is a movie in which the video and sound elements must remain synchronized, or else you end up with something that looks like one of those badly-dubbed Godzilla movies (you know—the kind in which the motion of a character's mouth has nothing to do with the sounds coming out of it).

You might be wondering what QuickTime has to do with DV, and if you are, you get extra points for thinking ahead. As a DV producer, QuickTime is important to you for two main reasons.

> ➤ You can use QuickTime tools to create, edit, and then convert video and sound elements to import into your iMovie movies. You are likely to encounter elements that you might want to use in your iMovie movies in many different places, including your own hard drive, CD-ROMs, and the Web.

> ➤ You are going to want to share your iMovie creations with other people. One good way to do this is to convert the iMovie project into a QuickTime movie that you can distribute in many different ways, such as by email, on the Web, or on CD-R discs. The people who receive your movies use the QuickTime tools installed on their computers to view your creations.

For both of these reasons, QuickTime is an essential part of your DV toolkit. Understanding what QuickTime is and how you can use it should prove to be very useful to you.

There are two versions of QuickTime. The first is the basic version that is installed whenever you install the Macintosh operating system (unless you specifically tell the Mac OS installer not to install it). The second, which is called QuickTime Pro, is an upgraded version that provides significantly more features.

The basic version of QuickTime is useful for viewing (or hearing) the various types of QuickTime files that you encounter. You'll learn about viewing QuickTime movies in Chapter 9.

QuickTime Pro provides you with all the capabilities of "regular" QuickTime, including the following features that are especially important for DV work:

> ➤ Editing QuickTime movie clips to prepare them to go into iMovie.

> ➤ Exporting QuickTime movies in the DV format so that you can import them into iMovie.

> ➤ Viewing files in a wide variety of formats.

> ➤ Downloading and saving QuickTime movies that you see on the Web; this is cool because you can then use these movies in your iMovie projects.

Upgrading to QuickTime Pro requires no new software—all you need is an upgrade code. The upgrade process takes only a few minutes and costs about $30.

There are several ways to upgrade. When you open the QuickTime Player, you might see a prompt suggesting that you upgrade to QuickTime Pro. In that prompt, click Upgrade Now. When you do, follow the on-screen instructions to upgrade. You can also upgrade by going to the QuickTime Web site at

`http://www.apple.com/quicktime/download/` and then
clicking the Buy Now button. You can also upgrade by using the
Registration button in the QuickTime pane of the System
Preferences utility (Mac OS X) or the Registration pane of the
QuickTime Settings control panel (Mac OS 9). Just in case these
options aren't enough, from the QuickTime Player's Edit menu,
choose Preferences and then choose Registration.

Whichever method you choose, you will receive the registration
code that you need from Apple (in most cases, via email).

To register the Pro version in Mac OS X, open the QuickTime
pane of the System Preferences utility, click the Registration button,
and enter your code. To register the Pro version in Mac OS 9,
open the QuickTime Settings control panel, choose Registration
from the pop-up menu at the top of the window, click Enter
Registration, and complete the form.

When you check the registration information for QuickTime, you
will see your registration number and that QuickTime is now the
Pro Player Edition. You will then have access to QuickTime Pro's
features.

You will learn how to convert QuickTime movies into the DV format using the QuickTime Player Pro so that you can import them
into iMovie in Chapter 6.

Planning Your Movie

Your first decision in the planning process should be about the
kind of movie that you want to make. There are two general types
of movies that you are likely to make with iMovie: *spontaneous*
movies and *directed* movies.

Spontaneous Movies

Spontaneous movies are those in which most of the action occurs
spontaneously; that is, the action is not specifically directed by you.

Examples of spontaneous movies are home movies of your family vacation or a quick flick showing the results of last summer's water fight. Many professional documentaries are also spontaneous because the moviemaker doesn't know exactly what is going to happen.

Most people use a camcorder to create these sorts of movies. Within the general category of spontaneous movies, there are two subtypes: "Grab and Go" movies or "Planned Event" movies.

Grab-and-go Movies

In a "grab-and-go" movie, something unplanned, but interesting, happens and you want to capture it in a movie, so you "grab" your camcorder and "go" shooting. The point is that you don't really know when one of these moments will happen, but when it does, you go.

Interestingly, all three phases of the movie-making process still apply, although they come in a slightly different order. In the case of a grab-and-go movie, the phases happen in the following order:

> ➤ **Production**—You do the production phase on the fly with no idea as to what you should be capturing. You just have to do the best you can to get clips that make an interesting movie.

> ➤ **Planning**—The planning phase for these sorts of movies is a bit different. Rather than asking the question, "What is my movie and how do I make it?," your question is, "I have these clips that are interesting; how should I make a movie out of them?"

> ➤ **Post-production**—The post-production phase is similar to that of the classic process. In it, you build a movie from the bits and pieces you have or that you create.

Planned Event Movies

The second sort of spontaneous movie is similar to the grab-and-go type in that you don't actually determine the events that happen. The difference is that you have some foreknowledge that some events are going to happen. There are lots of examples, including everything from a bike race to someone's surprise party (not yours, of course). In all these events, you know the where and when of the event, but you don't know the specific things that are going to happen.

When you create these movies, the classic process is also modified, but in a different way than the grab-and-go type. The process for this type of movie is the following:

> **Partial planning**—Because you know that an event is coming, you can do some of the planning tasks to prepare for that event. For example, you can scout the location at which the event is scheduled to occur and plan your camera locations.

> **Production**—During the event, you capture your clips.

> **More planning**—Because you don't really know beforehand what sort of clips you will end up with, you must wait until you have your clips before you can decide how to best use them.

> **Post-production**—The post-production phase is also similar to that of the classic process.

Directed Movies

Directed movies are those in which everything that happens is specifically planned (or directed), down to what the people on-screen do and say. Most movies that come out of the Hollywood process are directed movies, even some that try to appear not to be (anyone remember *The Blair Witch Project*?).

Catching a Vision

After you decide what kind of movie you are going to create, you need to develop a vision for your movie. What is it that you want to do with your movie?

Try to answer some of the following questions:

> ➤ **What is the point of my movie?**—To entertain? To document an event? To provide some insight into the world around you? The answer to this question should guide the rest of the work that you do.

> ➤ **What do I want the look and feel (and sound) of my movie to be?**—Are you going for the "MTV" look in which a scene remains on-screen only for a second or two? Or do you want a more traditional documentary sort of movie?

> ➤ **Who is going to watch my movie?**—Knowing your audience is always important. If you are showing your movie to everyone under the sun, you probably want to avoid including anything too embarrassing in it. (You can save that for the Special Edition!)

> ➤ **How much time, effort, and money, do I want to invest in my movie?**—The grander the scale of your vision, the more resources it consumes. The answer to this question can help you avoid biting off more than you can chew.

You might want to jot down the "vision" for your movie so that you can refer to it later. During the production and post-production phases, your vision can help you make specific decisions.

Writing a Script

A script defines certain aspects of what a movie will be; in a directed movie, the script defines almost all aspects of a movie. Whether you actually write a script for your movies is up to you, but you certainly should consider one for anything more than a minute or two of spontaneous video.

Scripts have several uses. A script helps you know what scenes you need to capture. Secondly, it helps you set up your shooting sessions by providing a location for each scene. And finally, it helps you piece together clips that you already have into a movie that makes some sense.

Your scripts might be pretty general, or they might be very specific. It all depends on how much you want to control the outcome of your work. The more time you put into creating a script, the better your final product will match your vision for it.

Writing Scripts for Spontaneous Movies

For grab-and-go movies, you usually write the script *after* you shoot the clips. Rather than defining the scenes in the movie and then shooting the scenes, these scripts define how you put a movie together from the clips you already have.

For planned events, your script should define the scenes that you would like to capture. For example, if you are making a movie of a local biking event, your script would define the parts of the event that you want to capture (such as the start, finish, or other interesting points). In addition to the location of each of these scenes, you would describe specifically what you want to capture on tape.

After you tape the event, you might want to modify your script to adjust for any unforeseen events that took place that you now want to incorporate into your movie (or if perhaps a scene did not develop as you planned).

Writing Scripts for Directed Movies

In a directed movie, the script is the movie. You need to define everything about your movie—from where and when the scenes take place to each word that every character in your movie speaks. As you move into production, the script guides what happens and how you capture that action.

This sort of script writing is a skill that must be acquired through education and lots of practice. If you plan to develop directed movies, you also must learn how to write detailed scripts.

Creating a Storyboard

The storyboard is another traditional movie-making tool that moviemakers use to define the details of how they put their movies together.

A storyboard serves as a visual representation of a movie's script. Each scene is described with one or more graphics. These graphics, usually in rough sketch form, depict everything that is happening in a particular scene. This includes where the subjects are standing in relation to one another, where they are located, what is happening in the scene, and so on. Notes on the graphics might describe the action or the dialog that is occurring. The camera angles and other production information are also determined. For example, in a scene that contains a close-up, that close-up is sketched to capture how close that close-up is (for example, how much of the person's face do we see?).

Storyboards are used to communicate the director's vision of the movie to the people who are making that vision into a reality on the screen. They are also used to guide the production process so that the appropriate scenes are captured during shooting. And last, but not least, the storyboards are used as a visual guide for the post-production tasks.

Storyboarding for Spontaneous Movies

For grab-and-go movies, you can use a storyboard to help you quickly rough out how you want the clips you have already captured to be sequenced. Using a storyboard process helps you get an idea of what your movie might look like in total before you spend all the time and effort actually putting the clips together.

For planned events, you can sketch out how you want to video each of the major scenes you have defined in your script.

Storyboarding for Directed Movies

Your storyboards for directed movies should be both more numerous and more detailed than those for grab-and-go movies. Because other people might be involved in production (and maybe even in post-production), you should have storyboards that are sufficiently detailed so that the other members of your team understand what you want to accomplish.

Planning the Shoot

After you have defined what your movie will be, you should begin to plan its production. Because you won't want to waste a lot of time shooting your movie, you need to carefully plan how you will shoot the movie.

Scouting a Location

One of the most important things you should do is to scout the locations of your shoot before you start videotaping. This might involve traveling to a far-off location, or it might be simply walking into your living room. Whichever the case, you need to explore your shooting area before you begin videotaping in it.

You are probably familiar with the image of a director walking around holding his two hands in front of him with his thumbs together to form a "box" that simulates a camera's perspective. Although this looks sort of silly, it's a legitimate tool you can use to get a general idea of how your location might look on camera.

The reason why this works is that a video camera records like your eyes do, only with a more restricted field of view. Using your hands to form the "viewfinder," you can get a quick idea of how your location might look on camera.

As you pan around with your hands, consider the following factors:

> **Lighting**—What is the lighting like in the area? If you can see comfortably, there is probably enough ambient light for the video shot (you might have to augment that with supplemental lighting). If you have to squint or strain to see what is going on, you definitely need to use supplemental lighting. If you have to squint in certain directions because of a bright light, you need to make adjustments while shooting.

> **Sound**—How is the sound environment in the area? Check for background noise. Make some noise yourself to check for echoes. See if sound carries in the area or if it dies prematurely. Just as with lighting, you can use your own senses to assess how your camcorder might handle the environment.

> **Camera positions**—Using your hand-cam, check out different camera locations from which you can cover the area. Identify several spots that you might want to use, and then take a closer look at each (check the sound and light in more detail) to see which positions you want to use. It's often a good idea to have a couple of locations for your camera to get different perspectives for your clips.

> **Backgrounds**—Another consideration is the background that you see from the camera locations you choose. Are there unpleasant or distracting things in the background? Is the background too bland? Look "past" what you will be filming to make sure that the whole image is what you want it to be. As you begin to edit your movie, the background becomes more prominent, and at that point, you aren't able to do anything about it. So make sure that your backgrounds are acceptable before you tape.

> **Interference**—Are there things in the area that will interfere with your shoot? For example, are you shooting across a street that has a lot of traffic? Are lots of people going to be strolling through the room in which you are taping? If you are likely to be interfered with during the shoot, you need to either change locations or choose a shooting time at which interference is less likely.

There are two basic shooting locations: indoors and outdoors. Each provides its own environment and challenges.

Shooting Inside

Because you have more control over the environment, shooting inside is usually easier than shooting outside. However, there are some difficulties shooting inside, including lack of room to work, poor acoustics, bad backgrounds, and so on.

Indoor Lighting

Two sources of lighting are used during your indoor shoots: ambient lighting and supplemental lighting.

Ambient lighting is the lighting that exists in the location before you add any light to it. Sources of ambient lighting include sunlight through windows, ceiling lights, floor lamps, and so on. You can control the ambient light inside by closing window curtains or blinds to lower the outside light coming in, or by turning ceiling lights and floor lamps on for more light or off for less.

> ### A General Lighting Rule
>
> Remember that a general rule is that if you can see comfortably, the ambient light is probably sufficient for your shooting session. Ideally, the light is slightly brighter than is normally comfortable for you, because camcorders tend to shoot slightly darker than light appears to the human eye.

If the ambient light is not sufficient, you must add *supplemental lighting*. All sorts of supplemental lighting options are available. Many camcorders either have supplemental lights built-in or have a shoe into which you can connect a light. You can also use various sorts of portable lighting such as lamps, droplights, and specialty filming lights.

You are likely to use two basic types of supplemental lighting. Spot lights focus light on a specific part of the scene, such as a person or a significant object. Indirect or diffuse lighting adds light to the entire area. Depending on the clips you are filming, you might need to use both types.

A second source of lighting—or perhaps I should call it anti-lighting—is shadow. You can often use shadows to create interesting visual effects, such as making a scene appear to be more three-dimensional. You can also focus the audience's vision on an object or person by using shadows to de-emphasize everything else in the scene.

BACKLIGHTING

When you shoot in front of something that is bright, such as a window that has sunlight streaming in, you have a backlit situation. This means that the objects you are filming are darker than the background. Most of the time, this is not a desirable situation because the audience can't see what you are filming—they only see a silhouette of the person or object. Although you can use this for a dramatic effect, most of the time, you should avoid backlighting. Many camcorders have a backlight control, which compensates for this somewhat, but the resulting image is often washed out. Often, you are better off if you can change your camera location to avoid the backlight.

Indoor Sound

When it comes to sound, the good news is that your ears routinely filter out all sorts of background noise so that you aren't even aware that it exists. The bad news is that the microphone that you use doesn't. The sound that is happening is what is recorded on tape.

This means that you must be really careful about the background noise in your location. Lights and fans hum, electrical equipment buzzes, the bass of your next-door neighbor's stereo rumbles, and so on. All of these noises appear on your clips, and because your ears tend to filter them out in everyday life, they will sound much louder to you when you listen to your movie.

The best way to judge the background noise level of your location is by using the "eyes-closed" test. Stand in the center of the location and close your eyes. Be still for a few moments, and your hearing sense becomes more sensitive (when your brain no longer has visual information to process, it places more of its resources on the sound input that it is receiving). Listen for a few minutes to hear what is happening.

If you hear objectionable background noise, you should do something about it before you shoot. Some sound sources you can stop permanently or temporarily. Others are simply part of the scene, and you either have to shoot with them or find another location for your shoot. If you get lucky, the background noise fits in with your movie and actually makes it better, but that doesn't happen very often.

The other option when dealing with too much background noise is to use a directional microphone that captures the sounds you want and minimizes the sounds that you don't want.

Indoor Camera Positions

As you check the scene using your hand-cam and the eyes-closed test, identify the locations from which you get the best views and minimum background noise of the area that you are filming. Pick a couple of camera locations so that you can add some variety to the shooting session by moving the camera to give the audience different perspectives. As you identify locations, make sure to use your hand-cam to evaluate the background that you see when you shoot from those spots.

Shooting Outdoors

Shooting outside presents more challenges than does inside shooting primarily because controlling the light, sound, and interference aspects of the location is much more difficult.

Outdoor Lighting

When you shoot in the daytime, the ultimate light, the sun, provides most of your light. Even though the sun can provide lots of light, using sunlight does present some challenges. One of the biggest is that the light provided by the sun is always changing. As the earth rotates, the relative angle of the light to your location changes. In the morning, the sunlight comes from low in the eastern sky. As the day progresses toward noon, the light comes from directly above you. As evening approaches, the fading light comes out of the western sky.

If you are filming over an extended period, all this change can cause problems for you (unless the changing conditions are part of your plan, of course).

Even in the short term, the sun's brightness requires that you take it into consideration when planning your camera locations. Generally, the sun should be behind the camera so that it shines on what you are taping. However, you don't want it to be directly behind you because of the shadows that it casts, particularly when the sun is low in the sky. Shadows that come when the sun is directly behind you can make your image hard to see, and your own shadow can sometimes appear in the scene (definitely not desirable). Usually, keeping the sun behind you, but so its rays are at about a 15- to 30-degree angle to your line of sight, works fairly well.

Another problem with sunlight is that it can cause many people in your scene to have to squint when they look toward the camera (which is where you want them to be looking at least some of the time). You can't do much about this except film on a less bright day. Keeping the sun off at an angle also minimizes the squinting problem because your subjects aren't looking directly into the sun when they look directly into the camera.

> ## WORKING BACKWARDS
>
> For a different effect, you can shoot with the sun behind the sub-jects, especially if it is fairly high in the sky. This can create a dra-matic halo effect.

Of course, there might be cloud cover on some days. This makes shooting conditions ideal if there are light clouds that block the direct sun but allow lots of indirect light to come through. If the clouds are moving rapidly, you have to deal with lots of changing lighting conditions.

You might want to use supplemental lighting when you are shoot-ing outdoors, even if you're shooting in the daytime. The easiest way to add lighting is to use reflectors to redirect sunlight to where you want it to be. (You can make an inexpensive reflector by paint-ing a piece of cardboard white.) Position the reflector so that it redirects sunlight into your scene to reduce shadows or to add a spotlight effect.

Shooting outdoors at night requires substantial additional lighting because, unlike the indoors, there are no walls or other surfaces to reflect the light that you add. All of your light goes streaming out into the night, which means that less of it stays focused on your scene.

Outdoor Sound

As with lighting, controlling noise on your set is much more diffi-cult outdoors than it is indoors. The sources of undesired back-ground noise are many and varied. They can include traffic, aircraft, and just about anything else. You usually can't control any of these noise sources. You must either accept them and deal with them as they are or change your shooting time or location.

The best way to assess the noise levels for your outdoor shoot is the eyes-closed test. Try it to see how much background noise your location has.

About the only way to deal with background noise outdoors (besides changing shooting time or location) is to use a directional microphone that has a very limited pickup field of view.

Outdoor Camera Positions

As with an indoor location, you need to check many different locations for your camera (considering the lighting, sound, and background) to determine several different locations to use.

Composing Your Shots

After you have established your camera locations and the sound and lighting at your shoot location, it's time to consider how you want to compose your shots.

Use the Rule of Thirds

Good image composition uses what is called the *rule of thirds.* This means that you draw two vertical and two horizontal imaginary lines across the viewfinder. These lines should divide the screen into thirds in each direction. Think of placing a tic-tac-toe game on your viewfinder, and you get the idea. You should use these lines to give your shots symmetry and balance while avoiding placing important elements in the exact center of the screen (this is called the *dead space* of the screen).

Use the imaginary lines to line up objects in the scene so that your shot appears to have a design. As you shoot, try to maintain this structure as you shift the focus of the shot around so that the images appear orderly to your viewers.

Provide Buffer Space

One of the most important things to remember is to always maintain some space above the central object in a scene. (You can use the upper "rule of thirds" line to help with this.) This buffer space (called *headroom*) gives your viewers better perspective on the subject and also helps you avoid cutting any of the subject off by letting it get to close to the top of the screen.

> ## HEADROOM AND CLOSE-UPS
>
> When you are shooting close-ups (such as during an interview), you often can violate the headroom and the shot looks good anyway. When we get close to something, as it looks like we are when someone is interviewed, we don't expect to see all of her. Many interview shows, such as *60 Minutes*, use this technique.

Speaking of headroom, you might have a person who doesn't entirely fit into the shot as you have planned it. If this is the case, try to "cut off" the person at an appropriate place on her body. If you only have room for a headshot, try and get the shoulders, neck, and head in the shot rather than just the head. The basic concept is to cut off people at a somewhat natural location. This makes the cutoff less noticeable to the audience.

Lead Your Target

Unless you are doing a "head-on" shot, the subjects or objects in your scene are looking or pointing in a specific direction. It makes the scene more realistic if you leave some screen space in the direction in which the objects in the scene are facing. For example, if you are videoing an airplane flying, lead the shot so that more room appears in the direction it is flying (in other words, in front of the plane) rather than keeping the space before and after the plane the same. This leads the audience in the direction that the action is happening, and it makes the audience feel more in touch with the scene.

> ## A SPEEDY RULE OF THUMB
>
> Generally, the faster something is moving, the more you should lead it. More lead increases the viewer's perception of speed.

Design Your Backgrounds

As you shoot, pay attention to the background of your shots. Backgrounds can make or break a clip; and after the clip is shot, there isn't much you can do about the background.

If you are shooting indoors, try to find an interesting—but not too interesting—wall to use as a background. Avoid windows as backgrounds (unless the blinds or curtains are closed). Fireplaces can also make good backgrounds, depending on the scene. Bare walls usually do not make very good backgrounds. Some kinds of furniture make good backgrounds. Avoid anything that has its own motion as a background. For example, a TV makes a terrible background; the motion of the TV image is much too distracting (and you can get the "flicker" effect).

Shooting the Shoot

As with composing your shots, there are also some principles and practices that you use when it is time to push the Record button and start filming your movie.

Plan on Waste

When you shoot, be generous with your record button. Take extra footage before the scene and include some at the back end, as well. When in doubt, hold the record button down. You should expect to use 25% or even much less of the video that you shoot in your final movie, so make sure to take lots of video from which you can choose and that you will edit later in post-production.

At the moment you're shooting, it's often hard to tell whether the clip you are capturing is going to be usable. A good practice is to take as much video as you can during the shoot; this ensures that you have plenty to work with later.

This does not mean that you should be sloppy or careless with what you take. Use the practices you have learned in this chapter and try to always get the best clips you can. Just realize that there is little hope of shooting exactly what you end up using in your movie, so plan on "wasting" much of what you shoot. This is just part of the moviemaking process.

Keep a Light Touch on the Zoom Button

The zoom feature is probably the most touted and overused feature on your camcorder. Many people make the mistake of substituting the zoom function for setting a proper camera location. Others zoom simply because they can.

I recommend that you use the zoom feature sparingly. Zooms are distracting and disorienting for the audience, primarily because there is no equivalent feature in the human eye. When we want to look at something more closely, we move the object to us or we move to the object. This changes our perspective as well as our position relative to the object. It also takes some time to make the change to the closer view.

However, your zoom feature works differently. There is no sense of motion, and the perspective does not change. There is also little time to adjust. A simple "zip," and the view zooms in or out. The object gets larger or smaller in the screen.

Another problem with zooming is that the image quality degrades somewhat, especially with digital zooming. This is more pronounced in lower-quality cameras, but it exists to a certain extent on all cameras. The best image quality is achieved in the non-zoomed mode.

> ### BREAKING THE RULES
>
> Hopefully, you are learning lots of useful tips to help you capture great video clips from which you can build a great movie. But don't feel bound by any rule in any particular situation. You should
>
> *continued...*

> generally follow established practices for shooting video, but that doesn't mean that you should always follow every rule. Throw in something offbeat every once in a while to give your video some additional texture. For example, although it is usually better to minimize the speed with which you zoom in on something, mix in an occasional quick zoom. Be creative with your shooting techniques—just don't go overboard.

However, the zoom feature can be used to change the scene in some important ways. When you use the zoom, do so slowly and smoothly (no zipping in and out, please!). And don't jump back and forth between the views. Slowly zoom in, give your audience some time to adjust, and then zoom out as needed.

> ### Pan and Zoom
>
> You can often lessen the impact of a zoom on your audience by panning the camera (moving the camera) at the same time.

Keep the number of zooms in a single scene to a minimum.

> ### A Good Use for Zoom
>
> Sometimes, you can use a zoom as an establishing shot. For example, if you are shooting a play, you can zoom all the way out so the scene shows the stage, camera, and the audience. This shows the audience where they are and gives some perspective on what they see. As the action on stage begins, you might zoom in so that the stage fills the frame.

Move the Camera

As you shoot, you usually have to move the camera. There are several ways to move it. You can move the whole camera forward or backward and left and right (called tracking). You can pan the camera, which means to rotate it about its axis. You can also rotate the camera up or down (called *tilting*), and you can move the whole camera up and down (called *craning*).

In whatever direction you move the camera, there are some basic rules you should follow as much as you can.

Use Image Stabilization

Almost all cameras use some form of electronic image stabilization. This feature minimizes camera shake as you shoot. Sometimes, you can turn this feature off; but you should almost always leave it on.

Use a Tripod

A tripod is a fundamental tool for shooting video. All camcorders have a tripod socket that you can use to mount the camera on a tripod. Tripods enable you to both precisely position and hold the camera, and they also help you make moving the camera more smooth and precise. Unless you are physically moving with the action that you are filming, your results will be much better if you shoot from a tripod.

Change Locations and Shoot at the Same Time

Sometimes, physically moving a camera during a scene with no clues for the audience can be confusing. For example, if you are filming a soccer game and move from one side of the field to the other, the directions that the teams are moving change. If you make this switch with no reference to the fact that the camera has moved, your audience might be confused when the scene changes.

Rather than stopping the camera, moving, and then starting again, you can try filming while you move. Or you can shoot during the initial part of your movement, stop the camera, move, and then shoot during the last part of the movement. Such clues help your audience maintain their orientation.

Move Smoothly to Keep Your Audience from Getting Sick

You move your camera during filming, make steady and smooth motions. Avoiding any really quick movements keeps you from losing your audience along the way. Sometimes, you must move quickly to keep up with the action, but do so only when it's really necessary.

> **MOVING A BUNCH?**
>
> If you find yourself constantly moving the camera while you shoot, you might not be in the best camera location. Try pulling the camera back away from the scene a bit to see if some of the need for so much movement goes away.

Switch to Manual

After you've used your camera for a while, experiment with some of the manual controls that it has. At the least, you can probably use a manual focus. Use the manual focus control when what you want to shoot isn't in the correct position for the automatic focus to focus on it. This usually happens when you are framing a shot. For example, you might want to focus on something closer to you but have most of the screen filled with the background. Using the manual focus, you can focus on the object and let the background become a bit blurred, for effect.

You might also have a white balance control that enables you to adjust the color properties of the image for various lighting conditions and for specific effects that you want to achieve.

Falling down this narrow course,
I'm about to fill the L-shaped void.
Would you seek to beat me?
Ha! Try catching the pixel in a net.

Chapter Six

Creating a Video Track

In the previous chapter, you learned that a lot of the movie making process has to happen before you ever start editing video within an application, such as iMovie. However, since this is *The iMac Way,* most of the material in this part of the book focuses on the post-production phase of the movie making process, which is the one in which your iMac is usually involved. It is in this phase that you combine the planning work you did with the video clips that you captured previously to create a movie with all the requisite parts: video track, special effects, sound, music, and so on.

The foundation for your movie is the video track (after all, what is a movie without video?—the answer: just a lot of noise!). You can use iMovie's video editing tools to create a basic video track. After you have the basic video track, you can add transitions, titles, and special effects (which are covered in the next chapter).

In this chapter, we are going to look at:

> ➤ Preparing your iMovie project

> ➤ Importing the video clips from which you will build a movie

> ➤ Editing those clips

Preparing for Your Movie Project

Now that you know the basics of making movies, it is time to get started with your movie project. To get your movie project going, you need to do the following tasks:

1. Prepare disk space on which to store your project.

2. Make sure that you have as much screen real estate and that you use as many colors as possible.

3. Launch iMovie and create the iMovie project.

4. Check some preferences.

THE BENEFITS OF MAC OS X

If you are using Mac OS 9 instead of Mac OS X, you should also do some fine-tuning of your system for maximum DV editing performance. DV work is extremely processor- and RAM-intensive, and you need to make sure that your iMac is devoting most of its resources to iMovie. The most important thing to do is to create a minimum set of extensions to use while you are working with iMovie. This will enable you to devote as much of your iMac's resources, such as RAM and processing output, to DV work as possible. For help creating and using extension sets and managing your Mac's RAM, see the book The Guide to Mac OS 9 (published by Hayden Books).

If you use Mac OS X, you don't have to worry about extension and RAM management because Mac OS X takes care of those tasks for you.

Making Room for DV Work

There is one inevitable fact of DV work—DV files are *huge, really* huge. You can expect even a modest iMovie project to require several gigabytes of disk space to store all the clips, special effects, and other project components. Plus, when you export your movie, you need space to store the various versions of the movie that you create. At the least, you must have a disk with 1 GB of free space to build an iMovie project (Apple recommends that you have at least

2 GB available, but for a short movie, you might be able to get by with just 1 GB). Even with the large disks that come with today's iMacs, disk space can be a problem. You can easily consume 10 GB or more for a single project.

Check for Free Space

First, see if your hard drive has enough free space to store your DV files. Open the Computer directory (Option+⌘+C) and select the volume on which you are going to store your iMovie project (if your disk has never been partitioned, you will only have one directory available to you). Open the Inspector (⌘+I) and choose General Information from the Show pop-up menu. If you have 2 GB or more available, you have enough to get started; however, you won't be able to store very many minutes of DV footage. If the free space is between 1 GB and 2 GB, you can get started, but you will have to carefully manage your disk space as you work. If there is less than 1 GB of free space, you need to move some of your files off your disk because you won't have enough room for anything except the briefest of movie projects.

> ### MAC OS 9
> Under Mac OS 9, open the volume on which you are going to store your project and check the status area to see how much free space you have.

Add an External FireWire Hard Drive

If your hard drive is pretty full, consider adding an external FireWire hard drive to your system. At the time of this writing, you can get a 75 GB drive for less than $500. That much storage space gives you lots of room for your iMovie projects. These drives are simple to connect (all you do is plug the drive's FireWire cable into a FireWire port on your iMac)

> ### FIREWIRE DRIVES
> A good source for hardware, including FireWire drives, is Small Dog Electronics, located at `www.smalldog.com`.

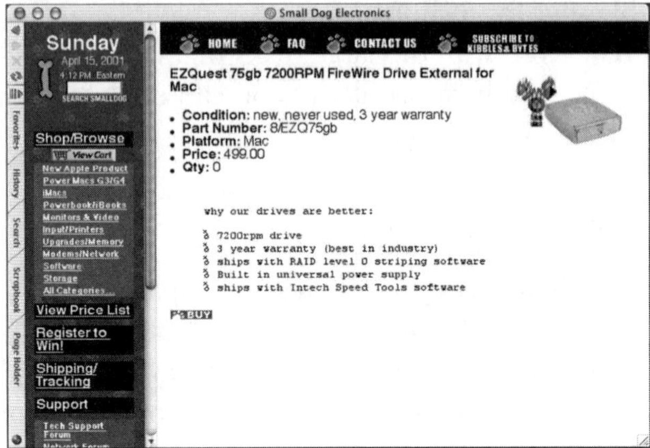

Figure 6.1 A FireWire hard drive, such as this one from EZQuest, can be a good way to make room for your DV projects.

If you add an external FireWire drive to your system, make sure that it features a data transfer rate suitable for DV work. Check with the manufacturer to make sure, but look for a rotational speed of at least 7,200 **RPM** (this doesn't ensure that the drive can handle DV, but anything less definitely can't). Many FireWire drives can be used for DV work, but check with the manufacturer before you buy one.

THE DISK SPACE SHUFFLE

If you have a slower drive, such as a FireWire hard drive, you can move your less demanding applications and data (such as most productivity applications and almost all documents) onto that "slower" drive and move your DV files onto the faster internal drive

Add a CD-RW Drive

Newer iMacs include an internal CD-RW drive that you can use to write CD-R and CD-RW discs (such as when you create audio CDs using iTunes). If your iMac doesn't have one of these drives, you can add an external USB or FireWire CD-RW drive to your system.

These drives are not fast enough, nor is there enough room on a disc, to be able to work on projects from them. But what you can use them for is to clear off space on your hard drive so that you have more room for DV work. You can also archive parts of your movie projects on CD, as well as the QuickTime version of the movie that you create (thus freeing room on your hard for more DV projects).

Replace Your iMac's Hard Drive

In order to get more space on your internal hard drive, you can consider replacing the drive that came in your iMac with another one of larger capacity. This can be a bit tricky because you have to ensure that the new drive will fit, and you need to be more careful installing it. Unless you are pretty savvy technical-wise, I don't really recommend this option.

Setting Up Your Display for iMovie

Two display settings affect your iMovie project: monitor resolution and color depth. To be able to have more working room and to get the best results, use the highest resolution and color depth that your iMac can support. For most iMacs, this is a resolution of 1024 x 768 with a color depth of Millions.

In Mac OS X, use the Monitors icon on the Dock (or the Displays pane of the System Preferences utility) to set the resolution to 1024 x 768 and the color depth to Millions.

In Mac OS 9, use the Monitors control panel to make these settings.

Preparing the iMovie Project

Open iMovie. If you have not used iMovie before, you will see a dialog box with three buttons: New Project, Open Project, and Quit. In this dialog box, click the New Project button. (If you have previously worked with iMovie, it remembers your last project and automatically opens it for you. In this case, start a new project by opening the File menu and choosing New Project.)

In the Create New Project dialog box, name your movie. Move to the volume on which you are going to store it and click Create. Unlike many other applications, the "thing" you just created is not a file but rather a folder that contains all the elements of your project.

Open the project folder that you just created, and you will see two items: a folder called Media and an iMovie file. The media folder is used to store all the clips, images, additional sounds (such as a music track), and other components that you use in your project. The iMovie file, which has the same name as your project, is a small pointer file that contains references to all the files in the media folder that you are using. If you want to open your project by double-clicking something, this file is the icon that you double-click.

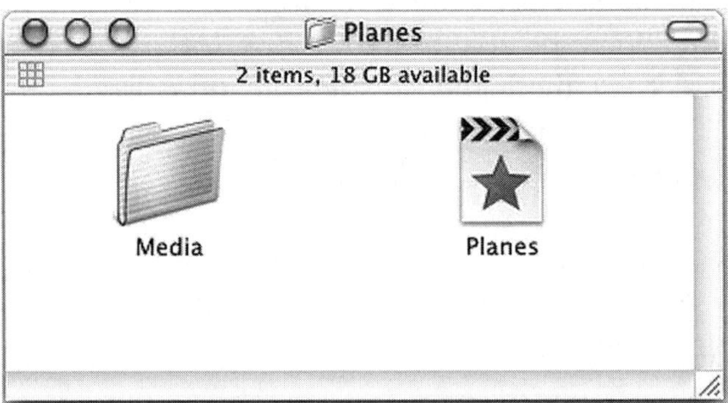

Figure 6.2 When you create a new iMovie project, you create a folder that contains the Media folder and an iMovie reference file.

Checking iMovie Preferences

iMovie has several preferences that you should check so that your experience will match the steps in this chapter (you can always change them later if you want).

From the Edit menu, choose Preferences. The Preferences window has four tabs: Import, Playback, Views, and Advanced.

Click the Import tab. These preferences determine how clips are brought into iMovie from a camcorder or other DV device. Make sure that the "Automatically start new clip at scene break" checkbox is checked. This makes iMovie start a new clip in a new slot on the Shelf whenever it detects a "break" in the video feed from the camera. Click the Shelf radio button so that clips that you import from the DV camera are placed on the Shelf. Leave the Still Clips setting at the default value (5 seconds).

Click the Playback tab. You will see two radio buttons (you can only select one at a time). The Smoother Motion button makes your iMac play video with smoother motion but with lower visual quality. The Better Image option increases the image quality, but the video may appear choppy. Use whichever preference you like. Your choice doesn't matter as far as your movie goes because these options only affect playback in iMovie. When you record to videotape or to a QuickTime movie, both the image quality and playback smoothness are the best they can be.

Now click the Views tab. These options affect certain elements in the iMovie interface. You can leave most of them at the default settings for now, but the next few bullets explain what they do:

➤ "Show Thumbnails in Timeline" places a thumbnail view of your clips on the Timeline Viewer; you should leave this on because it makes the clips easier to recognize.

➤ "Use Short Time Codes" removes the leading zeros in the Timecode, when a clip is less than a minute long (for example, if a clip is exactly 10 seconds long, you will see 10:00 rather than 00:10:00); again, you should leave this checked in most cases.

➤ "Show More Details" adds additional information to the clips in the Timeline Viewer including name and

> time code. I suggest that you check this box to turn this feature on.

➤ You can lock an audio clip to the Playhead to make it easier to locate. The "Show Locked Audio Only When Selected" preference hides the locked icon except when the locked audio is selected. Leave this one unchecked for now.

Now click Advanced. You probably won't need to adjust these preferences, but here is a quick summary of what they control:

➤ You can paste a video clip over an existing clip to replace it. If the "Extract Audio in Paste Over" checkbox is checked, the audio from the clip you are pasting over will be extracted and saved when the video is replaced. If it is not checked, the audio will also be replaced when you use the Paste Over command. This option is on (checked) by default.

➤ To improve quality, iMovie filters the audio that is imported from a DV camcorder. If you uncheck the "Filter Audio from Camera" checkbox, this filtering is turned off. Unless you have a specific reason not to filter audio, leave this checkbox checked.

➤ You can play video on your camcorder at the same time it is being played on the iMovie monitor. If you want this to happen, check the "Video Play Through to Camera check box".

Click OK to close the Preferences dialog.

Filling the iMovie Shelf

Now you are ready to begin to build your movie; you need to fill the iMovie Shelf with the clips from which you will build your movie. There are several sources for the clips you will import:

➤ Clips from a DV camera

➤ QuickTime movies

➤ Still images

PLANES

The movie that you will see being created in the figures in this and the following chapters is an example of a planned, spontaneous movie. The purpose of the movie was to get some interesting video of various airplanes taking off from local airports. It was planned in that I knew where and when I would be shooting, but was spontaneous in that I didn't know exactly which planes I would be seeing.

Importing Clips from a Digital Video Camera

Setting up a FireWire camera to work with iMovie is a snap. Power up your iMac and turn the camera on. Connect the small end of a FireWire cable to the DV camcorder and the larger end to your iMac. If the plug doesn't slip in easily, take a closer look. FireWire connectors are relatively fragile, so don't push too hard.

POWER IT UP

Because you are likely to operate your camera for quite a while as you import clips, you should power it with its power adapter rather than running it off its batteries.

Turn the camera on to its VCR setting—this is sometimes labeled VTR. You will see a message in iMovie's Monitor window confirming that iMovie is in touch with your DV camcorder. In addition to the Camera Connected message, notice that the button just under the Monitor is now Import. This means that you are ready to begin importing your clips into iMovie.

The really neat part about an iMovie-compatible DV camcorder is that you can control your DV camcorder using iMovie's controls. The Play, Fast Forward, Stop, and other buttons in the Monitor will control your DV camcorder. If you aren't using a camera that is iMovie-compatible, you will have to control the camera by using

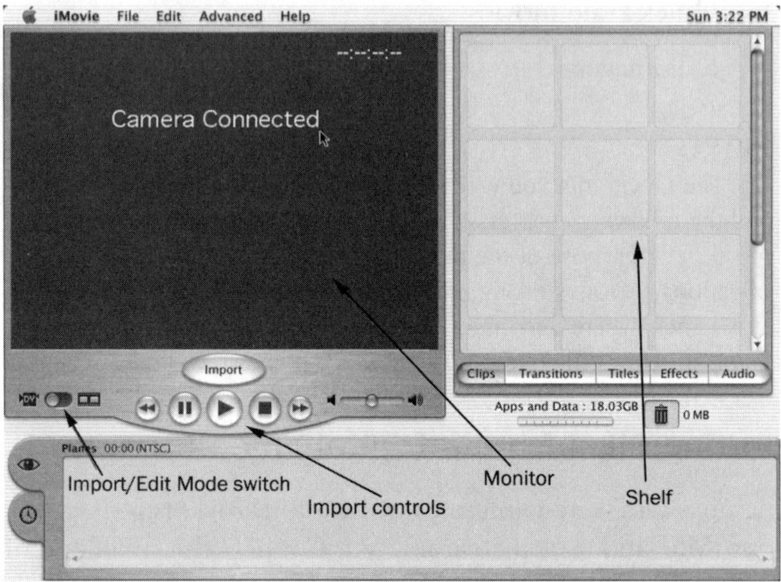

Figure 6.3 This message means that iMovie is ready to begin importing your clips.

its controls and manually controlling iMovie as well (for these steps, I assume that you are using an iMovie-compatible camera).

CAMERA BUTTON

If for some reason you aren't getting the screen shown in Figure 6.3, try clicking the Camera/Edit Mode switch. With most cameras, this is automatically selected when iMovie realizes that it is connected to a camera.

Get to the Clips You Want to Import

To begin playing the tape in your camcorder, click the iMovie Play button. The clips on the tape begin playing in the Monitor. Use the iMovie controls to move to the point on your tape at which you want to begin capturing clips from the tape.

It's a good idea to take a few moments to get used to controlling your camera using the iMovie interface. It can take a little while to get comfortable. In the Monitor, iMovie provides messages to you to make it clear what the camera is doing even if you don't see video in the window (such as when you are rewinding the tape).

Here are the controls that iMovie provides (from left to right and bottom to top):

> **Import—**You use this when you want to import clips to the Shelf.

> **Camera/Edit Mode—**This switches iMovie between the camera mode (which you are in now) and the editing mode, which is the mode you use to edit your movie.

> **Rewind/Review—**When the tape is not playing, the Rewind button rewinds the tape at top speed. When the tape is playing, it plays the tape backward (you see the video, but there is no audio). In the Review mode, you have to "hold" the button down to keep the review going (in other words, if you let up on the button, it goes back into Play mode).

> **Pause—**This one freezes the video at a specific frame.

> **Play—**Need I say more?

> **Stop—**The Stop button halts whatever is happening with the camcorder.

> **Fast Forward/Preview—**When the tape is not playing, the Fast Forward button moves the tape forward at top speed. When the tape is playing, it plays the tape forward at a high speed (you see video, but don't hear any audio).

> **Volume—**Drag the slider to the right to increase the volume and to the left to decrease it. Note that this affects only the playback volume and doesn't actually change the movie at all. This control affects your system volume level.

Import the Clips

Click the Import button (or press the Spacebar); iMovie starts the camcorder and begins capturing the clips. It stores the first clip in

the first available slot on the Shelf. When it gets to a scene break
(the point at which you hit the Stop Recording button on the DV
camcorder), it stops that clip and immediately begins capturing the
next scene, which it places in the next available slot on the Shelf.

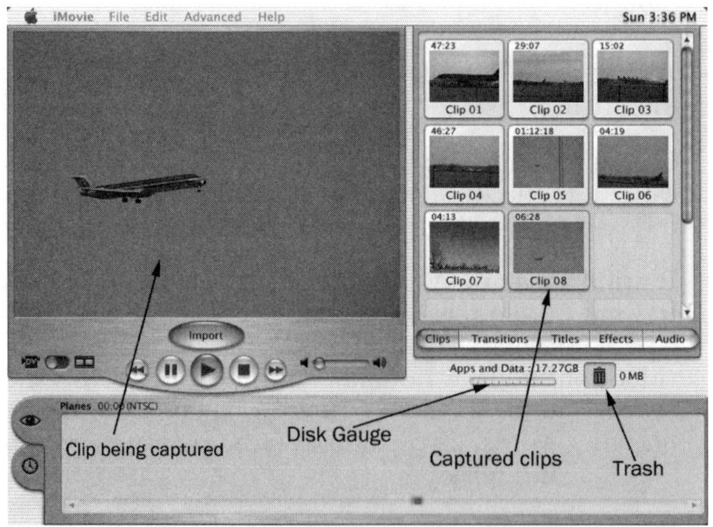

Figure 6.4 When you import clips from a DV camera, iMovie
stores them on the Shelf.

iMovie continues this process until it runs out of disk space to store
clips. If you don't want to wait that long, click Import again to stop
the capture process (or press the Spacebar).

As you import clips into iMovie, keep a close eye on the Disk
Gauge that is just under the Shelf. This gauge shows you how
much free space is available on the disk on which your project is
stored. When you are in good shape space-wise, the gauge shows
green. When it turns yellow, you are starting to run out of room.

> ### DON T SEE THE SHELF?
> If you don't see the Shelf, click the Clips button to show it.

When it turns red, the disk you are using is full, and you need to clear more space on it to continue.

Use the iMovie controls to move the tape to the next set of scenes that you want to capture, and begin again. Continue until you capture all the scenes that your script and storyboards call for, your disk runs out of space, or your Shelf is so full of clips that you have trouble dealing with so many (whichever comes first). Your Shelf now has some nice clips (and probably some not-so-nice ones), ready for you to edit and use in your movie.

When you are done, disconnect your camera and turn it off.

DITCHING CLIPS

As you capture clips, you will realize that some of them just aren't any good and you don't think you will end up using them. That is the time to get rid of the defective clip so that it doesn't consume any precious disk space. On the Shelf, click the clip that you want to dump to select it. Drag it to the Trash (or press Delete)—it disappears from the Shelf.

Placing a clip in the Trash gets it off the Shelf, but the clip still consumes disk space. To free up that disk space, you must empty the Trash. To do so, open the File menu and choose Empty Trash. Depending on how big the clips in the Trash are, you might see a dialog box asking you to confirm that you want to empty the Trash. Click OK, and the contents of the Trash are deleted. The space that this junk consumed on the disk is free for other purposes. (The increased space will be reflected on the Disk Gauge.)

MANUAL CLIP BREAKS

If you want to control how clips are broken instead of letting iMovie do it for you, uncheck the "Automatically start new clip at scene break" checkbox in the iMovie Preferences dialog. When you import video, the clips will come in as one continuous clip unless you start and stop the importing process manually.

Stocking the Shelf with QuickTime Clips

You might also want to use QuickTime movies in your iMovie project. These QuickTime movies might be some that you have digitized yourself, or they might be some that you have downloaded from email or from the Web.

Using QuickTime movies in iMovie is a two-step process. Step 1 is to use QuickTime Player Pro to convert the movie into DV format. Step 2 is to import the movies into iMovie.

Convert Your QuickTime Clips into DV

All clips in iMovie must be in the DV format. Native QuickTime movies are not in DV; they are in QuickTime (duh). To be able to use a QuickTime movie in iMovie, you first must make it into a DV movie.

First, find a QuickTime movie that you want to use in your iMovie project. Open the QuickTime Player application and then open the movie file that you want to convert into the DV format. It appears in the QuickTime Player window.

> ### GOING PRO
> Converting movies into DV format is one of the features enabled with the QuickTime Pro upgrade. If you haven't upgraded QuickTime on your machine, you won't be able to do this.

Open the File menu and choose Export. The Export dialog box shows up on-screen. Move to the location in which you want to save the DV movie version of the clip. Choose Movie to DV Stream from the Export pop-up menu. Click Save. The movie is converted into DV, and it is saved in the location you specified. (If the clip is more than a few seconds long, this process can take a while.) Eventually, you will return to the QuickTime Player window, which means that the clip has been converted.

Use the same process to continue converting your clips until you have them all in the DV format.

Put the DV Clips on the Shelf

To use a DV clip that you have converted, do the following steps. Back in iMovie, open the File menu and choose Import File. In the Import File dialog box, choose DV Stream file from the Show pop-up menu. Move to the first clip that you converted into the DV Stream format. Select the DV stream clip and click Import.

You will see a progress bar showing you how the import is moving along. If your clip is fairly lengthy, this process can take a few moments. When the importing process is complete, the clip appears on the Shelf, and it is automatically selected so that you see it in the Monitor. From this point on, it behaves in the same way as any other clip on the Shelf.

Importing Still Images

You can include still images in your movie, or if you want to create a slideshow, you can have a movie composed entirely of still images.

You can import image files in all of the common Mac image file formats, such as JPEG, TIFF, PICT, and so on. For best results, you should size your images so that they have a resolution of exactly 640 x 480 because iMovie will scale them to that size anyway, which can result in some distortion if the image's size is much different than this.

Moving your photos into iMovie is as easy as importing video. From the File menu, choose Import File. You will see the Import File dialog box. Move to the folder in which you saved the photos that you want to use in your show. Hold the Shift or ⌘ key down and click all of the images that you want to import. When they are selected, click Import. A progress window appears, and after a few moments, you will see your images on the Shelf.

> **QUIT AND EMPTY**
> The Trash is automatically emptied every time you quit iMovie.

Previewing, Naming, and Editing the Clips

Now that you have all of your clips in your iMovie project, you are ready to edit them and prepare for your movie.

When you are editing clips, you should have two goals. One is to understand the clips that you have. The other is to edit the clips so that they contain only the video that you want to include in your movie (in some cases, this might mean that you delete the entire clip). As you read in the previous chapter, you should expect to ditch *most* of the clips you captured, and you should expect to cut a lot from the clips that you do keep—this is a normal part of the editing process.

The steps to editing a clip are:

1. Preview a clip to see if it is has usable material (if not, delete it).

2. Understand and rename the clip.

3. Edit the clip down to its useable parts.

Previewing a Clip

Select a clip by clicking it on the Shelf. The clip is highlighted with a yellow border—this means that the clip is selected. More telling is the first frame of the clip that the Monitor shows.

Notice that when you select a clip, iMovie also moves into the Edit mode, in which you can manipulate your clips (if it isn't in the Edit mode, slide the Camera/Edit Mode switch to the right).

In Edit mode, the controls that you see at the bottom of the Monitor are slightly different than they were in the Camera mode. From left to right, they are:

> **Rewind/review**—This is the same as in Camera mode. Click it to rewind the movie at high speed; click it again to stop the movie.

> **Home**—This moves you to the first frame in the selection (whether you have selected a single clip or several).

> **Play**—Click to play and then click to stop playing whatever is selected (one or more clips).

> **Play Full Screen**—Click this to play the selected clip in full-screen mode in which the iMovie interface disappears and your clip fills the screen.

> **Fast forward**—Click this to move ahead through the selected clip at high speed.

> **Volume**—If you don't know what this is, I have failed miserably....

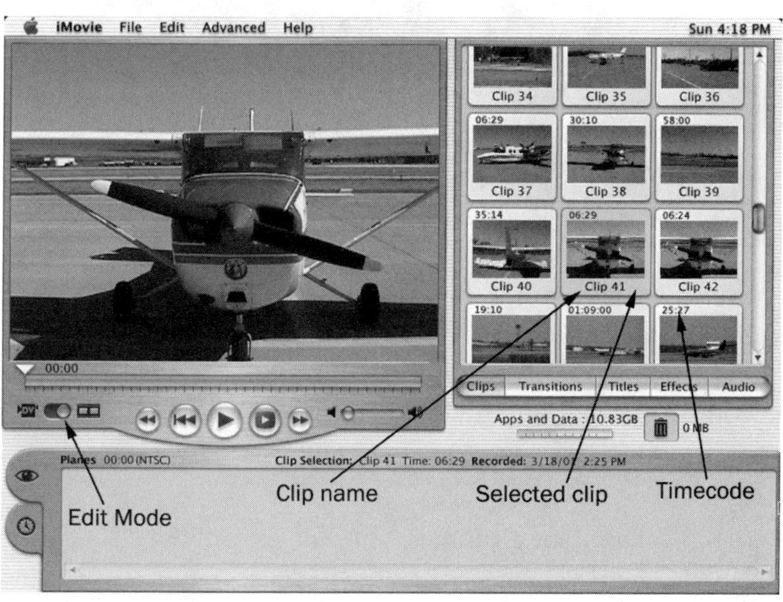

Figure 6.5 Clip 41 is selected on the Shelf; its first frame is shown in the Monitor.

Click Play to watch and hear your clip. Click Play again to pause your clip. You can also start and stop play by pressing the Spacebar.

As the clip plays, notice that the Playhead moves across the Scrubber Bar. The Playhead shows the exact frame that appears in the Monitor as it appears; you use the Playhead to determine where you "are" in a clip. The precise location of the Playhead is shown by the timecode that "floats" next to the Playhead.

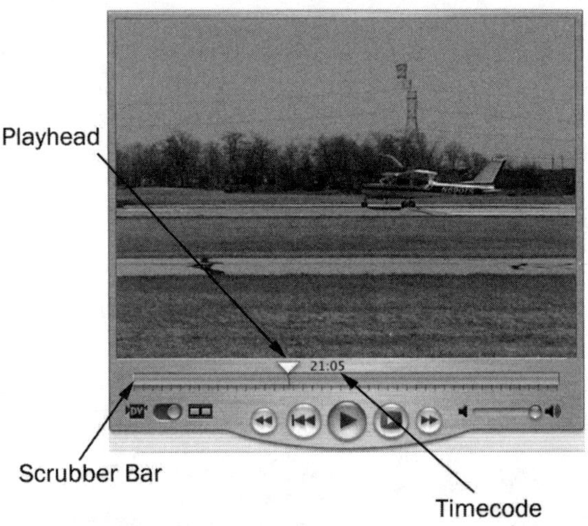

Figure 6.6 This clip is playing and is on the 5th frame of the 22-second of the clip.

The timecode is an important piece of information with which you need to get comfortable. As its name implies, the timecode provides information about the time aspects of a clip or of your movie. Timecodes appear in the following format:

```
Minutes:Seconds:Frames
```

If your clip is less than a minute, you will see only two sets of numbers: Seconds and Frames.

The Frames part of the timecode is a counter that measures the number of frames in a single second of the clip. Most clips that you capture have 30 frames per second, which is the number that is required for smooth on-screen motion. Within each second of the clip, the frames are numbered from 00 to 29 (for a total of 30 frames).

The Frames part of the timecode tells you where in each second of the clip you are. For example, a timecode of 36:21 means that the clip is 36 seconds long and has gone 21 frames into the 37th second (so it is actually almost 37 seconds long).

FRAME RATE

The technical term for number of frames per second is frame rate. Because video is actually composed of a series of still images that "flip" rapidly to give the appearance of motion, the more frames per second, the less change there is between individual frames. This makes the video smoother. A frame rate of 30 frames per second appears very smooth, and you won't notice any jerkiness. If the frame rate gets below 20 frames per second, you will start to notice "jumps" between movements on the screen, and it doesn't look very good to you. Fortunately, you don't have to worry about this when you use iMovie, because it manages the frame rate for you.

As you start editing, the timecode becomes very useful, especially when you are able to interpret it immediately. The first few times it can be a bit confusing, but just keep remembering that the last number in the timecode is the frame number; it'll eventually sink in.

You can preview (called *search forward* in iMovie lingo) by clicking the Fast Forward button while a clip is playing. The Playhead zooms across the screen until you click the Fast Forward button again. You can do the same thing in the reverse direction by using the Rewind/Review button (called *search backward*).

Adjust the playback volume using the Volume slider. Note that this only affects the current volume of the clip and in no way changes the clip itself (you will learn how to change a clip's volume in Chapter 8).

KEYBOARD SHORTCUTS

To fast forward a clip, you can press ⌘+] instead of clicking the Fast Forward button. Pressing ⌘+] again stops the clip. You press

continued...

> ⌘+[to rewind/review. An easy way to control volume is by using the Up- and Down-arrow keys. Pressing the Up arrow key increases the volume, while the Down arrow decreases it.

As you edit, you are constantly moving around a clip to get to specific areas to edit. There are a couple of ways to do this.

Click the Playhead and drag it to the right to move forward in the clip (or to the left to move backward in the clip). When you release the mouse button, the Playhead is at the exact position that you left it, and you can see the frame indicated by the timecode. Use this method for gross but quick movements in the clip, such as moving from the beginning to the middle.

You can also move the Playhead much more precisely by using the keyboard; this is essential when you get to detailed editing because you can move by increments as small as a single frame. To move the Playhead one frame at a time, use the Left- and Right-arrow keys. As you probably guessed, the Right-arrow key moves the Playhead forward one frame, and the Left-arrow key moves you backward one frame.

You can also move the Playhead forward or backward 10 frames at a time by holding the Shift key down while you press the Left- or Right-arrow keys. This movement is very useful when you are doing detailed editing because it also enables you to quickly move to a precise location in the clip, but you get there a bit faster than by moving one frame at a time.

A fast preview technique is to select a clip and fast forward through it (press ⌘+]) so that you get a good idea of what it contains. If it looks like it contains no usable footage, delete it. If it looks promising, watch it again at regular speed.

> **WORKING EFFICIENTLY**
>
> Make sure that you learn and use the keyboard shortcuts I mention in this chapter. Editing video is a time-consuming process and every bit of efficiency helps.

Renaming and Getting Information on the Clips

When you import a clip, iMovie gives it a name; but the names aren't very meaningful. The application simply tacks a number on the word Clip; this number comes from the order in which you imported the clips.

> ### A CLIP BY ANY OTHER NAME
>
> The exception to this is when you import a QuickTime clip into your project. In that case, the clip name is the name of the file that you imported.

You can make the names of your clips more meaningful. Click a clip to select it and then click the clip name (or just click the clip name directly). The clip's name box is highlighted to indicate that the name can be edited. Type a new name for the clip that helps you identify it and then press Return. Continue naming your clips until you have named them all.

Use a naming scheme that helps you identify the clips easily. For example, you might provide an idea of the clip's contents. Or you might include a number indicating what the clip's sequence in the movie should be. You can't see that many characters in the clip's name when you view it on the Shelf, but with a little creativity, you should be able to use meaningful names.

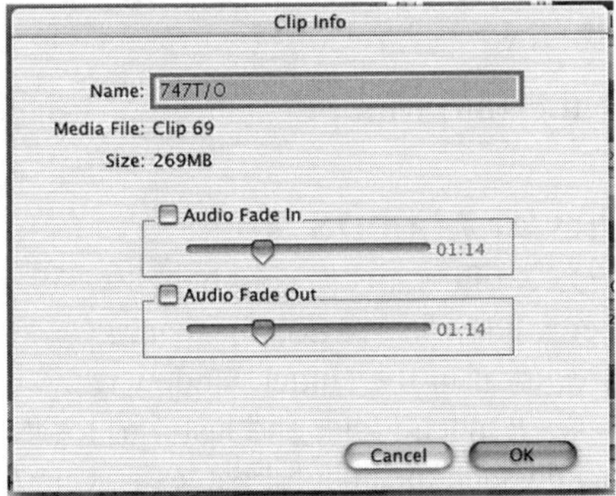

Figure 6.7 The Clip Info window enables you to see the clip's entire name.

You can also open the information window for any clip that you select. To do so, select a clip and double-click it (or press Shift+⌘+I). Its Info window opens.

In the Clip Info window, you see the following information about the selected clip:

> ➤ **Name**—This is the name that you gave the clip. Many clip names will be longer than what you can see when the clip is on the Shelf—you can see the full name in the Clip Info window. You can also edit or rename the clip by using the Name text box.

> ➤ **Media File name**—This is the name of the file in the Media folder for the project. When you rename a clip in iMovie, its file name does not change—the name of the reference inside iMovie is the only thing that changes. The Media File information can help you reuse clips more easily in other projects. For example, to use the clip selected in the previous figure in another project, I would copy the file called Clip 69 to the other project's Media folder.

> ➤ **Size**—This shows the file size for the clip. For example, the clip shown in Figure 6.7 is 269 MB; its timecode is 1:16:22, which means that it is 1 minute, 16 seconds, and 22 frames long.

> ➤ **Audio Fading controls**—You can have the audio part of a clip fade in or fade out. You learn about this in Chapter 8.

Click OK to close the Info window.

MORE BENEFITS OF MAC OS X

Using Mac OS X offers lots of cool benefits. For example, when you view a Finder window in the Columns view, you can select a DV clip and then preview it in the Finder window without ever opening the file. This makes it much easier and faster to locate files to which iMovie has attached such meaningful names as Clip 69.

Moving Clips Around the Shelf

As you delete clips that you aren't going to use, you might end up with empty slots on the Shelf. This doesn't hurt anything, but if you prefer to fill the empty slots, simply drag a clip from its current slot to the empty one. The location and placement of the clips on the Shelf doesn't make any difference because it has no relationship to when the clip appears in your movie. The Shelf is only the tool that you use to store and organize your clips before you place them in a movie.

Editing a Clip

The first step in editing a clip is to select the part of the clip that you want to edit. You do this with the Crop Markers.

As with most Mac applications, you select the material that you want to edit—in this case, frames of the clip—and then perform some action on them.

Click the clip that you want to edit to select it. The clip appears in the Monitor. Using the movement tricks that you just learned, move to an area in the clip that you want to remove. You can remove frames from the clip from any point, such as at the beginning, end, or somewhere in-between.

Move the pointer to the underside of the Scrubber Bar and two "ghost" Crop Markers will appear to show you where the Crop Markers will be located when you click. When you are ready to set the markers, click and drag. When you do, the Start Crop Marker becomes solid, and its location is fixed. Drag to the right to move the End Crop Marker to select a series of frames. The area of the clip that you have selected is indicated by the gold-colored portion of the Scrubber Bar. When you release the Crop Markers, the Playhead jumps to the right Crop Marker.

When the Playhead is aligned with a Crop Marker, it "sticks" to it. This enables you to make very fine selections, even down to the individual frame. You can also make the Crop Marker stick to the Playhead by dragging the Playhead so that it is directly over a Crop Marker (a small line extends down from the Playhead so that you can see precisely where it is located).

Figure 6.8 The Crop Markers indicate the portion of the clip that is selected; you can also see the selected frames by the gold colored (lighter in the figure) portion of the Scrubber Bar.

When the Playhead is "stuck" to the Crop Markers, you can make very fine selections by using the arrow keys. To increase the selected frames by a single frame, press the Right-arrow key one time (to shorten the selection by one frame, press the Left-arrow key once). To change the selection by 10 frames at a time, hold the Shift key down while you press the appropriate arrow key.

UNSTICKING THE PLAYHEAD

If you play a clip, the Playhead becomes "unstuck" from the Crop Marker and moves as it normally does.

To get rid of the selected frames, open the Edit menu and choose Cut (or press ⌘+X). The Crop Markers disappear, as do the selected frames, and they are removed from the clip. Play the clip to see how it is without the frames that you just cut. If you don't like the result, you can undo it by choosing Undo from the Edit menu (or press ⌘+Z).

If you want to remove everything that is *not* selected instead, use the Crop command. This is useful when you want to remove frames from both the beginning and end of a clip at the same time. Select the portion of the clip that you want to *keep* by using the Crop Markers; when you crop it, everything else is removed.

The editing commands that you can use on a selected portion of a clip are summarized in the following table.

Table 6.1 Editing Commands

Command	Keyboard Shortcut	What It Does
Cut	⌘+X	Removes selected frames from clip and places a copy of them on the Clipboard.
Copy	⌘+C	Leaves selected frames in the clip and places a copy of them on the Clipboard.
Clear		Removes selected frames, but does not place them on the Clipboard.
Crop	⌘+K	Removes all frames that are not selected.

> ### STICKY CROP MARKERS
>
> These Crop Markers are tough; once you put them down, they like to stay put. To get rid of them, click the clip on the Shelf and the Crop Markers are banished from the Monitor. You can recall them again by pointing to where you want them to be (you see them in ghost form) and clicking and dragging to set them.

Copying and Pasting among Clips

As with all other Mac applications, you can cut and paste frames in a clip or among clips. Use your editing skills to select the portion of the clip that you want to paste elsewhere in the clip or in another clip entirely. Copy the selection if you want those frames to remain in the clip, or use Cut if you don't want them to remain. Now move the Playhead to the point at which you want to paste the selected frames (select another clip first to move them to a different clip). Choose Paste (or ⌘+V) and the frames are pasted into the selected clip at the current location of the Playhead.

> ### PAY ATTENTION TO SOUND
>
> If your clips have sound in them, pay attention to that sound as you edit. Make sure that you don't remove sound that you want to be included in your movie along with the video. And try to avoid cutting sounds off in the middle—unless the sound isn't important, and you plan to mute it later anyway. In Chapter 8, you will learn how to separate a clip's audio from its video so that you can remove video frames without affecting the audio.

Splitting a Clip

Sometimes, it's useful to be able to break a clip into parts so that you can work with them individually. When would you want to do this? There are at least two situations. If a clip has a "bad spot" somewhere in the middle, you want to get rid of the bad spot. If you just cut the bad spot out, the clip suddenly jumps from one frame to another, which might be quite jarring. When you split a clip, you can add a transition in the gap you create to make the clip

flow more smoothly. Another situation might be when you imported several scenes as one clip. You might want to split this long clip
into scenes.

To split a clip, position the Playhead at the point where you want
the first clip to end and the second to begin. From the Edit menu,
choose Split Clip at Playhead (or press ⌘+T). The clip is broken
into two parts, which then become two separate clips. One clip
remains in the original location on the Shelf and the other (which
has /1 appended to the clip's name) is placed in an open Shelf slot.

Editing All the Clips

Use the editing skills you have to do rough edits of all the clips that
you want to use in your movie. Trim them down so that each clip
contains roughly what you want to appear in your movie. Don't
worry about getting them exactly right, because you will edit the
clips more as you build your movie. In fact, it's usually a good idea
to leave a couple of spare frames at each end of the clips so that
you have some "extra" to work with when you do the final editing.

When you're finished, you should have shorter and fewer clips
than you did after you imported all of the clips into the project.

> **PROJECT MAINTENANCE**
>
> As you work, remember to save your project to make sure that
> you protect your work. You should also empty the trash every
> so often so that you free up disk space as you remove frames from
> the clips.

Building a Movie

After you have done the rough editing of your clips, you can begin
to create your movie.

Hopefully, you have constructed a script or a storyboard to guide
you in the movie-making process. How detailed these are depends
on the type of movie you're making. You might simply have a list

of the scenes that shows the order in which you want them to appear in the movie. Or you might have a detailed storyboard an script that describes exactly how your movie moves from scene to scene. In any case, use your script and storyboard to guide your movie making process.

ARE YOU KIDDING?

I mention the script and storyboard again because these tools can really help you make a movie. Rather than just slamming clips together on a whim, your movie will usually be much better if you give some thought to the story that you want to tell (even if you are documenting an event).

You assemble your movie by placing clips on the Clip Viewer in the order that you want them to be in the movie.

Click the Clip Viewer icon, which is the eye, to bring the Clip Viewer to the front (it will probably be in the front already). To begin assembling your movie, simply drag clips from the Shelf onto the Clip Viewer. You can drag them onto the Clip Viewer in the order in which you want them to appear; you can reshuffle them later if you want to.

PARTING THE CLIPS

If you drag a clip from the Shelf to be between two clips on the Clip Viewer, those clips will move apart to allow you to place the clip between them.

When you select one or more clips on the Clip Viewer, the Monitor will contain the clips that you have selected on the Clip Viewer. Vertical lines in the Scrubber Bar mark the boundaries of each clip that you have selected.

If you don't have any clips selected, the Monitor will show the contents of all the clips on the Clip Viewer, in other words, your entire movie.

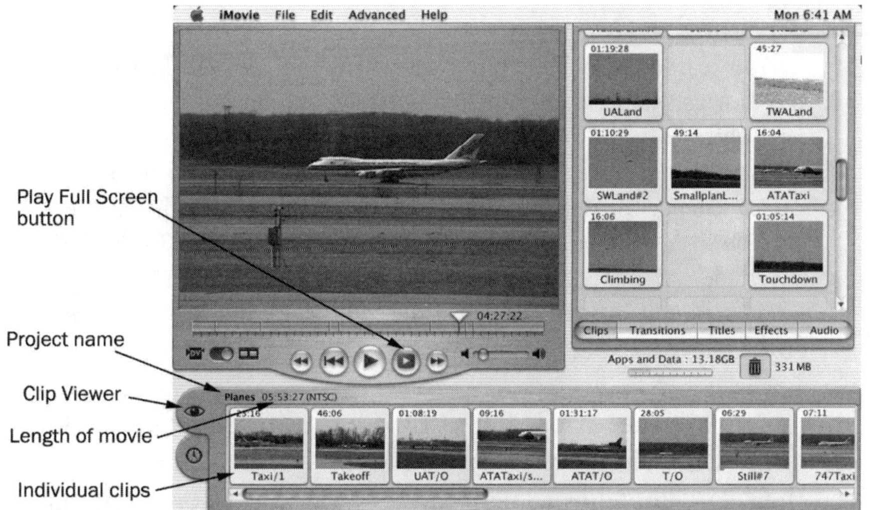

Figure 6.9 I have moved clips from the Shelf to the Clip Viewer; the Clip Viewer shows the sequence in which the clips will be played in your movie.

If the Clip Viewer gets full, use its scroll bar to reveal empty space for more clips.

How Long Is This Movie, Anyway?

The total time of your movie appears to the right of the project name in the Clip Viewer.

Press ⌘+D to deselect any clips that are selected. As the movie plays, a red location marker is in the Clip Viewer in each clip as it plays; its function is similar to the Playhead in that it shows the part of the clip that is playing.

Press Home to move to the start of your movie. To preview your movie, press the Spacebar. Your movie plays. You can use the same movement and editing controls with an entire movie as you can when dealing with an individual clip (such as fast forward). (You can play a single clip again by selecting it on the Clip Viewer.)

MOVING STILLS

You learned earlier that you can easily include still images in your movies. Rather than using a frame rate, still images use a duration, which is how long the image appears on-screen. By default, this is 5 seconds, meaning that the still image appears for 5 seconds. You can change the default value if you want, and you can change the duration for a still image when you add it to your movie. To do the latter, add the image to your movie. Select the image in the Clip Viewer and edit the value in the Time field to be the new duration for the image.

You can change the order of clips by dragging them from one location on the Clip Viewer to another. As you move a clip between two other clips, the clips move apart to show you where your clip will be placed when you release the mouse button.

You can remove a clip and place it back on the Shelf by dragging it from the Clip Viewer to the Shelf. You can delete a clip by selecting it and then pressing Delete.

You can work with an individual clip again by selecting it in the Clip Viewer. It appears in the Monitor as it did when it was located in the Shelf. Press ⌘+D to deselect the clip so that the entire movie appears in the Monitor.

To see your movie in full-screen mode, click the Play Full Screen button. Your movie plays back so that it takes up the entire screen. This helps you focus on your movie without any distractions from the iMovie interface. To stop your movie and return to iMovie before your movie has finished, click the mouse button or press the Spacebar.

Continue placing clips in the Clip Viewer until you have all of them that you want to appear in your movie. You don't have to use all of the clips on the Shelf; you can leave clips there for later use or delete them when you are sure that you won't use them in this movie.

Watch your movie and edit clips as you need to until the movie begins to meet your vision for it. Don't skimp on this process; take the time to whittle down the video track so that it contains only material that you want to actually appear in your movie.

Sprinkling pixels wide –
for the iMac,
the click.

Chapter Seven

Adding Transitions, Titles, and Special Effects

After you have created the basic video track, it is time to jazz up your movie with transitions, titles, and special effects—iMovie provides fairly sophisticated tools in each of these areas. Amazingly enough, even with their sophistication, these iMovie tools are relatively easy to use.

In this chapter, we are going to look at:

- ➤ Adding transitions between clips
- ➤ Adding text to your movie
- ➤ Using iMovie special effects

Using Transitions to Make Your Movie Flow

The segment between two clips in a movie is called the *transition.* You can use different transitions to smooth the flow from one clip into the next so that your series of individual clips doesn't look like a series of clips, but rather a movie that flows smoothly from one scene to the next. All video uses transitions of one sort or another.

The three most common types of transitions are the straight cut, cross dissolve, and fade to or from black.

The straight cut isn't a transition that you have to apply; this is what happens when you don't add a transition. A straight cut transition occurs when one scene runs right into another. As long as the adjacent scenes are similar "enough," the straight cut seems very natural, and you don't even notice it.

The cross dissolve is also very common. One scene dissolves into the next. This transition can be useful when the adjacent scenes are somewhat similar, but enough different that a straight cut is a bit jarring.

The fade to (or from) black is also a very useful transition. With the fade, a scene fades to black (or fades in from a black screen).

iMovie enables you to add a variety of transition effects to your movies with a simple drag-and-drop procedure. The basic transitions that you can use in your movie are shown in the following table.

> **ADD MORE TRANSITIONS**
> You can expand the number of transitions that iMovie enables you to use by adding new transition effects to your iMovie installation. You learn how and where to get more transitions in Chapter 10.

Table 7.1—*Standard iMovie Transitions*

Transition Name	Description
Cross Dissolve	One scene dissolves as the other becomes visible.
Fade In	From a black background, the clip slowly becomes visible.
Fade Out	The clip ends in a fade to black.
Overlap	The two clips exist on the screen for a brief time before the previous one fades and the next one begins.
Push	One clip is "pushed" off the screen in one of the four directions (left, right, up, or down).
Scale Down	With the next clip in the background, one clip gets smaller and smaller until it disappears and leaves the next clip in full possession of the screen.

You're likely to enjoy adding transitions, and it's amazing how much nicer they make your movies. Before you jump into them, however, take a moment and think about which transitions you want to add.

Choosing Transitions

Don't go crazy with transitions. When you first start playing with them, you might find them so compelling that you want to use a different one at each juncture between clips. Go ahead and do that just to see how they work, but your final movie's transitions should be more carefully thought out.

DON T BE A KIDNAPPER

When you are using transitions, don't succumb to what has been called the ransom note effect. This effect was first experienced back in the early days of the Mac when people realized how easy it was to add different fonts and sizes to their documents. And because they could, they did. They added numerous different fonts, and even different sizes of the same font, to a single document. The result was something that resembled a ransom note like one you might see in your favorite tale of kidnapping. Even though you have lots of transitions that you can use, use them sparingly. Most short movies should include only two or three different types of transitions.

When deciding upon a transition, you must carefully consider the clips on each side of it. The idea of a transition is to smooth the flow, so you should use transitions that do not interfere with the movie. Ideally, you want viewers to barely notice your transitions. If that is the case, your transitions are working well, and you should be proud. If your viewers make lots of comments about how neat your transitions are, they are probably paying more attention to your transitions and less attention to your movie.

If the clips next to one another are of dramatically different scenes, stick to transitions that make the transition as clear as possible. For example, the fade works really well for these sorts of situations because the fade out tells our minds to get ready to change gears and to expect something different to happen.

On the other hand, if your scenes are fairly similar, it might be beneficial to have both scenes on the screen at the same time so that the viewer "gets" that the next scene is simply a continuation of the previous one; the cross dissolve does this nicely. You might also want to try one of the Push transitions because this often gives the impression that time has passed.

You can usually tell whether the transition you're using is the right one by previewing it. If you find yourself thinking that the transition is really neat, try something less dramatic. If you find yourself being "jerked" from one scene to the next, you probably need a stronger transition effect.

Adding a Transition to Your Movie

To get started, open the Transitions palette by clicking the Transitions button. The Transitions palette pops up, and you see the Transitions tools.

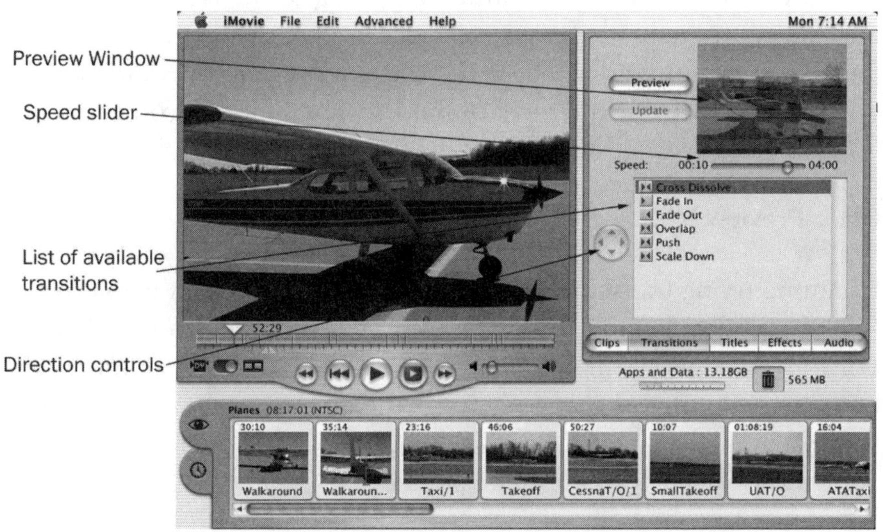

Figure 7.1 When you click the Transitions button, the Transitions palette replaces the Shelf so that you can add transitions to your movie.

You can preview a transition by clicking it on the list of available transitions. In the Preview window at the top of the Transitions palette, you see the transition applied to the clip that you have selected; if you don't have a clip selected, you see that transition applied to the first clip in your movie. When you click Preview, you see a preview of the transition applied to the clip shown in the Monitor window. Since the transition will be applied to the end of the clip, place the Playhead there before you select the transition that you are going to apply.

> ### A SILLY TRANSITION
>
> If you haven't moved the Playhead to the end of the clip, the preview shows the clip transitioning to itself. Not very useful, but you still get the idea of the transition well enough.

You can control the amount of time over which the transition effect is displayed by using the Speed slider that is just above the list of available transitions. Moving the slider to the left makes the transition last a shorter amount of time. Moving it to the right stretches the transition out so that it takes longer to play. After you release the slider, you immediately see the transition in the Preview window. In the lower-right corner of the Preview window, you can see how long the selected transition takes with the current setting.

Click Preview to view the transition on the Monitor.

Continue trying transitions to see those that you have available. When you find a transition that you want to use, you can apply it. For this example, I am applying the Cross Dissolve transition between a clip that shows a plane on the ground and one that shows a similar plane taking off. The general steps that you use to apply other transitions are quite similar.

Selecting and Timing the Transition

In the Clip Viewer, select the clip after which you want the Cross Dissolve transition to appear and move the Playhead to the end of the clip. Click Cross Dissolve to choose it. Watch the preview. Set its duration with the slider; try placing the slider in the middle of its range. If that is too long or too short, use the slider to set the proper amount of time for the transition. When the timing looks "close," click Preview to see how it looks on the Monitor.

When you're happy with the results, you're ready to place the transition in your movie.

Placing the Transition

Adding a transition to your movie is similar to adding a clip. You simply drag the transition from the Transitions palette to the Clip Viewer and drop it between the two clips that you want to transition between. The transition appears as a green box with arrowheads that indicate the direction of the transition.

In this example, I dragged the Cross Dissolve from the Transitions palette to between the clip called Walkaround#2 and the clip called CessnaT/O.

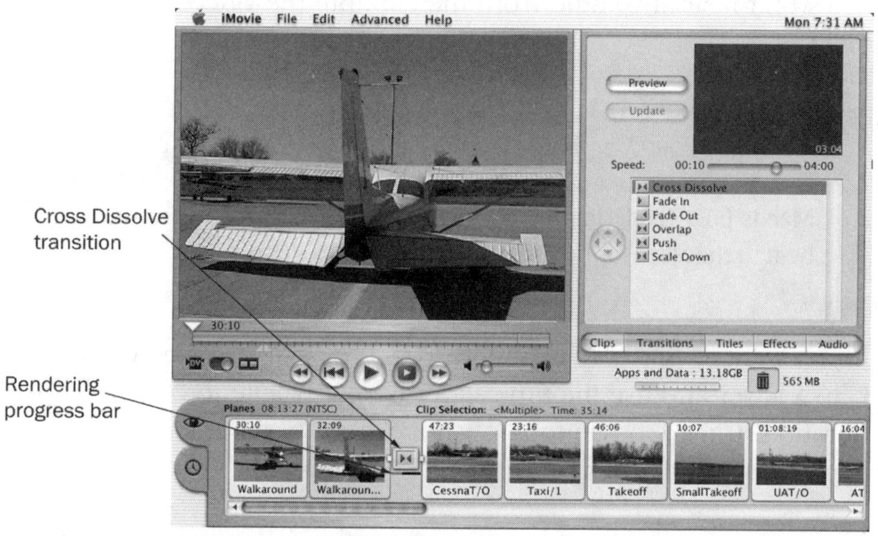

Cross Dissolve transition

Rendering progress bar

Figure 7.2 Adding a transition is quite similar to adding a clip; the main difference is that transitions have to be rendered.

Transitions are fairly sophisticated effects, and they require your iMac to do a lot of work to apply them. This process is called *rendering.* When your Mac renders a clip, it applies the proper amount of transition effect to each frame of the clip. When you apply a complex transition with a long duration, this can take a while. Fortunately, you can continue to work while your iMac renders your transitions.

When you place a transition on the Clip Viewer, your Mac immediately begins to render it; you see the small render progress bar at the bottom of the transition clip (see the previous figure for an example). When the rendering process is complete, the progress bar disappears. While a transition is being rendered, you can preview the transition, or you can move on to something else.

As your iMac is rendering the transition, you can preview it by selecting it in the Clip Viewer and pressing the Spacebar. When you do this, the transition and the first few moments of the following clip play. (If your iMac hasn't completed the rendering process, you won't hear any audio from the clip, but the video works just fine.)

> ## ONE THING THAT YOU CAN T DO
>
> While your Mac is rendering one or more clips, you can't save your project. If you try, you will see a warning telling you that your Mac is busy rendering. If you try to save your movie, the transitions being rendered will be deleted from the Clip Viewer.

If you want to make adjustments to the transition, select it in the Clip Viewer and use the time slider on the palette to change its duration. Click Update to apply the change to the transition. (The clip will be rendered again.)

You can just as easily add another transition between any two clips. Try adding a Push transition between two clips that are of similar scenes. In the palette, click Push. Notice that the Direction controls now become active. You use these controls to set the direction of the transition. For example, to get a push up, click the Up arrow. One clip "pushes" the next up the screen. Similarly, the Left arrow makes one clip push the other off the screen to the left.

Set the duration of the push with the slider. Watch the preview and make adjustments until the transition looks like it is "close." Click the Preview button to see the transition on the Monitor. Keep adjusting it until you are satisfied.

Then drag the transition and drop it between two clips (your iMac then renders it). Press the Spacebar to see the transition in action.

Finishing the Transitions

Continue adding transitions until you have made your movie really flow. At the least, add a Fade In at the beginning and a Fade Out at the end.

> ### STACKING TRANSITIONS
> You can place two transitions adjacent to one another. For example, to have one clip fade out and then the next fade in, place a Fade Out and a Fade in between two clips.

Don't feel as though you need to have a transition before and after every clip. Sometimes, the default straight cut works just fine. This is where your creativity comes in, so experiment until you achieve an outcome that is pleasing to you.

After you have your transitions in place, you will see the new movie timeline in the Clip Viewer.

Use the movement and editing techniques to watch your movie. Modify any of the transitions that you aren't satisfied with.

> ### PLAYING PORTIONS OF YOUR MOVIE
> You can play only portions of your movie by selecting the clips that you want to play in the Clip Viewer (including transitions). When you press the Play button (or the Spacebar), only the selected parts of your movie play. This saves time and helps you focus on particular parts of your movie.

Titling Your Movie

When it comes to titles, credits, and other text, your iMovie movies can certainly hold their own. There are many title effects that you can add to your movies in almost limitless ways. You will be amazed at how much improvement you can make to your movies with the right title effects.

Although adding on-screen text is called *titling,* this term refers to much more than just the movie's name. Basically, titling is iMovie's term for overlaying all sorts of text on the screen. The titles that you might want to use in your movies include the following:

- **Captions**—As with figure captions, you can use "clip captions" to add information to the image on-screen. You might want to add some explanation of what is happening on the screen, the date on which the clip was captured, or you can even add subtitles if you want to. Captions are the term for basically any informative text relating to a scene that you want the viewer to see. Captions can appear anywhere in your movie.

- **Credits**—I'm sure that you are quite familiar with credits, because most modern movies have several minutes of credits at the end (which you always stay for, right?). Credits are just what the term implies: the opportunity to take, or give, credit for something in the movie. For example, you can list all the people who appear in the movie. Or if someone helps you with the movie, you might want to give her some fame by mentioning her name. Even though you can use credits anywhere in the movie, most credits appear at the end.

- **Titles**—Titles are introductory text that can introduce a movie, a scene, or anything else you think warrants an introduction. Titles normally appear at the beginning of something, whether it is a movie or a scene.

Titling iMovies

The standard iMovie installation comes with quite a number of title styles for you to use. The following table lists them, describes what they do, identifies the type-specific tools used (explained in the next section), and provides some ideas as to when you might want to use particular titles.

> ### TITLE STYLES ARE EXPANDABLE
> Just like transitions, you can expand the title styles that you have available to you by downloading additional title styles from the iMovie Web site. You learn how to do this in Chapter 10. All titles use the same set of tools and features, so if you know how to apply the standard styles, you can also use any new ones that you add to your system.

Table 7.2 Standard Title Styles

Title Style	Effect	Type-Specific Tools	Good Uses
Bounce In To Center	Two lines of text "bounce" into the center of the window from opposite sides of the screen.	Direction, Pause	Credits, titles
Centered Multiple	Two lines of text fade into the center of the screen at a time; you can add multiple sets of text.	Add, Pause	Credits, dates, titles
Centered Title	Two lines of text fade into the center of the screen.	Pause	Credits, dates, titles
Drifting	Two lines of text drift in the center of the screen.	Direction	Credits, dates, titles
Flying Letters	Words fly into the window one letter at a time.	Direction, Pause	Credits, titles

continued...

Flying Words	Lines of text fly into the screen one word at a time.	Direction, Pause	Credits, titles
Music Video	A block of text appears in either lower corner of the screen.	Direction	Captions, dates
Centered Rolling Credits	Centered lines of text roll up or down the screen.	Add, Direction	Credits, titles
Rolling Credits	Lines of text dots roll up or down the screen.	Add, Direction	Credits
Scroll with Pause	Lines of text scroll on the screen with a pause in the center of the screen.	Direction, Pause	Titles, credits
Scrolling Block	A block of text scrolls on the screen.	Direction	Captions, credits, titles
Stripe Subtitle	Text appears in a colored stripe at the bottom of the screen.	None	Captions, dates, titles
Typewriter	Lines of text appear on-screen as if they are being typed.	Pause	Captions, dates

Using iMovie Title Tools

iMovie provides lots of titling tools that you can use to add almost any sort of text to your movie. Titles are added with tools that are similar to the Transitions tools that you learned to use earlier in this chapter.

You add and manipulate titles by using the Titles palette. To see the palette, click Titles.

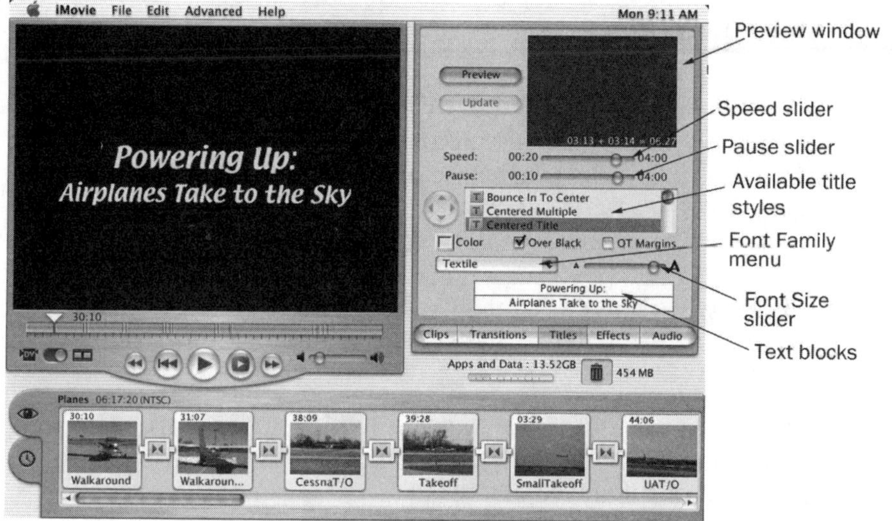

Figure 7.3 The Titles palette provides all the tools you need to add great text effects to your movies.

The following tools are included on the Titles palette:

> **Preview window**—This works just like it does on the Transitions palette. When you click a title style, you see a preview of it in the preview window. You also see a preview whenever you make changes to the title.

> **Preview button**—When you click this, you see a preview of your title in the Monitor.

> **Update button**—If you make changes to a title that you have already placed in your movie, click this button to update the title to include the changes that you have made.

> **Speed slider**—Just like transitions, all titles have a set amount of time that it takes for the title effect to occur. You can use the duration slider to set this time. Drag it to the left to make the title "faster" or to the right to make it "slower."

> **Pause slider**—If there is a pause element in a title's motion, use the Pause slider to control how long that pause is. Drag the slider to the left to make the pause last longer or to the right to make it a shorter pause.

> **MORE TIMECODE FUN**
>
> When you use a pause, the timecode that you see in the Preview window changes. Instead of a single number, you see two. The first is the speed of the title. The second is the length of the pause. iMovie even adds these together for you so that you can see the total length of the title.

➤ **Title style**—You click a title style to use it. The tools that are active on the palette change, depending on the style that you select.

➤ **Direction arrows**—Some styles involve motion for which you can set the direction. You choose a direction by clicking one of the active arrows.

➤ **Color menu**—Click this to change the color of the text in the title (it also affects the stripe color in Stripe Subtitle).

➤ **Over Black checkbox**—By default, when you place a title, it's applied over the clip that is selected or on which you drop the title. When you place the title on a clip, the clip might be split in such a way that there are two clips. One contains the title effect, and the other contains the remainder of the clip. If you want the title to appear in the first part of the clip, drop the title on the left side of the clip. If you want the title to appear on the end of the clip, drop it on the right side of the clip. The adjacent clips slide apart to indicate where the title clip is placed.

If you prefer the title to appear over a black background, you can check the Over Black checkbox. Instead of being applied to a clip in your movie, the title appears in a new black clip that is added to your movie wherever you drop the title.

➤ **QT Margins**—A QuickTime movie has different proportions than does a standard TV screen. For title styles that appear on the bottom edge of the screen, this can be a problem as those titles can get cut off when the movie is viewed on a TV. Unchecking the QT Margins checkbox moves the title up on the screen so that it won't be cut off when you show the movie on a TV. Checking it moves the title back down again so that it appears in a better location on the screen. You should leave this unchecked unless the style you use leaves text at the bottom of the screen. The only styles for which you need to use this are Music Video and Stripe Subtitle.

➤ **Font Family menu**—You can choose a font family for a title with this pop-up menu.

➤ **Font Size slider**—This slider enables you to make the selected font larger (drag it to the right) or smaller (drag it to the left).

➤ **Text blocks**—You can type the text for your title in the text blocks that appear on the palette. You see two styles of text block, depending on what style you use. Most styles use single lines of text. Others use a larger text block into which you can place a fair amount of text.

➤ **Add/Remove buttons**—Some styles allow you to add text blocks to the title. When it is active, click the Add button (the +) to add text blocks to your title. Click Remove (the -) to remove text blocks.

SCROLLING FOR TEXT

The scroll bar just to the right of the text blocks enables you to scroll up and down the text blocks that you are using.

You see different tools and options on the palette, depending on the title style that you use. Some styles (for example, Centered Multiple) allow you to add more lines or blocks of text. With these styles, the Add button (+) is active. Other styles (for example, Scrolling Block) involve motion for which you can set the direction; the direction arrows are active for these types.

Adding Titles to Your Movie

Here are the general steps that you use to add titles to your movies:

1. Decide what sort of text you want to add (caption, credit, date, or title) and to which clip you want to apply the text (or whether you want to apply it to a black background).

2. Based on the kind of text you add and where you apply it, decide on a title style to use (see Table 7.2 for help with this).

3. Open the Titles palette (click the Titles button) and click a title style to select it.

4. Type your text in the text boxes for that style. Use the Add button (if available) to add more text to the title.

5. Choose a font, color, and size for the title.

6. Set the direction of the motion (if applicable).

7. Set the speed and pause (if applicable) of the title.

8. Preview the title in the Preview window and by clicking the Preview button (to preview it in the Monitor).

> **RENDERING**
>
> Just as the transitions effects have to be rendered before they can be added to your movie, titles must be rendered before they appear on-screen. Rendering can take a while, so use the preview function to get your titles in great shape before you actually add them to your movie. Just like transition effects, you see a red progress bar in the title clips as they are rendered. You also see a progress counter that displays the rendering progress, frame-by-frame (as in 16 frames complete of 385 total frames in the title). If you update a title, its clip must be re-rendered.

9. Make adjustments to the title until it is "right."

10. Place the title in your movie by dragging it to the Clip

Viewer.

11.   View the section of your movie that contains the title to make sure that it works the way you want it to.

12.   If it doesn't, select the title and make changes to it using the Titles palette.

13.   Click Update to update the title.

Even though you do most of these steps, you might choose to do them in a different order than I suggest. Just experiment to find the order that suits you best.

Adding Titles: Examples

You know everything that you need to know to add titles to your own movies. In the following sections, you'll see some examples of titles I added to my movie.

SOME TRANSITIONS GET IN THE WAY

Sometimes, existing transitions block you from adding a title clip. If this happens, delete the transition, add the title clip, and after the title has been rendered, add the transition back in. If you are going to use a lot of titles in your movie, it can be easier to add the titles before you add transitions.

Introducing Your Movie with a Title

You probably want to add a title to most of your movies. For example, I called the movie that I created for this book "Powering Up: Airplanes Taking to the Sky." I chose Centered Title for its style.

NAMING TITLE CLIPS

When you add a title clip to your movie, iMovie uses the first part of the text that you enter for the title as the name of the title clip. If you don't like that name, you can rename title clips just like any other clips in your movie.

On the Titles palette, click Centered Title to choose it. Click the Over Black checkbox. Type the title in the text boxes (with this style, you can have two lines of text). Choose a font and the color for the text (leave the color in its default since you are using a black background). Use the Speed and Pause sliders to set the title's duration. As you make these selections, the title will be shown in the Preview window.

When you think the title is getting close to being ready, click Preview to preview it in the Monitor (see the previous figure for an example). When it is correct, drag the title style from the Titles palette to the Clip Viewer before the first clip in the movie.

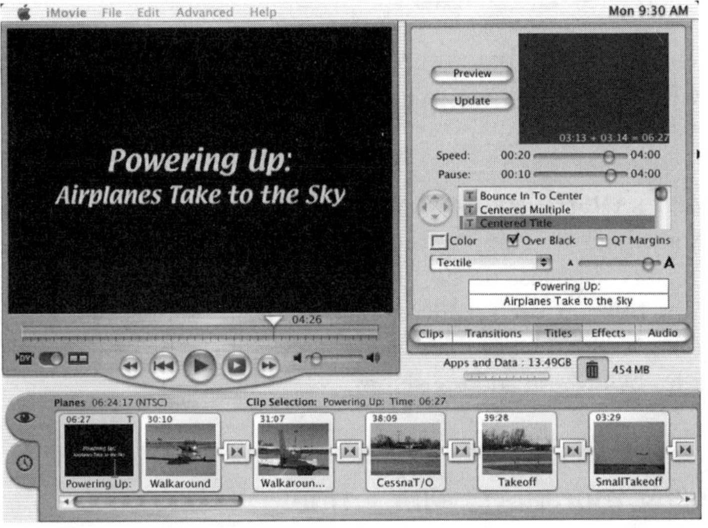

Figure 7.4 This movie now has a title screen at the beginning.

View the clip. If you want to make changes to the title clip, start by selecting the title clip. Make the changes you want to make and click the Update button. The clip will be rendered again.

Adding Credits

Adding credits is a good way to give people or organizations a quick thank you for contributing to your movie.

Open the Titles palette by clicking Titles. Check the Over Black checkbox. Select the type style that you want to use for your credits; Rolling Credits is a good choice. A preview appears in the Preview window.

In the first text box, type the first credited item. In the second text box, type the text to which you are giving credit. On the screen, it looks like this:

```
Credited Item.........Credit to
```

Enter a second set of credits. If you have more than two sets of credits to give, click + (the Add button). Another text pair appears. Type the Credited Item in the first box and then the Credit to entry in the second. Continue adding pairs of credited items and credits to text until all your credits have been entered.

> ### ORDER, ORDER!
> You can change the order in which the credit pairs are listed by dragging a pair up or down in the pair window.

Use the Direction arrows to set the direction that the credits will scroll on the screen. Click the Up arrowhead to have the credits scroll up or the Down arrowhead to have them scroll down the screen.

> ### SPEED KILLS
> If you add additional text pairs to the rolling credits, iMovie automatically makes the title last longer. After you add a pair or two, the title will last much too long. Just use the Speed slider to make them move more quickly.

Use the Speed slider to set the amount of time that the credits appear on-screen. Click the Preview button to see your credits in the Monitor.

When you are satisfied with your credits, drag the Rolling Credits item to the end of your movie on the Clip Viewer. The credit clip is then rendered. This takes a while for a long credit clip, but you can continue to work while it is rendered.

WHERE S THE TEXT?

After you place a title, the text for that title remains with it. If you choose another title type, you will see the text from the previous title in its text boxes. You can replace this text to make a new title. If you want to change a previous title, select that title and its text will appear on the Titles palette. Make your changes and then click Update to replace the title with the new version.

Adding a Caption

Sometimes, you might want to explain something that is happening on the screen. For example, you might want to add a date and location to a clip that shows some event.

TITLES AREN T LIMITED

Although the amount of text that you can add with a single title is limited, the number of titles that you can add to your movie is not. To add more text than one title allows, you can add more than one of the same titles in a row or string different types of titles together.

Decide what clip you want to add a caption to and select it. Open the Titles palette and click the Music Video title style.

REMEMBER THE PREVIEW

Remember to watch the Preview window because it shows the effects of each change as you make them.

In the text box, type the text that you want to appear in the caption. Choose the font, color, and size. Uncheck the Over Black checkbox so that the title appears over the clip. Click the Left arrowhead to have the caption appear on the left side of the screen. Use the Speed slider to set how long the caption appears on-screen. If you plan on exporting your movie to videotape for viewing on a TV, uncheck the QT Margins checkbox. Click Preview to see the results of your work

Make any needed changes to the caption. When the caption is ready, drag the Music Video icon and drop it in front of the clip on which you want the caption to appear. The clip in front of which you drag the title will be split into two clips. The first clip contains the part with the title applied. The second clip contains the remainder of the clip. iMovie gets to work rendering the title.

BOTHERSOME TRANSITION

Remember that if there is a transition connected to the front of the clip, you may have to delete it before you can place a title there. After the title is in place, you can add the transition back in—just place it before the clip containing the title.

Select the title clip and the clips on each side of it. Press the Spacebar to play the selected section of the movie. Make any needed changes to the title and click Update to implement them.

TITLES ARE CLIPS, TOO

The clips containing titles placed onto part of the video clip are just like other clips in your movie. You can rename them, store them on the Shelf, and so on. You can also, of course, add transitions to a title clip.

MIX AND MATCH?

Even though you can use multiple types of styles for the same sort of text, it is usually a good idea to stick with the same title style for a particular kind of text throughout a movie. For example, use the

continued...

Music Video style for all the captions in your movie. You should usually use a consistent text font, color, and size for the same text elements (such as captions) throughout your movie as well.

Adding Special Effects

iMovie has plenty of tricks left up its digital sleeve. You can add all sorts of interesting visual effects to make your movie look better and be more interesting.

Making a Clip Play in Reverse

You can make a clip play in reverse in your movie. Why would you want to do this? There are a couple of possible reasons. One is for comedic effect. Another might be to create an instant replay sort of effect (you will want to increase the speed of the clip to do this, and you will learn how later in this section).

Select the clip that you want to play in reverse. Open the Advanced menu and choose Reverse Clip Direction (or press ⌘+R). On the Clip Viewer, a direction arrow appears indicating that the clip plays from right to left. The first scene of the clip becomes the last one in the movie, and the thumbnail view that you see becomes the last frame (which is now the first frame). When you play your movie, the reversed clip indeed plays backward.

You can restore a clip to its proper direction by selecting it and using the Reverse Clip Direction command again.

REVERSING CLIPS AND TRANSITIONS

A transition impacts the clips to which it is attached. If you reverse a clip that has an attached transition, a warning dialog box appears and tells you that reversing the clip invalidates the transition. It then asks if you want to re-render the transition. If you proceed with the reversal, the affected transitions are re-rendered.

Applying Special Effects to Your Movie

The Effects palette contains a number of other special effects that you can apply to your clips.

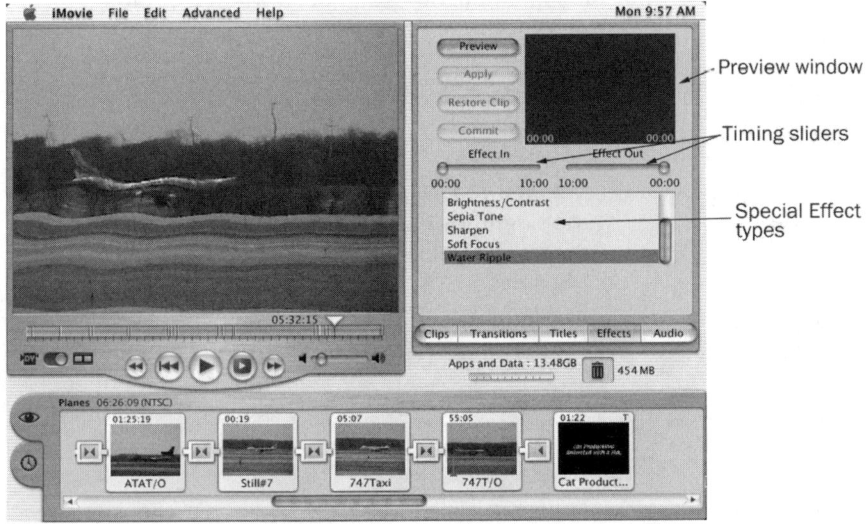

Figure 7.5 You can use the Effects palette to apply a variety of special effects to your clips (in this case, the Water Ripple effect is being applied to a clip of a 747 taking off).

The Effects palette is a bit different from the Transitions and Titles tool palettes—these tools are related to each other only in that they are effects that you apply to the video track (this differs from the Transitions palette, on which all the tools are related to transitions).

Even though this is true, it is also true that all these effects work similarly—after you use a couple of them, you can easily use all of them. Table 7.3 lists all the effects on the Effects palette and provides some examples of when you might want to apply each effect.

Table 7.3 iMovie Special Effects Tools

Tool	What It Does	When to Use It
Adjust Colors	Enables you to adjust the hue, color, and lightness of a clip.	When a clip has poor color or when it seems sort of dingy.
Black-and-White	Converts a clip into black-and-white.	For artistic effects.
Brightness/ Contrast	Enables you to adjust the brightness and contrast of a clip.	When a clip is too dark, too bright, or has poor contrast.
Sepia Tone	Applies a "wood grain" texture to the clip.	For artistic effects (often used to make a clip appear as if it were filmed a long time ago).
Sharpen	Adjusts a clip's sharpness.	When a clip is too "fuzzy."
Soft Focus	Applies a blur to the images in a clip.	For artistic effects.
Water Ripple	Makes the image look as if it is being viewed through water.	For artistic effects.

The Effects tools work similarly to the other tools you have used. First, you choose a clip to which you want to apply the effect; then you choose the effect that you want to apply. Next, set the time it takes for the effect to be applied, the time over which it disappears, and use the other controls that are provided to adjust that effect's properties, while previewing the effect along the way. When you are ready, apply the effect to the clip.

The Effects palette features a couple of buttons that you haven't seen before. These are Restore Clip and Commit. When you apply an effect to a clip, iMovie reworks that clip by using the effect that you apply. However, it saves the "un-effected" clip so that you can go back to it if you want to (this is sort of like an undo that you can use at any point in the future). If you decide that you don't want an effect anymore, select the clip and click Restore Clip. The clip is returned to the condition in which it was before you messed it up.

That's nice, but saving two versions of a clip (the effected one and the pure one) consumes extra disk space that you might not be able to afford. To keep the clip with the effect applied and remove the original (so that it doesn't use disk space), select the clip and click Commit. When you do that, iMovie deletes the original version, and you're stuck with the version that you have "improved."

Avoid using the Commit button as long as you can. Being able to go back to a pristine version of your clip is often highly desirable. After you are sure that the changed clip is what you want, click Commit to free up some disk space.

> ### ONE AT A TIME, PLEASE
>
> With the early versions of iMovie 2, you can only apply one effect to a clip at a time. If you want to add more than one, you have to add the first, use the Commit button, and then add the next one. This is sort of a pain to do. This may be a slight bug and hopefully will be corrected by a later version update. However, you probably won't want to apply more than one effect at a time very often so it isn't all that painful.

Applying Special Effects: Examples

The following examples of applying specific effects should help you understand how to apply any of them.

Making a Clip Look Old

You have probably seen a movie or documentary in which there were video clips of something that just couldn't have been filmed. For example, at the opening of the movie *Tombstone*, there is an "historical" sequence in which you see Wyatt Earp and other Westerners in the late 1800s. There were no film cameras in those days, so how did they get these old-looking clips? The answer is through special effects.

One of the effects that you can use to achieve this "aged" effect is to apply Sepia Tone to a clip. This makes the clip appear in hues of beige and gray; it has also been described as a wood-grain sort of effect. This effect gives the impression of age, in some ways, even more than black-and-white does.

Select the clip to which you want to apply the effect. Click the Effects button and from the Effects list, click Sepia Tone. You see a preview of the effect in the Preview window on the palette.

Use the Effect In slider to set how long the effect takes to transition in; if you want the whole clip to be in Sepia Tone, leave the slider set all the way to the left. The further to the right that you drag the slider, the longer it takes for the full effect to kick in.

> #### EFFECT TIMECODES
>
> As you set the sliders, you see two timecodes in the small preview window. The one on the left shows you the Effect In time, which is how long it takes for the clip to go from its normal appearance to being fully "Sepiaized" (that isn't a real word, but you get the idea). The timecode on the right tells you how far from the end of the movie that the Sepia Tone begins to be removed from the clip (by the end of the clip, it is returned to normal).

Use the Effect Out slider to determine when the effect begins to go away, thus returning your clip to its previous appearance. If you leave the slider all the way to the right, the clip remains in Sepia for its duration. The further you move the slider to the left, the earlier in the clip the effect begins to disappear.

When you think that you are close to where you want to be, click Preview. You will see a preview of the effected clip in the Monitor. Continue refining the effect until it is just right. When it is, click Apply, and the effect is applied to the clip. The clip has the letters "fx" in the upper right corner of its thumbnail to indicate that a special effect has been applied.

MORE RENDERING IS REQUIRED

As with other features, such as titles and transitions, these visual effects have to be rendered in your movie. If the clip to which you apply the effect has a transition attached to it, the transition has to be re-rendered, as well.

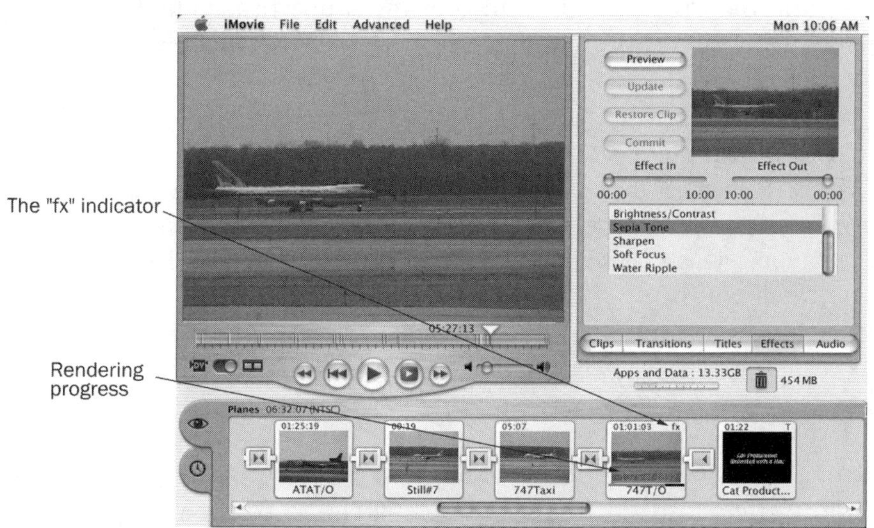

Figure 7.6 The Sepia Tone effect has been applied to this clip of a 747 taking off (of course, there were a lot of 747s in the old days).

Sharpening a Clip

Some clips you capture might look a bit fuzzy or blurry. You can use the Sharpen effect to make these images look crisper.

Select the clip that you want to sharpen. On the Effects palette, click Sharpen. You see the Sharpen tools, which are the Effect In and Effect Out sliders. You also see the Amount slider; this determines the amount of sharpness applied to the clip. Drag the slider toward High for more sharpness or toward Low for less.

Use the sliders to set the time it takes for the effect to be applied and for it to be removed (to apply the effect over the whole clip, leave the Effect In slider all the way to the left and the Effect Out slider all the way to the right). Use the Amount slider to set the level of sharpness you want applied to the clip. Use the Preview window and the Preview button to preview your work. When you are happy with the results, click Apply to render the clip with the effect.

> **RESTORE THAT CLIP**
> Remember that you can restore a clip to which you have applied an effect by selecting it and clicking Restore Clip. This works unless you previously clicked Commit, in which case, you're stuck with the clip like it is.

Correcting the Colors in a Clip

If you aren't happy with the colors in a clip, you can use the Adjust Colors effect to make changes. Select a clip to adjust and click Adjust Colors on the Effects palette. In addition to the Effect In and Effect Out sliders, you see three more sliders.

The Hue Shift slider changes the hues of the colors in your clip. Drag it to the right, and the colors have a greenish tint. Drag it to the left, and red tones become more prominent.

The Color slider affects the brightness of the colors. Dragging it to the left mutes the colors; if you move it all the way to the left, your clip becomes black-and-white (this does the same thing as the Black-and-White effect). Move it to the right again to make the colors as vivid as they get.

The Lightness slider changes the overall brightness of the colors. Move it to the right, and the clip becomes brighter. Move it to the left, and it becomes darker.

UNDOING EFFECTS

Sometimes, when you remove an effect from a clip that is attached to a transition, the effect remains on the transition even though you removed it from the clip. If this happens, delete the transition and then add it back in again.

These tools work similarly to the others that you have used. Use the sliders to make adjustments, preview your changes, and when you are satisfied, apply the effect to the clip.

Changing the Speed at Which a Clip Plays

To this point, you have used only one of iMovie's two viewers. The Clip Viewer is a good place to focus on the video track of your movie. But as you get into finer levels of detail in the editing process and when you start working with audio, you switch over to the Timeline Viewer. This view provides a more detailed view of your movie, and you "see" all the tracks that make up your movie.

To switch to the Timeline Viewer, click its tab (it has the clock icon). You see the Timeline Viewer in all its glory. This viewer looks more complicated than the Clip Viewer, and it is. This complexity enables you to do lots of great things, especially with your movie's audio track.

Figure 7.7 The Timeline Viewer enables you to see all the tracks in your movie.

In the top bar of the viewer, you see a graphical representation of the video track of the movie. Each clip is in its own section, and you see a thumbnail view of the clips. You also see the clip's name and timecode in its bar. Transition and title clips have the same symbols as they do in the Clip Viewer.

You use the Timeline Zoom pop-up menu to choose a "magnification" level for the view that you see. The larger the magnification level, the larger the clips appear (and the less of a clip that you can see on the viewer without scrolling). Choosing a lower magnification "zooms out," and you see more clips, but less detail for each clip. As you work, you should use this control to change the view to make your tasks easier. For example, when you are synchronizing sound with video, increase the magnification so that you have finer control over the process. When you are moving clips around, choose a lower magnification so that you can see more of the movie at one time.

> ### FULL AUTO
>
> If you choose the Auto setting on the Timeline Viewer Zoom pop-up menu, the Timeline Viewer zooms to a level that iMovie considers to be optimum for editing. This may or may not be optimum for you; if not, choose a specific magnification level.

Speaking of which, you can do everything on the Timeline Viewer that you can on the Clip Viewer. You click a clip to select it. The clip is highlighted in yellow, and then you can apply effects, transitions, and titles to it. You can also edit in the Monitor just as you did when you selected a clip on the Shelf or in the Clip Viewer.

Use the Clip Viewer when you want to make large changes to your movie, such as placing and moving clips, adding transitions, and so on. For finer work, such as adding sound effects, use the Timeline Viewer.

There is one special effect located on the Timeline Viewer (which is why I introduced it here). This is the Clip Speed slider that you can use to make a clip play faster than normal or slower than normal.

Using the slider is easy. Select a clip in the Timeline Viewer and drag the slider to change its speed.

To make the clip play faster, drag the slider to the left. When you play the clip, it plays at the faster speed. It appears as "compressed" on the Timeline Viewer to show that it requires less time to play than it did originally; you also see the fast forward symbol in the clip's bar.

> ### NO RENDERING, PLEASE
>
> Notice that with clip speed changes, iMovie does not have to do the rendering process. It applies the speed change instantaneously. Believe it or not, very few video editing applications can manage this.

> ### TRANSITION TROUBLES?
>
> As with other changes you make, any transitions or other effects that are attached to a clip that you change have to be re-rendered at the new speed. Otherwise, the speed will suddenly jump between the transition and the clip (and that wouldn't make the flow smoother, would it!).

To slow the clip down, drag the slider to the right. Now, when you play the clip, it plays more slowly. The clip expands on the Timeline Viewer, and the play slow symbol appears in the clip's bar.

Put the slider back in the center to return the clip to its normal speed.

> ### INSTANT REPLAY
>
> You can combine the direction and speed effects to add an "instant replay" to your movie. Select the portion of the clip that you want to replay. Paste it twice so that you have the three clips in a row. Choose the middle clip and make it play in reverse. Use the Clip Speed slider to make this "rewind" quickly. When you play this section, it appears as if the clip is rewound at high speed before replaying, thus looking just like instant replay.

Eyes closed, ears awaken:
To the left, to the right;
No light, no shade.
Here all images come alive.

Chapter Eight

Creating Sound Tracks

Ever since the "talkies" were invented, sound has been a very important part of any movie. In addition to the sound that you record along with video clips, you can also add and manage sound effects, and of course, a sound track for your movies.

In this chapter, we are going to look at:

- ➤ Working with the native sound from your video clips
- ➤ Adding sound effects
- ➤ Adding music

Adding Sound to Your Movies

Using iMovie, you can create rich and full sound tracks for your movies. You can include four types of sound in your movies, which are the following:

> ➤ **Native sounds**—When you import clips into iMovie, any sound that was part of those clips comes in, too. If your clips had sound, you've already heard it numerous times while you were assembling your movie from those clips. You can use iMovie tools to control some aspects of your movie's "native" sounds.

> **NATIVE?**
>
> By native, I mean sound that was imported to your movie along with the clips. Thus, without you doing anything, the sound is already there.

> ➤ **Sound effects**—You can add sound effects to your movie to bring it to life. You can use iMovie's built-in sound effects, and you can import other sound effects to use.

> ➤ **Narration**—If you want to explain what is happening in a movie or add your own commentary, you can record narration for your movie. You can also use the narration tool to record sounds from a tape player or other audio device.

> ➤ **Music**—The right music makes a movie a better experience. You can import music to your movies from many sources, such as audio CDs, MP3 files, and so on.

You use the Timeline Viewer to control the audio portion of your movie. As you saw in the previous chapter, the Timeline Viewer enables you to see all of the tracks that are part of your movie. Click the Timeline Viewer tab (the clock icon)to see the Timeline Viewer.

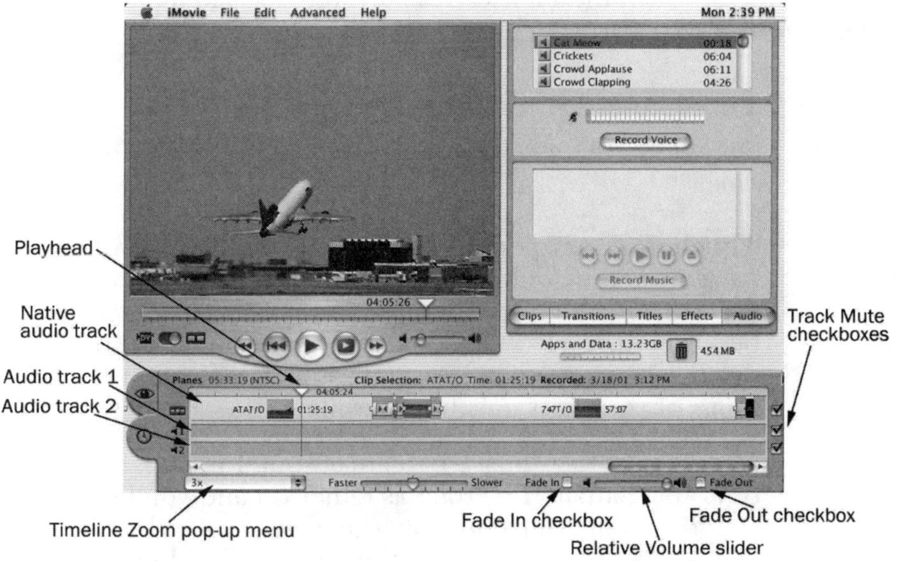

Figure 8.1 The Timeline Viewer and the Audio palette provide the tools that you need to create sound tracks for your movies.

Each track on the Timeline Viewer is used to create and edit one of the three audio tracks that you can have in your movie. The top track displays the native sound in your clips. Typically, the Audio 1 track is used for sound effects and narration and the Audio 2 track is used for music. Functionally, there is no difference between these tracks, and you can use them however you'd like.

In the previous figure, you also see the Audio palette, which you use to add sound effects, narration, music, and other sounds that you record to your movie.

As you learned in the previous chapter, the tracks that you see are all time-based "views" of your movie. The left side of the tracks represents the beginning of your movie, and the right side represents the end. You also see the Playhead, which works like it does in the Clip Viewer and the Monitor. For example, you can move it in the same ways, and the timecode shows its location in the movie.

The frame at which the Playhead is currently located appears in the Monitor window.

Some of the controls that you see on the Timeline Viewer do the same things for each track (or selected clip). These are the following:

> ➤ **Timeline Zoom pop-up menu**—Use this to control the "magnification" of the viewer. Choosing a higher magnification enables you to make more detailed changes because each second in the movie is shown in more detail. Choosing a lower magnification enables you to see more of your movie without scrolling.

> ➤ **Mute controls**—Using a particular sound track is an all-or-nothing affair. The track is either on and you hear its sounds, or it isn't and you don't. You use the Mute checkboxes to turn a sound track off. If the Mute box at the end of a track is not checked, that track is muted. You're most likely to use this on the Native track, but you might occasionally use it with the others, as well.

MUTE AND EXPORT

When the time comes to export your movie, you can mute a sound track to make the movie file smaller. When you mute a track, that track is not exported with the rest of the movie.

> ➤ **Fade controls**—The Fade In and Fade Out controls do what you would expect them to do. They make a selected sound clip fade in or fade out, depending on which boxes are checked.

FADING LIKE A PRO

If you double-click a sound clip or a video clip, its Info window appears. In the Info window, you see two fade sliders along with checkboxes. If you check a fade checkbox, you can use the slider to set the duration of the fade.

If you fade the clip with the checkboxes on the Timeline Viewer, you always get the default fade duration for the clip.

➤ **Relative volume slider**—You use the Relative Volume Slider to set volume levels of clips relative to one another. For example, if you don't want your sound effects to drown out the sounds on the Native track, you can control how loud the effect is relative to the native sound.

Working with Native Sound

Your movie probably has some sound that came with the video clips. If you recorded your clips with a DV camcorder, these sounds are whatever you recorded, for better or worse. Each clip has its own sound track, which is what you see represented in the Native track of the Timeline Viewer. The bars that you see show the beginning and end of each audio clip (and by no coincidence, each video clip).

Muting Native Sounds

The most basic change that you can make is to mute the Native track so that you don't hear any of its sounds. To mute the Native track, uncheck the Mute checkbox located on the right end of the Native track. Now when you play your movie, you don't hear any sound from it. To hear the native sounds again, check the Mute checkbox.

Changing Relative Volume Levels

Because your clips probably came from different sources or were recorded under different conditions, the sound level from one clip to the next might vary quite a bit. Although some variation is natural (you expect the roar of a jet plane to be louder than a cat walking across the road), too much variation (or the wrong variation, such as if the cat is louder than the airplane) can be annoying or distracting.

Use the Relative Volume Slider to set the relative sound levels of the various sound clips on the Native track.

On the Native track, select a clip that should be at the "average" volume level; after you do, the clip's bar on the track becomes highlighted in yellow to show that it is selected.

> ### SOUND, TRANSITIONS, AND TITLES
> Be aware that when you create transitions between clips and add title clips, part of each scene is separated from its clip and becomes part of the transition or title clip. The sound goes along with the clips, too. So you should check the sound of transition and title clips as well as the video clips. If you need to adjust the sound of the clip attached to a transition, you might need to adjust the volume level of the transition also. You can do this easily by selecting the clip and any transition or title clips attached to it and adjusting the volume of all the clips that you select at one time.

The clip that you want to be the average volume depends on the particular movie that you are creating. For example, if your movie has a lot of talking in it, choose a clip that has the talking recorded under the most common conditions. You use this average clip to set the relative sound levels for the others. With your average clip selected, move the Relative Volume Slider toward the middle of its range. This sets the volume level of the selected clip at an "average" level.

> ### CHANGING VOLUME ON THE FLY
> You can change a clip's relative volume while it is playing.

Now move through each clip in the movie and use the Relative Volume Slider to set its volume relative to your "average" sound level. Select the first clip in your movie that has native sound (assuming that your first clip isn't also your average clip, of course). If you want its sound to be louder than your average clip, drag the Relative Volume Slider to the right of the position that you set as the average volume level; if you want it to be quieter, move the slider to the left. Or, if you want it to be about the same, place the slider in about the same position as it is for the average clip.

> ### CHANGING SEVERAL SOUND LEVELS AT ONCE
>
> You can change the relative sound levels for several clips at once by holding the Shift key down while you select the clips. With the clips selected, move the Relative Volume Slider. The relative volume of all of the selected clips will be set at the level you choose.

Continue this process with all the clips that have native sound.

When you play your movie, don't be concerned if the Relative Volume Slider isn't where you set it for a particular clip. The slider only shows the position of the first clip that you select; or, if you don't have any clips selected, it is all the way to the right. This doesn't mean that your work has been lost. Select a clip, and the volume slider jumps to where you set it for that clip. The slider only shows the level for the selected clip (or the first one you selected if you have selected more than one). It doesn't move from that position when you play the clips, even though it seems like it should.

Also, the position of the Relative Volume Slider during playback is not indicative of the volume level of the movie. You hear the volume level of the movie as you set the volume levels of its clips. The position of the slider doesn't mean anything when you play more than one clip.

Now when you play your movie, the sound should make sense. Loud parts are louder, quiet parts are quieter, and the average is just right (relatively speaking, of course).

> ### CHANGING PLAYBACK VOLUME
>
> The Volume slider located in the Monitor changes the volume level that you are hearing at the moment. It doesn't change the relative volume settings of the movie in any way. It simply makes all of the sounds that you hear louder or quieter; it doesn't actually change your movie, unlike the Relative Volume Slider, which does.

Fading Sounds

If you have assembled your movie from a series of clips, the sound probably jumps from one clip to the next. For example, if your clip has music in its native sound track, it is highly unlikely that the editing you have done has resulted in smooth cuts in the music; more likely it is a rough cut from one part of the music to the next. This can be really jarring, and it disrupts the flow of your movie.

You can use the fade controls to make the sound of a clip fade in or out smoothly. If you make a clip's sound fade in, it starts out completely silent and smoothly comes to its full level. Similarly, if you fade out a sound, its volume smoothly becomes quieter until by the end of the clip, it has faded to silence.

> ### FADING SOUND WITH FADING TRANSITIONS
> If you add a fade out or fade in transition to a clip, its sound also fades so you don't need to use the Timeline Viewer fade controls on that clip.

To make a clip's sound fade in, select the clip and check the Fade In checkbox. If you want it to fade out, check the Fade Out checkbox.

You can control how long the fades are by opening the Info window for a sound clip (double-click it or select it and press Shift+Cmd+I to open its Info window). Check the Audio Fade In checkbox and use the slider to set its duration. Check the Audio Fade Out checkbox and use its slider to control how long the fade out takes. Click OK when you are done.

> ### FADE SEVERAL CLIPS AT ONCE
> You can also set fading for multiple clips at one time by selecting the clips (hold down the Shift key while you select clips) and checking the appropriate checkboxes.

Editing a Clip's Native Sound

As you learned when you began editing your clips, whatever you do to a clip's video, you do to the clip's sound (this works the other way, too; changing the sound affects the video)—unless you extract the sound from the clip (you will learn how to do this in the next section). You should play each clip and listen carefully to its sound. Crop or trim the clips as needed to eliminate sounds that you don't want or to include sounds that you do want (without messing up the video portion).

Extracting a Clip's Native Sound

You can extract the audio portion of the clip so that you can work with it independently from the video clip. Extracting the audio from a clip also enables you to move it relative to the video clip. This is useful if you don't want to use all of the audio, but want to keep all of the video in the clip.

One of the best uses for the extracting audio feature is when you have a clip containing background music that should be at least somewhat synchronized with the video, such as a ballet performance. You can extract the audio, and then you can edit the video part of the clip without hacking up the music that goes with it. You can then "spread" the extracted music so that the single music clip covers all of the video. While the music may not exactly match what is happening in the video anymore, this is a lot less distracting than music that jumps around as the edited scenes play.

To extract a clip's sound track, select that clip on the Timeline Viewer. From the Advanced menu, choose Extract Audio. The audio portion of the clip is extracted, and is placed on the Audio 1 track. When you extract it, it's still in synch with the video clip from whence it came.

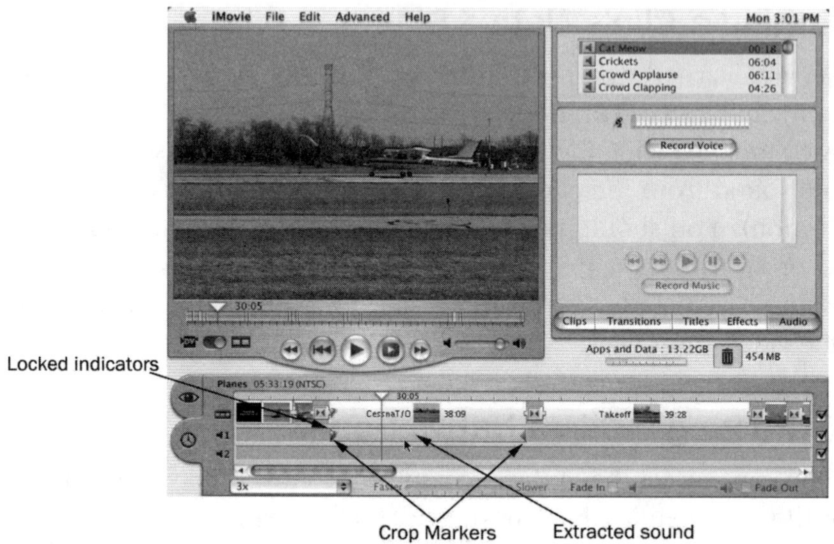

Figure 8.2 Here the Extract Audio command has been used to extract the audio portion of the clip named "CessnaT/O;" the extracted sound appears on the Audio 1 track directly below the clip.

After the audio clip is extracted, you can use the audio editing techniques that you learn about in the rest of this chapter to work with it. For example, you can move it around, lock it in place, and so on.

TECHNICALLY SPEAKING

When you extract audio from a video clip, the audio actually is copied to the audio track rather than being cut from the video clip. The volume of the audio that is part of the video clip is set to zero so that you never hear it again. Does this matter? Not really, but you shouldn't extract an audio clip unless you really need to. Because it is not actually removed from the video clip, your movie file will be larger than if you didn't extract the audio (since iMovie will carry two versions of that sound around). If you only want to mute the audio clip, set its relative volume to zero instead of extracting it.

continued...

> This also means that you can hear the sound of a video clip from which you have "extracted" the sound by selecting that clip and using the Relative Volume Slider to increase the sound of the clip again. You can use this for some interesting sound effects as you can have multiple versions of the sound playing at the same time, with each being slightly out of synch with the others.

Speaking of locking, you can lock audio to a video clip so that when you move the video, the audio goes along for the ride and always remains in synch with the video. When a clip is locked, you see the locked icons. One appears at the beginning of the locked audio and the other appears at the point at which the audio is locked on the corresponding video clip.

> **LOCKED PREFERENCE**
> By default, iMovie displays the locked indicators all the time. If you only want to see them when you have selected a clip that is locked, open Preferences, click the Views tab, and uncheck the Show Locked Audio Only When Selected checkbox.

Working with Sound Clips on the Audio Tracks

As you can see in the previous figure, sound clips in the Timeline Viewer look suspiciously like video clips in the Clip Viewer. This is no mere coincidence either; working with sound clips in the Timeline Viewer is very similar to working with video clips in the Clip Viewer. You can move them around by dragging and dropping, use their Crop Markers to select parts to edit, and so on.

Adding Sound Effects to Your Movie

One of the more fun aspects of making a movie is adding sound effects to it.

> ### WANT MORE EFFECTS?
>
> Even though the Audio palette comes with a number of sound effects, you can easily add more. Using QuickTime Pro, you can also convert almost any sound into a sound effect. You will learn how to do this later in this chapter.

You add sound effects by using the Audio palette. To open the palette, click the Audio button. The palette pops up and at the top of the palette you see several sound effects that you can use (scroll through the list to see and hear all of them). To hear one, click it. The effect that you click plays so that you can preview it. Continue clicking sounds until you find one that you want to use in your movie.

When you find the perfect sound effect, drag the sound effect from the Audio palette and drop it onto the Audio 1 track. When you move it over the track, a yellow line appears on the track where the clip will be placed when you release the mouse button; this line indicates the point at which the sound effect will start playing. Where you place the effect on the track determines where in the movie the effect is heard. When you release the mouse button, a small square appears on the track. This square represents the sound effect that you have added. You can work with the sound effect, just like the other elements in a track. For example, if you select it, you will see its name and duration at the top of the Timeline Viewer.

Drag the Playhead to the left of the sound effect that you just placed and press the Spacebar to preview it. To move the sound effect, click it to select it (its box is darkened to indicate that it is selected) and drag it to a new location. When you select the effect, the Playhead jumps to the beginning of the sound effect. At that point the Playhead "sticks" to the sound effect, and you can move it frame by frame using the Left and Right arrow keys (hold the Shift key down to move it by 10 frames at a time).

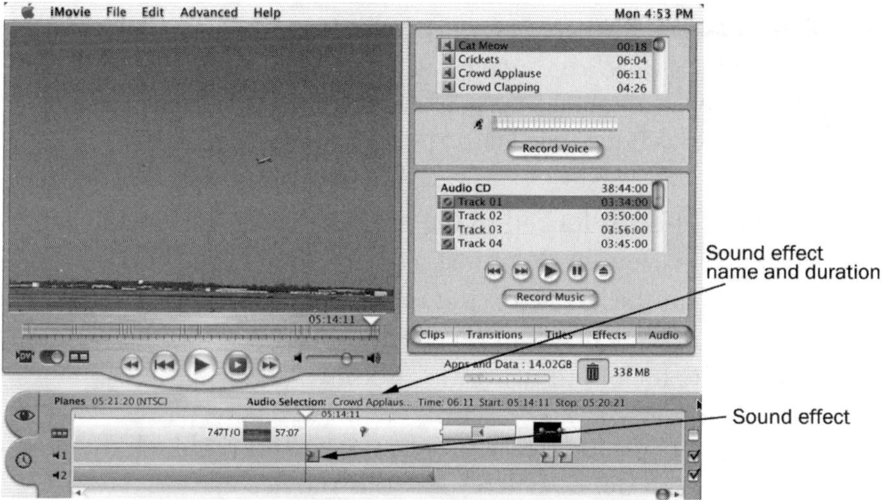

Figure 8.3 Here the Crowd Applause sound effect is added to the end of the movie.

> ### STICKY PLAYHEAD
>
> If you move the Playhead away from the effect and want it to stick to the effect again, drag the Playhead to the beginning of the effect. Like magic, it sticks again so that you can use the keyboard to position it.

When you have the effect positioned so that it plays at the perfect point in the video, it is a good idea to lock it to that spot so that should you move the video, the sound effect will still play at the right time. To do so, select the effect and from the Advanced menu, choose Lock Audio Clip at Playhead (or press ⌘+L). You will see the locked indicators and from that point on, the sound stays with the video.

If you want to move the sound relative to the video track again, select the clip and choose Unlock Audio Clip from the Advanced menu (or press ⌘+L).

> ### CHANGING A SOUND EFFECT S LENGTH
> Unlike a video clip or other kinds of audio clips, you can't change the length of time that a sound effect plays. The only way to do that is to edit the sound effect outside of iMovie.

Note that the effect is locked to the location of the Playhead wherever it was when you used the lock command. There is no reason that the Playhead has to be on the effect when you lock it. The effect will begin to play whenever the Playhead reaches the position it was when the lock command was used.

After all of your sound effects are placed, you should lock them so that they don't get out of synch with your movie.

The Fade and Relative Volume Slider controls work on sound effects just as they do on native clips. To have an effect fade in or out, select it and check the Fade In or Fade Out checkbox. To change an effect's volume relative to other sounds, select it and use the Relative Volume Slider. You can open the Info window for a sound effect to use the fade duration sliders on it, too.

You can also overlap sound effects. To do so, simply drag one effect on top of another. At those moments where the sound effects overlap, both effects play. You can more easily manage overlapped sound effects by placing one in the Audio 1 track and the overlapping sound in the Audio 2 track.

> ### DITCH THE SOUND
> To remove a sound effect, select it and press Delete. It is removed from the track. You can always add it back again by using the Audio palette.

Narrating Your Movie

Using the Audio palette, you can record your own sounds to play during your movie. One obvious use for this is to add narration to various parts of your movie.

> ### DON T LET THE BUTTON NAME FOOL YOU
>
> The record button in iMovie is actually labeled Record Voice. But don't let that fool you—you can use this button to record any sound that you want. For example, you can attach the output of an audio tape player to your iMac through its microphone jack to record the sound output of that device to use in your movie.

To record sound, you can use your iMac's internal microphone or add an external mike.

> ### OVERDUBBING
>
> If dialog in your movie is unclear or it just didn't come out the way that you want it to, you can overdub it by having your actors record new dialog using the Narration feature.

Back in iMovie, click Audio to open the Audio palette, if it isn't open already. Test your microphone setup by speaking into it. If everything is working, you'll see a sound level bar in the area just above the Record Voice button that shows you the level of the sound that is being input. This bar should be moving to levels at least above halfway across the bar. If it isn't, move closer to the microphone so it gets better input.

Now you're ready to record your narration. Drag the Playhead to the point in your movie at which you want to begin recording. Click Record Voice. Your movie begins playing. Speak into the microphone (or start the audio playback device). When you want to stop recording, click Stop.

In the narration track, you will see that your sound has been recorded. The recorded sound is represented by an orange bar with a Crop Marker at each end.

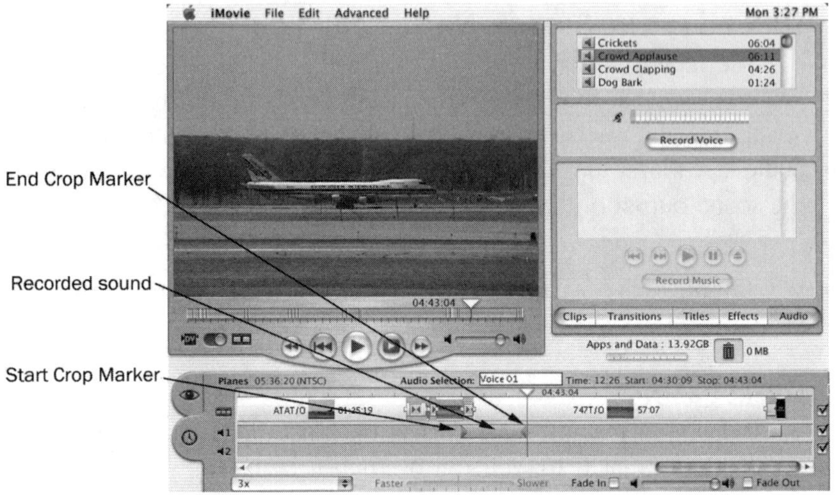

Figure 8.4 The bar shown in the Audio 1 track is a sound that was recorded via the iMac's microphone.

You can edit a recorded sound in ways that are similar to the ways you edit other elements of your movie. When you click the bar that represents the recorded sound, the bar darkens to show that it is selected. You can do the following tasks:

➤ Move the sound by selecting it and then dragging it to a new location. (If you are narrating something specific, the sound might become out of sync with the video.)

➤ Lock the sound in its relative place.

➤ Apply the Fade and Relative Volume Slider controls to the recorded sound.

➤ Move the sound's Crop Markers (which are always visible, unlike those for a video clip) so they enclose the part of the sound that you want to keep. Choose Crop from the Edit menu to remove all the sound except that between the Crop Markers.

> ### YOU DON'T HAVE TO CROP
>
> When you move a sound's Crop Markers, the part of the sound outside the markers won't play anymore. You can use this to fine-tune what you want to play before you actually change the sound clip. When you have it set to what you want to play, you should crop it so that the movie's file size will be smaller.

➤ Name the recorded clip by selecting the clip and then typing a new name in the Audio Selection box (or double-click it to open its Clip Info window and rename it there).

➤ Overlap sound effects with the recorded sound by dragging an effect on top of the recorded sound.

> ### OUT WITH THE SOUND
>
> To remove a recorded sound, select it and press Delete. The sound is removed from your movie and placed in the Trash. As you work, remember to empty the trash once in a while to free up disk space.

Adding Music to Your Movie

Adding a music sound track to your movie can make the difference between your viewers saying, "Nice movie," and, "Wow, great movie!" A music sound track can help you convey a full range of emotion or simply make your movies more enjoyable to watch. There's just something about music; we love to hear it, even when our main purpose is to watch something.

Adding Music to an Audio Track

Since working with music is much like the other sounds that you have already learned about, you already understand almost everything you need to know about adding music to one of iMovie's audio tracks. You can use the Audio 2 track to store the music that you want to play during all—or during parts—of your movie. You can use several different pieces during your movie, or you can have one piece play throughout.

You can use two methods to add music to your movies. One is to record music from an audio CD by using the tools on the Audio palette. The other is to import music that is contained in an MP3 or AIFF file.

Since you are now an iTunes expert and know how to create MP3s of any music that you have on CD, you should usually create an MP3 file for your music and import that into iMovie, rather than recording directly from the CD. Working with MP3 files is easier and faster than recording music from a CD directly.

Staying Out of Trouble with Copyrights

At this point, you might need to be reminded about a little thing called *copyright*. Basically, copyright laws exist to protect creators of non-material property (such as music, books, art, and so on) from people using and profiting from that material without providing some compensation to the creators of the material. The bottom line to all copyright laws is that you can't use copyrighted material without agreeing to the copyright that applies to that material.

Generally, all the music that you listen to, unless you created it yourself, is protected by some sort of copyright. Mostly, these copyrights prohibit you from distributing the copyrighted work as your own or profiting from its distribution. Many copyrighted works can't be redistributed by you in any form; the copyright entitles you to personal use of the material only.

> ### MUSIC IN THE PUBLIC DOMAIN
> If you can find music that is in the public domain, you can use it in any way that you see fit.

Practically speaking, if you are using copyrighted music in your movies and you are keeping the movies to yourself (you are only viewing them at your home or on your computer), you don't have to worry about violating the copyright. Stretching this a bit, even if you are emailing movies to a few *specific* people or are sending them to one or two people using a CD that you created, you are okay—unless you are charging for your work, which is never permissible if you are incorporating copyrighted material without obtaining the appropriate licenses. After you get beyond that, you had better be very careful about distributing your movies if they contain work that is copyrighted by someone else. If you are discovered doing so, you can be sued or even prosecuted.

The way to be able to use music that other people have created in your movies for so-called nonpersonal use is to obtain the proper license to use that material. Although you aren't likely to be able to license popular music groups or singers, there is lots of great music for which you can buy a license to be able to use it in your movies—even if you distribute it for profit. Royalty-free music, also called music with a buy-out license, can be used in any manner that you see fit.

You can order all sorts of royalty-free music on CDs, and you can download it from the Net. This music costs more than music on typical audio CDs does, but what you get for the additional money is a license to legally reuse the music as you see fit.

> **BAKING MUSIC**
>
> You can purchase all sorts of music that comes with a buy-out license from The Music Bakery at www.musicbakery.com. At the time of this writing, you can get a CD full of music for $59.

Adding Music from a CD

Adding music from an audio CD is very simple; the hardest part is figuring out which music is right for each scene in your movie.

Open the Audio palette. Insert an audio CD into your iMac's CD or DVD drive. Use the Play, Rewind, and Fast Forward controls to find the song that you want to use in your movie.

> ### JUMPING TRACKS
> You can jump to a specific track on a CD by clicking it on the Audio palette.

Now move the Playhead to the point in your movie at which you want the music to begin. You don't have to be terribly precise here, because you can always move the music around on the audio track later. Use the controls on the Audio palette to get the music to a point just before you want to start recording, and click the Play button. Start recording by clicking Record Music.

Your movie begins to play as the music is recorded. You see the purple music clip being laid down in the Audio 2 track. When you are done recording, click Stop. The Audio CD track will be imported into your movie.

> ### YOU WON T HEAR OTHER SOUNDS
> Don't worry that you can't hear the other sounds in your movie while you're recording from an audio CD. That's normal.

Continue recording tracks from CDs until you have all the tracks that you want to use in your movie. You can have as many different tracks as you have room for.

> ### DRAGGING MUSIC
> You can also drag a track from the CD window onto either of the Audio tracks to add that music to the track.

Editing the Music

Now that your movie has some music in the music track, you can use the sound controls, with which you are already familiar, to edit it.

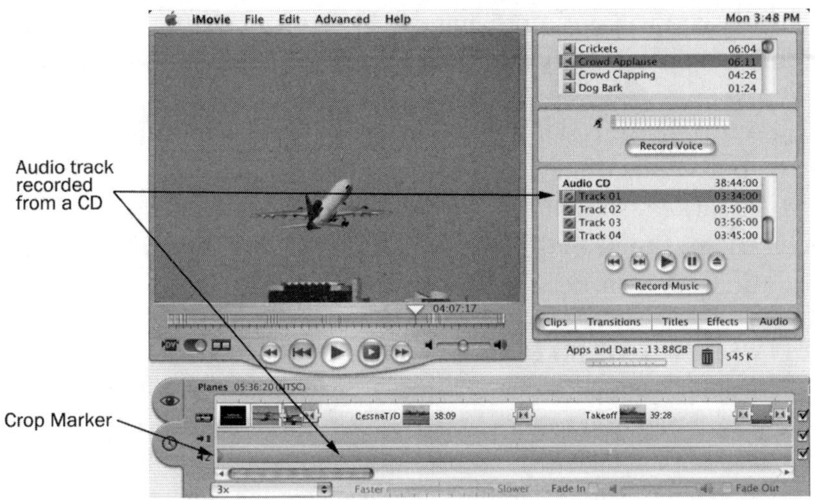

Figure 8.5 The Audio 2 track contains music that was recorded from an audio CD.

NAMED MUSIC

If you have used the CD from which you have recorded in iTunes, its name (along with the names of the tracks on it) will appear in the CD window rather that the generic names shown in the previous figure. This makes choosing tracks easier.

Name the music clip by selecting it (the bar darkens to indicate that it is selected) and typing a name for it in the Audio Selection box. If the song's title is already there (because you have previously identified the song title), you can leave it as is.

Position the music clip by dragging it on the track. Align the Playhead with the left or right Crop Marker to make it stick to the clip and then use the arrow keys to precisely position it. When it is properly aligned, use the Lock Audio at Playhead command to lock it to the video clip.

Use the Fade In, Fade Out, and Relative Volume Slider controls just as you did with the native sound and the sound effects. To use these, select the music clip and then use the appropriate control to apply it. (The Info window works with these music clips, too.) Most of the time, you will end up using the Fade Out control on music clips, unless you get lucky and they end at precisely the right time.

You can crop the music if it is too long or if you want to remove either or both ends of it. Select the clip that you want to edit. Move the Crop Markers so that the music that you want to keep is between them. Open the Edit menu and choose Crop. The music outside the Crop Markers is removed from the track.

BETWEEN THE MARKERS

Only the portion of the music clip between the Crop Markers will play, even if you haven't cropped it yet. It is a good idea to set the markers and then play the clip to make sure that you have the part selected that you want to retain. Then crop the clip.

Move the Playhead to the start of the music clip and press the Spacebar to view the movie and hear its new music track.

Adding MP3 Music to a Movie

The best way to add music is by importing MP3 files into your iMovie project. In Part 1 of this book, you learned how to use iTunes to create MP3 files for your music. You can import these files into iMovie to use as sound tracks.

LOOPING MUSIC

One of the more difficult things about using music is having the music end at a point that sounds "right" because it's highly unlikely that any piece of music you choose just happens to end at the same time as a video clip. Most of the time, you can use the Fade Out control to alleviate this problem.

When you are butting two clips together, another solution is to use looping music. Looping music is designed in such a way that you can piece it together at just about any point, and it sounds fine.

Move the Playhead to the point you want the MP3 music clip to begin to play. From the File menu, choose Import File (or press

⌘+F) and then move to the MP3 file. Select the file that you want to use and click Import. A new music clip shows up on the Audio 2 track.

Editing MP3 Clips

The now-familiar sound editing tools work on imported MP3 files just as they do on other sounds that you use. You can move, lock, fade in, fade out, change the relative volume of, and crop the clip.

You can also copy and paste the clip to make it longer. This works especially well if the music clip is designed to be looped. To do so, select the clip (or use the Crop Markers to select only a portion of the clip), press ⌘+C to copy it, and move the Playhead to the point at which you want to paste it. Press ⌘+V to paste the clip. Use the crop and fade controls to make the music match the video and to smooth the transitions.

Adding and Using Your Own Sound Effects

Although iMovie comes with several sound effects, you can import any Audio Interchange Format (AIFF) file and use it as a sound effect in your movie. This means that there are a ton of sounds available on the Internet for you to use. The better news is that you can convert practically any sound on your iMac into AIFF and then use it in iMovie.

You can bring an AIFF file into iMovie in one of two ways.

You can install the file in the Sound Effects folder (which is within the Resources folder in the iMovie for Mac OS X folder). Any AIFF sounds that you install in this folder appear on the Audio palette. You can easily reuse these sounds by dragging them from the palette onto one of the audio tracks. Use this option when you want to install a sound effect that you think you might want to reuse often.

The other option is to import the AIFF file into iMovie. With this
method, the sound is placed on the Audio 2 track at the current
location of the Playhead. You can then treat it as you do a sound
effect that you recorded. You should use this option if you want to
use the sound only once or only very rarely. Importing and using
an AIFF file works in exactly the same way as importing an MP3
file.

Adding the Sound from Any QuickTime Movie to Your Movie

You can "lift" the sound track from any QuickTime movie to use
as a sound in your movie. For example, if you have converted
some clips from a VHS tape into QuickTime, you can use portions
of their audio tracks in your iMovie movies.

> ### ARE YOU A PRO?
> You have to be using QuickTime Pro to be able to convert
> sounds into the AIFF format.

Using QuickTime Player Pro, open the QuickTime movie that
contains the sound track that you want to use. Save the movie with
a different name so that you don't change the original. From
QuickTime Player Pro's Edit menu, choose Delete Tracks. In the
Delete Tracks window, click Video Track and then click Delete.
Your movie now has only a sound track—you don't see the video
window at all.

Play the sound. Use the Crop markers to trim away any sound that
you don't want to use in your iMovie project. When you have the
sound the way that you want it, save it.

Now export it as an AIFF file. From the File menu, choose Export.
In the Export dialog box, choose Sound to AIFF in the Export
pop-up menu. Name the file and save it.

Go back into your iMovie project. From the File menu, choose Import File. Move to the sound file that you just exported and click Import. The sound is placed on the Audio 2 track at the point where the Playhead was located. You can manipulate it just like other elements in your movie. When the Playhead moves over it, you hear the sound.

Mixing Audio Tracks

After you have added all of the audio to your movie, play it. Listen to the individual tracks (use the Mute buttons to turn off tracks) and listen to how the various sounds interact. Use the editing controls to change the relative volumes of the tracks. For example, your music should be quieter than any sound effects that you want your audience to hear. You can use the Relative Volume slider to make this happen.

You can also move music and sound effects between the two Audio tracks. This can be especially useful if you want to use part of one track, but mute the rest of it. You can drag the sound from one track to the other and mute the one that you don't want to hear.

> ### EXTENDING A MOVIE
>
> If any of your sound tracks extends beyond the end of your video track, it will continue to play while the video track shows a black screen. When you change video after you have added audio, make sure that you preview the entire movie again.

Past, present, future: immeasurable
Yet clear as digital stars
Late at night the room cold as ice
But the moonlit screen on fire.

Chapter Nine

Finishing, Distributing, and Watching Digital Video

Now that your movie has a video track and sound tracks, there are two final steps to completing your movie: polishing it and distributing it. After those steps are done, all that remains is to enjoy the result of your work by watching your movie.

In this chapter, we are going to look at:

- ➤ Editing your movie as a whole
- ➤ Distributing your movie on videotape
- ➤ Distributing your movie electronically
- ➤ Watching your movie

Editing Your Movie

After your movie has all the essential elements—video, transitions, titles, sound effects, narration, and music—you might be tempted to think that your masterpiece is complete. The fact is that there is still one important task to be done to turn your collection of bits and bytes into a movie. That task is editing your movie as a whole.

As you added the various elements to your movie, you should have been reviewing and editing each element. Now it is time to do the same thing with your entire movie, treating it as an entity rather than a collection of individual elements. Your goal here is to polish your movie so that it is something that you are proud of and that others will enjoy viewing.

By now, you have seen all the elements of your movie several times (probably many times). But it is likely that you have not viewed it as a whole all that much. Now is the time to do so.

Open your iMovie project and click the Play Full Screen button. The screen goes dark, and the iMovie interface disappears. Your movie begins to play, and when it does, it fills the entire screen.

Figure 9.1 When you play your movie in full-screen mode, you can view it in the same way that your audience will—without the iMovie interface.

Critiquing Your Own Work

As you watch your movie, be critical. Pay close attention to all the details. Ask yourself about the following aspects of your movie:

> **Video scenes**—How is the composition of the scenes? Is the video easy to see, or are some parts of such poor quality that they are not valuable? Are some scenes too long or too short? Do some parts of the clips need to be cut?

> **Transitions**—Does your movie flow smoothly from scene to scene? Are there points at which the movie jumps too abruptly? Is there some variety to the transitions you used? Do the different transitions you used make sense (for example, are the more disruptive transitions used between major scene changes)? Do you have too many different kinds of transitions for one movie? Are there spots at which a new transition is needed?

> **Titles**—Are the titles meaningful? Do they add to the movie, rather than being there just because iMovie has a titles feature? Do the titles appear in the right places? Are the titles on-screen long enough to read, but not too long that they become boring? Are the titles easy to read? Do you see any misspellings or other types of mistakes?

EDITING PIECES AND EDITING THE WHOLE THING

By the way, if you've been editing each element as you add it to your movie, there shouldn't be any major surprises when you view your movie as a whole. At this point, you should be finding only minor areas for improvement. If you didn't edit the elements as you added them, editing your movie as a whole takes a lot longer, and the end result isn't as good.

> **Native sound**—How does the native sound that came with your video clips fit with the rest of the elements? Are the native sounds too loud or too quiet? Would your movie be better off without some of the native sound?

➤ **Sound effects and narration**—Are the sound effects and narration easy to hear? Do they occur at the right places? Are there too many of them? Do they add to the movie, or are they so prominent that they distract from it? How are the relative volume levels among the different sound effects? Do the relative volume levels make sense (louder effects for louder action)?

➤ **Music**—Can you hear the music well enough? Is it loud enough or does it tend to drown out the rest of the sound in the movie? Do the various music clips start and stop smoothly and at the right places?

➤ **Overall effect and enjoyment**—Do *you* enjoy watching your movie? Does it tell the story that you want to tell in the way that you want to tell it? Is the overall "package" something that you are proud to have your name associated with?

As you watch, take notes so that you develop a list of changes that are needed; you can use this change list as a guide as you make the changes later. Don't try to fix each problem as you watch your movie—that approach simply doesn't work. You must identify all the changes needed first, and then you can make them all later. If you try to fix all the problems that you find as you watch, you will miss the point, which is to identify problems at the "movie" level rather than at the "parts" level.

It usually takes many critical viewings of your movie to evaluate it properly and to develop your full change list. You might want to focus on particular elements during specific viewings. For example, on one pass, you might want to concentrate on the video. On another, pay particular attention to the sound effects.

Asking Someone Else to Criticize

It is usually a good idea to have one or more people watch your movie and help you critique it. After you watch your movie a few times, you become somewhat blind to the details; the more times that you view it, the worse this blindness becomes. Having someone else look at it brings a fresh perspective to your movie and helps you get a better view of what needs to be fixed.

If you do ask other people to critique your movie, make sure that you are emotionally prepared to deal with the criticism. Depending on how much emotional ownership you have invested in your movie, it might be painful to hear others criticize it. The fact is that criticism, while necessary and valuable, can hurt.

However, you need to learn to listen to comments that people have. Don't argue with someone who is providing comments to you. Just listen.

Add the useful comments that you receive from others to your change list.

Making the Changes

After you have developed your change list, start making the improvements that need to be made. Because you now understand all the ins and outs of using iMovie's editing tools, you already know how to make these changes. It has come down to rolling up your sleeves and getting to it.

> **DESELECTING**
>
> As you edit, sometimes it can be more difficult than it should be to deselect what you have selected. The best way to deselect things is to press ⌘+D. Getting familiar with this particular shortcut will end up saving you lots of mouse clicks.

The most common mistake in movie making is making a movie that is simply too long to be its best. Like a visitor, a movie should never wear out its welcome. When your movie is over, viewers should be wishing for more rather than heaving a sigh of relief because they can finally do something else. Be brutal with yourself when it comes to evaluating your movie's length. During the editing process, if you have even a trace of doubt that your movie is too long, it almost certainly is.

The second most common mistake is the ransom-note effect that you read about earlier in the book. There shouldn't be too many different types of elements in your movie. For example, having a zillion different types of transitions in your movie might be fun for you, but it probably isn't good for your movie. All the elements of your movie need to add up to a good whole rather than calling attention to themselves.

> ### RESTORE THAT CLIP!
>
> If you find that you have really messed up a clip and want to restore it, open the Advanced menu and choose Restore Clip Media. Sometimes, it is easier to start over with a clip than to fix all of your edits.

Use all the tools that you have learned about throughout this section to make your changes. In the next two sections, you will learn about a couple more techniques that you might want to use.

Splitting a Clip

When you edit your movie as a whole, you sometimes find that a specific clip just doesn't work. The clip might be too long, or you might want to take some frames out of it. You can edit frames from within that clip, but this usually makes the clip "jump" from one image to the next. It is usually better to use the Split Video Clip at Playhead command to create two clips out of one clip. Then you can add a transition between the two parts to make the edited version move more smoothly.

To split a clip, position the Playhead where you want the clips to be split. From the Edit menu, choose Split Video Clip at Playhead (or press ⌘+T). The clip will split at the point where the Playhead is located. The two clips become independent, and you can treat them as if they were never part of the same clip.

Pasting Over a Clip

Sometimes, you might want to replace some or all of the video in a clip. You might do this because the video is not up to snuff. Or, you can do it just to create interesting effects.

For example, if you have shot a scene using a couple of cameras, you can use the footage from one camera as the "baseline" and add frames from the other to give additional perspective. You might use one camera to capture a close-up view that you want to intersperse among the pulled-back shot.

Or you can achieve some MTV-like scenes by pasting over a bunch of different frames in a clip so that it rapidly jumps from scene to scene.

To paste over video, select and copy the frames that you want to paste (the source clip can be left on the Shelf). Position the Playhead at the point at which you want the frames to be pasted. Open the Advanced menu and choose Paste Over at Playhead to replace the selected frames of a video clip.

The audio from the clip that you are pasting over will be extracted and placed in the Audio 1 track; this ensures that the paste does not affect the audio. Then the frames that you copied will replace the frames over which you paste them. The new frames become part of the clip in which you paste them.

PASTING OVER AUDIO

The "Extract Audio in Paste Over" preference on the Advanced tab of the Preferences dialog controls whether audio is extracted or not. If this preference is unchecked, the audio will be replaced along with the video. Unless you are going to mute the audio for the clip in which you are pasting, it is usually better to have it extracted.

PASTING OVER

If you select frames in the clip over which you are pasting the replacement clips, the command becomes just Paste Over. The

continued...

> frames you have copied will be pasted in the selected frames, even if the lengths are not the same. For example, if the frames that you copied are shorter than the frames you selected to paste over, you will have blank frames at the end of the paste.

Finishing It

As you edit your movie, you will start to understand why it is such a big deal to edit each element as you add it. Because all the elements affect the others, when you make a change in one part of your movie, it can impact the other elements in a negative way. For example, if you discover that a particular clip is simply too long, cutting frames from it might cause a sound effect to play in the wrong place or might mess up the music track. Editing your movie as a whole can be quite a juggling act. The closer that the individual elements are to how you want them to be as you add them to your movie, the less juggling you will have to do.

Continue the "critique then edit" process until you can't find any more changes that are needed, or until you run out of time or patience (whichever comes first). Make sure that you save your movie and then quit iMovie.

> ### SAVE EARLY, SAVE OFTEN
> Remember to save your project frequently as you work on it. You never know when something might happen. If you lose hours of work, it can ruin your whole day. After all, it only takes a simple press of ⌘+S to save you hours of grief.

Leave your project alone for a while. Then come back and view it a couple more times. If it still meets with your approval, declare it to be a wrap!

Getting Your Movie "Out There"

Watching a movie in iMovie is okay, but iMovie is not really intended to be a viewing application. After you have finished your movie and are ready to release it to the world, you can export your movie from iMovie. What you export it to depends on how you want your viewers to be able to watch your movie.

Your movie will be watched in two primary ways. You can record your movie on videotape that others can watch with a VCR. Or you can export your movie to a QuickTime file that can be viewed on a computer; you get your movie file to others in a variety of ways, including email, on the Web, or on CD-ROM.

The good news is that you can export the same movie by using any or all of these methods to get your movie to as many people as possible.

> **ANOTHER OPTION**
>
> With Apple's SuperDrive and the iDVD application, you can put your movies on DVDs that play in standard consumer DVD players. At the time of this writing, the SuperDrive in only available in high-end Power Mac G4s. If you know someone who has one of these machines, you can use it to get your movie on DVD.

Distributing Your Movie on Videotape

Distributing your movie on videotape offers several benefits. The first is that the quality of your movie appears to be higher because you don't have file size or other technical limitations to deal with (as you do when you want your movie to be viewed on a computer). The second is that almost everyone has access to a VCR and TV, and it's pretty easy to watch a videotape. A third benefit is that it is very easy to store a movie on videotape (a tape doesn't hog valuable disk space, for example). Using videotape results in good viewing quality, as well as easy viewing and storage.

The primary downside of distributing your movie is that you have to get the videotape to the viewer. In addition to the cost of the tape itself, there is the cost and difficulty of physically transporting the tape to your viewer. Hand-delivering a tape can be time-consuming, and sending a tape can be a hassle and is also expensive. Plus, you have to record the movie onto the tape; and unless you have access to a high-speed duplicator, this is a pain in the neck.

Consider using a videotape to distribute your movie in a couple of cases. The first is when you have only a handful of people who want to view your movie (such as family and close friends), and you don't mind the expense and hassle of getting the tapes to them. The second case is one in which you are distributing your movie for professional reasons, in which case the quality and ease of viewing a videotape might outweigh the costs and time required.

GET SERIOUS

If you plan on sending lots of tapes out, you should explore some of the companies that sell shorter tape lengths in bulk. For example, you can get tapes that are only 10 minutes long, 20 minutes, or just about any other length. These are much cheaper than a six-hour tape at your local retailer. Search on the Web for videotape distributors, and you will find lots of them.

Recording Your Movie on Your Camcorder

The first step to getting your movie on videotape is to export your movie from iMovie to your DV camcorder. This process works similarly to getting clips from the DV camcorder into iMovie.

Connect the FireWire port on your camcorder to the FireWire port on your Mac (this is the same setup that you used to import clips from the camcorder into iMovie). Now open your iMovie project. The Monitor will display *Camera Connected.*

NOT COMPATIBLE?

If your camcorder is not iMovie-compatible, you'll have to make some adjustments to the steps in this chapter because they assume that the camcorder you are using is iMovie-compatible.

Use the iMovie controls to move the tape in the camcorder to the point at which you want to begin recording your movie.

Open the File menu and choose Export Movie. In the Export pop-up menu, choose To Camera (it is probably already selected). If you want more than the default one-second of black to appear before your movie begins and after it ends, increase the value in the Add _ Seconds of black before movie and the Add _ Seconds of black to end of movie fields. Click Export.

> ### How Much Black Is Enough?
> Try to add at least three to five seconds of black before and after your movie. If you have ever tried to erase something from the very beginning of a tape, you know why....

Several things happen, all of which are automatic, so you can sit back and relax. iMovie sets your camcorder to record and then waits a few seconds to make sure that your camcorder is ready. The camcorder begins recording while displaying one second (unless you set it to a different amount) of black screen. After the black screen, your movie begins to play, and your camcorder records it. A progress bar shows you how much longer you have to go (because your whole movie plays, the process takes as much time as your movie is long). You won't hear any sound as your movie is recorded—this is normal operation.

> ### Slow Camera?
> When you click Export, iMovie waits for your camera to be ready before it begins. If you miss some movie because your camera is slower than iMovie expects, increase the value in the Wait _ Seconds for camera to get ready field on the Export Movie to Camera screen.

When your movie is finished, iMovie stops your camcorder. You now have your movie captured on the camcorder; from here on, you can treat it just like any other movie that you have recorded. That's all there is to it!

> **PROTECT YOUR INVESTMENT**
>
> If you want to prevent others (or yourself) from recording over your masterpiece once it is on VHS, pop out the record prevention tab on the VHS tape before you give the tape to anyone.

Transferring Your Movie to VHS

To get your movie onto a VHS tape, connect the output of your camcorder to the input jacks on a VCR and set the VCR to take its input from those jacks. Start your movie and press record on your recording device. When the movie is done, the videotape is ready for prime time!

> **JUST PASSING THROUGH**
>
> Some DV camcorders enable you to pass-through a signal. This means that you can output to VCR at the same time that you are inputting to the DV camcorder through FireWire. This is good because you can make a first-generation recording directly on the VCR at the same time that you record it on your DV camcorder. In fact, you might not even have to record it on the DV camcorder at all. To find out if your DV camcorder has this feature, connect it to a VCR at the same time as you connect it to your Mac. If you see a picture through the VCR while you export the movie to the DV camcorder, you can pass on through.

Distributing Your Movie Electronically

You can also distribute your movie in digital form for viewing on a computer. The primary advantage of this method is that it is an easier and much less expensive way to get your movie to a lot of people than using videotape is.

The primary disadvantage to viewing your movie on a computer is that the quality is largely dependent on the computer that is being used and the technical savvy of the person to whom you have sent the movie. (Although it's easy, playing a QuickTime movie requires a bit more knowledge than playing a videotape does.)

Another drawback is that there are many more choices to be made when preparing a movie for computer playback; one of these choices is the means that you use to get your movie to its audience.

Whichever choice you make, you first export your movie to QuickTime; then you transfer the QuickTime file to the viewer who uses the QuickTime Player to watch it. How you export the movie depends on how you transfer it.

WINDOWS USERS CAN DO QUICKTIME, TOO

QuickTime is very popular on Windows computers, as well as being part of the default installation of the Mac operating system. You can provide the QuickTime version of your movies to Windows users as well as Mac users. This provides a much larger audience for your movies.

You have the following transfer choices:

> ➤ **CD or other removable media**—You can store a movie on a CD or other high-capacity disc and then send that disc to the person who wants to see your movie. This method provides the highest quality, but it also requires the largest file size. It also requires that you have the equipment you need to write to the disc that you choose (such as a **CD-RW** drive to burn a CD). And you are faced with the same delivery issues as with a videotape (such as mailing costs).

> ➤ **Email**—Given that almost everyone has email access, one of the best ways to get your movie to people is to email it to them. Emailing a movie is usually free, and you can email it to many people with one email. Attaching a movie to an email message is very simple. The drawback to emailing a movie is file size. Movie files are really big. To get the file size down to a reasonable level for most people to be able to download it in email, the quality of the movie must be compromised. Additionally, many email systems limit the size of files that you can attach to email; even with the relatively small file sizes iMovie generates, a movie file might still be too big to attach to an email message.

> ➤ **Web**—You can post your movie to a Web site so that others can go to that site to view the movie. As with email, you must compromise quality to keep the file size down. And it can be complicated to find a Web site on which to post your movie (assuming that you don't have your own Web site, of course). The benefit of having your movie on the Web is that anyone who can access the Web can view your movie; it's a great way to get your movie exposed to lots of people all over the world.

When exporting to QuickTime, you must always trade off file size versus quality. The better the quality of your movie, the bigger the file is (and the more resources that it consumes to send or store). For example, the following table shows the resulting file sizes for various export formats for the same movie, which is 5:21:20 long.

Table 9.1 File Sizes for Various Format Options

Export Format Choice	File Size (MB)
Email Movie, Small	3.4
Streaming Web Movie, Small	7.9
CD-ROM Movie, Medium	25.5
Full Quality, Large	1,100

When choosing quality and file size, always keep the recipient of the movie in mind. If you know that the person to whom you are emailing uses a 56K modem, keeping the file size small is important. If you are using a CD, maximize quality; it doesn't matter how big the file is (as long as it isn't bigger than the 650 MB the disc can hold, of course).

The method you choose depends on what you want to do with your movie. You might choose to distribute it in all three ways (four if you count via videotape).

The next three sections show you examples of how to distribute your movies using all three of the methods mentioned previously. You can use these examples to guide you as you get your own movies "out there."

Putting Your Movie on CD

This method is the most hardware- and software-intensive one, because you need a CD-RW or CD-R drive. (CD-RW drives are better because you can erase and reuse CD-RW discs; this makes it easy and inexpensive to experiment.) You also need a CD burning tool such as Apple's Disc Burner or Roxis's Toast.

> **OTHER DISKS WORK, TOO**
>
> You can use the "CD" method to distribute your work on a hard disk, over a network, or even by a Zip or other disk. The export settings you use depend on how much room you have on the disk you are using to store your movie. For example, unless your movie is pretty short, you probably won't be able to store the highest quality version on a 100 MB Zip disk, but you will be able to fit a lower quality version (such as an email version) on it.

Preparing the QuickTime File

The first step is to create the movie file that you will burn onto a CD. Open your iMovie project, and from the File menu, choose Export Movie. Choose To QuickTime from the Export pop-up menu. You will see the Export Movie window; the window now has a Formats pop-up menu. You can use this menu to choose a format in which to export your movie.

Click the Formats pop-up menu. You have several options. The option that you choose depends on how long your movie is, and thus how large the file is. Because a CD is limited to 650 MB, you don't want to have a QuickTime file larger than that.

To figure out which option you should use, try the CD-ROM Movie, Medium option. Select that choice from the pop-up menu and then click Export. You will see the Export QuickTime Movie dialog box. In that dialog box, name your movie, choose a save location, and click Save.

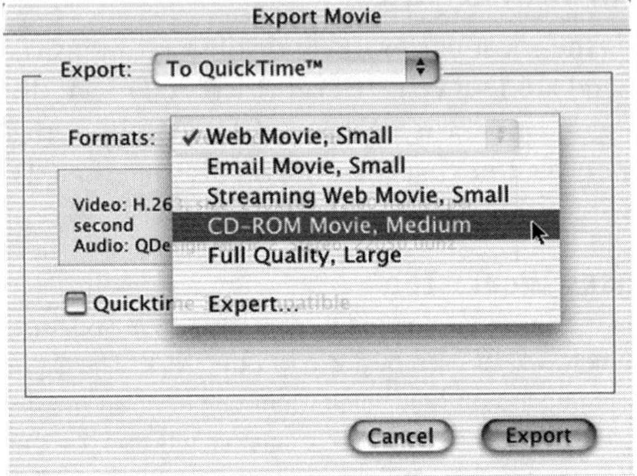

Figure 9.2 You use the Formats pop-up menu to choose a format in which to export your QuickTime movie.

iMovie begins to export your movie, and a progress bar that gives you an idea of where you are in the process will appear on-screen. You can also see the Playhead moving and the movie plays in the monitor in the background. Unless your movie is really short, the export process takes a long time, so plan on doing something else for a while. Eventually, the progress bar goes away. When it does, you are finished exporting the movie. You have created a QuickTime version of your movie!

> **INTERRUPTED**
>
> If you move out of iMovie and then back into it while the export process is occurring, the movie in the Monitor will be replaced by the text "Exporting to QuickTime." This is a normal operation.

Open the file that you just exported. QuickTime Player opens, and through it you can watch your movie (you will learn how to use QuickTime Player to watch a movie later in this chapter). If the file size is significantly smaller than 650 MB, try exporting your movie with the Full Quality, Large format to see what effect that has on quality and file size. Use the highest quality version that you can fit onto a CD—that is, one that is 650 MB or smaller.

Recording Your Movie on a CD

The second part of the operation is to place the QuickTime movie that you just created onto a CD. How you do this depends on the hardware/software combination that you are using. For example, if you are using an iMac with a built-in CD-RW drive and Apple's Disc Burner software, you can just drag the QuickTime file onto a CD-RW or CD-R disc. If you are using another CD burning application, such as Roxis's Toast, the process is similar.

> ### NAME THAT CD
>
> When you burn it, don't forget to add a meaningful name to the CD.

When you have burned the CD, test it before you send it to anyone else (insert the CD and double-click the movie file). If you can test it on several different machines, that is usually a good idea.

> ### CDS FOR WINDOWS
>
> If you are sending the CD to a Windows user, make sure that you format the disc in the ISO 9660 format so that they can mount the disc. Also ensure that all the files on the disc are named with Windows file name conventions (for example, add the ".mov" file extension to the name of the QuickTime file).

Shipping the CD

If everything works the way it should, you should record your movie on a CD-R disc (you can use a disc image to make this even easier). All that remains is to mail out the CD to whomever you want to have it.

> ### MAKE ONE FOR YOURSELF
>
> You should also make a copy of the movie CD for yourself. Storing the QuickTime movie version on a CD rather than on your hard drive makes more sense for long-term storage. After all, you need all the hard disk space that you can get for your next iMovie project!

> ### THE NEED FOR SPEED
>
> For best playback (especially if the CD/DVD drive you use is slow), the person receiving the movie should copy the movie to his hard drive before playing it. You can add a text document saying so to the CD as well (call it something like Read Me). But most people are likely to play it directly from the CD, which usually works just fine.

Sending Your Movies via Email

Creating a movie to send out via email is similar to creating one for distribution on a CD. The difference is that you need the file to be much smaller. Typically, you should limit the size of files that you attach to email messages to be 5 MB or less. This is a fairly severe limit for all but the shortest of movies.

Preparing the Movie for Email

Use the same steps that you used when you created a movie for CD distribution with one exception. This time, choose Email Movie, Small from the Formats pop-up menu. The other steps are exactly the same (but the file is created a lot faster because it is a lot smaller).

When the file is done, play it. Don't be shocked at how poor the movie looks. That's the price you pay to get a file that is sized reasonably for email transfer.

> ### SMALL MAY NOT BE SMALL ENOUGH
>
> Many email systems limit the size of attachments that you can add to email messages that you can send. Even with the Email Movie, Small format, the file might still be too large to send. Also, if the recipient uses a slow connection to the Net, such as a 56K modem, consider using another distribution method. Many people do not like downloading large files via these slow connections.

Emailing Your Movie

Now all you have to do is attach your QuickTime file to an email message. The exact steps you use depend on your email application. In most email applications, you simply drag the file onto a new email message.

> #### SIZE IS RELATIVE
>
> One way to make the movie file smaller is to mute any sound tracks that are attached to it, particularly a track with music on it. When a sound track is muted before you export it, the track is not exported; this can make a file quite a bit smaller. Of course, the viewer does not get to hear the sounds, either, so this is another compromise.

Watching It

When the recipient receives your email, he is able to save your movie to disk and then watch it. Depending on the email application used, the recipient might see the movie as part of the email message and be able to watch it from there.

> #### SPEED IS ALSO RELATIVE
>
> The export formats are simply predefined sets of configurations that have been designed for particular situations, such as email. There is no reason why you can't use one for another purpose. For example, if your recipient has a cable or DSL connection to the Net, receiving a 40- or 50-MB file might not be a problem (although sending it might be for you). In that case, you might be able to use the CD export format to export the file instead of the email option. The file is much larger, but the quality of the movie is much higher, too.

Showing Your Movies on the Web

You can also upload a movie that you create onto a Web site so that anyone visiting that site can view your movie. You probably can already guess how to create the movie file; the only challenge is finding a Web site on which to post your movie.

Exporting Your Movie for the Web

Everything is the same as the last two exports, except the export format that you choose from the Exports pop-up menu.

When exporting a movie for the Web, you have two preconfigured options: Web Movie, Small and Streaming Web Movie, Small. The most important difference between these is that the second requires that the server on which you post the movie must support QuickTime streaming (you have to find out from the organization that serves the Web pages on which you post the movie). If you can use QuickTime Streaming, it is the better choice because the viewer will be able to watch your movie as it downloads.

> ### QUICKTIME 3 COMPATIBLE?
>
> If you check the QuickTime 3 compatible checkbox, your movie can be played by using QuickTime 3. However, QuickTime 4 has been available for a long time, so you can stick with it by leaving the checkbox unchecked.

Export the movie, choosing Streaming Web Movie, Small from the Formats pop-up menu. This one takes longer than the email format to export, but it doesn't take as long to export as the CD format.

When you're finished, you can post the file to a Web site.

Posting Your Movie on a Web Site

If you have your own Web site, you can post your movie to your site and direct people to your URL to view it. If you don't have your own Web site, you must find a site that will allow you to post your movie. Many of these enable you to create your own Web site, and some are free (although since movie files tend to be large, a site's file size limit might be a problem for you).

> ### SIZE DOES MATTER ON THE WEB
> Note that most Web sites limit the size of the files that you can post (you can usually pay more to post larger files).

> ### YOUR MAC OS X WEB SITE
> Under Mac OS X, every user account has its own Web site. You can create a Web site for your movies and place it in the Sites folder that is in your Home directory. You can host this site to your local network so others on your network can view it, and you can serve that site to the Internet.

One of the best options that you have for posting your movies on the Web is Apple's own iTools. iTools enables you to create a Web site quickly by using templates and then posting your movie to the site that you create. While the details of this process are beyond the scope of this chapter, here are the general steps required to create an iTools Web site and post your movie to it:

1. Create your iTools account.

    Under Mac OS X, you can do this when you install the operating system or at any time by opening the System Preferences utility and using the Internet pane.

    Under Mac OS 9, visit the iTools Web site at `www.apple.com/itools`. You will have to download and install the iTools software.

2. Sign in to your iTools account (under Mac OS X you don't have to do this, you only have to move to the iDisk directory).

3. Mount your iDisk on your Mac.

4. Copy your movie file from your Mac into the Movies folder on your iDisk.

> **iDisk Space**
>
> Your iDisk can contain up to 20 MB of data. Unless your movie is only a few minutes long, it might be larger than this when you export it. If so, try muting any music tracks and then re-export the movie. If it is still too large, you have to cut some of the video and sound effects as well. If you do, make sure that you create a new project and import all of your clips into it. Or duplicate the project folder for your movie so you can hack that version without changing the full-length version. In effect, you have to create a second iMovie project specifically for the Web. Don't replace your full-length feature with the shortened version—you still want the full version for disk or videotape viewing. Another option is to pay for more storage space on your iDisk.

5. Move back to the iTools Web site and use the Home-Page tools to build your Web site.

    You can choose from several format options using the templates provided for you. For example, you can add an iMovie page to serve your movie. You can edit the existing text on the templates to customize it for your site.

> **Sites Is Sites**
>
> In your iDisk, you also have a Sites folder. You can use this to post your own Web site that you build using tools other than the iTools templates. For example, you can place the same Web site in the iDisk folder as is in the Sites folder in your Mac OS X Home directory.

6. Add your movie to the iMovie Web page.

7. Preview and publish the page.

8. Add other pages to your iTools Web site.

9. Send your iTools Web site URL to those whom you want to watch your movie.

> ### HELP WITH ITOOLS
> You can find help with iTools on the iTools Web site or in the books Special Edition Using Mac OS X and The Mac OS X Guide.

> ### YOU CAN DO EVEN MORE
> You can build a fairly substantial Web site by using thc iTools HomePage. You can have more than one movie page, and you can have all sorts of other pages, such as a page to display photographs. Take some time to explore iTools; you'll be impressed with how easy it is to build your own Web site. It is truly amazing that Apple provides this great resource for free! If you want to build a large Web site, you need to purchase more storage space, but even so, iTools is a great way to get on the Web.

Using Expert Format Settings to Export Your Movie

Most of the time, one of the standard format options will be what you need to use. However, you can use the Expert format to specify all aspects of how your movie is formatted. When you choose Expert from the Formats pop-up menu, you will see the Expert QuickTime Settings dialog.

While a discussion of the specifics of all of the options you have is beyond the scope of this book, a quick overview will give you some idea of how this works.

> ### APPLE WASN T KIDDING
> There is a reason that these options are accessed by a format option called Expert. Understanding the details of these settings requires some study and experimentation. However, you should be aware that they exist so that you can use them as you grow in your iMovie expertise.

Basically, when you export a movie, you control the image and audio settings for that exported movie and how the movie is prepared for the Internet. You can control the resolution of the movie's video, the compression that is applied to it, and so on. You can also control the compression and other settings for the audio portion of the movie. And you can choose the type of Web server that will be serving your movie (standard or QuickTime Streaming).

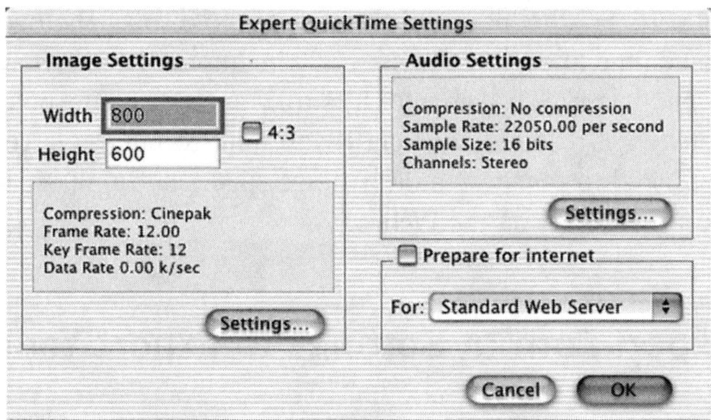

Figure 9.3 You can control many aspects of how your movie is exported by using the Expert format option.

In the Image settings area, you can set the width and height of the movie (its resolution). If you click the Settings button, you will see the Compression Settings dialog that enables you to choose the compressor, depth, quality, and motion settings for the movie.

UNDERSTANDING THE OPTIONS

It is interesting to select one of the predefined options and read the information box just below the Formats menu. Here you see the settings that Apple has input for the various format choices (such as for Streaming Web Movie, Small). This can give you some insight into the options you see if you use the Expert format settings.

If you click the Settings button in the Audio area, you will see the Sound Settings dialog.

Watching Your Movie

Now that your work is done, it is time to enjoy the fruits of your labor.

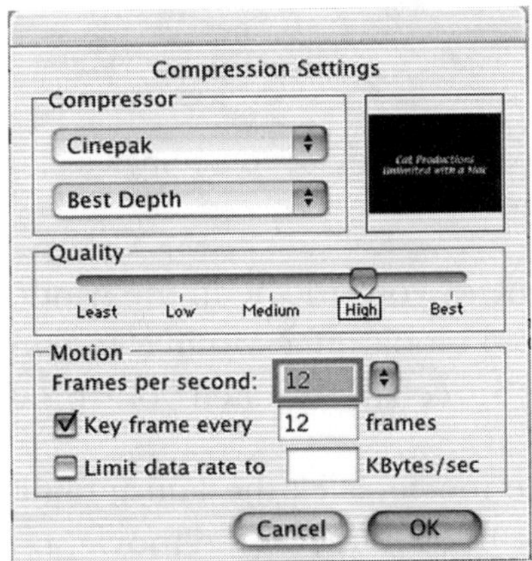

Figure 9.4 You use the controls in the Image Compression settings dialog to control the quality and file size of the movie.

Watching Your Movies on Videotape

The simplest way to watch your movie is to record it to videotape and pop it in your VCR. This method eliminates any technical problems, and the performance and quality of the movie are quite good.

Watching Movies with QuickTime

There are a couple of ways to watch your movie in the QuickTime format: using the QuickTime Player application or watching your movie from a Web site.

Watching Your Movie with the QuickTime Player

Open your movie file (choose the highest quality version that you exported). The QuickTime Player application will open, and you

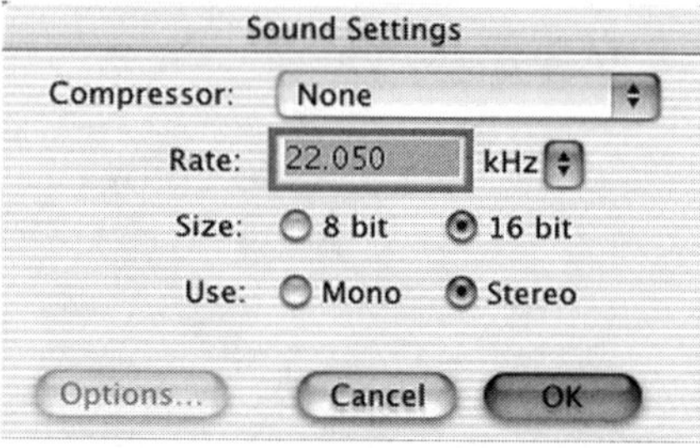

Figure 9.5 You can use the Sound Settings dialog to control the audio in your movie.

will see the first frame of your movie in the window. Most of the controls you see should look quite familiar to you. Click the Play button (or press the Spacebar) to watch your movie.

To stop or pause the movie, click the Pause button (or press the Spacebar). To adjust the volume of the movie, use the Volume slider. To move to a particular point in the movie, drag the Playhead to the point at which you want to be (as you move the slider, you will see the frames of the movie change). (You can also click a point on the Scrubber bar to jump to that point instead of dragging the Playhead there.) To resize the QuickTime movie, drag the Resize handle until the window is the size that you want it to be (the QuickTime Player ensures that the window stays in the intended proportions).

RESIZING THE WINDOW

You can also resize the QuickTime Player window with the commands on the Movie menu.

YOU RE STRETCHING IT NOW!

When you use QuickTime Player to resize a movie, you aren't changing that movie's resolution. If you make a movie larger, QuickTime has to "stretch" the same amount of information over a larger area. The result is that the movie may not look as good at the larger size if it was created at a smaller resolution. You won't hurt anything doing this, but the movie may end up looking pretty bad.

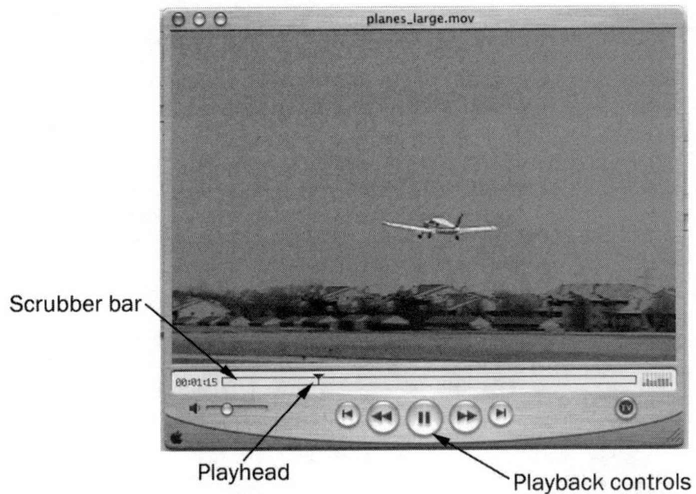

Figure 9.6 Watching your movie in the QuickTime Player is similar to watching it in iMovie.

Watching Your Movie on the Web

When you view a QuickTime movie on the Web, you use the QuickTime plug-in for your Web browser. Click a movie to view it. It begins to be downloaded to your iMovie, and it *streams,* meaning that it will play at the same time that it is downloaded to your iMac.

The controls you use are quite similar to those in the QuickTime Player application.

When enough of your movie has downloaded so that it can be played with no pauses, it will begin to play. You can use the download progress bar to monitor how much of the movie has been downloaded to your Mac.

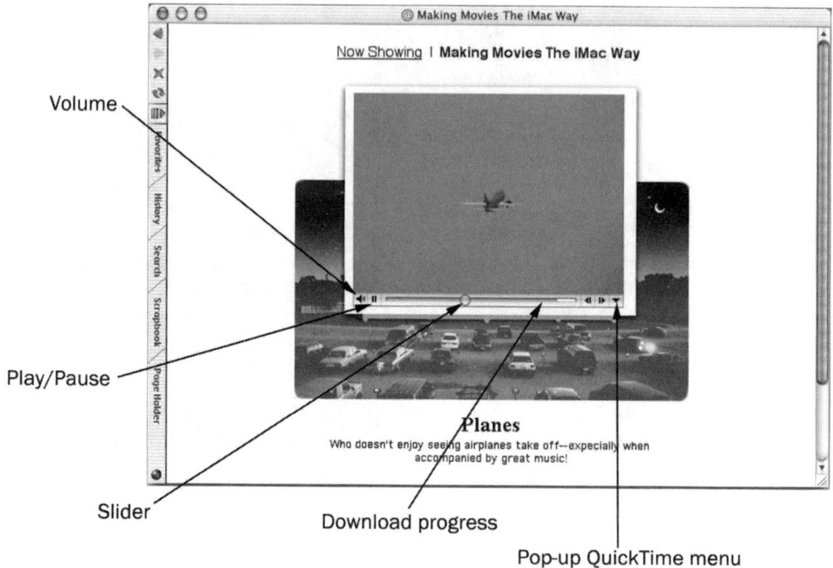

Figure 9.7 Here's a movie posted on an iTools Web site for easy viewing.

BROADBAND

QuickTime is a good reason to upgrade to a broadband Internet connection. With a 56 K modem, watching QuickTime movies can be a drag because you spend more time waiting than watching. With a cable modem or other high-speed connection to the Net, you can watch QuickTime movies just like watching TV—the results are instantaneous. You can also watch the high-resolution versions, which makes them much more enjoyable.

The image clear, the edit deep,
Each particle, each instant a reality,
A bird call shills through mountain dawn:
Look where the iMac sits, a rock, in Ten.

Chapter Ten

Advanced Digital Video

In the previous chapters in this section of the book, you learned quite a bit about iMovie. Hopefully, you feel comfortable making your own movies and have all the information you need to be as creative as you'd like to be. And those chapters contain everything you need to know to make sophisticated DV movies. However, there are other things that can help you make your movies even better. That is where this chapter fits in.

In this chapter, we are going to look at:

> Archiving your completed iMovie projects

> Exploring iMovie Web resources

> Adding to and maintaining the iMovie application

> Taking a look at some other video applications

Archiving Your Movies

As you have seen, DV files are really big. As you create your movies, it is likely that you will have GBs of data for a single iMovie project. Unless you have an infinite hard drive storage capacity, it is likely that you will run out of storage space long before you run out of ideas for more iMovie projects.

You will probably want to remove the iMovie project folders from your iMac's hard drive so that you will have room for other iMovie projects.

The thing to remember here is the fundamental structure of iMovie projects that you learned about back in Chapter 6. Remember that in the folder for your iMovie project, there are two items. One is a reference file that contains pointers to the various elements of your movie. The other is the media folder that contains all of the media (video clips, sounds, etc.) that you used in your movie. In order to be able to make changes to your movie, you need to be able to access both of these items.

When you have finish a movie project, consider the following steps:

1. Make sure that you have exported your movie to videotape.

2. Export your movie using all of the electronic format options that you think you might need (such as a small one for email, a medium size for the Web, a larger one for CD-R, and a full quality version to store on your hard drive).

3. In your iMovie project, delete all of the clips that you didn't end up using and that you can't envision using in the future. Then empty iMovie's Trash.

After you have completed these tasks, the question you have is what to do with the iMovie project files themselves. Here are some options:

> **Ditch them all because you won't need them again**—This is an option, but isn't a very good one. If you ever want to make changes to your movie or even export it into a different format, you will have to recreate all of your work.

TAPE IS CHEAP

You should keep the tapes on which you originally recorded the clips that you used in your movie rather than recording over them. Tapes are relatively inexpensive and should you ever need to restore some footage, you will be glad that you kept the originals.

> **Record your movie's media to videotape**—You can add any clips that aren't used in your movie to a "trailer" at the end of your movie and export all of that material to your video camera. If you need it again at some point, you can import the movie and the additional clips later. Editing the movie is much harder since it will come in as a single unit (of course, you can manually break the large clip into shorter clips when you import it); however, if you don't have a way to store the data digitally, this option is better than nothing.

> **Save the media files to a CD**—This is a good option; however, you should expect to use several CDs for a single iMovie project. Make sure that you place all of the files in your project's media folder on a CD. You also need to make sure that all of the files keep the same names. This will enable you to reconstruct your iMovie project on a hard disk should you need to work on it again.

> **Save the project to a high-capacity, back-up drive**—This is your best option because it enables you to save your iMovie projects in their current form, which makes restoring them to a hard drive easy and reliable.

A VERY MAC-FRIENDLY RESELLER

When you need to obtain hardware and software for your iMovie toolkit, check out Small Dog Electronics. Visit Small Dog at www.smalldog.com or call 802-496-7171.

➤ Good choices for this purpose are FireWire tape drives, such as Imation's Travan FireWire Tape Drive; the tapes for this drive have a 20 MB capacity. Tape drives have a huge capacity, and tapes are relatively inexpensive. The downside is that you can't use a tape directly; you must restore the files to a hard drive before you can use them.

➤ Another good choice is a FireWire DVD-RAM drive; DVD-RAM discs have a capacity of 2.6 GB per side. The downside to these drives is that the discs are relatively expensive at about $40. But you can mount the discs on your desktop so they have many uses.

Figure 10.1 A FireWire tape drive, such as this Imation Travan FireWire Tape Drive, is a critical component if you intend to make very many iMovie movies.

➤ Most of these drives include the outstanding Retrospect application that you can use to back up and restore your iMovie projects.

> **TIME TRAVEL**
>
> And now just one more warning about this before we move on. If you don't archive your iMovie projects, you won't be able to change your movie at a later date. If all you have is the QuickTime version or the version on videotape, making changes to the movie will be very difficult, if not impossible. It is inevitable that you are going to want to remove your old iMovie projects from your hard drive. If you are serious about iMovie, you should obtain and use a high-capacity, removable media drive.

Exploring iMovie Web Resources

Two major Web sites are fundamental to DV on the Mac. Apple provides both of these sites. One is the iMovie site; the other is QuickTime's home on the Web. You'll find lots of other sites useful, as well, including those of hardware and software manufacturers, retail sites, informational sites, and so on.

Visiting the iMovie Web Page

The main iMovie Web site is provided by Apple (no surprise there, huh?). This site contains tons of useful information; this includes everything you need to know— from which camcorders are iMovie-compatible to an online tutorial to additional resources that you can download and use in your movies.

Open your favorite Web browser and go to `www.apple.com/imovie/`.

Hopefully, this book will provide you with a lot of the iMovie information and help that you need. However, if you want to learn more, the iMovie site contains online information and tutorials through which you can work. The learning resources are located at `www.apple.com/imovie/gettingstarted`. If you want some additional iMovie help, check this page out.

Figure 10.2 At Apple's iMovie Web site, you will find a world of iMovie information and resources.

As with all software, Apple is continually working to solve any problems with iMovie and to improve the way it works. You can use the Apple site to download updates to the iMovie application (and for any other Apple software that you use).

> **AUTO UPDATES**
>
> You can use the Software Update feature of the Mac OS to check automatically for updates to Apple software that you have installed on your Mac.

As great as all of these parts of the iMovie site are, I've saved the best for last. Apple provides lots of additions to the special effects you can use in your movies, and they are all free! You will learn a bit more about this later in this chapter.

Visiting Apple's QuickTime Web Site

Throughout this book, you have learned how important Quick-Time is to your movie studio. In addition to being an important way to watch your movies, QuickTime also enables you to get all sorts of content (that doesn't come directly from a DV camcorder) into iMovie. Apple devotes a substantial area of its Web site to QuickTime, and you can really benefit from spending some time exploring it.

Fire up your Web browser and visit `www.apple.com/quicktime/`.

Visiting Other Useful Pages

As you might imagine, there are tons of useful Web sites that relate to DV and iMovie (some directly, and also many indirectly). Here are a few of them just to get you started.

Figure 10.3 Apple's QuickTime Home Page should be a regular stop on your Web journeys.

Table 10.1 Great Web Sites Related to DV and iMovie

Site	Summary	URL

About.com	An extensive collection of DV information organized by subject (there is an area devoted to iMovie, but don't limit yourself to just this part of the site).	`destopvideo.`
		`miningco.com/`
		`compute/`
		`desktopvideo/`

Apple Tech Info Library	Apple's technical information library contains numerous technical articles; you can search these for specific topics of interest.	`til.info.apple.` `com/`
Canon DV	Information on Canon's fine line of DV camcorders.	`www.canondv.com/`
DV Insider	A news site devoted to DV information.	`www.dvinsider` `.com/`
Small Dog Electronics	Great Web retail site that is very Mac friendly; you can find all of the DV tools you need here.	`www.smalldog.com/`
Panasonic USA	Information on Panasonic DV camcorders.	`www.panasonic` `.com/`
Short Courses	This site offers several short courses that will help you make better movies.	`www.shortcourses` `.com/`

Sony Electronics	Lots of information on Sony's DV camcorders .	`http://www.sel`
		`.sony.com/`
		`SEL/consumer/`

Adding Additional iMovie Resources

Although iMovie comes with a good collection of transitions, sounds, and other effects that you can use, there is no reason to limit yourself to those. You can download lots more from Apple, install them, and then use them in your movies.

Downloading iMovie Resources

To get started, go to the iMovie site at `www.apple.com/imovie`.

Find the iMovie 2 Plug-in Pack link. The plug-in pack contains additional title and transition effects that you can load into iMovie. To download the pack, simply click the link. The file is downloaded to your Mac.

CHECK THE VERSION

Make sure that you download the version of the Plug-in Pack that is appropriate for the version of the Mac OS that you are using.

Move to `www.apple.com/imovie/freestuff`. This page has backgrounds, sound effects, and looping music that you can download and use.

Figure 10.4 You can download and add these resources to your iMovie application.

Downloading any of these extras is a matter of pointing and clicking.

Prepping the Files

After you have downloaded the files to your Mac, you need to prepare them before you can install and use them. Open the folder to which your files were downloaded.

The files that you downloaded are compressed in the .sit (StuffIt) format. Depending on how your Mac is configured, they might or might not be uncompressed automatically. If the files were uncompressed automatically, you will see a folder named with the same name as the file you downloaded, and you also will see the original .sit files.

If the files were not uncompressed for you, use StuffIt Expander to uncompress them.

Installing iMovie Resources

You can install the items you download in several ways. Fortunately, none of them requires more than a few moments.

Plugging in the Pack

To use the titles and transitions in the plug-in pack, you need to do the following steps. First, quit iMovie if it is running. Then open the iMovie folder and open the Resources folder. Now drag the iMovie Plug-in Pack 2 folder into the Plugins folder. Open iMovie and then open the Transitions palette. You will see the additional transitions that have been installed. You can work with these new transitions just as you do with the preinstalled transitions. You also have additional titling effects to use.

Using Resources One-by-One

You can use the backgrounds, sound effects, and music that you download on a case-by-case basis rather than installing them in the application. The benefit of this approach is that they do not add to the memory or processor requirements for the application (adding resources to the application tends to slow it down). The disadvantage is that you must import them each time you use them rather than choose them from a palette.

> **BACKGROUNDS ARE DIFFERENT**
> You can only use the background files on a case-by-case basis. There is no way to install them on a palette.

To add one of these resources to an iMovie project, use the Import File command.

Adding Resources to the iMovie Palettes

If you find that you want to be able to reuse some of the free stuff easily, install the files in your iMovie palettes so that you can use it with a simple drag.

Quit iMovie. Open the Resources folder that is within the iMovie folder. Drag the sound effects or music that you want to be installed on the palette into the Sound Effects folder. Open iMovie. Then open the Audio palette, and you will see the sounds that you installed in the Sound Effects folder. Click a sound to hear it. Drag it to the Clip viewer to use it in your movie. You can reuse these sounds as often as you'd like.

Exploring Advanced Digital Editing Applications

While iMovie is the most approachable digital video application, it is also very powerful. You should be able to do almost anything you want to with it. However, there are some other applications that you should be aware of in the event that you want to take your DV work to "the next level."

Figure 10.5 Apple's Final Cut Pro provides more powerful video tools for you, but it is also harder to use and requires more powerful hardware.

Apple Final Cut Pro

Apple's Final Cut Pro can be thought of as iMovie's big brother.

Some of the features that Final Cut Pro offers are the following:

➤ Multiple video and sound tracks

➤ More sophisticated video editing tools

➤ Audio editing tools

➤ Compositing and other video effects

➤ Support for plug-ins

Final Cut Pro is not for the faint of heart; at around $1,000, you aren't likely to get a copy just to play around with. And its interface is quite complex and requires a steep learning curve compared to iMovie.

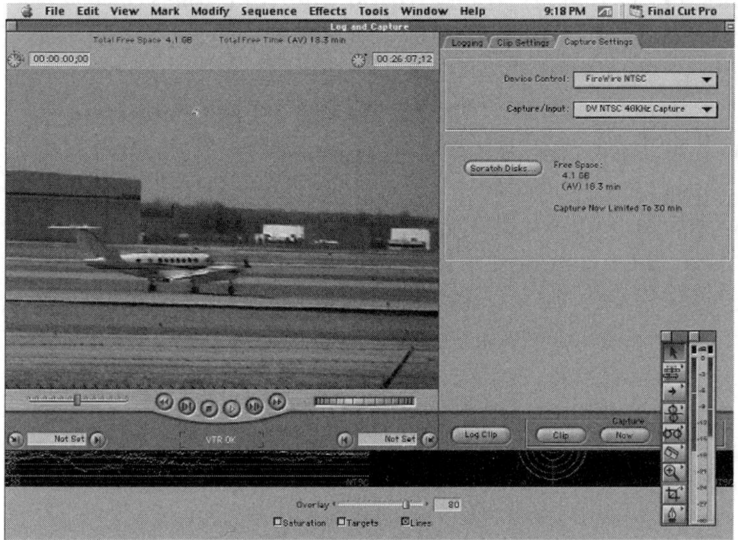

Figure 10.6 Apple's Final Cut Pro is a professional level video-editing application.

Still, if you grow beyond iMovie's capabilities, check out Final Cut Pro at www.apple.com/finalcutpro/.

Adobe Premiere

Adobe's Premiere is another professional video editing application. Currently in version 6, this application has been around much longer than either iMovie or Final Cut Pro. It offers similar advantages to those of Final Cut Pro and also comes with similar barriers (although it is not as expensive as Final Cut Pro is).

TRY BEFORE YOU BUY

You can download a demo version of Premiere from the Adobe Web site at www.adobe.com/products/premiere/.

iDVD and the SuperDrive

Apple's iDVD (free) and iDVD Pro (not free) applications enable you to put your movies on DVD-R discs that can be played in most consumer DVD players. These applications enable you to create a nice menu for your movies somewhat like the menus that you see on DVD movie discs.

The catch is that to use the iDVD applications, you must have an Apple SuperDrive that can write to DVD-R (as well as CD-R and CD-RW discs), and which currently ships only on the high-end Power Mac G4 machines. Some external DVD-R drives are becoming available, but at the time of this writing, iDVD does not support these third-party drives.

For information about iDVD and the SuperDrive, see `www.apple.com/idvd/`.

Digital Graphics

Graphics are evolving. Your iMac is an amazing digital graphics machine: with its speed you can work with huge digital image files, manipulate complex geometry, and render physically accurate light-sources on 3D models.

Your iMac is an amazing digital graphics tool: sophisticated software allows you to enhance photographs, draw detailed illustrations, or lay out entire books with your iMac whether it's a Web page, a poster for an event, or this book.

Your iMac is an amazing digital graphics work of art: the beautiful high-resolution display in your iMac allows you to create and present your visual creations in a stylish compact design.

So, whether you want to experiment with digital photography, draw a picture, lay out a page, a magazine, or a book, design and animate 3D characters and scenes, or even produce professional graphics, the iMac is an amazing computer to use.

In this section we'll explore digital graphics, the iMac way:

> Chapter 11: Digital Photography

> Chapter 12: Digital Image Editing

> Chapter 13: Printing Pictures

> Chapter 14: Advanced Digital Graphics

Red, green, and blue, break upon the screen,
There's a span to my view—depth to my eyes.
One-thousand-twenty-four pixels, sixteen-point-
seven million colors:
From which the water flows, the butterfly dreams.
for the listener,
a beep.

Chapter Eleven

Digital Photography

Digital photography is a great example of the convergence of digital and traditional technology. No more film developing costs and environmentally unfriendly chemicals. No more waiting to see the results, and then discovering that you didn't get the picture you were hoping for. And best of all, no more sorting through negatives to get more prints made of your favorite pictures. With mega-pixel digital cameras and inexpensive photo-quality printers, and, of course, the Internet, everyone can use his or her own computers to explore digital photography.

Your iMac is the perfect companion to a digital camera. Once you have your images captured or scanned, you can easily view them, perhaps even organizing them into slideshows. You can share them on the Internet. You can edit and manipulate them. You can even animate your pictures and mix them into iMovies. Digital photography and your iMac can be a lot of fun.

In this chapter we're going to look at:

- Capturing pictures using a digital camera

- Scanning pictures using a flatbed scanner

- Viewing your pictures on your iMac

- Acquiring pictures on the Internet

- Creating pictures artistically from scratch

Using Digital Cameras

We are in the midst of a revolution in photography. Digital cameras are available with amazing resolution and clarity at quickly decreasing prices. The latest models with 3 mega-pixel resolution can produce images rivaling 35mm professional cameras. Automation of exposure makes using a digital camera just as easy as the most simple point-and-click film cameras, achieving great results every time.

Figure 11.1 The Nikon CoolPix is a typical digital camera featuring removable data storage and a built-in viewing screen.

KNOW YOUR PIXELS

At first, the terms used when describing digital images may be confusing: image size, pixel, resolution, color depth, color value, color palette, color channel, hue, saturation, and brightness. But all digital images are basically the same—they all have two essential components: size and color. Digital images are a gathering of data that can be interpreted into a viewable image, whether it is a large rectangle of a single solid color without any detail, or an intricate representation of a masterful painting containing subtle shades of colors and minute detail. Digital images all have a size, and they have colors assigned to their pixels.

Each digital camera has different software and connection options. Some connect directly to your iMac by using the USB or FireWire interfaces, others require special adapters for the camera's storage media. Most of the latest cameras use small (even tiny) digital storage media cards to hold image data they capture. If you are using a PowerBook, there are PC-card adapters that hold the camera's media and allow it to be accessed directly. On an iMac you can get small external smart-media interfaces, which can take the removable camera media and mount it on your desktop like a hard drive via a USB or FireWire interface. Before purchasing any digital camera equipment, be sure that it supports a connection method that works well with your iMac.

Most digital cameras are very easy to use. Simply point and click. The camera takes care of exposure, focus, and storage of the digital image data. How many images you can capture will depend on the data storage capacity of your camera (or its removable memory card) and the resolution and compression quality. Memory in a digital camera is comparable to film in a regular camera, and memory can be quite expensive. Be aware that there are many methods used by different cameras to fit as many images as possible into less space. On many cameras you can choose lower resolution images or decreased data-compression quality to hold more pictures in the same amount of space. Of course, having multiple memory cards, or a very large card, can be helpful.

Many digital cameras may have a built-in display to let you preview the picture you are going to capture, as well as to play back the images you have already stored in your camera without having to download them to your iMac. By browsing through the images, you can choose to delete pictures selectively, making more space in your camera. More advanced digital cameras have features for adjusting the color or even capturing pictures in grayscale or sepia-tone, which you can also preview on their display.

PIXELS IN THE PICTURES

A digital image is a two-dimensional matrix of pixels (picture-elements), *so many* pixels in width and *so many* in height—like a

continued...

---

graph with each square filled in with a color. This is an image's *size*. The display on your iMac, for example, is a digital image, and it can be set at a resolution that is 1,024 pixels wide and 768 pixel high—this is its size. Pixels are relative to each other by position. The dimensions of an image's data (pixels) don't tell you its size in a real-world physical way. This is where resolution comes in.

Resolution is always relative to something real, such as an inch. If you take 1,024 pixels and present them in an 8-inch wide view (perhaps a printout of some kind), you are displaying the image at a resolution of 128 pixels per inch (128 ppi). If you scan an image that is an 8 x 10-inch photograph at 300 ppi, you are generating a digital image with a size of 2,400 x 3,000 pixels. A digital image's size is always fixed in pixels, but its resolution is just a relative value, and it can be changed independently of an image's size.

Flatbed Scanning Pictures

Probably the most common method for getting photographs into a computer is by using a flatbed scanner. With a flatbed scanner, you can digitize all sorts of things: photographs, documents, drawings, and natural materials (leaves and flowers, for example). With some scanners using a special back-lit device, you can scan transparencies (there are also specialized slide scanners).

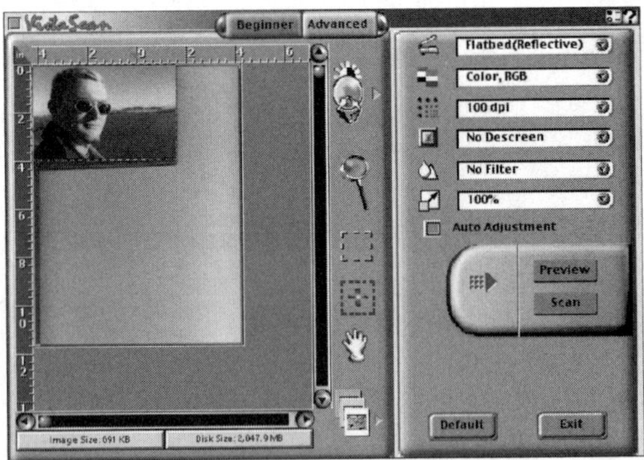

Figure 11.2 This is the scanner software interface for capturing images from a UMAX flatbed scanner.

Good quality scanners with USB interfaces are available for an extremely low price. A flatbed scanner that cost over $1,000 just two years ago can be found today for about $100. Be sure that the scanner has software that works with an iMac, and try using it at a computer retailer to see if the software makes sense to you and the image quality is good.

Many scanners will include the ability to capture images directly within software applications designed for working with images. If you use an application such as Adobe Photoshop, it can be very useful to be able to access your scanner from within Photoshop and have acquired images come up in a window for editing immediately.

In addition to capturing images yourself, there are many professional digitization services available to help get your photographs or documents turned into digital image files. The costs for these services can vary greatly, as can the results.

If you are a professional photographer and need the best possible scans of a set of slides, you can expect to pay between $40 and $80

Figure 11.3 You can get your film digitized onto Kodak PictureCD as part of Kodak development services, and delivered on CD-ROM with a cool interface for browsing and exporting your pictures.

an image, but the resulting data will be very accurate and have extremely high-resolution.

If you simply want the snapshots (film-based, of course) from a recent vacation turned into digital images for fun and enjoyment, there are many services that will put good quality, medium resolution scans on a CD and make normal photographic paper prints as well for just a few dollars more than normal development and prints.

Viewing Your Pictures

Of the various types of digital data you work with on your iMac, images are the most common and have the most support (when compared to sound and video). There are many software applications to look at and work with images. Some are simple to use, such as Picture Viewer, which came with your iMac, and others are more robust, such as Graphic Converter, which is available on the Internet as shareware. The most sophisticated, of course, are commercial products, such as Adobe Photoshop, and can cost hundreds of dollars.

Let's look at some easy solutions for looking at images of different kinds that you can use whenever you need them. We'll look at a couple ways to look at single images by themselves, as well as how to present slide shows of many images for your own amusement.

COLORS BY NUMBERS

Each pixel (picture-element) in a digital image has a single color that is created by assigning a numerical color *value*, from a range of colors in its *bit-depth* and defined by its *palette*. All digital images must have a depth and a color palette so that the values assigned to the pixels in the image have meaning. A "bitmapped" black-and-white image (without any grays) is an image with 1-bit of color depth, which means that each pixel has a numerical range of either *zero* or *one*, for a single binary bit.

continued...

Along with the depth, a color palette is defined that is an index for translating color values within the range of the color depth to perceivable colors—zero becomes black, one becomes white. But a different color palette might just as easily define pixel color values of zero to be blue and values of one to be yellow.

There are images with much larger color depths supporting larger color palettes than black-and-white, 1-bit images; there are also 8-bit color depths, 16-bit, and 24-bit.

An 8-bit image defines each pixel's color value by assigning it a number that is an eight-place binary number. This allows for 256 different values between 00000000 and 11111111, one of which might be 01101001. This value has to then be interpreted through a color palette index to find the color it represents. An 8-bit color bit-depth may seem like a lot of colors when compared to black-and-white, 1-bit images, but it is still quite limited.

With only 256 colors, it is hard to render full-color photographs, but a limited selection of colors can still render reasonable results. An 8-bit palette of colors is usually a hand-picked set of colors that facilitate a common need—such as the Mac OS system palette or the common HTML Web palette. However, 8-bits can also be used as what is known as a *color channel*.

CHANNELS OF COLOR

Another way of creating a color palette is to use the color range of 8-bits (256 values) to define a saturation and brightness scale for a single color: a color channel. For example, a grayscale image uses a white color channel, which starts with black as a low value and blends smoothly to white as a high value, providing 254 grays in-between. This is enough color steps to produce continuous looking results—your eye can't distinguish between two adjacent colors (grays). With a grayscale color palette (channel), you can reproduce a beautiful, full-range black-and-white photograph with realistic results. But what about full color?

To create full color in a digital image, there is a 24-bit color depth that can be used. These are actually the combination of three-

continued...

color channels: 8-bits for Red, 8-bits for Green, 8-bits for Blue. By combining and mixing the values for these three "additive" colors, you can create just about any color hue, with any brightness from black to a fully saturated color and all the way on to white, all from a possible 16.7 million color values. This is what your iMac display uses when it is set to millions of colors. It can realistically render just about any continuous tone, full-color photograph.

You may also have heard of 32-bit color. This is a color format that doesn't give you more colors, rather it is 24-bit color range with a fourth 8-bit channel added called an *alpha-channel* which provides transparency. With these additional 8-bits, a pixel can have any of 256 values of visual transparency—at one end being completely clear and on the other being completely solid, in the middle being 50% transparent.

One last common color depth to be aware of is 16-bit color. With a 16-bit color depth, a pixel can be any one of 32,768 colors. This is far fewer than 24-bit, but still quite good, rendering a full-color range with only minimal perceivable steps between continuous tones.

Images Everywhere

There are images everywhere on your iMac screen—it is itself a picture. There are pictures on Web pages, some embedded as elements of the pages, and others that are framed within pages for presentation. There are also images on CD-ROM available as stock photography. Many times you get to an image via an image viewer; for example, while browsing the Web you locate and view images all at once. However, if you should get image files themselves (perhaps someone sends you an image file attached to an email, you download one, or capture it with a digital camera), you will want to view it with something.

To view an image file, you'll need to open it with a software application that can read that file type and display it. You'll probably also want some options on how to display the image—fitting it to your screen if it is very large (too big to see all at once), or perhaps presenting it full-screen without a menu bar or other interface items next to, around, or on top of the image.

Figure 11.4 One of the many places to find pictures is `Zing.com`, which allows individuals to post their image collections.

DIGITAL COMPRESSION

Whenever you are dealing with digital data (image, sound, video), you'll run into the concept of compression. Normally, digital image data is linear, each pixel described individually. This can make image data very lengthy, slow for reading and writing, processing, and big to store—lots of bytes for each pixel of a digital image, increasing exponentially with size and depth. There have been many efficient methods invented for managing and storing this data in compressed forms so that it takes up less space and is faster to access. Compression of data comes in two general types: lossless and lossy.

LOSSLESS COMPRESSION

Lossless compression means that when data is encoded, none of the original data is lost. A good example of this is LZW compres

continued…

sion (short for the name of its inventor, Lempel Zev Welch), and it describes their dimension instead of spelling out each pixel. For example, if you have a string of 345 white pixels in an image, it is far simpler to just record the color white once with the length of that string of pixels, rather than recording 345 individual white pixels. If an image has few, if any, continuous regions of color, perhaps it is all a noisy pattern; then it won't compress well using this method. Of course, *lossless* compression makes more sense when you consider the term *lossy* compression

LOSSY COMPRESSION

Another common way to compress data is to throw away irrelevant parts of it, or details that cannot be perceived by the viewer, meaning that the decompressed image isn't quite the same as the one you started with. Lossy compression can achieve much higher compression rates than lossless methods.A good example of this is JPEG compression (short for the name of the group that came up with its algorithm, Joint Photographic Experts Group), which compresses either full-color or grayscale images of natural, real-world scenes. JPEG is designed to exploit known limitations of the human eye, notably the fact that small color changes are perceived less accurately than small changes in brightness. So a region with subtle color shifts gets reduced to a single hue, but areas of brightness, like a cloud in a sky, are left with more detail. Thus, JPEG is intended for compressing images that will be looked at by humans. If you plan to machine-analyze your images, the small errors introduced by JPEG may be a problem for you, even if they are invisible to the eye.

Another important aspect of JPEG is that decoding applications can trade off decoding speed against image quality, by using fast but inaccurate approximations to the required calculations. Some image viewers obtain remarkable speedups in this way. (Encoders can also trade accuracy for speed, but there's usually less reason to make such a sacrifice when writing a file.)

Easy Image File Viewing

The easiest way to view images on your iMac is to use a piece of
software that comes with QuickTime called *Picture Viewer*. While
this program has a few neat options for presenting an image, it has
one huge advantage—namely that it will view just about any file format you come across. It works because it uses QuickTime to
decode image data, and QuickTime is designed to support and
decode a wide range of data types for images, sound, and video.

Picture Viewer came with your iMac because your iMac has
QuickTime preinstalled. You can, of course, get the latest version
of QuickTime from the Apple Web site.

Figure 11.5   PictureViewer comes with your iMac as part of
QuickTime. It is a great simple utility for viewing just about every
image format there is.

To use Picture Viewer you can drag an image file icon onto its
icon, or possibly just double-click on the image file. If you don't
have the software that was used to create the image file originally,
your iMac will likely ask you which of the available applications
you'd like to view the file with, and Picture Viewer will be one of
them.

When you have an image open in Picture viewer, you can view the
image at different sizes by selecting them from the Image menu.
You can select half size, normal size, double size, and fill screen.
Picture viewer is a very simple application. While it does allow you
to resize the window an image is being displayed within, you can't
scroll around in an oversized image.

Picture Viewer can also be used to save an image to another file in any of the formats that QuickTime supports, which is very useful. You can open a TIF file and save it as a JPEG file for previewing in a Web browser, or open a PICT image and save it as a BMP file for your friends who use Windows PCs.

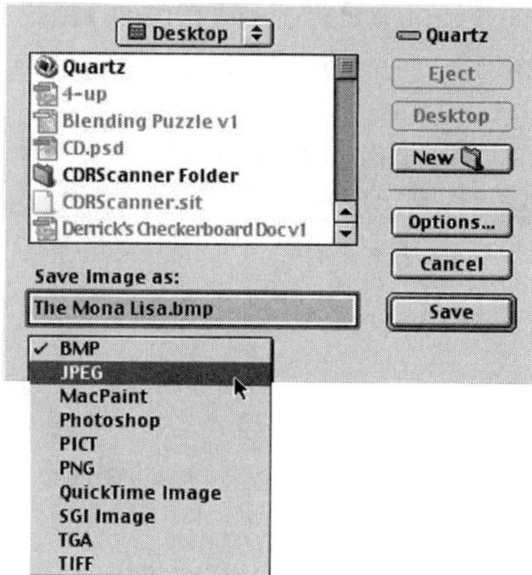

Figure 11.6 You can export any image open in PictureViewer to any of the formats in this menu.

When you are exporting an image, you can select any of the format types available for that file, and then by clicking the Options button, you can specify the setting for the file supported by that format. For example, when you select JPEG, you have options for color depth, compression quality, or alternately you can specify a target size for the data, which will limit the quality to meet that goal.

Viewing Pictures Using Mac OS X

Viewing image files is also very easy if you are running Mac OS X. Instead of using the PictureViewer application, use the Preview application. It will open and display image data in any of the dozens of formats that are supported directly by Mac OS X, including PDF (Portable Document Format), which is its native graphics language.

Easy Slide Shows

If you have a whole lot of pictures you'd like to look at, there is software designed for more robust viewing of images. Such applications have features for organizing image files as well as presenting them. One really good image presentation software application is iView Multimedia, a $25 shareware product available at `http://www.iview-multimedia.com/`. A good alternative to iView is Graphic Converter, which also has slideshow features.

Figure 11.7 iView Multimedia is a great application for creating slideshow presentations of images.

FILE FORMATS

The file types and formats in which digital image data are written affect the ability for that image to be opened and viewed on different computer systems with different software. Some formats are designed for specific computer platforms, others for containing specific compression types, and still others for portability and easy display such as on the World Wide Web. Let's look at a few of the most common.

Note that many software applications have their own variations of these file formats, or have their own proprietary formats, which only they can use (such as Adobe Photoshop image files), but, in general, standard image formats are interchangeable between applications.

continued…

PICT Images

All the images displayed on your iMac screen must have a common structure or a format so that software can create images for you to see. This format is called *PICT* (the Mac OS file type code for *picture*), and it is part of the system software called *QuickDraw*, which is used to display them. When you make a screenshot of your iMac screen (by pressing ⌘-Shift-3, for example), the image data is written into a PICT format file. PICT images can be in any color depth and at any size. They can even support different types of compression and even object-graphics. They are very flexible, and can be used by most Mac software applications. However, PICT files will not work well with Internet applications or other computer platforms.

BMP Images

The common image file format on Windows PCs is BMP (short for bitmap) and also known as a Paint document. It is similar to PICT in that it is a format that is native to an operating system. As an iMac user, you are unlikely to see many BMP files.

JPEG Images

The most modern format to use for display images on Web pages and for working with huge photographic images is JPEG. JPEG images are images formatted with JPEG compression, and they can be created from many image editing software applications. JPEG files must be in full-color or grayscale. They don't support alpha transparency channels.

JPEG is used heavily on Web sites because it can be very aggressive at reducing file sizes for fast downloading of low-bandwidth modems. It supports progressive rendering, which means that it can be rendered as it is downloaded, allowing the viewer to display the elements of the image that are available, and adding detail as it arrives.

GIF Images

Mostly used as a Web graphics format, GIF images (say *gah-if*; is short for Graphic Interchange Format) are designed to be easy to render on any computer system. This special format has a limited

continued...

color depth and simplistic organization so that computers of limited speed and display ability can receive the images efficiently over networks. GIF was created in the early 1980s, and it is patented by CompuServe. GIF version 89a is limited to an 8-bit maximum internal color palette and supports the use of transparency in a single color, interlacing for low-resolution previewing and multi-frame animation. GIF incorporates LZW lossless compression.

PNG Images

Portable Network Graphics is an extensible file format for the lossless, portable, well-compressed storage of raster images. While not yet in mainstream use, PNG provides a patent-free replacement for GIF and can also replace many common uses of TIFF. Indexed-color, grayscale, and true-color images are supported, plus an optional alpha channel. Sample depths range from 1 to 16 bits per channel.

PNG is designed for Internet browsing applications, and it is fully streamable with progressive display options. PNG is robust, providing both full file integrity checking and simple detection of common transmission errors. Also, PNG can store gamma correction and chromaticity data for improved color matching on different computing platforms.

TIF Images

Probably the most commonly recognized file format, TIF (or TIFF, Tagged Image File format) image files are an open standard. TIF is a flexible image file with tag fields for each element of an image's data, which allows TIF to be used for just about any combination of color image channels and uses, including RGB, CMYK, LAB, grayscale, duo-tone, alpha channels, and even application-specific custom fields. While TIF is understood by most image editing applications, not all forms of TIF will necessarily be compatible. TIF files can be different for Mac and PC use, and can contain compression. TIF images are not generally supported for Internet browsing.

Using iView, you can create catalogs of image files on your hard drive, give them an order, view the files as a list, view thumbnails of the images, and view each image individually. You can also present them full-screen as a slideshow, with smooth fading transitions and for different lengths of time.

Creating Images

Digital images can come from two sources: acquired or created. When you download an image from a Web site, capture an image with a digital camera, digitize an image with a flat-bed scanner, or have traditional photographic slides or negatives digitized professionally onto a Kodak PhotoCD, you are acquiring an image. When you make an image on your computer from scratch, perhaps by taking a screenshot or painting and drawing an image on your computer, you are creating it.

There are many ways you can capture images from the real world and bring them into your iMac. You can get images on the Internet, use a digital camera, scan a photograph at home, or even send out for professional digitization service.

Downloading Images from the Internet

There are millions of interesting images on the Internet available for you to use. There are thousands of personal and commercial sites dedicated to photography and digital imagery. While most good imagery that you'll find is copyrighted, you can use whatever you find for personal use—just on your iMac (you are not allowed to distribute or sell copyrighted materials).

You can capture an image from a Web site in a number of ways. If you are using Internet Explorer, you can simply drag an image from a Web page onto your desktop, automatically downloading it into a file on your hard drive. You can also Control-click on the image to reveal a contextual menu of viewing and downloading options.

There are also commercial sites with photographs which you can buy in different forms, including a downloadable image file, or even as a print in your choice of frame. When it comes to finding a

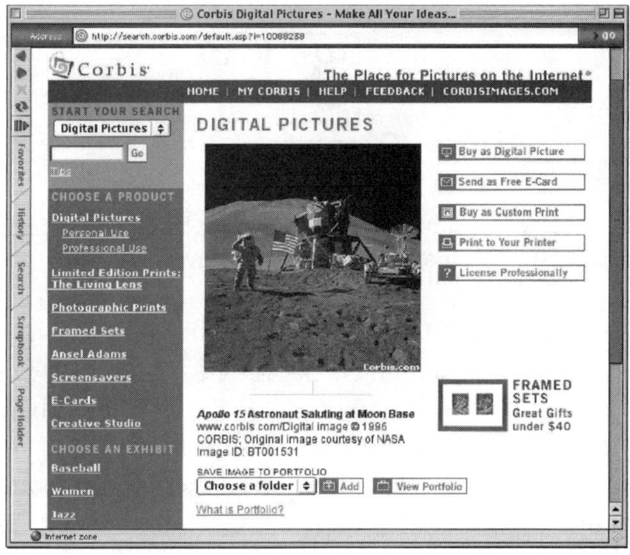

Figure 11.8 This image of astronauts on the Moon is available from Corbis as a downloadable (640 x 480 pixel) image for $3.

picture of something, no matter how obscure, the Internet is an amazing resource.

Making Images Yourself

If you feel so inclined, creating imagery from scratch on your iMac is a great alternative to capturing images from outside your iMac. You can capture images directly from the screen, paint original artwork, or draw detailed schematics.

Screenshots

If at any time there is something on your screen that you'd like to create a digital image file from, simply press ⌘-Shift-3, and your iMac will take a screenshot of it. When this command is executed, you'll hear a camera shutter-click sound and a PICT file will be created on the top level of your hard drive named Picture 1 (or numbered further in order). A screenshot will look just like what is on your screen, with every pixel and at the same resolution.

Figure 11.9 When you take a screenshot by typing ⌘-Shift-3, a file such as this is created on your hard drive.

You can also use a different screenshot command to capture a selected portion of the screen by pressing ⌘-Shift-4. When this command is selected, your cursor will become a cross-hair, and you can click and drag out a rectangle around whatever you'd like to capture. A file will be created in the same manner as before, but only will contain the area you marked. Clicking without moving the mouse will escape this function (as will pressing the Esc key).

If you enable the Caps Lock key while the ⌘-Shift-4 area capture function is active, you can capture the area of a window just by clicking once on it. This function will change the cursor to a bullet-target for selecting the window you want to capture.

There are also software applications and system extensions available as shareware and commercially that add more extensive screen capturing abilities. These are required for capturing things that tend to be in motion or are active only temporarily, such as pull-down menus, cursors, or other types of animation.

> ### GRABBING THE SCREEN
>
> If you are using Mac OS X, you'll need to use the special screen-capturing application called *Grab*. You can find it in your Utilities folder within Applications. Grab lets you capture a selection, a window, the whole screen, or a timed screen automatically after 10 seconds, which is useful for catching animated interfaces when you need to be clicking to reveal something like a pop-up menu, rather than on the controls for Grab.

Painting

There are many great software applications for painting your own digital images. Such applications vary from the simplistic and child-oriented, to advanced ones with realistic material simulation for the professional artist. Of course, every painting application can be the tool of choice for any skill level.

Your iMac may have come with several software applications which have painting capabilities, including: AppleWorks, KidPix Deluxe, or Kai's Photo Soap. With any application that allows you to paint, you can save your artwork as an image data file that can be opened and imported into other software applications.

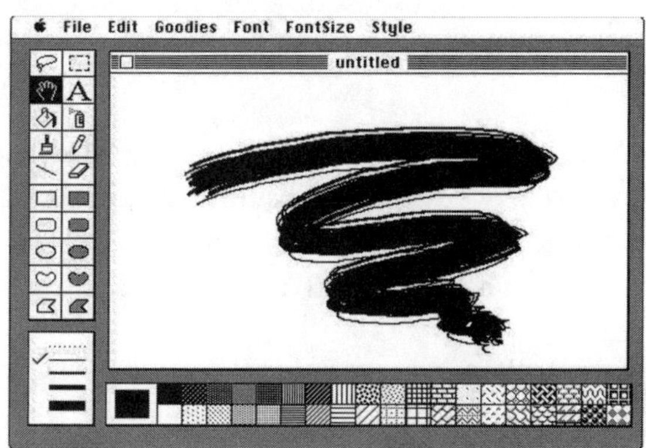

Figure 11.10   It all started with MacPaint on the original Macintosh in 1984, the most basic of painting applications.

Paint is a specific computer term to describe using software tools such as a pencil, paint brush, or airbrush, which apply color to a pixel-based image by pressing the mouse button while dragging the tools around on the screen. MacPaint was the very first painting application, and much of what it was, is still a part of AppleWorks today (which is directly descended from the original MacPaint, MacWrite, and MacDraw software applications).

Figure 11.11 KidPix Deluxe is essentially an advanced form of MacPaint with special features and sounds geared to the child artist.

Painting on a Mac is a great past-time of young iMac users, and there are several great software applications geared toward the inventiveness and imagination of the young-at-heart. Among these, the most developed is KidPix Deluxe. It has the same painting

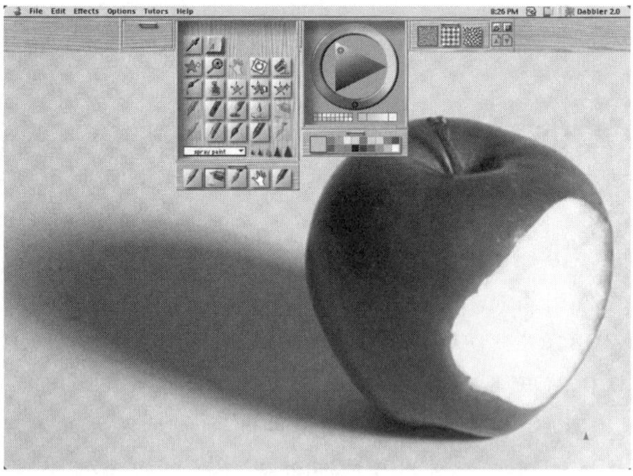

Figure 11.12 Corel Dabbler and Painter are advanced painting applications that are capable of producing very natural looking artwork by using simulated media such as oils, watercolors, pens, and pastels.

tools as most basic paint programs, but it adds sounds to punctuate each brush-stroke, as well as special animated tools that do unexpected things that are best discovered on your own. Finger painting was never this good.

For the advanced artist who wants realistic looking results with traditional materials and textures, there are some amazing commercial applications. The best of these is probably Corel Painter (which has changed ownership several times, formerly Fractal Design, and then MetaCreations). It has hundred of tools for different types of media including inks, charcoals, pastels, watercolor, oils, and even artificial metallic flowing paints. It also uses paper-like textures to give the media a realistic appearance on rough or smooth surfaces. Lower-end versions of the application geared for a consumer audience (Painter Classic and Dabbler) have many of the same capabilities but a simplified interface.

With any of these painting applications, you can also use pen-based input devices, which allow you to use an electronic pen on the surface of a special tablet to digitize your finger movements, much more naturally. Devices such as the Wacom Graphite tablet sense the movement of the pen at high resolutions, as well as the pressure of touch and even the angle the pen is held, allowing software to produce very realistic simulations of ink and paint flow and movement.

Drawing

Technically, drawing is not a function of digital image data, rather it is an object-oriented environment where the boxes, lines, text, and other objects are each mathematical descriptions of those shapes—not pixel renderings of them in a digital image matrix. However, if you need a more structured or technical look to your illustrations, you'll probably find it useful to use a drawing application rather than one designed with free-flow painting in mind.

Figure 11.13 Adobe Illustrator is a very advanced drawing application that supports elaborate color blending of geometrically defined shapes.

There are many software applications devoted to drawing and illustration, such as AppleWorks, which has MacDraw-like tools, or Adobe Illustrator, which has advanced, path-based drawing capabilities. Most drawing applications can render an image to a pixel-based image data file for you to use and manipulate, perhaps for including on a Web page.

One minute of sitting, one inch of glass,
Like lightning all images come and pass.
Just once look within the screen:
Where everything has ever been.

Chapter Twelve

Digital Image Editing

Perhaps the best part about digital images is editing them. You can do a lot to a digital image while maintaining its quality and realism. You can do simple things to adjust an image's size and proportions, you can use dark-room like tools to adjust an image's color or contrast, and you can do advanced compositing of images together to create special effects. You can even run algorithmic digital filters to change the overall quality of an image, such as sharpening it, adding motion blur, or even making it look like a watercolor painting. In fact, many of the most advanced Hollywood film effects are created with Macs by using these very same techniques.

There are many software applications that are good at image editing—the best is Adobe Photoshop, but there are others that are very good and cost much less. One of them that is good and inexpensive is Graphic Converter, which is shareware and available on the Internet at `http://www.lemkesoft.com`. It even runs native under Mac OS X. Let's look at some of the basic image editing functions you can do on your iMac. You can crop, resample, modify, rebalance, and filter digital images to enhance and change them.

In this chapter we're going to look at:

- ➢ Cropping the dimensions and resampling the size of images
- ➢ Retouching and compositing images
- ➢ Adjusting the tone and color of images
- ➢ Filtering to blur, sharpen, distort, or modify images
- ➢ Preparing images for use on Web pages

Making a Good Image

A digital photograph that looks its best is very much the same as making a traditional photographic print. You use the same artistic techniques used in the darkroom to take an image and enhance it to achieve the most appealing results. You can crop your subject, adjust the contrast, brighten colors, sharpen details, and even burn in highlights and dodge out shadows. Fortunately, no chemical baths are needed, and you don't have to work in the dark.

The key to any artistic expression is experimentation. Try different settings and options. Also use the features of image editing software to undo and redo a change to quickly see its effect—you may be

Figure 12.1 Before and after, this original, unadjusted image gets a makeover. It is from Point Reyes, California (photo by Hans Hansen).

surprised to make an adjustment which you think is very subtle, but when quickly hidden and reshown, is dramatic.

Cropping and Resampling Image Dimension

When you want to change the size of an image, you are either cropping it or resampling it. Cropping an image is the same as cropping in the real world—you are trimming off sides of the image to change its horizontal and vertical dimensions. However, if you want to change an image's size, either to lower or raise its resolution—perhaps you want to take a very high-resolution image of many megs in size and reduce it to a much smaller file that you can put into a Web page—you'll need to resample it.

Figure 12.2 Using image-editing software to crop an image entails selecting a region to trim the image to.

Resampling an Image

Resampling is a digital process of interpreting the pixels of an image into fewer pixels (or into more pixels if increasing the resolution) by averaging the color of adjacent pixels into a single pixel (or into many more). As an image is resampled down, it will become somewhat blurred; however, this can be compensated for by sharpening the image by using a filter. Resampling is a very processor-intensive task that can take quite a long time to complete for large image files.

There are less perfect algorithms that are much faster, such as subsampling, which rather than averaging the pixels together, simply drops all but one of the pixels from a group of pixels (reducing an image to half drops every other pixel, reducing an image to one-third drops two of every three pixels).

Increasing the resolution of an image cannot add more detail to the image; however, it can give it a soft smooth look that sometimes can be more desirable than hard-edged pixels.

Cropping Your Subject

The first thing to do with any photograph is to crop it so that the subject of the photograph is well framed. However, this doesn't mean that you should center the subject in the image. The best

Figure 12.3 This image has been cropped tightly horizontally, putting emphasis on the skyline as well as the distance between the foreground rocks and the distant hills.

photographs have dynamic elements that tell a story—a subject that is presented in contrast to a background or other elements. So it is just as important to consider the entire image when framing your subject.

You might want to crop the image so that the subject is off-center, or even near an edge, allowing the background to be big and thus impart a sense of depth and vastness. Or you might want the subject cropped close to impart a sense of confinement in a tight space.

Retouching Image Details

In years past, modifying a photograph by retouching it involved extraordinary skill and artistic prowess, using Xacto knives to slice

Figure 12.4 The possibilities are limitless when you get into photo retouching.

up images and paste them together, or to airbrush the skin of a model to a creamy smoothness, or perhaps to simply clean up scratches and dust specks with spot-tone. Today, digital editing removes the challenges of realistic image manipulation, allowing new levels of imagination. The pyramids of Egypt can be moved for aesthetic perfection, a can of soft drink can be removed from the table in front of a world leader for the cover of a news magazine, or alien spaceships can hover over New York City.

In addition to somewhat traditional techniques, there are some image manipulation tools that are uniquely digital. For example, Adobe Photoshop has a clone tool that allows you to point to a location on an image and then paint it somewhere else on the same image or on a different image, allowing you to take a detail and blend it in somewhere else. While this can be used to give someone a third eye, or duplicate one person into a crowd of people, it is most useful for duplicating subtle textures from one part of an image to modify another part.

Adjusting Tone and Range

With a digital image, it is easy to change its color palette and the relative levels of pixel brightness, contrast, and saturation. You can invert the colors of an image, perhaps turning a scan of a film negative into a positive image. You can subtly or dramatically change the hue of the image turning all the colors into others—twisting the color wheel, for example, making reds to greens, greens to blues, blues to yellows, and yellows to reds. You can increase the contrast to make an image's shadows blacker and highlights whiter, or decrease the contrast to make the image grayer (sometimes for a more natural softness). You can increase the saturation of an image's colors making them stronger—a dull color becoming a bright and intense color—or decrease saturation to make a colorful image a black-and-white grayscale, or with only subtle coloring.

Any of these adjustments can also be done on sections of a digital image instead of the whole by selecting regions of pixels to affect.

Figure 12.5 You can adjust an image's color palette for realistic and subtle effects, or not.

Some image editing applications also allow you to make alpha-channel selections where the edges of a selection are soft and have transparency in them, so you could change the color of the sky independent of a foreground subject and have a soft natural edge between them.

Adjusting Contrast

The second step in making a good image is to adjust the color depth so that the highlights (whitest areas) and the shadows (blackest areas) are suitably bright and dark. Adjusting the color levels so that blacks are black, and whites are white will make the photo seem more real and make details easier to distinguish.

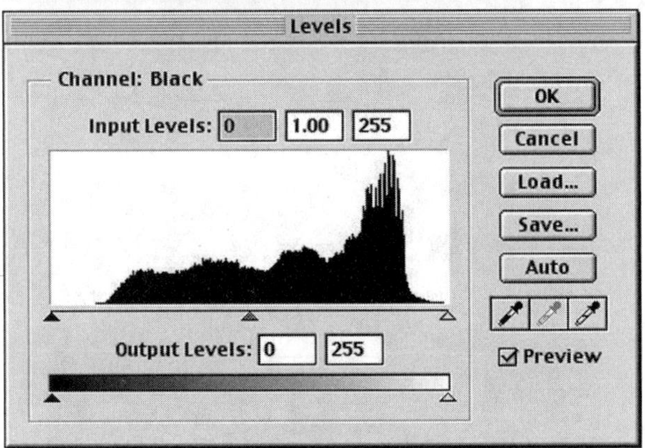

Figure 12.6 In this stage, the image has been leveled to reduce the grayness of the image, bringing the lightest point to white, and the darkest to black.

The goal of adjusting contrast (color levels) is to reduce the appearance of muddiness, or grayness, within the image. If you prefer to have a low-contrast image with a very soft appearance, first adjust the levels to optimize the contrast; then evenly reduce the contrast by adjusting the highlights darker and the shadows lighter.

Filtering Effects

Filtering used to be done by adding special lenses in front of cameras, some to soften an image, others to add distortion or texture. With a computer there are all sorts of filter operations that can be applied to the data of an image. All filters are actually mathematical computer programs that do something to the data of an image, be it a simple transformation or a complex one. A simple filter might be one that blurs an image by mathematically smearing the values of pixels into adjacent pixels. A complex filter might be one that distorts it into a spherical shape while considering the prismatic optical bending of glass over different wavelength of colored light (very complex indeed). Let's look at the effects of several common filter types.

Blur Effects

When you want to obscure an image, or a portion of an image, you can use a blur filter to blend its pixels together so that the image's details appear out of focus.

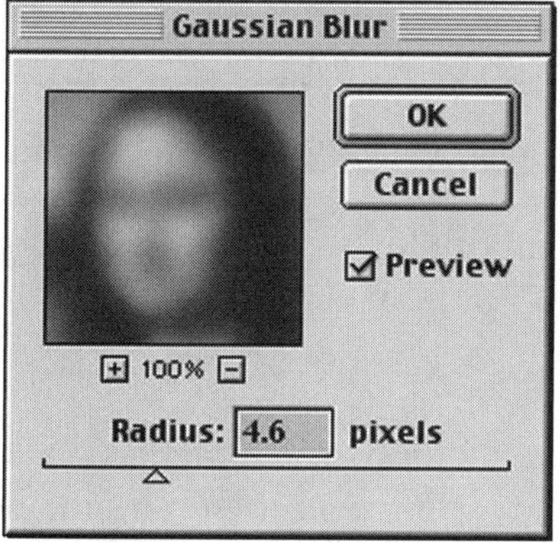

Figure 12.7 To create an out-of-focus appearance, blur your image.

There are many varieties of blurring methods and algorithms for different effects. Normal and Gaussian blur are natural looking focus adjustments, but there are also motion blur effects, which appear to blur along a straight line (only in one direction), giving the appearance of movement.

Sharpen Effects

When you want to increase the clarity of details in an image, you might want to sharpen it. This technique increases the contrast of an image only in areas where there is already contrast, such as along edges of objects or in textures. Sharpening is applied

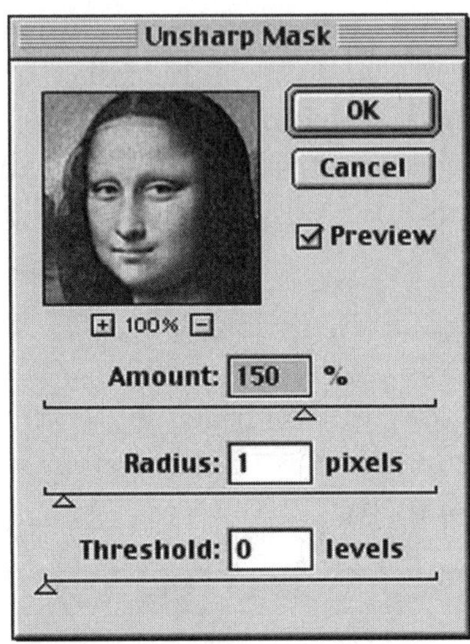

Figure 12.8 To bring out blurry details, try sharpening your image.

inversely of blurring. While the results of sharpening can be dramatic, they can also make an image appear blotchy and unnatural if oversharpened.

The best sharpening methods use a method called Unsharp mask, which combines sharpening over the entire image with a blurred mask of the image so that areas without detail such as smooth tones like a sky don't get sharpened, while the areas of detail are affected. One obvious defect of sharpening is the creation of halos along the edges of objects where light-colored backgrounds become even lighter near the edges of objects.

With your image framed and adjusted you should try sharpening its details and blurring things you want to obscure. When sharpening, try not to overdo it. Keep the image from appearing too textured or unrealistically hard-edged. Try to keep from introducing digital artifacts, such as jagged edges and white halos around your subject.

Alternatively to sharpening, blurring can be a powerful way to improve the dynamics of an image, allowing you to create more

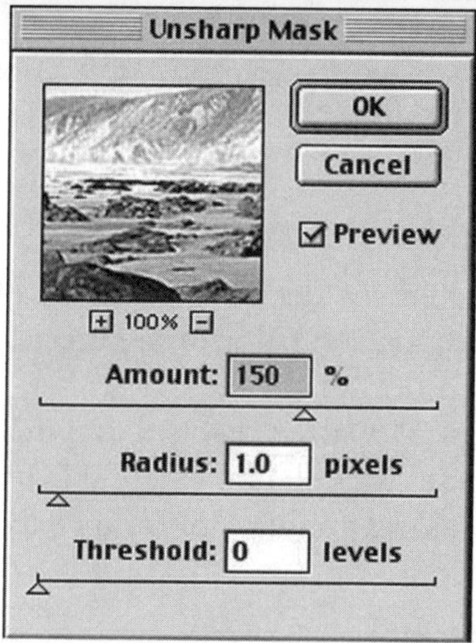

Figure 12.9 In this image, the whole image has been sharpened substantially to emphasize the textures on the rocks and hills. The sky has been blurred slightly to smooth out film grain and digital artifacts.

distance between foreground and background or by suppressing busy patterns that distract from the subject.

Distortion Effects

Other types of filters that can create dramatic effects are those that distort an image, bending it and twisting it at different angles and with different shapes. These algorithms are highly mathematical, usually taking the pixel data of an image and projecting it onto a geometrical extrusion.

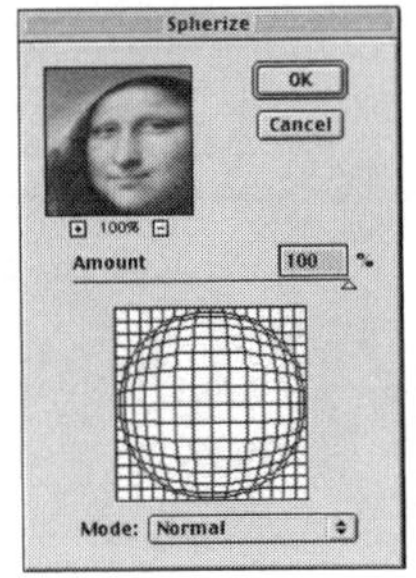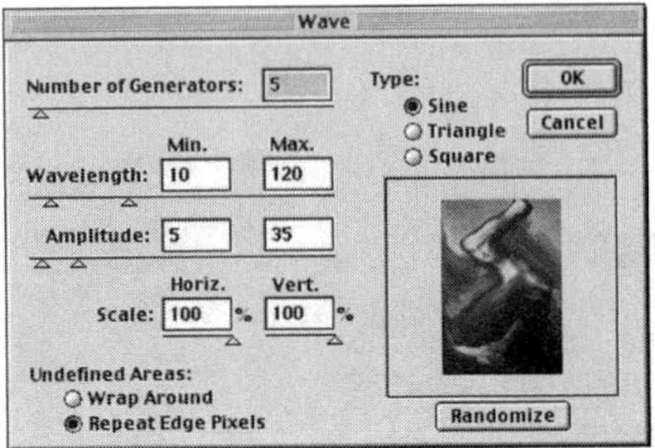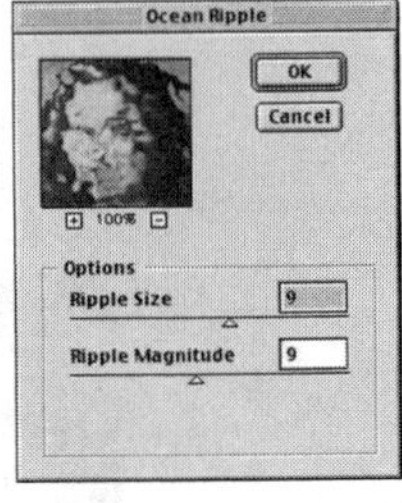

Figure 12.10 There are many filters to distort images, for example Spherize, Ocean Ripple, and Wave.

Lighting Effects

Some filters don't affect the detail or the shape of an image, but instead affect the lighting and color of the image. The most dramatic of these is Photoshop's lighting effects filter, which allows you to position and adjust virtual spotlights on an image to give it the appearance of being lit with natural external light. For example, this can be useful for creating a studio appearance to a photograph of a product or an object.

Another popular lighting effect is lens flare, which adds realistic-looking camera lens "sun spots" to an image to create an

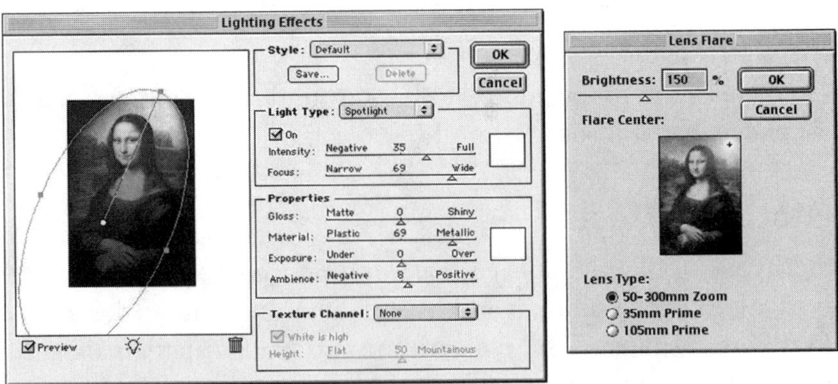

Figure 12.11 Some filters affect the lighting in an image, for example, Lighting Effects and Lens Flare.

appearance of a photograph being imaged by a 35mm camera with a complex compound lens. Several different lens options are available, and the position of the bright spot that the spots are reflecting can be moved.

Artistic Effects

The fanciest filters are those which use a combination of methods and techniques to create complex effects that tend to simulate traditional textiles and media, such as film grain, oil paint, watercolor, pastels and charcoals, pen and pencil drawing, and even surreal pointillist effects.

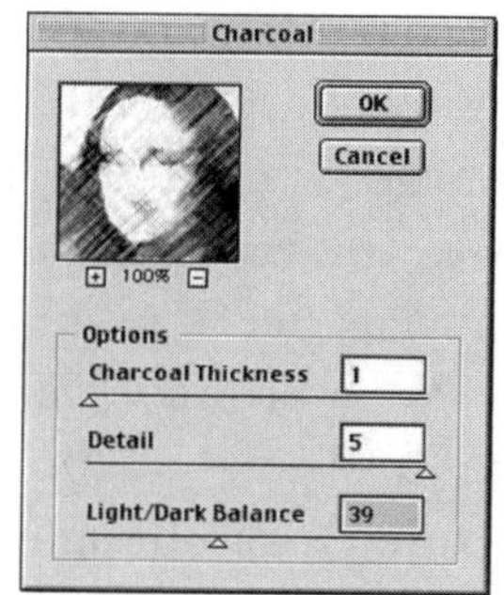

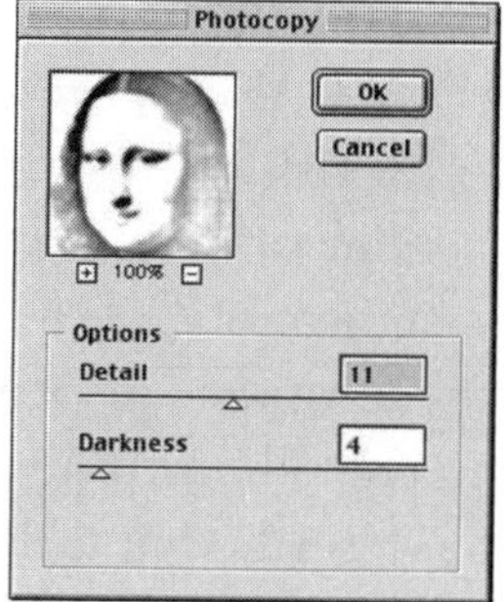

Figure 12.12 There are many filters to transform an image into a realistic texture effect, for example, Watercolor, Charcoal, and Photocopy.

Images on Your Web Pages

Putting images on your Web site can be very easy; you simply save them in a Web browser readable format such as JPEG or GIF. The difficult part is making your images small enough so that they transfer over slow modem connections efficiently. However, if you compress an image to make it very small (only a few thousand bytes) so it will download in just a couple seconds over a 56 K modem, you will probably find that it looks bad—its details blurred or its colors tinted and broken up. If you don't compress an image at all (retaining every byte of the original uncompressed image), it could take a very long time to download and be frustrating for anyone viewing your Web site. You need to balance the file size of a compressed image against the quality of the detail of the image itself.

There are two parts to optimizing an image for use on the Web: adjusting dimension (height, width, and color depth) and specifying compression options.

Adjusting Dimensions

Adjusting the dimension of an image is an obvious way to make sure that you're not providing more image data than is needed to view the details of your image. Many people overlook this because HTML Web pages allow you to specify the size (width and height in pixels) to present an image. Even if its natural dimensions are smaller or larger, a browser will resize the image on the fly to fit the specifications of the <img> tag. So, if an image is larger than a typical computer display, the Web browser can present a reduced image. The problem with this is that all those extra pixels have to be described and downloaded even though only a portion of them will be used when displayed.

Whenever you are making a Web page that will have images in it, you should adjust their size to match the space that they will take up on the page. And you should design your Web page so that the images can be reasonably small—so that the page isn't just one huge image (or even a bunch of huge images). If the purpose of the page is to present images that need to be large, use a thumbnail image menu so that the visitor can choose which to look at, one at a time.

Adjusting Size

Adjusting the size of your image is easy. Use your image editing software to resample or crop the width and height of your image to the dimensions you need for your page.

When you are designing your Web page, choose a standard width that you think is reasonable for people to view comfortably on the monitors they use. Most people typically have computer displays that have a pixel dimension of approximately 800 x 600, so most Web pages tend to be designed to be about 600 pixels wide. If your largest image is smaller than your Web page, you might choose for it to be about 450 pixels wide. Use your image editing software to resample the image's width to 450 (with the height proportionally equal, of course).

Adjusting Color Depth

In addition to the width and height of an image not being larger than necessary, you should also consider how much color depth your image requires. Both JPEG and GIF have different options for color depth, so for now simply consider the larger color depths of 24-bit, 16-bit, and 8-bit.

First, consider that if your image is a 24-bit (millions of colors) photograph, instead you can use 16-bit (thousands of colors), which is barely distinguishable from 24-bit but is a third less data (also consider that most computer users don't have the 24-bit display capabilities of an iMac).

Next, consider whether or not the quality and the detail of your image will work well in 8-bit (256 colors). If it is a natural scene photograph, it probably will not look as good as an 8-bit image—so plan on using JPEG compression, which is good for photographs. If the image is a graphic such as a logo with solid color areas, or an image with less color range, such as a black-and-white photograph or full-color photograph but of mostly similar hues (such as clouds in a blue sky), the image will probably work well with just 8-bit color (or even fewer perhaps). Plan on using GIF compression, which is good for custom color indexes and images with solid areas of color.

You can use your image editing software to change the color mode of your image before compressing it, or you can simply choose the color depth as part of the compression process. Often, you have more control over the image if you adjust the color depth before compression because most image editing applications don't give you options for manipulating the details of an image in the process of saving an image with compression.

Improving Color

If you are working with a full-color image (not a black-and-white grayscale image as reproduced in this book), you will likely want to improve the color saturation, and possibly adjust the color balance. Many digitized images have an undersaturated appearance (fewer appear oversaturated). This means that those bright colors you see with your eyes tend to appear a bit bland or understated on-screen. Use your image editing software to adjust the color saturation to an appealing point. While the inclination may be to turn up the saturation a lot, don't oversaturate an image either. If the colors are unnaturally bright, blowing out (losing detail), or bleeding into adjacent details in the image, turn the saturation down. For effect, you might also try turning the color saturation down very low to give the appearance of a black-and-white photograph with subtle hand-coloring (a saturation level of zero is pure grayscale).

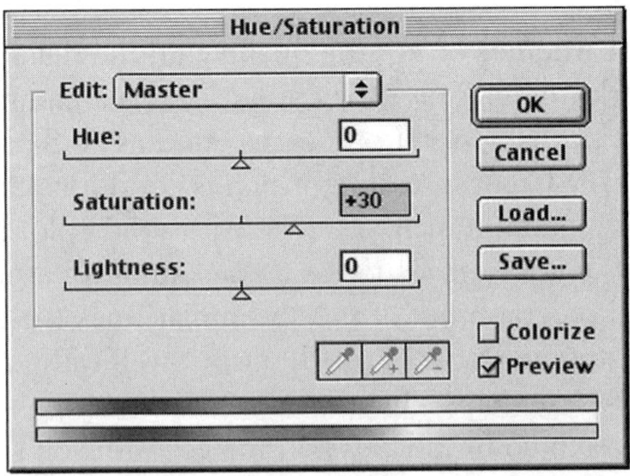

Figure 12.13 Adjusting the color of an image can be subtle yet very effective for bringing it to life, particularly increasing the saturation.

You might also find that the color in your image has shifted and is not very natural appearing. You can adjust the color balance (also known as the hue). The best way to do this is to look at the whites in an image and adjust the color so that they don't appear bluish or yellowish, but a natural white. Many image-editing applications have tools to help do this automatically, using a selected neutral gray within the image.

Specifying Image Compression Options

It is difficult to predict the outcome of compression, and ultimately you will need to try compressing an image several times with different compression methods and settings to perfect your results. You may be surprised to find that GIF works well on some full-color photographs, providing a very small file size while maintaining the best quality. Or you may find the opposite to be true, that JPEG gives you the best results for images that typically work better with GIF.

JPEG Quality Settings

When you are optimizing an image for the Web with JPEG compression, you essentially want to choose the lowest quality setting

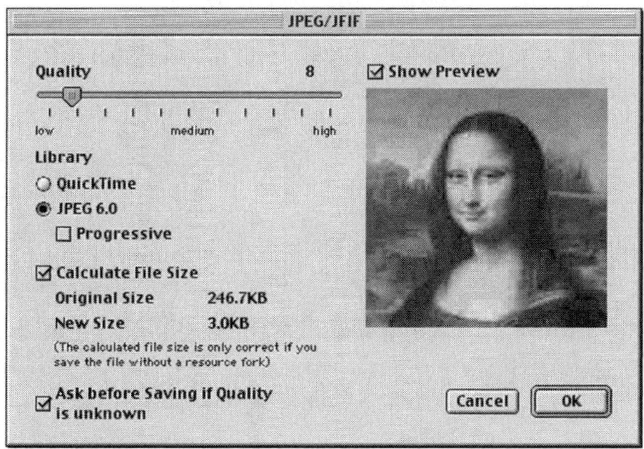

Figure 12.14 Adjust the JPEG quality setting to achieve the smallest possible file without compromising the detail of your image.

(from between 0 and 10), which provides the most compression while suitably capturing the detail of the image, probably so that the viewer won't look at it and notice any compression defects such as blurring or color-stepping.

The only JPEG option beyond the compression quality setting is the ability to encode the file in a progressive downloading method. This allows your Web browser to begin showing the image data as it is downloaded, beginning with a low-resolution preview of the entire image and adding in resolution as it is received.

GIF Color Palette Dithering

When you are optimizing an image for the Web using the GIF file format, you first want to adjust the number of colors to the fewest needed to capture the detail of the original. Different imaging software applications have different methods for changing color depth, but with some experimentation, you will find that you can reduce the number of colors substantially while maintaining your image.

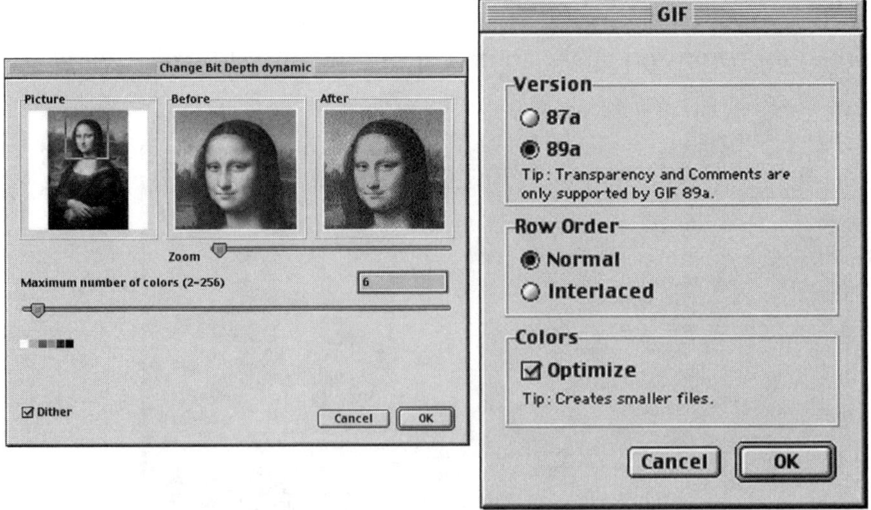

Figure 12.15 Adjust the number of colors to as few as possible without compromising the detail of your image before saving it as a GIF.

When you are working with indexed color palettes (used for 8-bit or fewer color depths), you will usually have an option for dithering that can create smoother color transitions and provide the appearance of color mixing.

After you have reduced the number of colors to a minimum, you can save the image as a **GIF** file. **GIF** has fewer compression options because all GIF file use the same built-in methods for encoding the image data (while JPEG has variable compression), so the GIF options are only related to special options such as transparency, interlacing, and GIF file version (87a or 89a). Transparency in a GIF file allows a single color to be chosen to become transparent, which is useful for images that you want to appear to be irregularly shaped rather than rectangular. Interlacing is similar to the JPEG progressive option, allowing for your browser to begin drawing the image at low resolution and increasing resolution as it downloads. The GIF file version should probably always be the newest, 89a, unless you are presenting your image to viewers who are using very old Web browsers that don't support the newer format.

Dodging and Burning

The last and most advanced photographic technique for improving an image is to dodge and burn. This is a traditional darkroom photograph term which describes the technique of making an area of a photograph lighter or darker by allowing more or less light exposure when printing the image to light sensitive photo-paper. Dodging usually uses a small light blocking tool, often a small solid circle attached to a wire, to keep part of an image from getting too dark and filling in details in dark shadows. Burning is often done with a card with a circular hole cut into it to protect an image from the light, while letting light through the hole to burn in the details in very light highlights, which need more exposure to darken them. This process take lots of practice and is akin to painting with light. On a computer, you have simpler controls that accomplish the same goals of darkening or lightening areas of an image.

Figure 12.16 In this last step, the finished image has been burned along the top edge to give the sky more depth, as have the hills. The rocks have been burned in while the beach has been dodged for a more natural sand appearance.

Using digital tools for dodging and burning is a powerful technique to increase the dynamics of an image, in both large areas and in small details. Making a background darker than your subject can create distance and emphasis. You can tone down bright spots for a smoother appearance, such as reflections off oily skin, or brighten dark spots, such as bringing out highlights in someone's hair, eyes, or clothes. Keep in mind the appearance of your image from a distance, and try to keep it from having one tone throughout.

Content with ink and paper,
The image forms on the branch.
The single task: conveying message, thought,
Indifferent to the leaves of the universe.

Chapter Thirteen

Printing Pictures

Inkjet printers are amazing. By squirting microscopic blobs of cyan, magenta, yellow, and black ink in very precisely arranged positions and patterns, an inkjet printer can simulate thousands of colors and print detail that was previously only possible with toner-based laser printers. For about $100, or even less, you can get a printer that can image your digital photographs with quality, rivaling a print from a one-hour service from 35mm film.

Of course, this might not be as easy at it sounds. You have to have the digital image you want to print, perhaps cleaned up from your image editing software. You have to select the paper and format the layout of the page to position your picture sensibly. And then you need to set your printer to use its high-quality settings to get the best resolution and color fidelity results. But none of these things is actually difficult, and once you know how to do them, you'll be able to produce prints of your favorite photographs anytime. Your iMac can be your very own digital photo lab.

In this chapter we're going to look at:

> Features of inkjet printers to consider when purchasing

> Connecting and setting up a USB printer with your iMac

> Formatting your documents for your printer

> Quality options on typical inkjet printers

> Choosing paper, ink, and color settings for the best quality picture

Picking Out a Printer

It used to be that purchasing a printer meant having to weigh the cost and features of laser printers, dot-matrix printers, or inkjet printers. Laser printers were and continue to be expensive, and they are mostly geared toward high-quality, black-and-white text. Dot-matrix printers were the consumer-priced, noisy cousin of the modern inkjet, printing text or images by slowly passing back and forth over the paper—with considerably low-resolution and rough-looking output. The advent of the inkjet has made high-quality color printing available for a low cost; so for most people, the decision about what type of printer to get is a foregone conclusion. Nonetheless, there are still issues to consider.

Choosing an inkjet printer is mostly a choice of paper size handling, resolution and speed, special photo-quality inks, and computer interface type. This last is the simplest for an iMac owner: USB. Most inkjet printers have USB interfaces, making them easy to set up and plug in to your iMac, as well as fast for your iMac to

Figure 13.1 Epson printers, such as the Stylus Color 777i, have built-in support under Mac OS X and are designed to be used with an iMac.

control and transfer the graphic data of your document. You need not worry about types of serial port or PC parallel port connections. However, keep in mind that most printers don't come with an interface cable (allowing them to be generic for different types of computer systems), so you'll need to get an appropriate USB interface cable when you pick up your printer.

> ### PRINTING ANYTHING
>
> A printer is the most common peripheral that people purchase with an iMac and for good reason since it is entirely useful. You can print so many things and take them with you, give them to other people, or simply enjoy them. Today, printing photographs that look as good as expensive 35mm prints is so easy that people are quickly adopting digital cameras and giving up on chemical based photo-processing. You can also produce very professional documents with beautiful typography and graphic design. There are tons of places to go to learn more about document design, digital photography, and printing technology; many bookstores have a section among their computer books devoted to desktop publishing techniques and technology.

In choosing a printer, you should first consider your printing needs. For most people a basic printer such as the Epson Stylus 777i costing around or below $100 is optimal in its features and economics. This consumer printer prints full-color with photographic quality on letter-sized paper. It also prints in black ink with similar quality to a laser printer, and with reasonable speed. Less expensive printers are hardly worth considering as they really are just limited versions of this type of printer, forced to be slower and lower-resolution, for only $20 or so less.

The next step up is a printer in the $250 range, which adds somewhat higher resolution and special photo-inks; instead of four inks, they use six, the addition of a light blue, and light red, to smooth out light or soft tones. This "Photo" printer is worth considering if you are a serious digital photographer and can discern the subtle difference in print quality; however, the additional cost for the printer as well as the additional photo-inks may not be worth it for most people.

Stepping up from these printers to the $400 to $600 range are those which handle larger paper sizes such as tabloid (11 x 17 inches, twice letter size). It can be very useful for designers and those of you who like to make signs and flyers at home with your iMac to have access to printing on larger size papers. These are also available in models with normal color or with enhanced photo-inks.

Figure 13.2 A high-end model, such as the Epson Stylus Photo 2000P, uses pigment-based, photo-inks for archival reproduction.

At the top end of the inkjet printers, at around $900, is a large paper printer that uses pigment-based inks. These special inks are designed for archival printing, which fades less than standard inks over days, months, and years. Indeed, most inkjet printing is far from archival in nature, fading quickly and noticeably when exposed to direct sunlight for several days, and washing away almost completely in longer periods of time. This is a fact of life with inkjet printing, but for the most part it isn't of concern because so few people print high-quality renderings with long-term archival intent. If you are planning to produce professional prints to be framed and presented for years to come, you may want to consider a pigment-based ink printer. There are, of course, many other issues besides ink that can affect archival rendering, such as paper and matting substrates.

> ### PRINTING CORRESPONDENCE
>
> The most common use for a home printer is not printing photographs or artwork, but simply text, usually in the form of a letter. It is easy to put a nice writing linen into your inkjet printer, select a traditional typeface, perhaps Caslon, at a small reading size, say 10-point, and produce beautiful, professional and personal results. Much nicer than email.

Connecting Your Printer

After you have your printer, you need to connect it to your iMac and set it up—this is actually quite easy. Simply set the printer near your iMac, plug in its power, and turn it on. Connect the printer with a USB interface cable to an available USB port on your iMac; you can get a USB hub if you are out of available USB ports. That's it. Now all you'll need to do is configure your iMac to recognize the printer.

If you're running under Mac OS 9 on your iMac, you will need to install the printer driver software that came on a CD with the

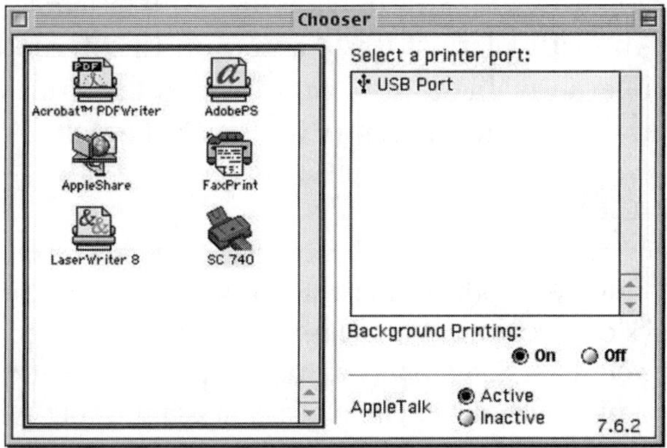

Figure 13.3 In Mac OS 9, use the Chooser to select your printer.

printer, or may be downloadable from the manufacturer's Web site (in fact, you should check the Web if you are able to, to make sure that you have the latest version to install). When the installation process is completed, your iMac will need to be restarted.

With the printer connected, the driver installed, and your iMac restarted, you can open the Chooser to select the printer. First, select the Printer driver on the left side of the Chooser window and then select the USB printer on the right side. With the printer selected, or "chosen," you can close the Chooser to begin using your printer.

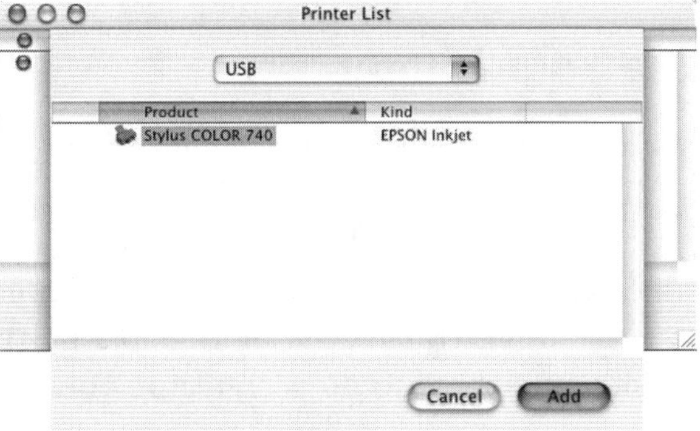

Figure 13.4 In Mac OS X, use the Print Center to select your printer.

If you are using Mac OS X, it may be that your printer's driver is already built-in, particularly if it is a common Epson model. To make the printer available to use, simply open the Print Center application in the Utilities directory and click the Add Printer but-

> ### PRINTING ENVELOPES
>
> When you have a bunch of envelopes to address, you should consider using your printer. Most inkjet printers will easily hold a small stack of envelopes. With a little setup in your word processor and with your Page Setup options, you can position the text on the small area of the envelope. Of course, you can use your printer to do more than just address an envelope; you might also decorate it with images and artwork.

ton at the bottom of the Printer List window. You may need to select USB from the printer selection sheet, which will drop down from the Printer List window. With the printer added to the Printer List, it is immediately available for use.

Your Document's Page Setup

With your printer online and selected, you're ready to print. But before printing any document, you need to format your document for your printer by selecting Page Setup from the File menu of the application you want to print from. The Page Setup window is used to determine the printer you want to format the document for, the page size, the paper's orientation, and a scale to enlarge or reduce the document printed on that paper.

For most people, you'll want to choose US Letter for common 8.5 x 11-inch paper and an upright orientation. Setting the scale to 100% will give you a print at normal or actual size; a smaller percentage will reduce the size of the document, and a larger percentage will increase its size.

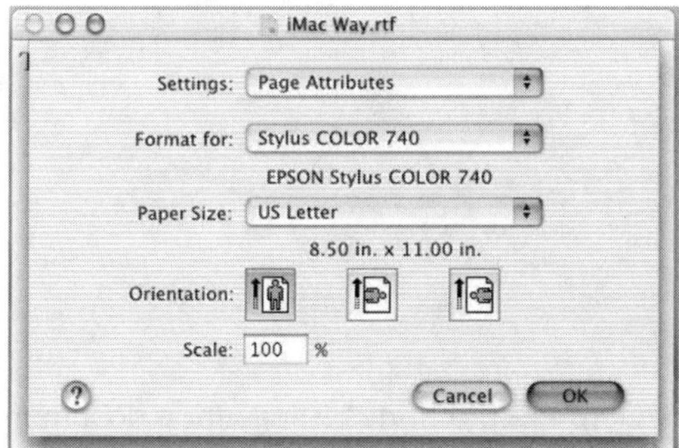

Figure 13.5 Use Page Setup to specify the paper size, orientation, and scale.

PRINTING LABELS

Whether for labeling packages or letters, or for organizing files or boxes, printing labels is easy and productive. Many database and

continued…

> word processing applications come with templates for common label
> sheets, but if you have trouble finding a template or making your
> own, try the manufacturer. One of the biggest label supply compa-
> nies, Avery, has templates for common software applications avail-
> able for download on their Web site at www.avery.com, as well
> as online formatting and downloading of PDFs prepared with your
> data for selected label types.

Changing Your Print Settings

When you're ready to print, and after you have specified the Page
Setup for your document, you have many more options to choose
from. To begin, choose Print from your application's File menu.
You will be presented with the Print settings where you can use a
pop-up menu at the top of the dialog to switch to a different
printer, as well as choose a predefined set of printer settings from
the Saved Settings pop-up menu. In the middle of the Print settings
is an area that you can choose to display any of your printers' various options.

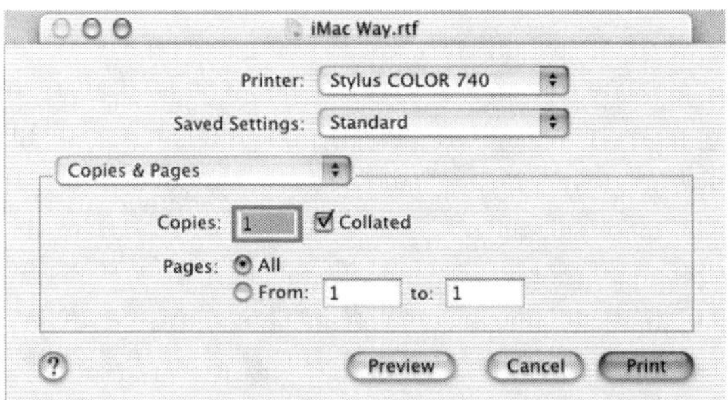

Figure 13.6 Here are the Print settings for a document in
Mac OS X.

At the bottom of the Print settings is the Print button, which initi-
ates the printing, as well as a Cancel button to dismiss the Print settings without printing. Mac OS X also has a special button labeled
Preview. This button will save the print job as a PDF file and display it in the Preview application, which you can use to page

through the print job and view the results of your printing, just as they would be formatted for your printer. You can go ahead and print from the Preview window.

Let's look at some of the specific printing options.

Copies & Pages

These settings allow you to determine the total number of copies to print and what page range to use. The default setting is to print one copy, but you can change this to any number of copies you like, as well as change them to be collated—each page printed in duplicate together, or the set of pages printed as sets. The Pages setting is by default set to All, but if you only want to print a portion of the pages of your document, you can specify the page to begin from and to end with.

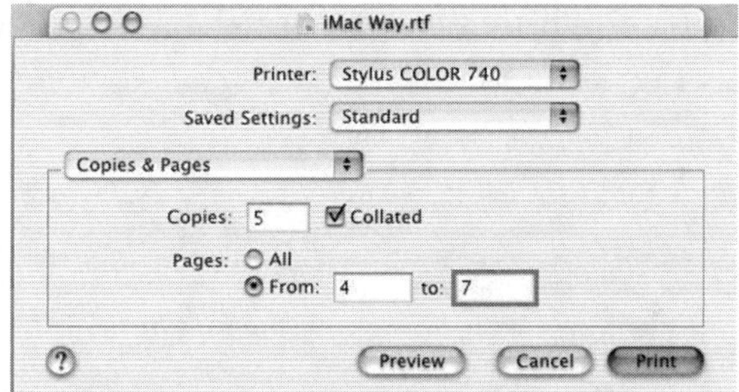

Figure 13.7 Use the Copy options to set the number of copies to make and the page range to print.

Layout

When you are printing more than one page, you have the option to combine several pages onto a single sheet of paper to save paper. You can choose the number of pages per sheet and the direction to flow the pages onto the paper when it is divided up. You can also choose to include a border so that the edge of the pages is distinguished.

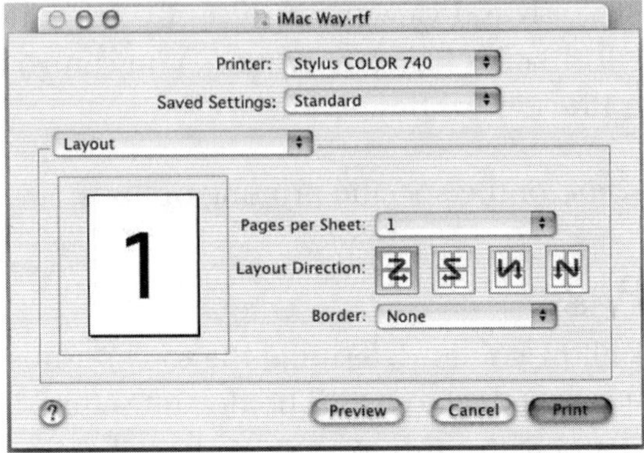

Figure 13.8 Use the Layout options to save paper by combining several pages together on a single sheet.

Output Options

This singular option allows you to choose to save the print job as a PDF file rather than print it. This is similar to using the Preview button, except that the print file will not be automatically displayed in Mac OS X's Preview application.

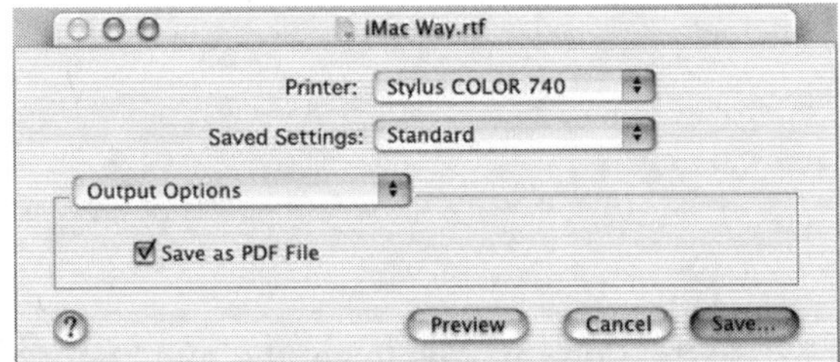

Figure 13.9 Select Save as PDF File to save the print job as a file rather than print it.

Print Settings

The print settings represent the options of the specific printer you are printing to, in this case an Epson Stylus Color 740. You can choose the media type, to specify the kind of paper to use, thus defining how much ink the printer will apply. You can choose to print in color or reduce a color document to black-and-white only.

You can also define the Mode options, to specify the quality resolution to use, which in turn determines the speed of the printing.

Figure 13.10 The Print Settings define quality options specific to your printer.

Advanced Settings

For more detailed control of the printer quality settings specific to your printer, use the Advanced Settings options. For an Epson Stylus you can define the Media Type and Ink to use, as well as the specific resolution and color toning methods. There are also spe-

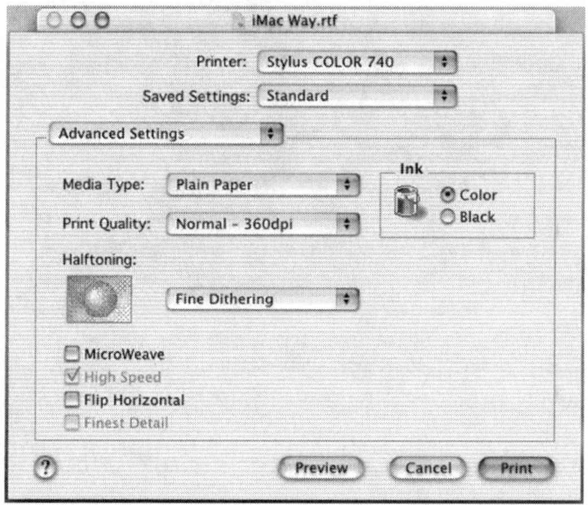

Figure 13.11 Similar to the Print Settings, these Advanced Settings reflect more specific and technical options for your printer.

cial options such as MicroWeave, High Speed, Flip Horizontal, and Finest Detail, which are useful for special papers and qualities. You can experiment with these settings to help you perfect a print's quality.

Color Management

The Color Management settings are very important for getting the best results from realistic images, such as photographs and scanned artwork. The default setting of Color Controls with a mode of Photo-realistic will probably produce the most accurate results; however, if your image is noticeably tinted with a particular color-cast, or you'd like to increase the saturation or contrast, you can use the slider controls to experiment with their effects. If you are using ColorSync color management with your digital images, you will want to override the color controls by selecting the ColorSync option.

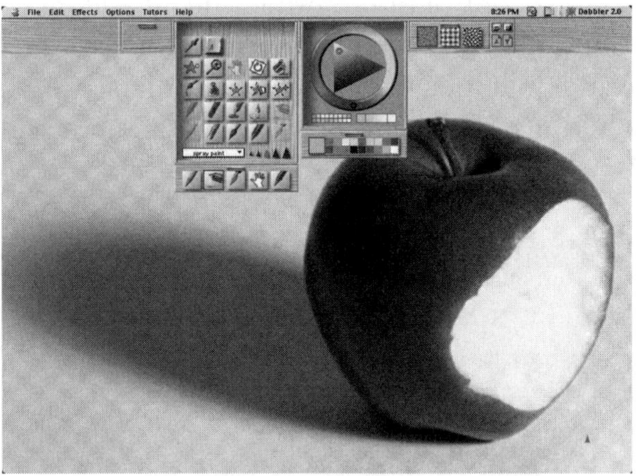

Figure 13.12 Color management can be quite tricky; the default settings usually produce the best results.

Summary

You can select Summary when you want to see a quick review of all the settings specified for your print job. Also note that you can find the print driver version in this listing. If you find you are using a customized setting often, you can select Save Custom Setting from the print options menu to save them as a saved set.

Getting the Best Results

Achieving the best results from your printer requires a combination of print settings and materials; in fact, the paper stock you use can

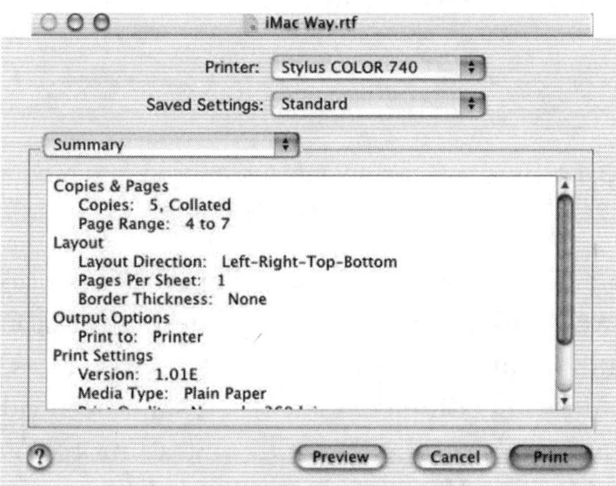

Figure 13.13   Use the Summary setting to view all the print options specified for your job.

have the most dramatic effect on the quality of your printing. The texture and body of the paper you use is critical to getting a bright, sharp image without the ink bleeding and smearing into the pulp, obscuring details and dulling the colors. Also setting the media type properly so that the printer lays down just the right amount of ink can make a big difference.

You can buy specially designed papers from the manufactures of your printer; for example, Epson produces a line of papers for producing different types of documents. The photograde papers tend to be smoother and brighter white, even-coated and glossy and thick, feeling very similar to traditional photographic papers. There are also special coated transparent films, which will adhere the ink of the printer. Unfortunately, papers produced and marketed by the manufactures of printers can be very expensive.

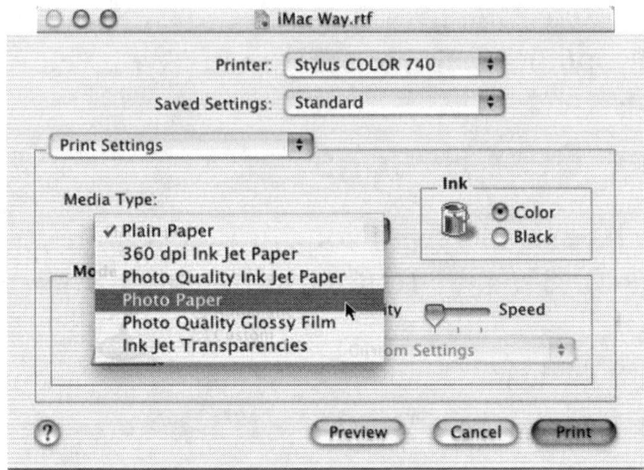

Figure 13.14 Here you can specify the appropriate media type for your paper stock.

You can also get excellent results with paper that is not specifically designed for your inkjet. A high-quality linen cover stock can produce beautiful and artistic results. Avoid thin papers as they tend to bleed more and to become cockled when saturated with ink. For example, great results can be had with a Strathmore Writing Cover Bristol, Bright White, Wove, Cover 88, Acid Free paper. This paper produces a very natural finish that is sharp and bright for photos, and is particularly nice when framed. This paper is also much less expensive at only about $12 for 125 letter-size sheets.

When printing to achieve photographic quality results, always select a photo quality media type and a mode with the highest quality setting (drag the slider all the way to the Quality end). These settings use the printer's highest resolution dot dispersal, and they will apply less ink so that it doesn't bleed into the paper as much.

Sky's not high, earth not solid —
Try to see! Look,
A vision of pixels,
The Northern dipper blazes south.

Chapter Fourteen

Advanced Digital Graphics

Just about everyone knows that the Mac is the graphics platform of choice for creating advanced digital graphics. You can manipulate photographs in the same ways that professionals do. You can create graphic design illustrations for charts, graphs, or anything. You can lay out books, and produce beautiful typography. Your Mac is also great for 3D modeling and rendering CG animation. You can do any of these things with your iMac.

Most of the software for producing advanced digital graphics doesn't come cheap or easy—these applications can be expensive and very complex to use. But spending your time and money investing in learning and producing with them can be both personally and professionally rewarding. By developing skills with an advanced graphics application, you may find yourself quickly expert in many aspects of using your iMac. And you may also find your professional life expanded and enhanced; even if at first the skills in digital graphics seem far from your work, they have many practical uses.

In this chapter we're going to look at:

- ➤ Advanced digital image editing techniques

- ➤ Graphic design illustration using vector-based tools

- ➤ Typographical and text technology support on your iMac

- ➤ Book design methods and page layout software

- ➤ 3D modeling and rendering techniques

Advanced Photo Editing

Already in this book we've explored a bit of digital image editing, by introducing image size resampling and filtering. An advanced application like Adobe Photoshop has many more advanced features: layering, effect styles, history, actions and batch processing, and color management. Let's take a closer look at the advanced features of Photoshop.

DEMOS AND TRYOUTS

The applications for producing digital graphics can be quite expensive given their professional application. However, most of them are available in demo or tryout versions that usually allow you to use the full features of the application, but limit you in either the number of days you can use the software without purchasing it or have disabled key features (such as Save or Print). Check the Web site of the developer of the software for availability:

```
www.adobe.com

www.macromedia.com

www.corel.com

www.aliaswavefront.com
```

Layers and Styles

The most powerful feature of an advanced image editing application such as Photoshop is arguably image layers. As you know, digital images are two-dimensional arrays of color pixels. These pixels can be cropped, resampled, brushed over, copied and pasted, filtered, and adjusted. But when you are combining parts of separate images together to composite them, Photoshop layers offer a powerful ability to keep elements separated and individually adjustable.

An image can exist as a layer with areas that are opaque and have color pixels, as well as other pixels that are transparent, either completely or just semi-translucent. By stacking and combining images

Figure 14.1 Layers provide a powerful way to composite images together.

on different layers, allowing images below to show through the transparent and translucent areas in the layer above, you can blend the layer together into a single composite image. But by keeping the images separated into layers, you can easily grab one layer and reposition it, or edit it (perhaps deleting more pixels to show

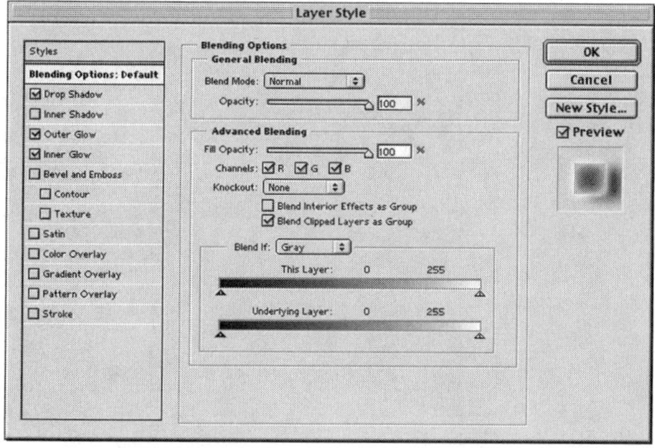

Figure 14.2 Layer styles create shadows and other global effects that can be edited.

through, or adding to the image to cover up something underneath) without disturbing the other layers. When layers are combined literally, flattening the stack of layers, the pixels take on their combined appearance and the elements on the originally separated layer can no longer be manipulated on their own.

Photoshop allows you to easily change the stacking order of layers, as well as to hide and show layers individually. You can even mask one layer into its directly superior layer without being combined with other layers above or below. And Photoshop has special layer styles that can be applied to add a drop shadow, or glow, or many other effects that are not permanently applied to the data of the layer and combined image until it is flattened.

History

Another very powerful Photoshop feature is the History. As you use Photoshop, it keeps track of each edit or adjustment you make to an image, allowing you to view the history of your changes and to select an earlier state of the image to return to. This is similar to having multiple levels of undo, but presented in a visual palette and with additional features for tracking and adding changes.

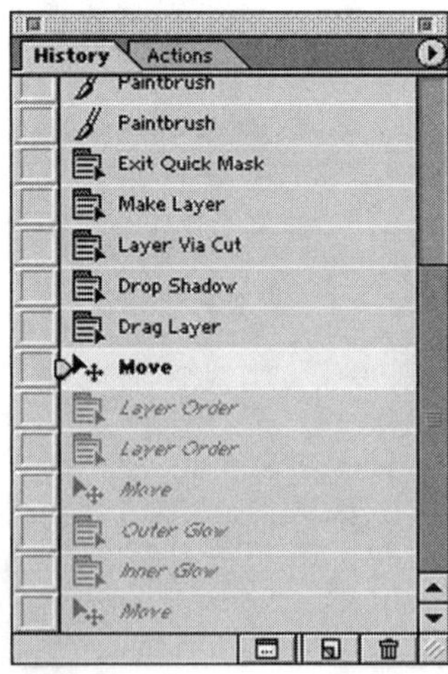

Figure 14.3 History provides multiple levels of undo, as well as special snapshots of your images.

The History of an image can be especially useful when you are making a bunch of variations of an image, perhaps trying different effects. You might start by applying a few global adjustments to an image, and then add some additional effect that you might want to take away and try differently later. Simply save a copy of the fully adjusted image, and then go back in the History to a previous state that you want to build upon again.

One twist on the History is the Snapshot. By clicking and saving a snapshot of an image, you can make changes to your image and then use the older version of the image retained in the snapshot to blend back into the image in any number of ways, including a special paintbrush tool.

Actions and Batch Processing

Because Photoshop is used by many professional graphics production shops that produce hundreds or thousands of images, often needing to apply repeatedly the same steps to adjust and edit them, the program includes automation features called *Actions*, as well as a batch processing command. Using the Actions palette controls, you can have Photoshop record all the commands and tools you

Figure 14.4 Use the Actions palette to record and play back sequences of commands.

apply to an image so that they can be applied again simply by running the saved sequence. Actions are a very powerful tool and include specialized features for editing the sequence and adjusting the parameters of specified commands. You can even set actions to be evoked at the press of a command key, giving you quick access to often repeated commands.

You can also apply any action to a batch of images automatically by using Photoshop's Batch command. With it you specify a selection of images, perhaps the contents of a directory of your iMac, tell it what action to perform on the images, and then how to save the affected images, either as new images or replacing the original. If you have many hundreds of images to adjust, using a batch action can save you hours of effort, letting your iMac do all the work by running on its own.

Color Management

Photoshop is perhaps the most color aware software application ever produced. It knows about every type of digital image color format, as well as how to apply color profiles that describe the color gamut of devices such as digital cameras and scanners, monitors, and printers so that the colors that you see on the screen are

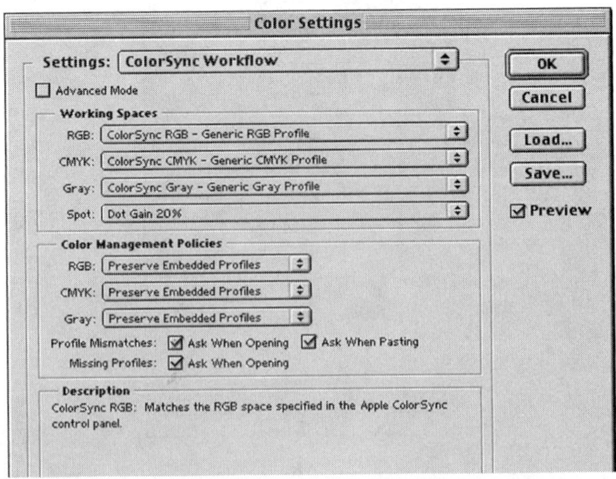

Figure 14.5 Photoshop's color management is highly evolved.

properly representative of those captured and trying to be described for output. Because every device has its own color qualities and calibrating them is so difficult, color management and the data workflows to maintain color averaging between devices is an amazing achievement.

If you want to use color management on your iMac, begin by opening the Monitors control panels and following the steps to adjust the color and save a profile of its settings. Then open the ColorSync control panels to select profiles for your monitor and any input and output devices that you use, such as a scanner and printer. Then by enabling color management in applications such as Photoshop, it can try to present the images from your scanner accurately on your monitor, and when they are printed they should look similar to what you see on the display. Color is a highly subjective and scientifically advanced field, but the good news is that your iMac is riding the edge of the technology.

THE HISTORY OF PHOTOSHOP

Photoshop has a long history on the Mac dating back to the late 80s. It began as a digital image format translation utility, designed only for reading in image data of one type and saving it as another format. It quickly expanded with features for displaying and selecting image data—and then further with filters and channels effects—and yet further with layers and actions and styles. Over the years it has been carefully added to and expanded continuously while maintaining high-quality image rendering and full support for all types of image formats. Photoshop is the leader in its field and without rival. While many other image editing applications have been created, many very good, none have the advanced level of features and the perfection of interface and programming that make Photoshop so great.

Graphic Design Illustration

Along with desktop publishing, the Mac has been a center of professional graphic illustration with software applications such as Adobe Illustrator and Macromedia Freehand. Illustration software "draws" by using pen tools and geometric shape tools, positioning and formatting them to create designs. You can create just about any graphics with an illustration application, from logos and type designs, to charts and graphs. What separates illustration from digital images is the use of vector-based objects to draw out the design geometrically, rather than being rastered from pixels like an image. Vector-based graphics can be resized and rendered at any resolution, always being drawn precisely.

Figure 14.6 Adobe Illustrator is a vector-based drawing application.

You can use an illustration application to create a full-page design to print directly from the application, or you can save the illustration in a format that can be imported into other applications. This format is generally an EPS file, Encapsulated PostScript, a file that uses the PostScript page description language to describe the geometry and layout of two-dimensional graphics. If you are creating a logo, for example, you can save it as an EPS file, which you can then place in page layout software or in the layout in a word processor to display the logo when your document is printed.

PENS AND MECHANICALS

Computer based graphic illustration applications such as Adobe Illustrator are based on the traditional and now defunct methods of

continued…

using pens and photo-mechanicals to produce designs for reproduction by printing or photography. It used to be that graphic designers would draw out a design very precisely using rules and pens. They would have type photo-mechanically set, which they could cut with Xacto knives and use wax to paste to a layout board. They would use masking film to fill objects with colors and patterns also photographically produced. They built up layers using transparent overlays carefully registered in place with tape and guide marks. The finished design could then be reproduced onto film by a copy camera and the film used for offset printing or for further photographic reproduction. It was, to say the least, a very expensive, slow and skilled, labor-intensive process. The advent of desktop publishing tools, and specifically PostScript, has essentially made these methods and skills obsolete.

Illustration with Vectors

Illustrating is all about connecting the dots, in this case by positioning points on a page and connecting them with curved or straight lines to create objects, and then applying colors and patterns to the object's border line and interior fill.

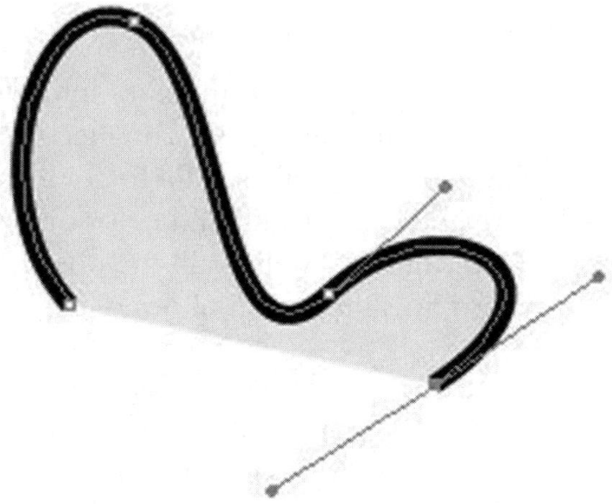

Figure 14.7 You can draw vector graphics by creating points and connecting them with lines.

Using a vector illustration application and its pen tool can be a bit tricky the first time. This method of illustration, rather than drawing out the length of lines like when using a pencil or brush, instead is planned as you go by placing a point to connect to. By clicking to place a starting point, and then clicking a second time somewhere else, you define a line. By clicking an end point for a line and dragging the mouse before releasing the button, you drag out a curve control handle, which will bend the line toward the handle. This line can later be moved and its curve adjusted by selecting it and dragging either the end points or grabbing the curved line itself to pull its curve out further or to reduce it. This sort of control can be used to create very precise and complex designs.

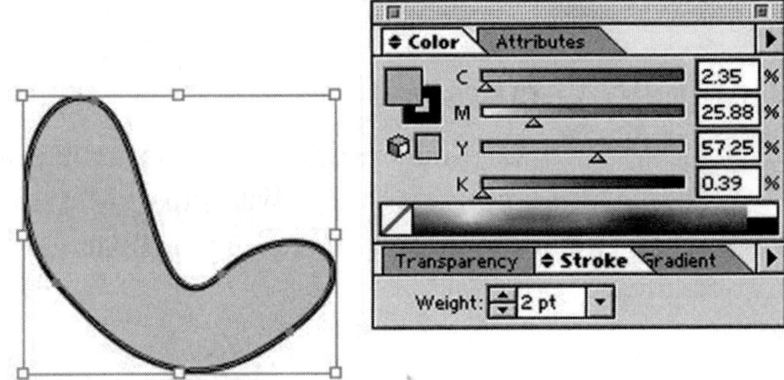

Figure 14.8 You can apply a color stroke and fill to objects.

After you've created lines or closed the lines into shapes, you have objects that you can position and layer. By selecting an object, you can apply a stroke (a line format) or a fill to color the object. You can apply a line weight of any width and color or a dashed pattern, including a stroke of none, as well as fill the object with any color, pattern, or gradation, including a fill of none.

Every object on a page has a draw-order or layer in front or behind the other objects. Determining what is in front of another object is crucial to building a complex design, and the software provides many commands for changing the order of objects, moving them to front or to back. You can also group objects into sets or hold them on defined layers to assist in building much more complex designs.

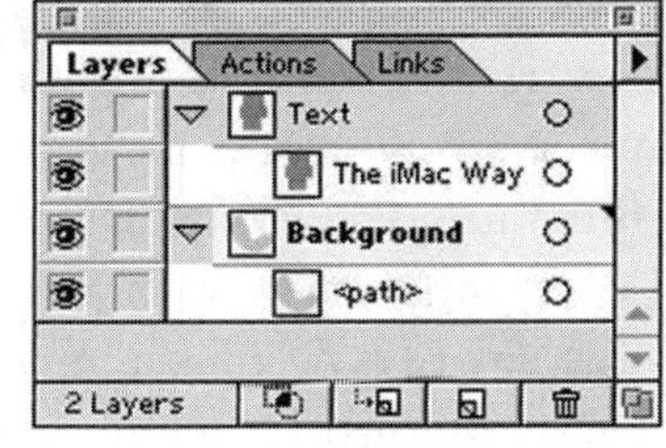

Figure 14.9 You can group objects together onto layers that can be rearranged and hidden.

A NEW LIFE FOR VECTOR GRAPHICS

The latest computer graphic technologies are those geared toward the creation and presentation of 2D graphic animation, primarily used on the Web in the form of Flash graphics. This technology allows graphic designers to create moving type and logos that can be integrated into the design of an HTML Web page and respond interactively to mouse pointing and clicking. The mechanisms for Flash animation are built in to the Mac OS now with QuickTime, allowing for graphic animation to be displayed in Web pages without the need of special plug-ins (sometimes they are still required), as well as directly in QuickTime movies (stand-alone or embedded in Web pages). Many graphics applications support exporting their graphics to Flash format, or to be edited by the original Flash application from Macromedia.

Desktop Typography

When the Mac was introduced, it was presented as the first WYSIWYG (What You See Is What You Get) computer display environment. It attempted to make all your productivity software application's documents appear on-screen just as they would look when printed out. A word processor, for example, would use and display the fonts just as they would be printed, a spreadsheet would present the cells and their numbers formatted as they appeared on the printed paper, and design software would reach a new level of sophistication rendering increased levels of detail and texture. The key to all this was fonts—type on-screen needed to look similar to the printed versions. At first, this was a bit rough, using screen fonts for display and printer fonts for PostScript printers. Then Adobe introduced technology for displaying the printer fonts on-screen (Adobe Type Manager), and as software has developed in recent years, the display of type on-screen has improved to the point where it is now the display technologies driving the printer rather than the printer technology being emulated on-screen.

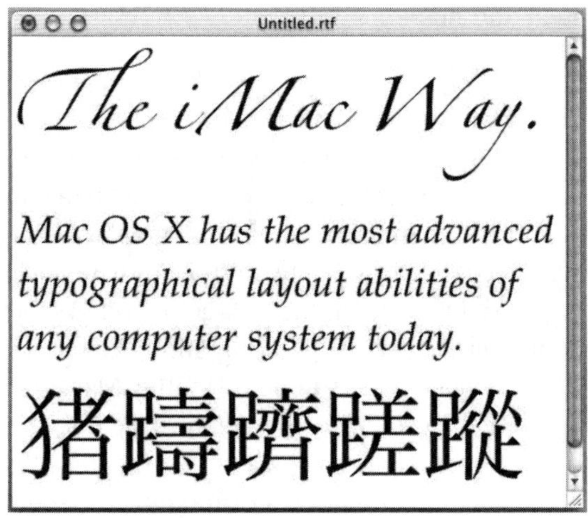

Figure 14.10 Mac OS X has the most advanced typographical layout capabilities of any computer system today.

The best and most current example of this is Mac OS X, which uses a PDF-based rendering engine called *quartz* that draws everything on the screen using advanced type and color layout techniques. All the type on-screen in Mac OS X is produced from the resolution independent OpenType format fonts, using anti-aliasing and color to render sharp, beautiful looking type.

Getting More Fonts

While there is not much to explain on using fonts on your iMac without getting carried away by the traditions of type design and use, what most people want to know is how to get more fonts. If you are looking for a typeface to give your projects or designs a unique flair, all you need to do is go out on the Internet. You will find that there are many type design houses (developers) and that the quality and cost of type varies quite a lot.

On the low end, when you are looking for something quick and dirty to add a bit of design grunge to your work, there are thousands of free typefaces available from individuals who have made them and share them. Simply search any online freeware or shareware sites.

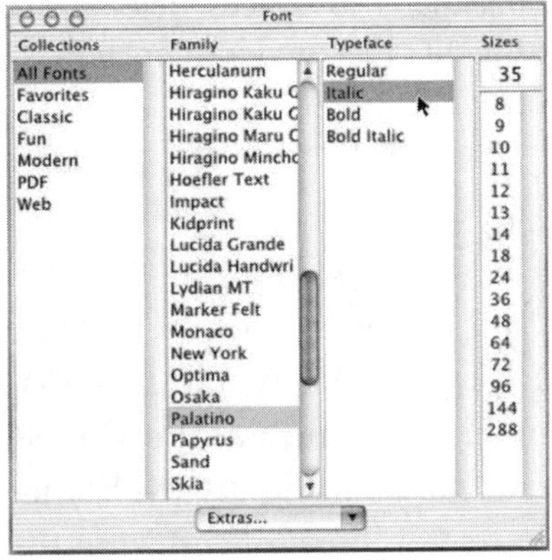

Figure 14.11 Mac OS X comes with many professional typefaces from which to choose.

On the high-end there are thousands of professionally drawn and digitized typefaces, with complete font families and extended character sets available. You might begin by going to Adobe's Web site (`www.adobe.com`) and viewing their fonts, which are available for purchase and download. A personal favorite of mine is Fonthead Design, an independent publisher who makes a variety of great decorative typefaces available online for customers at `www.fonthead.com`.

WHAT IS A FONT ANYWAY?

The term font has been bastardized by the computer industry and desktop publishing. In general when you are talking about fonts,

continued…

you are talking about type or typography, not fonts. A font is simply a specific casting of a type design in a specific style and size. Times italic 12 is a font, while Times Roman 12 is a different font. And while it might make sense to go to a Font menu to choose a font of a type design family in a style and size, it might make a lot more sense to go to a Type menu.

Of course, the typewriter is probably more responsible for the use of the term font, as most people can't think of type without thinking of typing. This is the same kind of misconception that has made everyone think that two spaces belong after a period, that apostrophes are straight, that underlining is a style, and that an ellipsis is three periods....

Laying Out Pages

Desktop Publishing is the mainstay of the Macintosh industry. The invention of the laser printer (the Apple LaserWriter was the very first commercial laser printer) and Adobe PostScript in the late 80s gave the Mac a niche it has held tightly ever since. Combined with the advanced graphics capabilities of the Mac for image editing, illustration, and typography—desktop publishing became a new

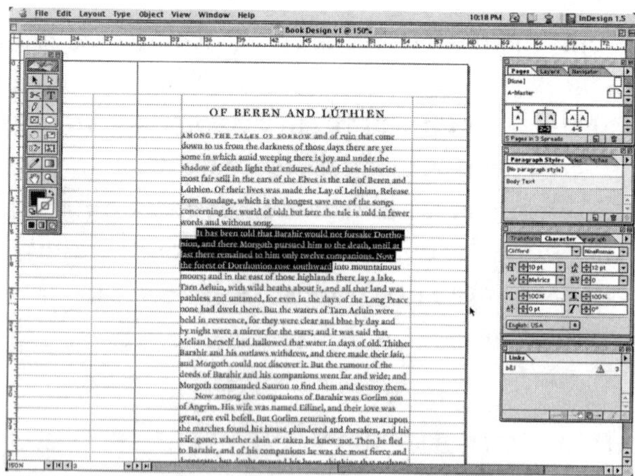

Figure 14.12 Adobe InDesign represents the state of the art in desktop publishing software.

paradigm for text and graphic production that has literally changed the entire printing industry in a short number of years.

Page Layout software combines the techniques and technologies of digital images, graphic illustration, and typography to produce multi-page documents such as books and pamphlets. While most word processing applications provide basic layout features, they cannot compete with software dedicated to designing and laying out pages. The first page layout application was Aldus PageMaker, designed to imitate the methods of the traditional newspaper production techniques—assembling together text blocks and graphics on a layout board, with room to set yet unused blocks and images on the surrounding pasteboard. Such applications have developed continuously over the past 15 years with the leaders being (now Adobe) PageMaker and Quark Xpress. For a taste of desktop publishing methods and technology, let's take a look at the latest in page layout software, Adobe InDesign.

Designing Pages

Building a document in the tradition of a book, magazine, newspaper, pamphlet, flyer, or broadside begins with shaping the page. Choosing dimensions for a page is a combination of aesthetic and technical interpretation. You must consider the limitations of the printing methods that will be used to reproduce the document, as well as consider the content you are presenting. If you are producing your document to be printed on a home inkjet printer, then you probably want to choose a letter-size paper and a page size that

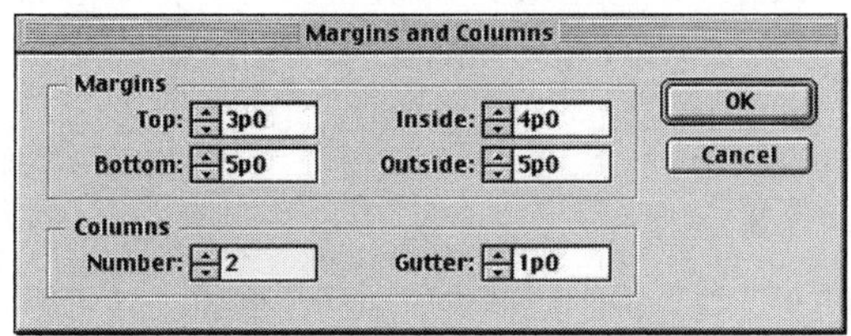

Figure 14.13 You should begin building a document by defining the page dimensions and margins.

either fills that paper or evenly divides into it, such as 5.5 by 8.5 inches being letter-size folded in half. Page layout software provides many default page sizes to choose from as well as setting the binding options of the pages, single-sided loose pages versus double-sided and facing pages, similar to those in a book.

The next step is to create a text area on the page by defining margins. It is common to have a larger margin on the outside edges of a book leaving space for thumbs to hold the page without covering the text, while also providing space for notes and additions. Defining margins is actually a more complex and artistic problem than most people would guess, leading to comfortable text line length and spatial harmonies. The layout software will provide default margins that you can customize. The margins will be displayed on-screen and will affect the behavior of text objects.

Another part of designing a page is to define a baseline grid. This is a vertical spacing down the length of the page on which the base of the body text sits, and on a well-designed page, everything lines up and fits in multiples of this spacing. The layout software can display this grid and use it to automatically position certain types of type objects.

Flowing in Text and Placing Graphics

Once you have the basic page design setup for your document, you can begin to import text and graphics. While modern page layout applications have sophisticated features for editing text and graphics, they are not generally considered word processing or graphic design applications. You should instead expect to create and edit large amounts of text with a separate word processor, as well as edit and create images and illustration with other specialized applications.

When you import text and place it on a page, it is put into a frame; this frame defines the area in which that text appears and is controlled. In the case of long lengths of text, many frames are linked together on page after page for the text to flow through. You use

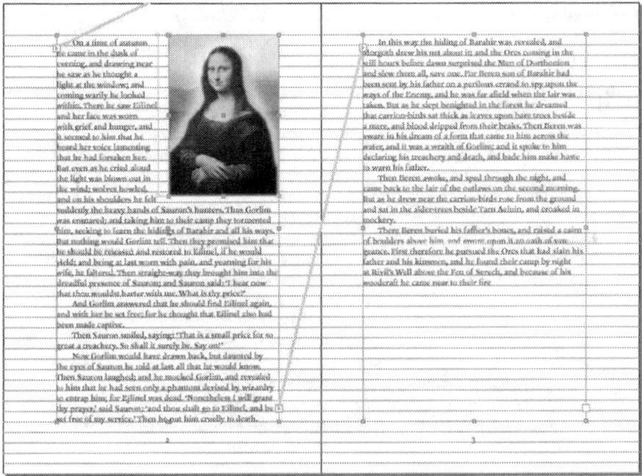

Figure 14.14 You can import text and graphics to place on the pages of your document.

separate tools within the application to edit the text within the frame, versus editing and manipulating the frame itself. You can autoflow the text into your document, automatically creating text frames within the text area of the pages, while adding additional pages until all the text is revealed.

Placing images and graphics into your document layout also uses frames to contain them. You can use the frame to crop and position the graphic on the page, as well as resize the graphic within the frame. Frames can also have automatic text wrapping, which forces the text in overlapping boxes to wrap words and shorten its lines to fit around the frame's edges.

Tagging Text Styles

Page layout applications, like many word processors, also use paragraph and character style tags to quickly format text. By predefining paragraphs' text designs for common elements of your text, such as titles, subtitles, body text, excerpt text, numbered and bulleted text, captions, and footnotes, you can apply these styles by tagging the text with them. The software can then automatically apply the appropriate text settings, such as type style and size, or indenting and justification.

The power of tagged styles is apparent when you want to modify a style, even subtly. By changing the definition of a paragraph style the software can automatically reapply it to all the appropriate paragraphs and reflow the text accordingly. If you were to try to change some aspect of your text design to a book length document manually, it could take days of work.

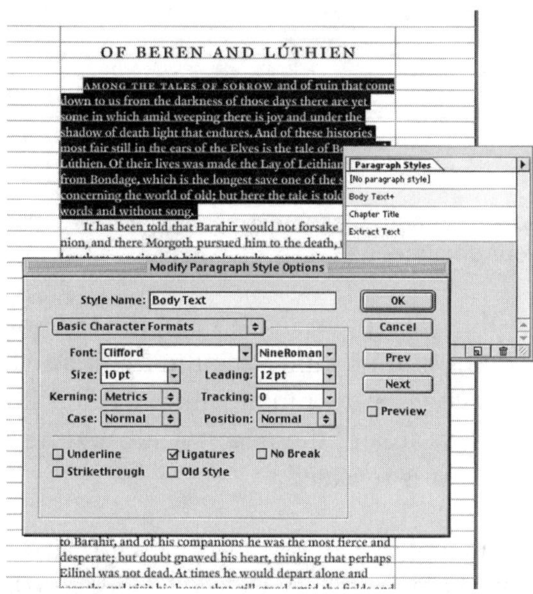

Figure 14.15 You can use paragraph style tags to automate the formatting of text.

Building a Book

The power of page layout software comes in managing long documents. A book of many chapters and hundreds of pages, with dozens of separate text stories, and perhaps thousands of independent graphics, can be very challenging to manage. Page layout software provides features and tools for building book length documents with varying page designs and sections.

The Pages palette is a diagram of the pages in the document, which is used to select and view pages, as well as to indicate page numbering and sectioning. You can use master pages to define different

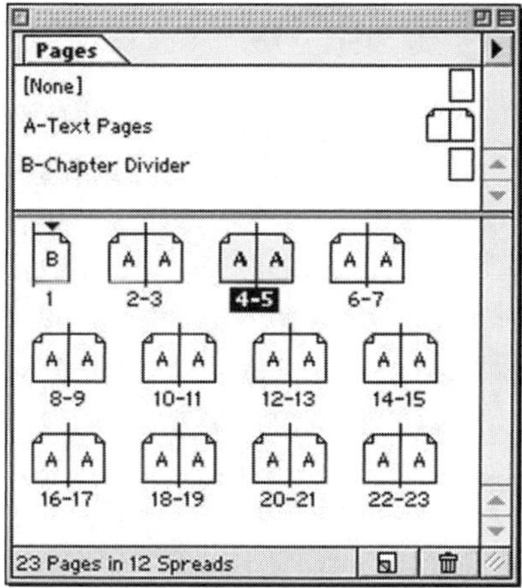

Figure 14.16 The Pages palette lets you set up and navigate large documents.

BOOK PRINTING: A 500-YEAR TRADITION

The book has been a paradigm of written language for several millennia—more convenient than a scroll (or a stone wall) and quite durable. Not surprisingly, the book as we have it today (even as this is in your hands) has changed little in all this time. While the technology of printing and manufacturing books has developed in leaps and bounds, the book itself still is essentially the same. Books are still built from gatherings of folded pages, bound at the spine. And the way content is presented in books has also changed little. Page numbers, running heads, titles and chapters, columns of lines of text, initial letters, paragraphs and sentences, indexes, and margins and footnotes all have examples dating back hundreds and thousands of years. Even the basics of type design and typographical marks have changed little in the last 500 years. Desktop publishing and your iMac may be new, but the book lives on.

---

page designs, some of which may be based on each other, and apply the designs to selected pages simply by dragging and dropping their icons onto the page icons that you want to apply them to.

Modeling and Rendering

Beyond the realm of desktop publishing technologies are computer graphics (or CG). CG generally refers to producing 3D computer graphics such as those featured in cartoons and movies. As our computers become faster and more powerful, the tools for designing complex models and then photo-realistically texturing and shading them are becoming very accessible. There are consumer-oriented 3D rendering applications that make putting together stock geometry into a scene and applying stock textures and lighting effects easy and surprisingly professional looking. There are also advanced applications that can take months to learn to use effectively, but have the power to create anything you can imagine, and, in fact, are used to create fantastic images you see in mainstream movies and advertising.

To create a photo-realistic image from 3D models involves several steps: modeling objects, positioning objects in a scene, setting camera viewpoints and animating objects, adding textures to paint objects and the scenery, lighting and shading the scene, and finally rendering it into a 2D digital image. Some applications have the tools for all these steps while others separate them into separate applications, or simply specialize in one area such as modeling, rendering, or texture production.

Modeling

The process of computer graphics begins with modeling. This is how an object is created in the computer, which can then be manipulated, positioned, and rendered. Modeling an object is very much like drawing the object in a vector-based illustration application, but instead of merely defining points to connect with lines on a page, you are creating points within a 3D space that are connected by surfaces. The surfaces of the object can be flat or curved and twisted.

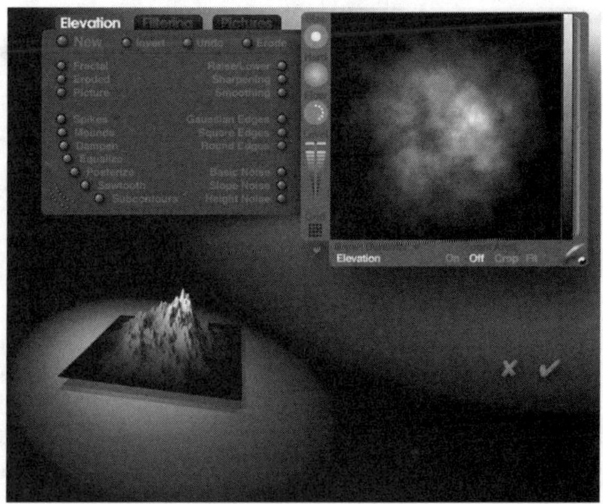

Figure 14.17 The 3D rendering application Bryce 4 provides special tools for modeling natural looking terrain.

Creating simplistic geometrical object, such as cubes and spheres, is very easy and most applications offer tools to create these, just as illustration software has tools for drawing circles and squares. More complex objects use specialized 3D tools to generate shapes such as lathe and extrusion tools. Many applications also let you combine several objects together and then automatically build a skin around them, creating a unique shape. You might then grab points on the object to stretch and mold the shape to perfect it. Yet other applications might have unique tools for creating specialized types of objects, such as mountains and cloud layers.

Advanced modeling applications also let you build skeletons, which define and control the movements of parts of the model. This is particularly useful in producing animation where you want to easily bend and position a model rather than re-create it from scratch for each position.

Scene Building

Once you have objects modeled, you'll want to use them, and usually this means placing them within a scene, after all most objects have no context without environment. A 3D model of an airplane might look neat on its own, but the context of a scene gives it dimension—in clouds and a sky versus on a table in a child's bedroom, for example.

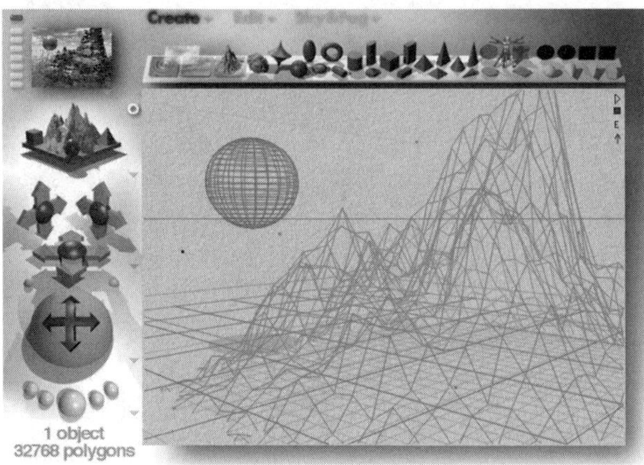

Figure 14.18 You can position models in a scene to create the context of their environment.

Building a scene generally involves defining the environment, beginning with the horizon, sky, and ground, as this is the typical world in which most things we experience live. You might then put up walls, a floor, and ceiling, leaving a window out into the outside world. Within this room you might position your models, setting them up realistically (or otherwise, your scene can be anything you want and with the power of CG modeling and rendering it could easily be something unreal).

Texturing

With the models built and positioned within a scene, you might begin to apply textures to everything. In general, this means the color and patterns that appear on the surfaces of objects. Without defined textures, all the objects and the scene are just gray or otherwise represented by a default appearance.

Applying texture is more than just coloring. You might apply a custom painted surface texture that provides the appearance of the

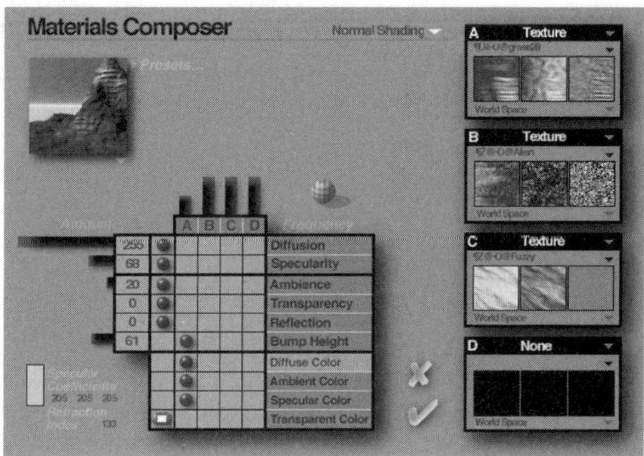

Figure 14.19 Applying textures to your models gives them tone and realism.

objects' surface details, perhaps with nicks and scratches, pores and hair, paint and decals, logos, and type, and even materials such as cloth, wood, or metal. Textures can also define special properties of the material so when lit they appear dull, or shiny, or even transparent, or liquid-like. Some material textures are not merely image-maps wrapped into the surface of the object, but are multi-dimensional simulations that can move and change with the shape and depth of the object—particularly useful for organic appearances such as wood and flesh.

Lighting and Shading

With objects in a scene and with textures applied, the last step in setting the scene is lighting the objects and defining shading properties. Any rendering is about light reflecting and refracting off the objects in a scene to create a photo-realistic appearance. This requires setting up lights just as you would in a studio.

Virtual lights in a scene can have any number of real-world properties. They can be diffused and glow in all directions like an unshaded light bulb. A light can also be directional and focused like a spotlight on a stage. And any of these lights can vary in intensity and color. They can also be positioned anywhere within the 3D

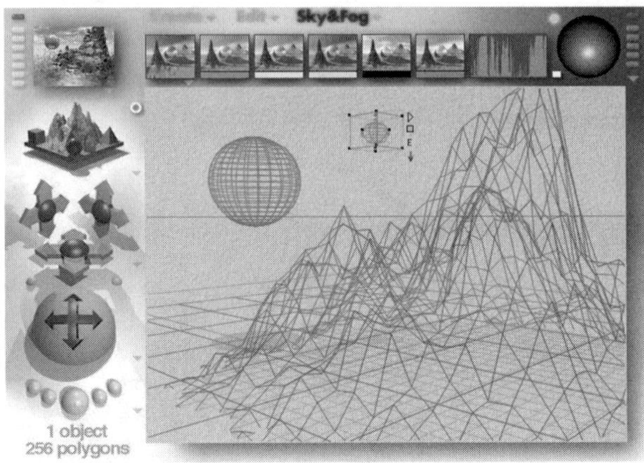

Figure 14.20   Adding and adjusting the virtual lights creates depth in your scene.

environment of your scene, even unnaturally right in front of the "camera" view and be programmed to reflect off objects while being invisible itself. Lights can also be programmed to project shadows or not, or even to be masked with a pattern, such as narrow level blinds similar to those found on a window shade.

Rendering

The last step in any CG work is the rendering. This is the stage when the scene is calculated into a two-dimensional image. A scene is always rendered from a fixed perspective, also known loosely as the camera. In fact, most rendering options include many camera simulating optical effects such as depth of focus, angle, and refraction.

Besides the obvious settings for resolution and image size, rendering involves many complex considerations. In order to realistically render lighting effects, object textures, reflections, and atmosphere dynamics, a process called *ray-tracing* is commonly used. This process analyzes the geometry of the objects from the perspective of the camera to generate the color of a pixel in the finished image as it should appear based upon the combined materials and lights that would affect a ray of light bouncing realistically through the

Figure 14.21 The process of rendering requires extensive calculation and can take many hours.

scene to that position. The rendering of 3D scenes can therefore be extremely computer processing intensive; it is not unusual for a high-resolution image of a complex scene to take many hours, even days, to be rendered. Of course, the speed of our computers today, including the iMac, is making this dramatically faster, as are specialized 3D rendering graphics processors.

THE MAC AND CG

Macs have long been used in conjunction with 3D-generated graphics, because after the images are rendered, the Mac is a great (and relatively inexpensive computer system compared to dedicated 3D workstations) platform for compositing and adjusting the images for final production. While the Mac has rarely been a part of the 3D rendering limelight, it has long been a near neighbor, and with Mac OS X, the Mac is poised to jump into 3D computer graphic rendering with both feet. Steve Jobs, the CEO of Apple who created the Macintosh and many years later returned with the iMac and Mac OS X, has a long personal history with 3D graphics since he is the CEO and founding owner of Pixar, famous for its CG movies Toy Story and A Bug's Life, as well as many other short and feature films. With Steve's influence in the Mac and the 3D rendering industry, we may see the Mac make new headway into this complex arena.

Part

Digital and Beyond

Your iMac is an amazing Web building workstation: today more Web sites (especially high-quality professional sites) are built using Macintosh computers than all the rest of the computer platforms combined. With its graphics friendly hardware and software, it isn't surprising that Web artists prefer it.

Your iMac is an amazing automation tool: the sophisticated AppleScript programming environment allows you to automate just about anything on your iMac you can do yourself. You can have your iMac carry out tasks completely on its own, or you can make a complex task that you perform often into a "one-button" operation.

Your iMac is an amazing networkable machine: its built-in, high-performance Ethernet interface, as well as its support for AirPort wireless networking make networking it easy to set up and fast to communicate. It even has the ability to boot off a network server—the first true network computer.

The Mac OS is an amazing operating system: it is filled with short-cuts and tricks that advanced users use to cut through the tedium of computer using. Learn just a few, and you'll be able to "mouse" circles around your friends, as well as impress yourself.

In this section we'll explore beyond digital media, the iMac way:

➤ Chapter 15: Making Your Own Web Page

➤ Chapter 16: Building Your Own Web Sites

➤ Chapter 17: Wireless Networking

➤ Chapter 18: Automating with AppleScript

➤ Chapter 19: Ten Quick iMac Tricks

Seventy-two clicks to browse
The HTML mirror.
Smashing through,
I'm on the Path!

Chapter Fifteen

Making Your Own Web Page

You've got your iMac connected to the Internet. You've got email, bookmarks of places you like to surf on the Web, and perhaps you've even developed a knack for chatting. Now you're ready to create your own outpost in the digital universe.

As you will quickly discover, the Web is all about HTML (Hyper Text Markup Language). *Hyper text* is text that has links to other text or resources—the *hyper* is the links. *Markup language* refers to the special codes that are inserted into the text to add formatting and structure—it is text that is *marked-up* in a special *language*. If this isn't clear to you now, that's because that's what this chapter is about. By the time you're ready to post your Web pages online, you'll know all there is to know about HTML.

In this chapter we're going to look at:

> ➤ Creating a simple Web page using Apple's HomePage

> ➤ Building a Web page from scratch using a text editor

> ➤ Making a Web page using a graphical Web page editor

> ➤ Exploring more elaborate HTML formatting options

> ➤ Posting your Web page to a Web server

Create a Page Online

Before we dive into the technical details of a Web page's HTML, let's take the express route to establishing a Web page of your own on the Internet that all your friends and anyone else can access.

There are many free services that you can use for creating and posting Web pages. These simplified services use prefabricated templates to let you build pages simply by filling out a form, filling in text, and locating some images you'd like used on the page. The automated services simply insert these into the template and post them to an address you can access.

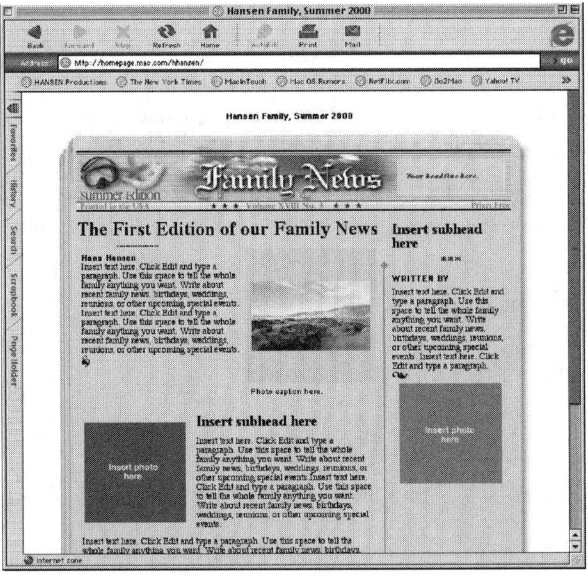

Figure 15.1 Using iTools' HomePage, you can create and post your own Web pages without knowing anything about HTML.

For this example we'll use Apple's iTools HomePage, which you can access for free if you have Mac OS 9 (or later) installed on your iMac.

WHAT TO PUT ON YOUR HOME PAGE

Making a personal home page is a great way to establish your own outpost in the digital universe—having a place where your friends can come and keep in touch with you, or a place to introduce yourself to new people. You can post information about yourself, about your hobbies, interesting anecdotes, pictures and snapshots, links to your favorite places on the Internet, and contact such as your email address or any other place you'd like people to be able to find you.

Be sure you lend your Web page some of your personality, too. Use colors you like, dress it up with images and graphics, and link it up to your friend's pages. Have fun with it, and share it—the Internet is a community that we can all be a part of.

Getting a HomePage

After you have signed up with Apple's iTools, you can choose the HomePage section of iTools to begin building a Web site. The HomePage section is where you control the Web pages—

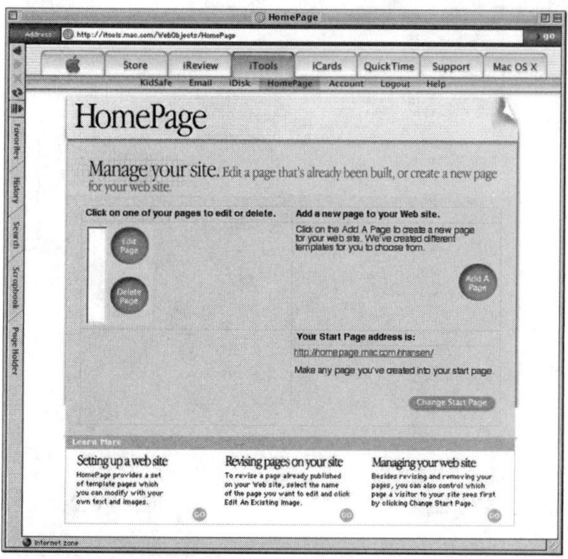

Figure 15.2 The main access to HomePage is where you add, edit, and delete pages from your HomePage site.

for example, where you can Add a Page, Edit a Page, Delete a Page, and Change Start Page. There are also help topics related to HomePage available at the bottom of the page.

You can access the Web pages to create and post via HomePage at `http://homepage.mac.com/[your iTools user name]/` from any Web browser anywhere on the Internet. And Apple doesn't use this free service to post advertising on your pages, like so many other free Web page hosting services.

Adding a Page

To add a page, simply go to the HomePage section of iTools and click the Add a Page button. You will be presented with a list of page types to choose from such as: photo album, iMovie theater, personal page, invites, baby announcements, resume, and education. You can select one of these areas for a specific page design theme, which you can then use as a template and add your content to it.

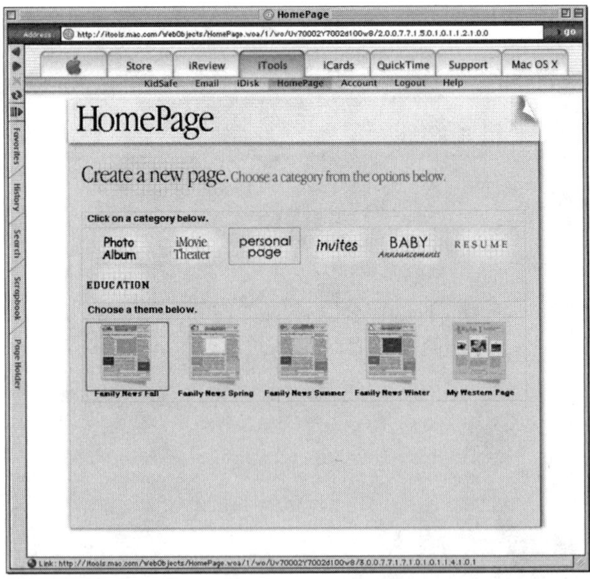

Figure 15.3 HomePage uses prefabricated template designs for pages of different types and themes.

Setting Up Your First Page

After you have selected a page theme, you can begin to edit the elements within its design. These will either be text or image fields, or text with link options.

Figure 15.4 After you have selected a template, you can edit its elements to customize the content.

Editing a Text Element

To edit an item on a page, click the Edit button adjacent to the item to enable its editing mode. The text field will become editable. Simply select and type over the text in the field to replace it with your content. You should try to be aware of the relative length of the text, as many items are designed to be short headlines. When you have finished entering your text, click Apply to accept your changes. If your text is too long or awkward looking, you can click Edit to revise it again.

Keep in mind that the Edit (or Apply) buttons are only visible in the creation mode for this page; later when you post the page, these buttons will be hidden and only text (or images) will remain.

Figure 15.5 Clicking the Edit button allows you to change text and then Apply it.

Selecting an Image

Some of the items on the page are fields that hold images rather than text. When you click the Edit button next to the field, you will be presented with a list of picture files stored on your iDisk.

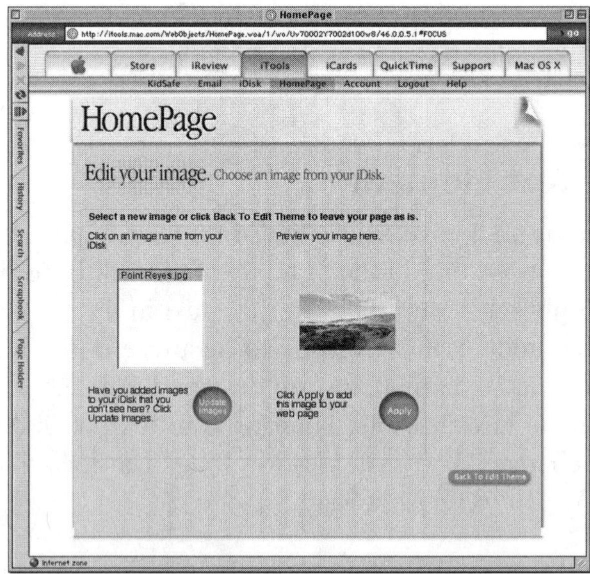

Figure 15.6 Editing an image item lets you select an image from those that have been copied to your iDisk.

In order to add images to your page, you will first need to copy them to the Pictures folder on your iDisk. Select an image from the list; a preview of it will be displayed, and you can click the Apply button to link that image into your page.

Editing a Link

Some page designs include link items. You have two editing options with these types of items: text or link. Clicking Edit: Text will allow you to change the text that is displayed on the page. Clicking Edit: Link allows you to change the URL that is activated from that text, which means, the Web page to go to when the text is clicked on.

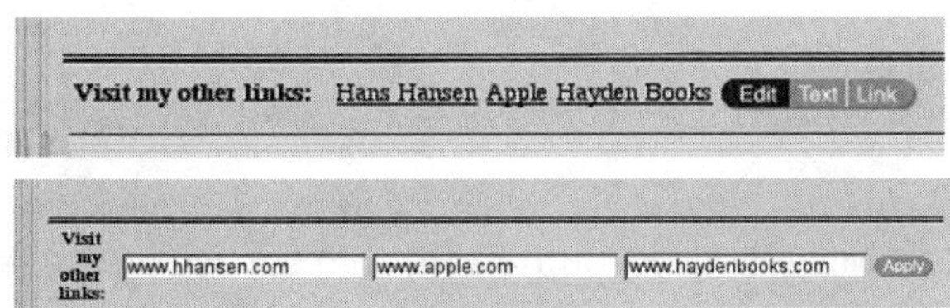

Figure 15.7 Use the Edit: Link button to change the destination of special link items.

Posting Your Page

When you are finished editing your page, you can click the Publish button at the top of the page to post it for the world to see. A message will come up identifying the URL for your new page, which you can use to access it. iTools will also provide you with a button to send email to your friends, letting them know about your new page.

Adding More Pages

At any time you can add more pages to your HomePage site by clicking the Add a Page button. You can add as many pages as you like; however, because all your pages are stored on your iDisk (which is limited to 20 megs), you may eventually run out of space for more pages or have to compete for space with other types of files you have stored on your iDisk.

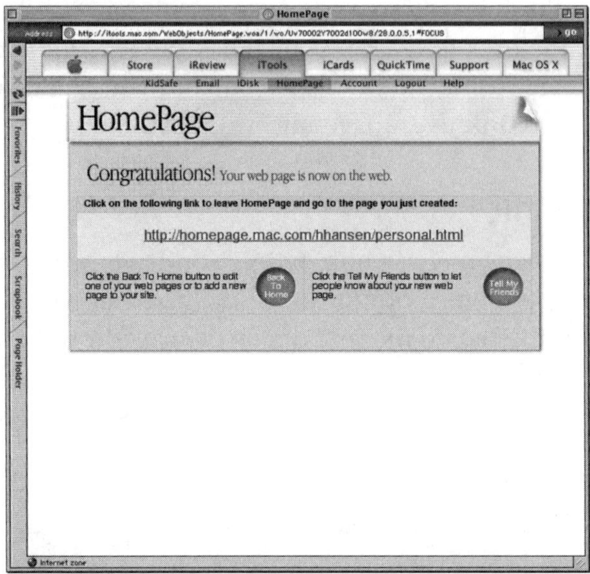

Figure 15.8 When you click Publish, your page will be posted and HomePage will tell you what the URL is to access the page.

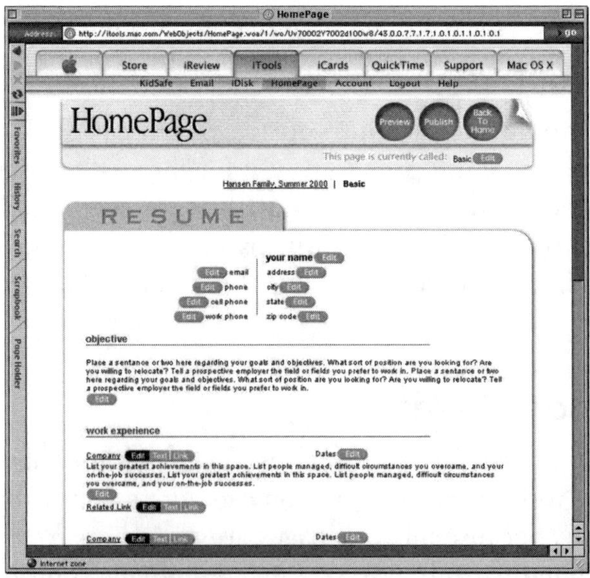

Figure 15.9 You can add as many pages as you like to your site; this page uses a resume template.

Changing Your First Page

When you have several pages on your HomePage Web site, you can select which one will come up by default as your home page when your site is accessed at the top level by visitors (`http:home-page.Mac.com/yourusername/`). Use the Change Start Page button to select your first page from your list of pages.

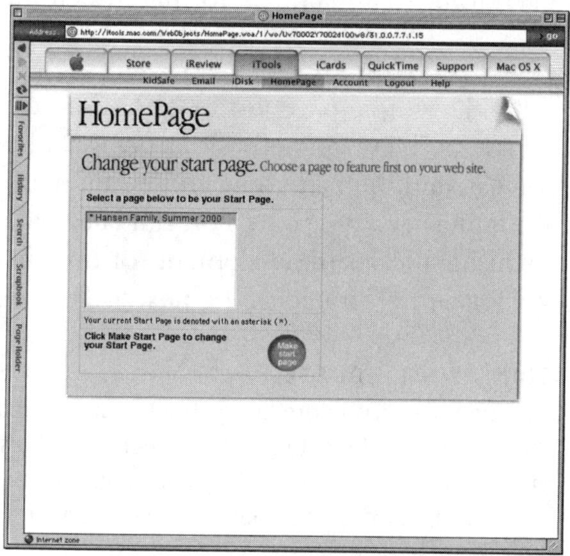

Figure 15.10 You can define which page on your site you want to load first by clicking the Change Start Page button.

For many people, HomePage provides all the features of a personal Web site that they will ever want or need. However, there is much more that can be done with a Web page, and if you want to create pages that aren't based on Apple's template designs, then you'll need to learn how to make your own Web pages.

Create a Page from Scratch

If you don't want to take advantage of templates for creating your own Web site, the best place to begin creating your own Web pages is simply by doing it yourself from scratch. And because all Web pages are just text that is marked up with formatting codes, anyone can do it. Simply open a word-processing application (such as SimpleText) and prepare to type some code.

Before you begin typing, you should understand that any formatting you apply to the text in your word processor is irrelevant; only the codes in the text matter. In fact, when you save your Web document, it will need to be in a plain text format, which will not retain text styling.

We're going to build a simple page just to demonstrate how HTML works. First, we'll create the basic structure, add some content, save and view it, and then add a bit more—an image, a link, some formatting, and a separator bar. You can later build a more complex page by using these simple elements or by using a graphical Web page editor demonstrated in the next topic.

> ### INFORMATION ABOUT YOURSELF
>
> Use your home page for information about yourself. Share your ideas and philosophies, and link them up to other related resources. If you're trying to find a new job, put your résumé on your home page. If you're an artist or designer, put together an online portfolio for visitors to browse and enjoy.

Basic HTML

A single Web page is a single text document that is HTML text marked up with codes that define formatting and function. An HTML viewer, such as a Web browser, reads the text and parses the codes in order to display the page with its formatting, images, and links. It doesn't care at all about any formatting that is already in the text, such as paragraph breaks or line breaks. The viewer only considers the HTML tags. It does, however, follow the order of elements as they are marked up in the file, placing them farther down the pages the farther into the HTML document they are.

HTML is all about using tags to define formatting or functions to be associated with text. A tag is a code within brackets, in this case the brackets are always a less-than and a greater-than sign that looks like this: <*tag*>. To use a tag, you simply insert it within the text where you want it to take effect. Some tags can stand alone and simply do something by themselves, such as the image tag <IMG>, which indicates the placement of an embedded image. Most tags, however, are designed to format a selection of text and need to have an additional closing or ending tag that adds a forward-slash into the tag code: </tag>; such as <B> and </B>, which will format all the text between these opening and closing tags as bold text.

Essential Tags

Each Web page text document must have three HTML tags that define its structure as an HTML formatted text. First, an HTML document needs to begin with an <HTML> tag (and end with an </HTML> closing tag) to mark that the text that is enclosed in this tag is formatted for HTML display. Within the <HTML> there are two main sections: the <HEAD> and the <BODY>.

The <HEAD> tag is used to enclose preliminary information that applies to the whole file, generally using special tags that affect global settings. In our example we'll use the <TITLE> tag within the <HEAD>.

The <BODY> tag is used to enclose the content or body of the page. This is where most of your HTML will reside.

Begin your HTML document by creating a new empty document in your word processor (we're using SimpleText) and typing in the following code:

```
<HTML>
<HEAD>
</HEAD>
<BODY>
</BODY>
</HTML>
```

Begin an HTML document by entering in these tags that define its structure.

Type in this code in plain text with a Return at the end of each line. This is the beginning of your HTML document.

Add Your Content

Next, let's add some content. We're keeping this example very simple and short, but you are welcome to paraphrase the text with your own.

First, we'll add a <TITLE> tag and some text. This will be the name of the Web page as it will appear in the title bar of the window when it is displayed in a browser, as well as what will be bookmarked as the name of the page in your browser's Favorites. This is not the name of the HTML document—that will come later. The <TITLE> tag is placed between the <HEAD> and </HEAD> tags, and it must end with a </TITLE> closing tag.

```
<HTML>
<HEAD>
<TITLE>Hello world!</TITLE>
</HEAD>
<BODY>
<H2>This is my first Web page.</H2>
<P>This is some text that appears on <I>my first</I> Web page.</P>
</BODY>
</HTML>
```

> Add the lines of code that are in bold to your sample HTML document, building the content of the page.

Next, let's add some content into the body of the document. We'll add a headline and a paragraph of plain text. There are many different tags to define different text styles; we'll list them all later, but for now I'll just give you one for a large bold headline: <H2>. This is the second largest headline text style; there are also <H1> and <H3> styles (and others). Enclose some text within an opening <H2> tag and a closing </H2> tag within the <BODY> section of your document to place at the top of your page. For the plain text paragraph we'll use the <P> tag, for paragraph. Enclose some text in an opening <P> and a closing </P> tag, after the <H2> tag within the <BODY> of your HTML document.

In our example, I've also used another formatting tag within the plain text to italicize two words by using the <I> and </I> tags.

Save It and View It

Once you have your HTML document underway, you can save it and view it in a Web browser to see what it looks like.

Save the file as a Plain Text document from your word processor.

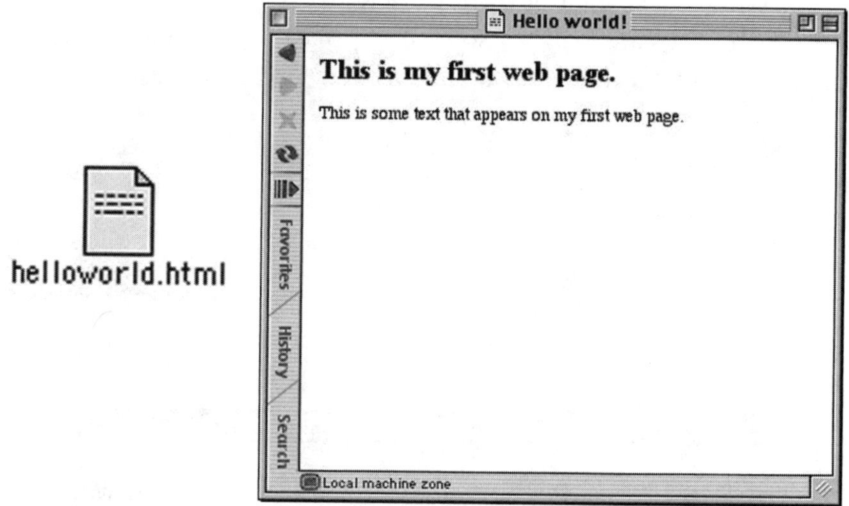

Figure 15.11 View an HTML document by dragging it into an open window of a Web browser.

Give it a name such as "helloworld.html." Always include ".html" at the end of your document's file name so that you and your software know that it is an HTML document. Some people, mostly Windows users, will use ".HTM" instead, but you're an iMac user.

After you have a file on your hard drive, simply open a window in your Web browser and drag the documents icon into the window to have your browser display it.

As you develop your HTML document, you can leave it open in your Web browser. Then whenever you make a change to the file and save it, you can switch back to the window in your browser and click the reload button to update the display with your changes. Some word processors such as BBEdit include commands to switch and reload a file in just one keystroke.

In most browsers you can view the source code of any Web page (such as in Internet Explorer) by selecting Source from the View menu. As you experiment with creating your own pages, you'll want to view the source code for other people's pages to discover new HTML tags and see how they accomplished complex formatting. These days the Web has grown to such an advanced level that most Web pages are built by software applications that automatically code the HTML and are capable of very elaborate displays.

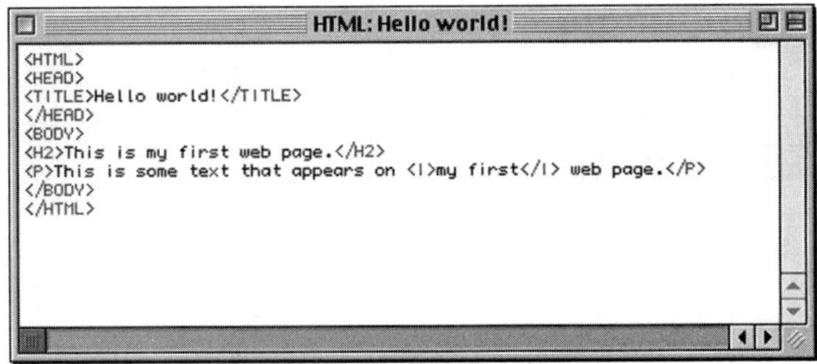

Figure 15.12 Viewing the source of a Web page in your Web browser is a great way to see HTML in action.

So now you have completed a simple Web page. Let's add a couple of common elements into it: an image, a link, centered formatting, and a separator bar.

> ### ANECDOTES AND HOBBIES
>
> Got something interesting to say? Something funny? Put it on your home page. Tell a story and link it to places and things from your adventure. Got a hobby? Share your knowledge of it on your home page. Find other people with pages and information that you can share and connect your page to. You can even sell your work from your page.

Add an Image

HTML is a great way to present text, but an image can be worth a thousand words. Including an image in a Web page is easy—just use the <IMG> tag. This tag defines the name (or URL) of a separate image file for the browser to load and display. The position of the tag within your text determines where an image file will be displayed. You'll notice that the <IMG> tag is a singular tag (no closing tag) and that it has several special parameters:

```
<HTML>
<HEAD>
<TITLE>Hello world!</TITLE>
</HEAD>
<BODY>
<H2>This is my first Web page.</H2>
<P>This is some text that appears on <I>my first</I> Web page.</P>
<P><IMG SRC="mona.jpg" WIDTH="238" HEIGHT="353" ALIGN="BOTTOM"
BORDER="0"></P>
</BODY>
</HTML>
```

Use the <IMG> tag to embed an image within a Web page.

When you use the <IMG> tag, you need to define several parameters that are located within the tag's brackets, each separated by a space. The first is the SRC parameter, which defines the source file and is written as *SRC="image.jpg"* with the name of the image file within quotes. The name of the file can be just the file name if the data file for the image is going to reside in the same directory location as the HTML document itself. Otherwise, it can be a

Figure 15.13 Our example Web page with an image added.

complete URL pointing to another location on the Internet or to a relative directory (UNIX based file structure codes).

Other parameters define the **WIDTH** and **HEIGHT** of the image, which you'll need to determine. The width and height don't need to be the same as the image's pixel dimensions, but may look odd if they are not. You can use an image editor to get the exact size of an image.

The last two parameters in our example are **ALIGN** and **BOR-DER**. The **ALIGN** parameter defines how the image should be positioned relative to the text that may be on the same line within the Web page. The **BORDER** parameter defines how many pixels of border to display around the image; for example, a setting of zero equals no border. There are also many other optional parameters for the **IMG** tag that aren't covered in this book.

In this example the IMG tag is within <P> tags to display the image as its own paragraph, separated from text above and below the image.

Add a Link

Adding a link to your Web page is what having Web pages is all about. Without links to other files on the Internet, it wouldn't be as vast and as useful an environment as it has become. The process of creating links involves using *anchors*. An anchor is a selection of text or an element such as an image within a Web page that defines a hyper-link to another place—it is the anchor of the link. Without an anchor, there would be nothing to click on to activate the link. To define an anchor within an HTML document, you use the <A> tag.

```
<HTML>
<HEAD>
<TITLE>Hello world!</TITLE>
</HEAD>
<BODY>
<H2>This is my first Web page.</H2>
<P>This is some text that appears on <I>my first</I> Web page.</P>
<P><IMG SRC="mona.jpg" WIDTH="238" HEIGHT="353" ALIGN="BOTTOM"
BORDER="0"></P>
<P>Click here to go <A
HREF="http://www.louvre.fr/">somewhere</A>.</P>
</BODY>
</HTML>
```

Use the <A> tag to define an anchor for a link. The HREF parameter defines the destination to load when the link is activated.

By enclosing a selection of text within an <A> tag and using the HREF parameter, it will become a link. The HREF tag is used to define where the link goes by placing a URL within its quotes: HREF="http://url.com/". Use the </A> tag to define the end of the anchor text or elements.

To make an image an anchor, simply enclose its <IMG> image tag within an <A> anchor tag.

Figure 15.14 Our example Web page with a link added within a new line of text below the image.

Center Your Elements

In addition to text styling format tags, there are also text (and element) positioning tags. One example is the <CENTER> tag, which center justifies a selection of your document to the middle of the browser window. For our example, we'll center the entire page by using the opening <CENTER> tag at the beginning of the <BODY> section and the closing </CENTER> at its end.

```
<HTML>
<HEAD>
<TITLE>Hello world!</TITLE>
</HEAD>
<BODY>
<CENTER>
<H2>This is my first Web page.</H2>
```

```
<P>This is some text that appears on <I>my first</I> Web page.</P>
<P><IMG SRC="mona.jpg" WIDTH="238" HEIGHT="353" ALIGN="BOTTOM"
BORDER="0"></P>
<P>Click here to go <A
HREF="http://www.louvre.fr/">somewhere</A>.</P>
</CENTER>
</BODY>
</HTML>
```

Use the <CENTER> tag to center justify text and other Web page
elements.

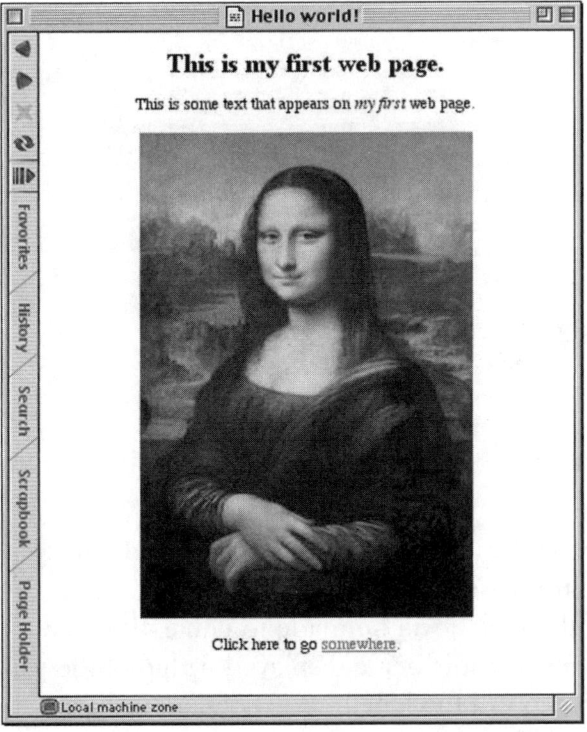

Figure 15.15 Our example Web page with all its body content
centered.

Centering has been handled in different ways over recent years, so
if you view the source of many Web pages, you'll see different
methods used. There are also many other formatting tags not covered here.

Add a Separator

Another example tag commonly found on many Web pages is the separator bar. This is a horizontal bar used to separate content and break up elements on a page. It uses the <HR> tag, which stands for horizontal rule.

```
<HTML>
<HEAD>
<TITLE>Hello world!</TITLE>
</HEAD>
<BODY>
<CENTER>
<P>
<H2>This is my first Web page.</H2>
<P>This is some text that appears on <I>my first</I> Web page.</P>
<P><IMG SRC="mona.jpg" WIDTH="238" HEIGHT="353" ALIGN="BOTTOM"
BORDER="0"></P>
<P>Click here to go <A
HREF="http://www.louvre.fr/">somewhere</A>.</P>
<P><HR WIDTH="40%"></P>
</CENTER>
</BODY>
</HTML>
```

> Use the <HR> tag to add a horizontal rule to break up your content. Use a <P> paragraph tag by itself to add an empty line of space.

The <HR> tag uses a **WIDTH** parameter to define the length of the rule. In this case, it is given as a percentage value of 40. This means that the length will be made to equal 40 percent of the width of the window that it is being displayed within; if the window changes size, so will the length of the separator bar.

The <HR> tag has been enclosed within a <P> tag to keep it in its own paragraph, apart from any text of the document.

I have also added a single <P> tag at the top of the content to add an empty line of space above the headline text to give it a bit more room.

Include an Email Link

One last commonly found element on a Web page is a link to an email address, which your browser can use to automatically address an email message. This is done in the same manner as a link, using the <A> anchor tag. Within the HREF parameter, use the "`mail-to:username@domain.com`" URL command. Note that there is *no space* inserted between mailto: and the email username.

```
<HTML>
<HEAD>
<TITLE>Hello world!</TITLE>
</HEAD>
<BODY>
<CENTER>
<P>
<H2>This is my first Web page.</H2>
<P>This is some text that appears on <I>my first</I> Web page.</P>
<P><IMG SRC="mona.jpg" WIDTH="238" HEIGHT="353" ALIGN="BOTTOM"
BORDER="0"></P>
<P>Click here to go <A
HREF="http://www.louvre.fr/">somewhere</A>.</P>
<P><HR WIDTH="40%"></P>
<P>Click here to send <A HREF="mailto:hans@hhansen.com">me</A>
email.</P>
</CENTER>
</BODY>
</HTML>
```

An email link is created by using the "mailto:" command within the HREF parameter of an <A> anchor tag.

My First Web Page

These are just the most basic HTML tags. There are many more for defining more complex elements such as tables, form fields, and multi-frame pages made of several HTML documents, as well as other tag languages, such as Java script, which can add even more features, such as button animation and programmable inter-action.

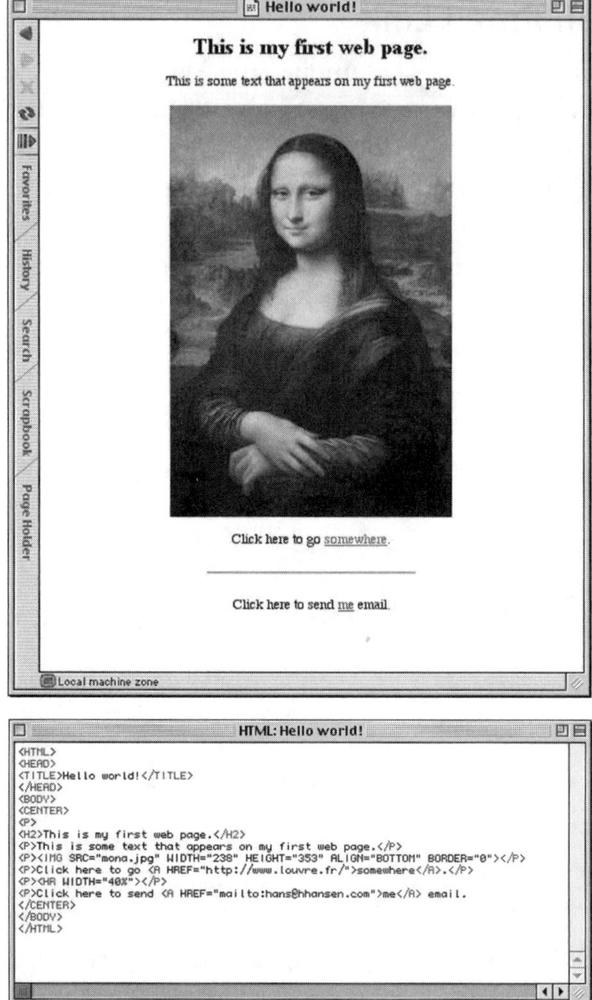

Figure 15.16 The completed Web page example HTML document, and its HTML source code viewed by the browser.

Save this example if you've followed along on your iMac. You'll find that it makes a good starting place to build your own future Web pages, or you can use other examples given later in this book. Later in this chapter, we'll look at how you can post your Web page on the Internet to share with the world.

Create a Page with an Editor

Understanding how HTML works is essential to making your own Web pages, but editing HTML directly can be a bit of a chore, especially when your Web pages get to be more complex. An easier way to create and format Web pages is to use a graphical editor that allows you to design your pages while displaying them as they will appear. Fortunately, many iMacs come bundled with an excellent software application for editing HTML documents, Adobe PageMill.

PageMill allows you to open HTML documents, edit text, select and format text, define link anchors, and create more complex page elements, such as tables, which can be difficult to create manually. PageMill also comes with a collection of many prefabricated graphics for use on Web pages as headers, buttons, and separators.

If you haven't already done so, install Adobe PageMill on your iMac from the bundled CD-ROM; then open up the application and check it out. PageMill comes with an excellent tutorial, and it has an extensive number of features, so we'll only cover the basics of creating a new page, editing it, viewing its source, saving it, and viewing it.

SNAPSHOTS

Tired of filling photo albums? Share pictures from your last vacations of you and your family (and of your pets). You might post pictures of places you've been and things in which you are interested. Having pictures on your home page is easier than carrying them around in your wallet.

A New Page

Creating a new HTML document in PageMill is as easy as choosing New Page from the New submenu at the top of the File menu. This will give you an empty page to add text and images to and to format. PageMill also has the ability to manage a Web site of many pages, which we'll get into later in the next chapter.

Figure 15.17 The example HTML document created by hand in the previous section of this chapter, shown as it is viewed in Adobe PageMill and ready to be edited.

You can also open HTML documents already created in PageMill by using the Open command in the File menu, or by dragging and dropping the file onto the PageMill icon by using the Finder. This will open the file and display it somewhat like it will be viewed in a Web browser. However, you should be aware that PageMill will change the HTML code structure to meet its own more mechanical methods if you save the file. This may not make any difference to you unless you hand code the HTML and prefer it the way you've entered it.

Edit It

Editing your pages with PageMill is just like using any word processor on your iMac. You type your text, make selections and apply formatting to them, and insert objects and manipulate them. Much of PageMill's editing interface supports drag-and-drop, so you can move selections of text around by dragging them, or you can move images and other objects.

Figure 15.18 The interface of PageMill is all geared toward editing Web pages. The Inspector palette is used to edit global page settings and object parameters.

Global settings are handled in their own interfaces. The title of the Web page is entered in a text field at the top of the window. Other global settings are specified in the Inspector palette. There are settings for the page itself, mostly related to the colors of the background, or links. There are also setting for special objects, such as the parameters for an embedded image, a separator bar, or table. You'll also see many special controls for building frame-based Web sites, which we'll cover in the next chapter. HTML also includes many tags for creating forms, which makes working with PageMill very easy.

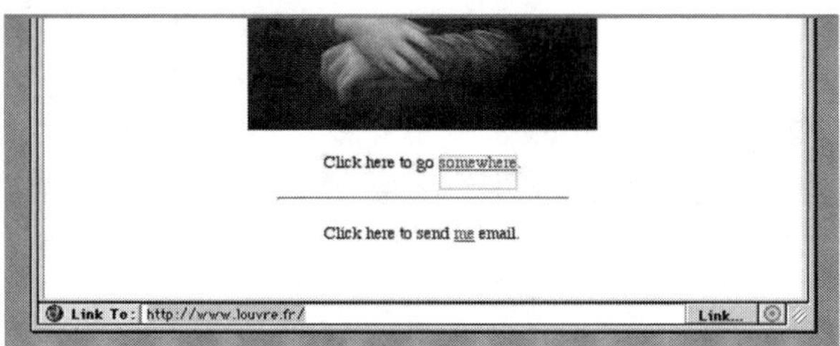

Figure 15.19 Specify a link by selecting text or objects and entering the URL in this field at the bottom edge of a document window.

Creating a link using PageMill is very simple. Simply select the text to become the anchor for the link; then click in the Link To text field at the bottom of the window to enter the URL for the link. Press Enter to accept the changes. You can also click the Link button at the right end of the text field to select a file on your hard drive, perhaps another page on your site, to link to.

LINKS

Do you visit a bunch of interesting Web sites regularly? Share your bookmarks and favorites with others. Organize them into categories for you and your friends to use. And be sure to ask your friends to put links to your home page on their sites. Don't isolate yourself; connect your home page to other people and places.

See the Source

In addition to editing your HTML documents visually, PageMill also lets you view and edit the HTML source code by choosing Source Mode from the View menu. You'll notice that the code for even a simple document can become very complex looking and prolific when created by a machine.

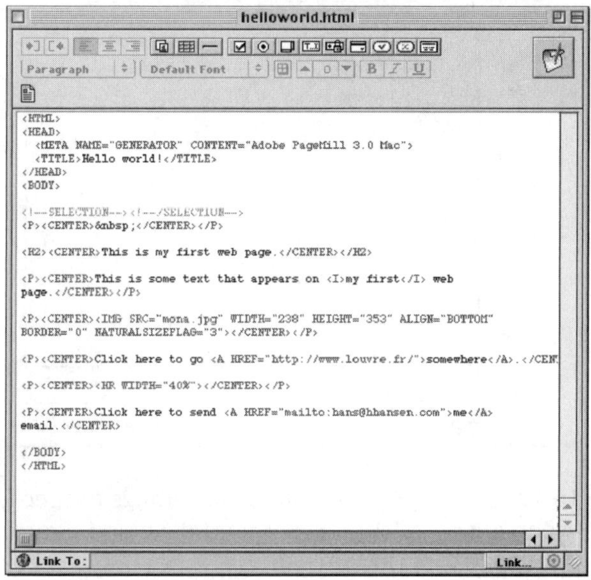

Figure 15.20 Use the Source Mode to view the HTML code of a document and edit it.

You may also notice a lot of commented out codes (commands within <!—and --!> bracketing) being used to track settings that are specific to PageMill. This is because all the information related to your PageMill documents are stored within the HTML structure, rather than having a separate master Web site file and exported HTML documents from that master (as some other Web page editing software applications function).

Save It

When you save your file, you can simply choose Save from the File menu like you would for the documents of any software. However, if your HTML page is going to be uploaded to the Internet, you many have to tell PageMill how to relate any embedded images or other HTML links to files that are currently located on your hard drive.

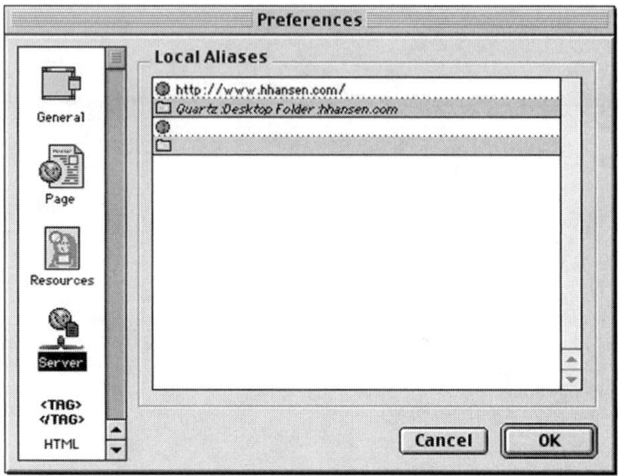

Figure 15.21 Use the Server preference settings to specify a relation between a local folder on your hard drive and a remote Web server location.

Using the Server settings within PageMill's Preferences, you can specify a URL that will be the location equivalent to the folder on your iMac where you currently are storing the files for your Web pages. With this setting, PageMill can save the link references so that they will work when located on the server with that URL, essentially aliasing the local file structure to the intended one.

PageMill also has features for checking the links of pages automatically, looking for any broken or unspecified locations. This is very useful for complex pages with many links.

View It

While editing your HTML documents in PageMill is very close to seeing what they'll look like in a Web browser, you can also use PageMill's Preview Mode to do the same thing. It is available from the View menu or by clicking the large button at the upper right corner of a document window. Using this function, you can turn off editing and view the pages easily. All the links will become active, allowing you to test links to other local pages and items.

Figure 15.22 Use the Preview Mode to see and interact with your document in a method similar to a Web browser.

You can use the Switch To command at the bottom of the View menu to quickly view your most recently saved changes in a Web browser of your choice. You can also use the Switch To command to open other items in other software applications, such as images in an image editor or HTML text in a word processor.

Other Web Page Elements

There are, of course, many great books and resources all about creating Web pages, so without going into very much depth, let's look briefly at a few of the more complex capabilities of Web pages: tables, forms, and using backgrounds and color.

Tables for Formatting

Tables consist of any organization of rectangular cells into a grid, each cell able to contain text, images, and objects, just like any Web page. Tables can be set up to a proportional grid, which can be resized with a page, or they can be set to exact pixel widths and heights to maintain a perfect layout. HTML tables can have borders and spacing of precise widths as well, even being hidden entirely so that you can't see the edges of the table. Tables can be a simple grid of cells, or a complex combination where cells are merged together to form complex designs.

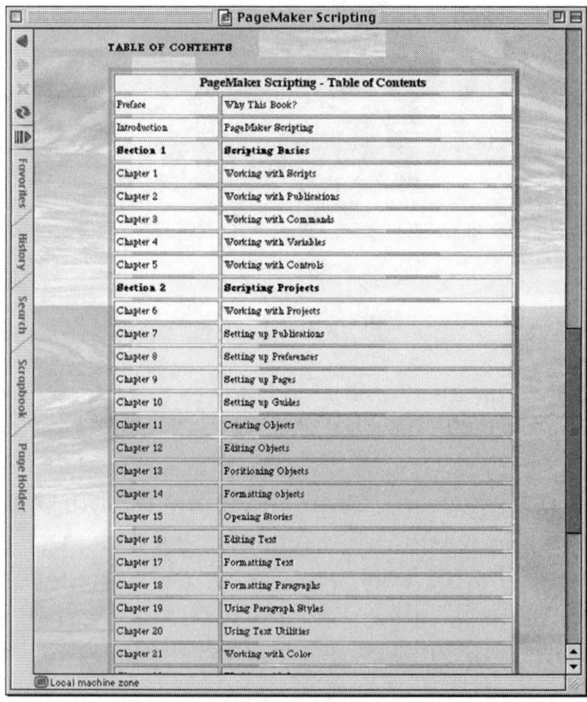

Figure 15.23   Formatting a list into a table can make it much easier to read and work with.

You'll generally see tables used for two purposes: organization or layout. A table is an obvious way to organize tabular data such as lists or charts. But tables can also be a very useful layout tool for formatting complex pages with precise positioning.

Figure 15.24 This Web page, *The New York Times* on the Web, uses tables to control its layout for a tight and organized structure.

Setting up tables can be difficult to manage by hand, and it requires careful planning of a page design. Most Web page designers will use a graphical editor or Web page layout software application to help set up the table structure and fill it in.

Form Fields for Acquiring Data

There are a rich set of HTML tags for defining form field within a page, which can be used by the Web user to enter information and send it into the server for processing. You can define text fields, obscured password fields, pop-up menus, checkboxes, and radio button sets. Each form item can have parameters that control the length of the input and how to relate some types of controls together into groups. There are also standard tags for creating submit and cancel buttons.

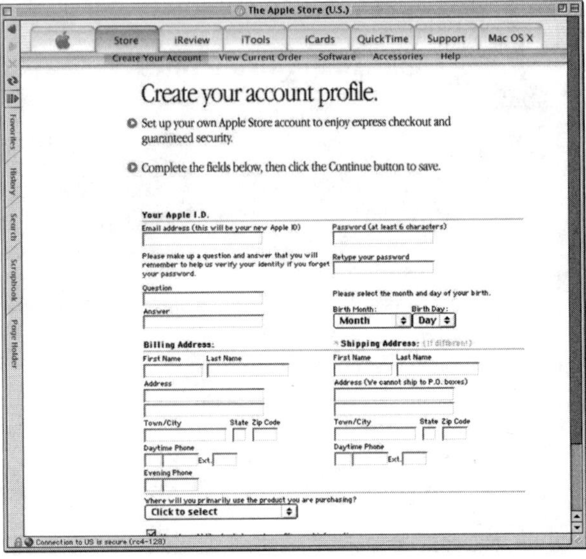

Figure 15.25 You use HTML form fields every time you purchase something online.

One thing that you can't do with HTML is actually process the data that is entered; for this purpose, special programs need to be written to accept data when it is submitted and then process it. Many forms will use special JavaScript features to make fields smart by only accepting data in particular patterns (such as credit card numbers) or by totaling amounts automatically.

Mixing It All Together

The most elaborate Web page designs use many techniques all at once and additional layer-like abilities. A background image will be used to create a foundation for a design; then a table is used to fit specially formatted images and text objects onto it so that everything lines up perfectly. There are also HTML features for filling spaces with colors and handling complex formatting of text such as using specific fonts, sizes, styles, and colors.

Figure 15.26 This very complex page uses a background image, tables, color fills, precise image alignment, and rich text styles.

Posting a Page on a Server

Once you have a page or two built, you'll want to share it with the world, and to do that you'll need to put it on a Web server. Getting space to put Web pages these days is easy. If you have signed up with iTools, you can use your `homepage.mac.com` site to host your pages. If you have an ISP (Internet Service Provider) such as Earthlink, you'll get free Web space with your account.

It is also possible to serve your Web pages directly from your iMac using Personal Web Sharing or a more robust Web server application.

CONTACT INFO

You might not want to share your home address and phone number with anyone who happens by your home page, but you might put up your email address and list any chat rooms where you can be found.

If you volunteer or contribute to some community or organization, you might want to list it and how to support it.

Using Your iDisk with `homepage.mac.com`

If you have signed up with Apple's iTools (once again, the free service for users of Mac OS 9 or later), you have 20 megs of online storage on your iDisk that you can use at least in part for Web pages. Within your iDisk is a folder called *Sites*, which is where you can store your HTML files and any linked images or objects. If you used iTool's HomePage to build pages online, they are stored here as well. This is probably the easiest way for an iMac user to get your pages online quickly.

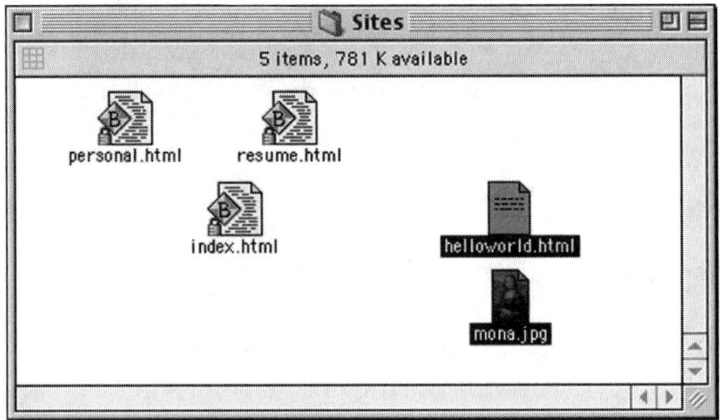

Figure 15.27 The Sites folder on your iDisk is an easy way to post your Web pages quickly for the world to see. Use the URL for your pages: `http://homepage.mac.com/yourname/yourpage.html`

To use the iDisk to host your Web pages, simply copy your HTML and linked images to the Sites folder. You can then immediately access them on the Internet by going to the appropriate URL. In this case it will include the name of the HTML file you want to view: `http://homepage.mac.com/hhansen/helloworld.html` is the URL for our example HTML document on my personal iDisk.

Using an ISP

If you use an ISP such as Earthlink to dial up to the Internet, it is likely that your account came with some free space for hosting Web pages. To access your Web server space, you first will need to go to your ISP (probably their Web site) to find out how to access your directory and access it with FTP. You will also need to find out what URL to use to view your pages.

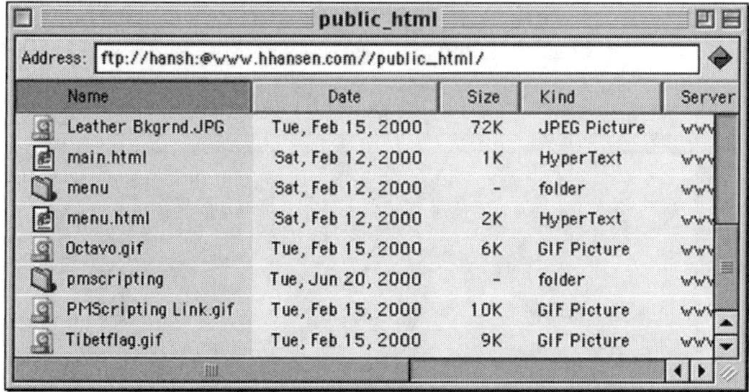

Figure 15.28 Access your Web server directory using FTP software, with information provided by your ISP.

Accessing Your Server Directory

After you have the FTP access information for your Web server directory, you can access it by using an FTP software application such as Anarchie. Get the directory of your Web server space and use your user name and password to access it.

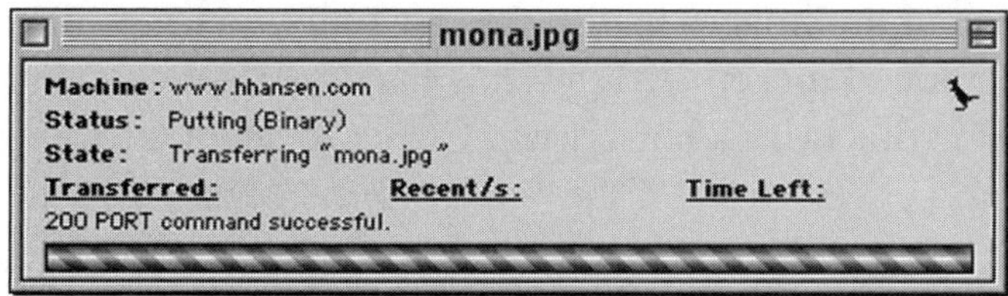

Figure 15.29 Upload your HTML files and any linked images to your Web server space.

Once you have a window open for your "site," you can drag files into it to upload them. Post all the files that are used in your pages, both HTML and any linked images and objects.

Testing Out Your Page

The last step is to test out your page by accessing it over the Internet with your Web browser. Enter in the URL and see if it loads. If not, check to make sure that the name of the HTML document is correct, as well as the domain and user subdirectory.

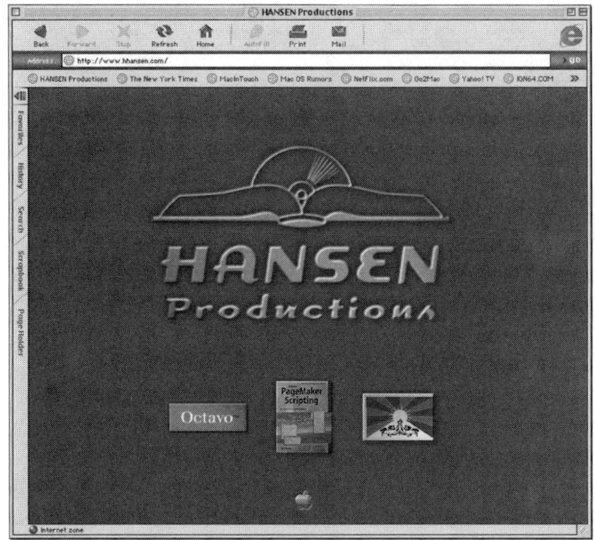

Figure 15.30 Here is my finished product.

Check that all the images load properly; if not, perhaps they are being referenced incorrectly, possibly because they were linked to a location on your iMac's hard drive. Check to see if all your links work. If not, check to see if the URLs are correct.

So that's it. An introduction to Web pages: HTML documents, a quick overview of special HTML formatting capabilities, using a graphical Web page editor, and lastly how to post your page to a server for the world to enjoy. There are an endless number of ways to make Web pages, and new technologies are being developed every day to add new features and capabilities to Web pages. If you want to learn more about creating Web pages, just go online. There are many great sites devoted to Web page development and design, as well as many great books.

Understanding how a Web page and HTML works has been the second step to becoming a sophisticated Internet user; the first was to get online and be able to get email and surf the Web, and the next will be to make a multi-page Web site of your own. But first, we have some ideas about things you might put on personal Web pages to inspire the newly found Web developer.

Under the hazy fluorescence, within the cold gray cube,
Between loose wires hanging from the ceiling,
An iMac encounters an error, beep!
Startled, the Web designer drops his mouse.

Chapter Sixteen

Building Your Own Web Site

Making your own Web site might be the most complex and rewarding thing you'll do with your iMac. Working with multiple pages, lending them structure and navigation, and building frame sets, bring the Web site to life. Special effects, embedded media, and getting feedback via submitted data, perhaps even serving your site right from your iMac also make it your own. New methods and technologies are being developed every day to enhance the Web for users and authors.

Building Web pages is easy, but building a Web site of many pages can be a bit trickier. Let's look at how you can construct a group of pages that work together.

In this chapter, we are going to look at:

- ➤ Organizing a Web site of multiple pages

- ➤ Building your site using frames

- ➤ Adding special effects, such as button roll-over animation and embedding media (QuickTime movies)

- ➤ Setting up a simple Web form for data submission

- ➤ Serving your Web site directly from your iMac by using Personal Web Sharing

Organizing Your Site

If you are using iTools HomePage builder, you already may have built several pages and know that HomePage automatically creates cross-references between them. But if you have an interest in building a more customized site for yourself, perhaps for personal interests or the needs of your business, you'll want to build a site from scratch—not from a template-driven page builder. Organizing a site, building navigation between pages, and developing a design that is consistent *and* flexible, all are a bit awkward the first time, but easier with practice.

Working with Many Pages

You need to plan and organize your site before you begin building it. Understanding the content you are presenting is essential. Perhaps you have a single page that is too big (too long and complex, resulting in slower download times), which might work better as several smaller pages.

MAKE A GREAT WEB SITE EVEN GREATER

The World Wide Web is a vast universe of sights and visions, some better than others. The Web has been around long enough now for certain types of presentations to become common and proven effective. When building a great Web site, there are several things that you should keep in mind. They are: content always comes first, location matters even in the virtual universe of the Internet, design of form and function should be balanced, your Web needs a personality, and your site should be alive with activity.

The best sites balance these elements with a good measure of each. A site with good content may not need to be as active (changing often), but it still needs to be easy to find, easy to load, and be interesting (have personality). When you explore a site, or when you build your own site, look at how well it manages each of these elements; most of the time you'll find that a site which is less captivating is missing one or more of these basic elements.

Start at Home

Every Web site needs to have a home page—a base that someone browsing your site can always find. The home page is typically the top (hierarchically) of your site with a summary of what can be found in the site, whose pages they are, and why they have been put together. The home page usually will have a menu, or directory, of the pages within the site.

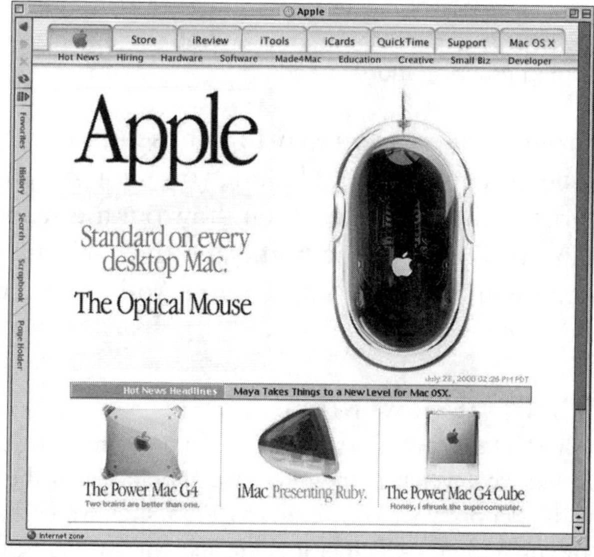

Figure 16.1 The home page is where every site begins. Apple's site presents a menu across the top and featured items within the body of the page.

There are many different structures in which information can be presented on a site. The most common is a menu-driven structure that allows readers to choose which subject interests them first, thus allowing them to browse around the site following their own interests. But for linear information, a series of pages that link only to the next or previous page is common (usually also with a link to the top or home). For very large sites, a combination of structures can work at different levels: a menu of subjects at the top, further menus within each section, and a linear series of pages at the lowest level.

393

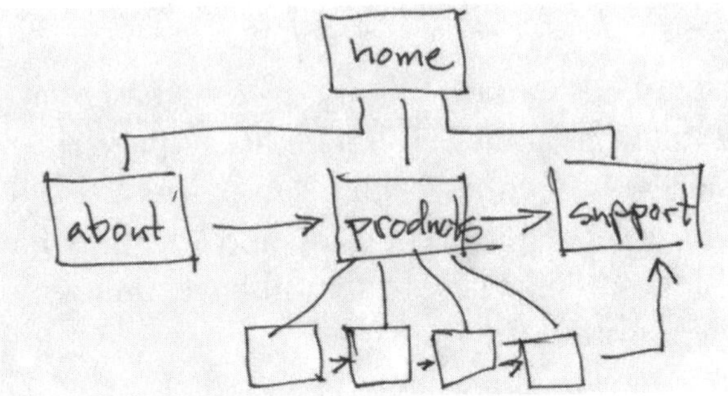

Figure 16.2 Drawing a diagram of your Web site organization will help you plan its navigational needs.

When organizing your site, you may find it useful to draw a diagram of the site and consider the linking you want to build among its topics. Start with a home page; then draw out the second-level subjects. Draw lines between the home and the subjects to represent the navigational links they will require. Add more pages below as are needed.

> ### CONTENT, CONTENT, CONTENT
>
> Clearly, content comes first. You have to put something on your Web site and whatever it is, nothing else should get in the way of exploring it. People visit and return to Web sites which have the most depth on a topic—whether it is the anatomy of sharks, the history of pong, or an online book store—if the content is weak, so will be the interest of your users.
>
> One method for developing great content is to create a community on your site. You can invite friends and associates, as well as people interested in your topics, to contribute to developing each other's ideas. The online bookstore Amazon.com does this by allowing users to write reviews of the books in their databases. Other sites develop message boards where users can interact and discuss topics on the site.

Navigation Elements

After you have your site organized, you can begin thinking about the navigational needs of your site. Do you want a menu to your

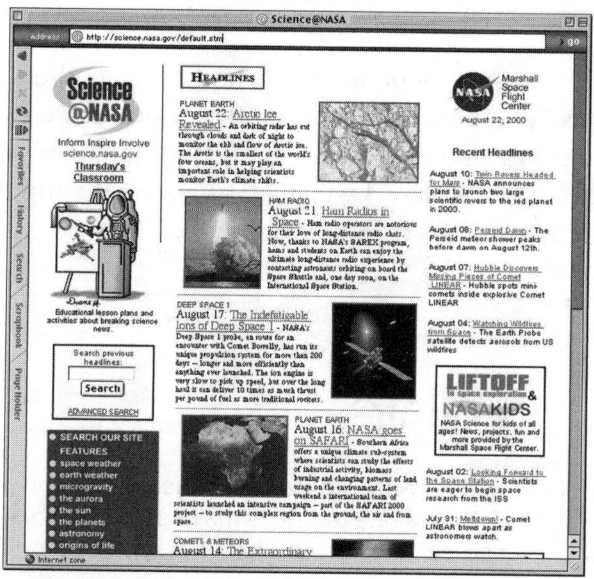

Figure 16.3 Granted, it may be hard to develop content as good as NASA's, but what is important to recognize is how well they have kept content first in their Web site design, featuring recent discoveries and useful reference resources. `(science.nasa.gov)`

subjects available on every page, or just on the home page, which the reader will have to return to before accessing a different subject? Do you want a graphical menu at the top of your pages, along one side or just a text-based menu at the foot of your pages?

Figuring out how you want to present your navigational elements shouldn't be too difficult. After all, there are millions of Web sites out on the Internet that you can browse for ideas and organizational concepts. Let's look at a few of the more common elements that are used on most Web sites.

Continuity and consistency are always very important on a Web site. It makes the pages appear to go together and helps the readers identify what is important as they browse through pages—the important elements are those that change.

Menus

Most Web sites use a menu to define and navigate their major subjects' sections. The design difficulty with a menu-driven structure is that the menu must be on every page of the site. More and more site menus are being drawn by using tabs across the top of a page, but there are many ways to convey a menu.

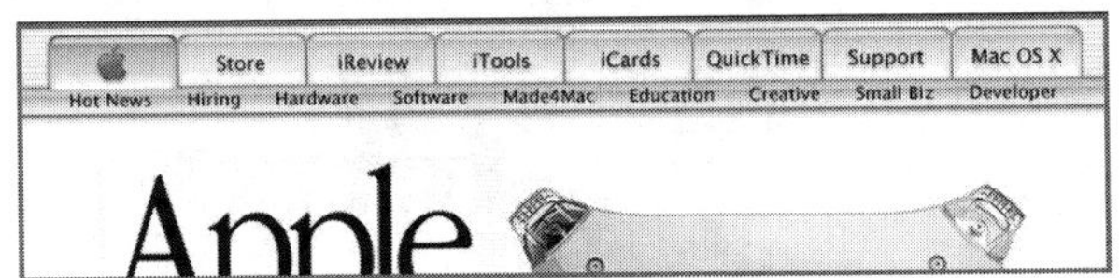

Figure 16.4 Apple's Web site uses tabs across the top of every page on the site to navigate the site's major sections. Beneath the tabs within each section of the site is a submenu of section-specific items.

A menu should always be in the same place and should never change its order or have items disappear—any change in continuity can be very confusing. One detail of a menu is that it should indicate the current selection you are within—don't simply drop the item for the section you are in (disrupting menu continuity), but rather highlight it in some fashion and deactivate its link.

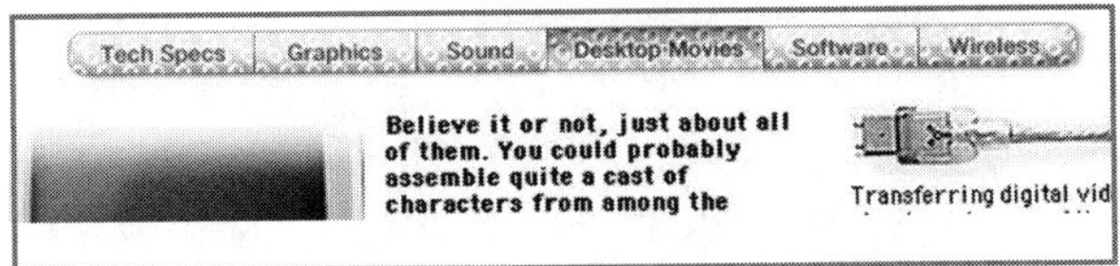

Figure 16.5 Apple's site also has an additional menu design to handle third-level pages.

Many large Web sites also need second level menus, which give you a directory of the subjects within the current section being viewed. The deeper your Web site goes, the more such submenus you may need.

Link Home

Every Web site that has many pages needs to have an obvious link back to the top or home page. Usually, the home link will be a logo or a site identifier. It should always be in the same place on each page within a site.

Figure 16.6 The Apple logo is used as the home button.

Footers

Another place that many sites put common navigational elements is at the foot of a page (the footer). Some sites put text versions of graphical menus at the footer, as well as additional navigational aids, such as search fields and pop-up menus. They also often put copyright information and contact info there.

Figure 16.7 The footer on Apple's Web site has a search field, common links, contact and legal information, and is the same on every page.

Thumbnail Images

When a site includes links to many images or files, using small thumbnail images to represent them makes browsing convenient. Selecting one of the images opens it as a larger image. Usually, the reader will need to go back to the gallery listing to access other images.

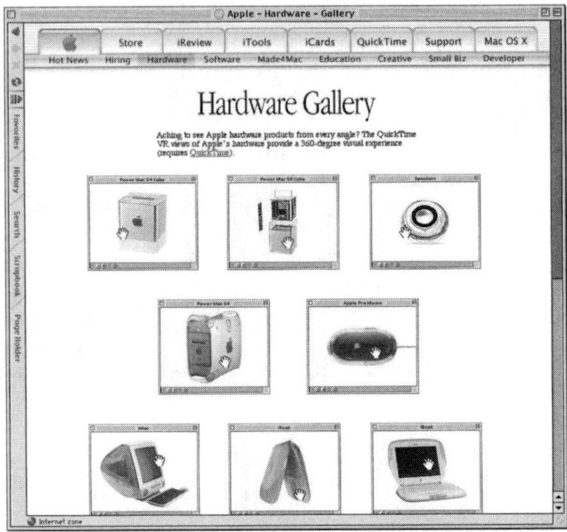

Figure 16.8 Many sites have galleries of pictures and media files that use thumbnail images as a directory for viewing them individually.

Subpage Navigation

While most of the time you browse a long page simply by scrolling up and down, it is possible to set up links that will go to a specific location scrolled down a page. This is useful in very long texts. For example, a page might begin with a list of chapters or topics and selecting one will take you down the page to it.

Using Design Templates

After you have determined what navigational elements you want, you'll need to make them. There are lots of books out there devoted to designing Web sites; however, you probably can manage on your own. You don't need to create elaborate graphics; a simple list of text-based links can be very effective.

The easiest way to create a consistent design is to begin with a page that has all your common elements and then use copies of it to build your other pages. You can also create templates for the different parts of your pages—one template file for the top (header) of your pages, several files for different content layouts that fill the middle or body of your pages, and a template file for the footer of your pages. You can then build the pages for your site by copying and pasting different elements together. This sort of template-driven design is a necessity when you are building a large site and there are many people working on its pages.

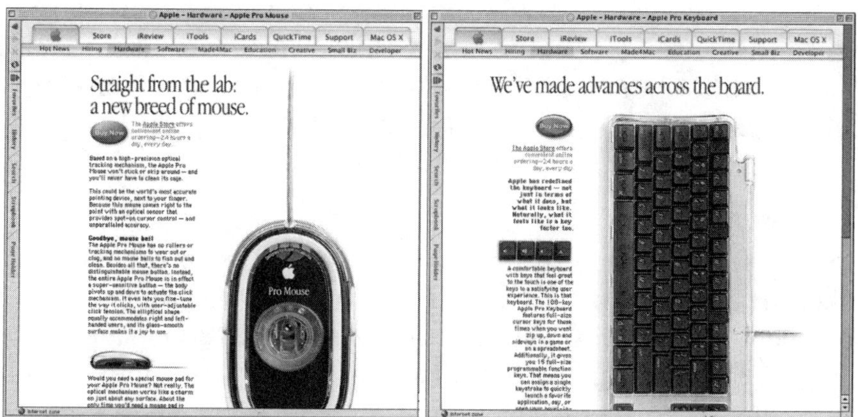

Figure 16.9 Building a consistent look to your pages can be a design challenge, but once an element is created, it is easy to use as a template to build additional pages. The Apple Web site is a great example of designing for global, content, and unique elements.

The key is to create a consistent design and stick to it. You can build yourself some templates to use as you implement your pages. Web site elements usually fall into three general types: global, content, and unique—each requiring different consideration and application.

Global Elements

Elements that appear in the same place and in the same way on every page of your Web site are considered to be global elements. These elements tend to be the easiest to implement, but can be the most difficult to design as you need to keep in mind the needs and functions they bring to each page, while not distracting from the needs of the different content to which they will be joined. Global elements tend to be menus, headers, and footers, with common text and images within them such as logos and slogans.

Content Elements

Content is what a Web site is all about, so you should find ways to make the layout and presentation of text and images consistent and pleasing throughout your site. You should set text in a similar manner on every page, using the same fonts and sizes and styles, while creating heads and subheads for your text that are also styled consistently. You should present images throughout your site in similar ways, such as always with a thin black line framing them (or not), and of similar quality, in full-color JPEG, for example.

Unique Elements

Of course, the more structure and consistency you build, the more likely that you'll have exceptional elements that need to be handled uniquely. Perhaps you will need to figure out how to fit an extra long bit of text or an image that has an irregular shape into your Web site. Handling such challenges is the fun of being a designer—breaking the rules to create new ones.

Working with Frames

You've probably found that many Web sites don't use a simple page-to-page linear approach to navigation, but instead break the Web browser window into rectangular regions that can be swapped out individually while keeping other regions static. This *frame* method is great for keeping common navigational elements static while switching between content selections, such as creating a narrow frame for a site menu along one side, while displaying selected content in a main body frame, and keeping common footer information static at the bottom. A frame layout can be used to create more efficient designs that download quickly and are fast to navigate.

Frame Basics

Frames are sets of HTML pages that are designed to work together. Each frame is its own HTML page, and all the frames in a set

LOCATION, LOCATION, LOCATION

Getting people to find your page easily can be half the battle of building a presence in such a vast arena as the Internet. One way to make it easy is to register your own domain name—www.your-name.com or www.mycompany.com. Hundreds of thousands of domains have already been registered, but there are still millions of dot-coms, dot-nets, and dot-orgs available. A good domain name is one that is either obvious or memorable—a word or name that naturally relates to your site and describes what it is, or one that is creative and unique that people will remember.

To register a domain name, you'll need to search for it to see if it is available and then pay a fee to use it. The management of .com, .net, .org, and other top-level domains is maintained by a company called Network Solutions, which you can visit at `www.network-solutions.com`. Registering a domain is something for which you have exclusive use on a renewable annual basis, currently costing $35 per year. When you register a domain name, you'll need to coordinate pointing it at your Web site server with your Internet service provider.

Figure 16.10 Location is all relative, but having a domain name that matches your business is an obvious place for people to find you on the World Wide Web. (`www.adobe.com`)

are defined by a special top-level HTML file called a *frameset*. The frameset uses special <FRAMESET> and <FRAME> tags to describe how to divide up the browser window into frames and what HTML files to load into them. The frameset HTML file also uses a <NOFRAMES> tag for HTML code to use when a Web browser doesn't support frame viewing.

Figure 16.11 This simplistic example has a menu frame along the left, a body frame filling the right, and a footer frame along the bottom of the body frame.

```
<HTML>
<HEAD>
        <TITLE>My Web Site</TITLE>
</HEAD>
<FRAMESET FRAMEBORDER=1 COLS="23%,77%">
<FRAME SRC="Menu.html" NAME="Menu">
<FRAMESET FRAMEBORDER=1 ROWS="88%,12%">
```

```
<FRAME SRC="Body.html" NAME="Body">
<FRAME SRC="Footer.html" NAME="Footer">
</FRAMESET>
<NOFRAMES>
<BODY>
Viewing this page requires a browser capable of displaying frames.
</BODY>
</NOFRAMES>
</FRAMESET>
</HTML>
```

In the HTML frameset code for the above example, note that it defines a frameset within a frameset.

Each frame is created by the <FRAMESET> tag, which defines how the window is split to create two or more frames; for a vertical split you use the **COLS=""** parameter, for a horizontal split you use the **ROWS=""** parameter. With these parameters you can define the splits by percentage of the window, by an exact number of pixels, or by an asterisk (*), which means all-that-remains. Within the <FRAMESET> and closing </FRAMESET> tags, you must define the content of each frame specified by using a <FRAME> tag, or you can define additional frame splitting within a frameset using another <FRAMESET> tag.

With the <FRAME> tag you define the source HTML page for the frame with the SRC="page.html" parameter. You also give the frame a name by using the **NAME** parameter for reference when targeting links to specific frame content.

Laying Out Your Frames

Coding frames can be quite involved, but using a graphical Web page editor such as Adobe PageMill can make the task very easy. With a blank document window open, you can hold down the Option key to drag out frame dividers from the edge of the window. PageMill automatically compiles the instructions to define the frames you visually create.

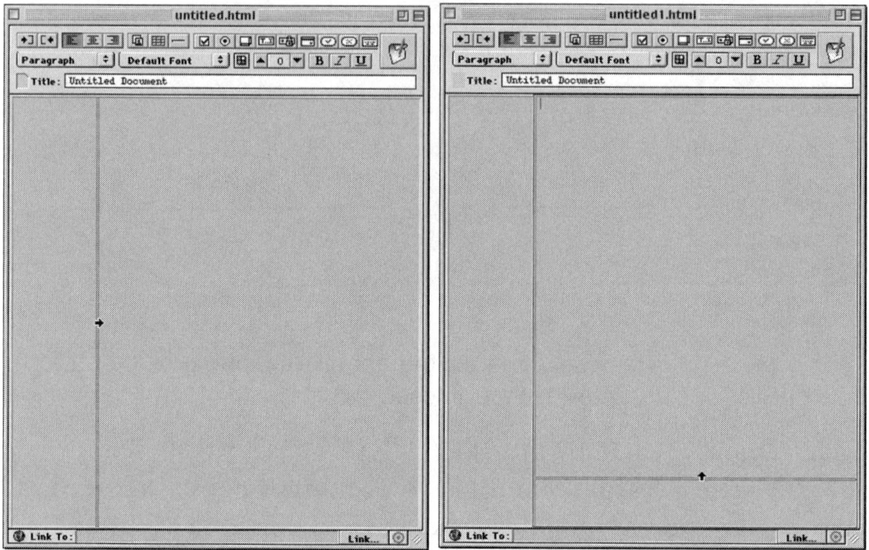

Figure 16.12 In Adobe PageMill you can hold down the Option key and drag frame dividers into position.

With your frames created, you can click within them to select them to specify their options. Using PageMill's Inspector palette, you can select the first tab on the left to see the selected frame's settings.

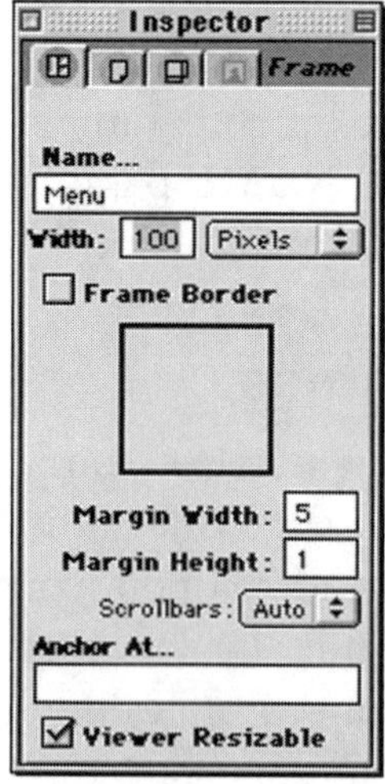

Figure 16.13 Frame options can be adjusted using PageMill's Inspector palette by selecting the tab at the top-left.

You can specify the frame's name, its width or height in percentages or pixels, how much border and margin to use, and whether you want the frame to be scrollable when its content is larger than its viewable space.

After you have defined your frames, you'll need to save your frameset. To save the master frameset file, choose Save Frameset from the Frameset submenu in the File menu. This will save the definition of the current frames, both their positions and the HTML pages that have been specified to be used within the frames. It does not save the content of the frames.

Frame Content

You can build the content of your frames right in PageMill, within the frames themselves, or you can specify external HTML pages to be used in your frames using the Insert Frame command in the Frameset submenu. When you edit frame content within PageMill, you'll need to save each frame individually or use the Save Everything command in the Frameset submenu.

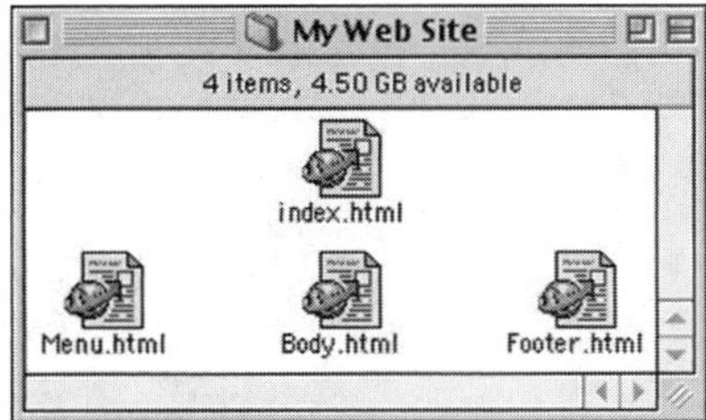

Figure 16.14 A site with frames uses a master frameset file (index.html) and individual HTML pages for the content of each frame.

Targeting Links

When you create a link within a frame, you may need to specify where and how the Web browser should display the content of the link's target HTML page. By default (if unspecified), the content will be displayed in the same frame as the page the link is within.

But if this is a menu frame, you probably don't want its page replaced; rather you want it to show link content in a larger body frame. To do this you must target the link.

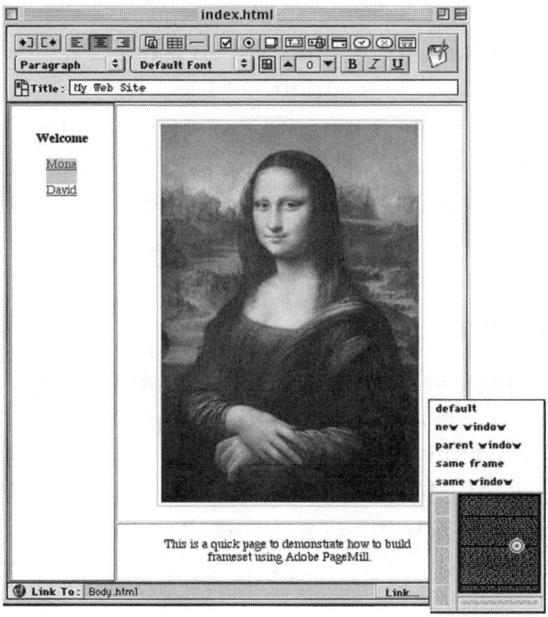

Figure 16.15 Use the Target menu to specify how to handle the display of a selected link's content; in this case, a menu link is targeted to the large *body* frame.

Using PageMill, you can easily target a link to a specific frame, or to open a new window, or even to replace the entire window content (replace the whole frameset). Select the link within your document and at the bottom-right corner of the PageMill window is a Target button; clicking on this will reveal a menu of targeting options for the link. You can either select one of the menu options or use the small representation of your frameset to point to which frame you'd like the link's content directed into.

Adding Special Effects

Many Web pages you see these days have elements that are live in some fashion. There may be simple looping animations of images creating dynamic logos, moving text, or cartoons. There may be interactive buttons that light up when you point to them and animate when you click on them. Or you may see embedded media such as QuickTime movies or Flash animation. These effects can help make a Web page more interesting and appealing, but they also can be difficult to create.

Methods used to add special effects to Web pages are generally not part of the HTML specification itself; rather, they use other browser-supported technologies like JavaScript or require browser plug-ins that add support for additional media types. There are many software applications, specially designed for creating animations and special Web effects, such as Macromedia Fireworks or Adobe ImageReady. With these applications you can design the artwork for your animations and interactive elements, define their actions, and automatically build the code that makes them work.

BALANCED DESIGN

Creating a design that is balanced—form following function, and function following form—is not unique to Web pages. However, this philosophy has some unique interpretations when applied to interactive and hyperlinked material, which is typically accessed via slow modem connections. You want pages of text and images to be compact so that you can quickly load them, and they should be filled with well-organized menus and links to facilitate easily maneuvering through them. The main goals generally are to keep it simple, keep it legible, and keep it fast.

The best Web pages are not necessarily the most beautiful; a site that functions well is just as important as one that has an aesthetic layout. Using HTML effectively by using text and table tags instead of images of prerendered text is more flexible for different types of Web browsers, resizable windows, and different size computer screens.

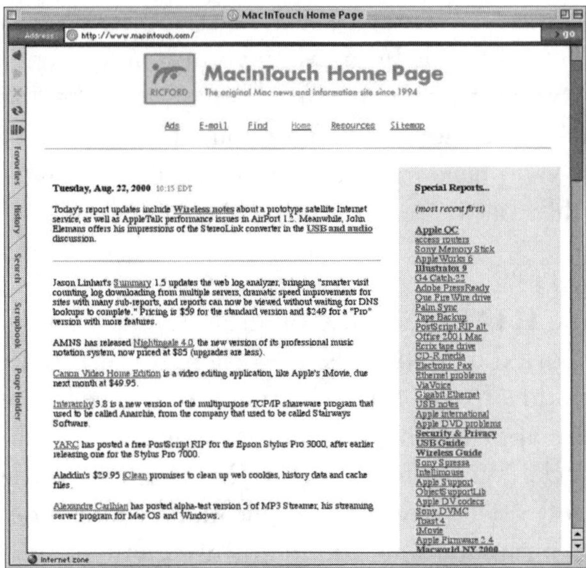

Figure 16.16 A site that uses HTML without reliance on images or fixed table widths makes it flexible for all users, no matter which Web browser they use or how big their computer screen is. (www.macintouch.com)

Image Animation

Animation is the most common special effect on the Web. Just about every advertisement is animated, and many people use animations in their logos and page designs. Usually, these animations are created with GIF image files that support multi-image animation. Sometimes, animations are created more elaborately with JavaScript or an external media (supported with a plug-in), such as QuickTime, Flash, or Shockwave.

Using GIF

The simplest way to add animation to a Web page is to create a GIF image file animation. The GIF image file format supports encoding several images together into a single file, as well as including instructions for how quickly to play back and how to loop through the frames of animation. With an animated GIF, you can simply insert the image file as you would normally place an image into a Web page, and it will animate automatically with no special HTML coding necessary.

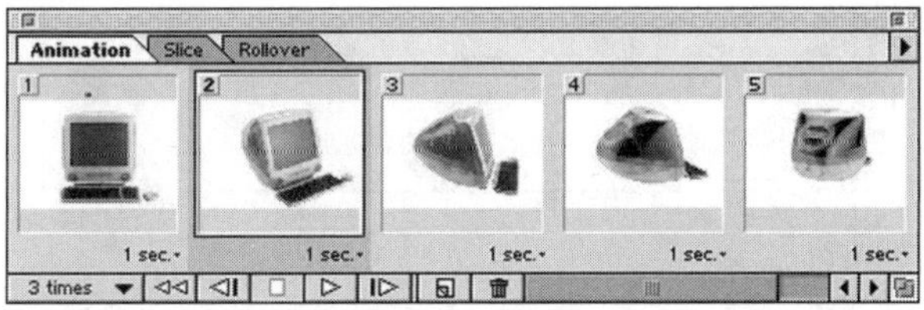

Figure 16.17 To build an animated GIF, you'll need to use an image editing application such as Adobe ImageReady.

To build a GIF animation, you'll need to use an image editor application that has features for handling multiple images as animation and that can save the animation as a GIF image file. Using an application such as Adobe ImageReady, you can create several images to use as frames of animation, organize them together specifying the time to wait between each frame, as well as how to loop through them. You can specify to play the sequence of frames once, several times, or continuously.

Button Rollover Animation

You'll find menus and buttons with rollover effects that highlight and animate when you point and click on them located on many professionally created Web sites. To accomplish this the designers of those pages needed to create separate image files for each button in each state of interaction: one for normal, one for hovering over, one for clicking, and perhaps additional versions for pressing down, holding, and letting up on the button. They also programmed the Web page with JavaScript to load each of these separate image versions and display them when appropriate. This sort of interaction is complex to create manually, but there are many great software applications that make it relatively easy.

Using an application such as Adobe ImageReady, you can create the frames of animation used in the button interaction, and ImageReady will save out each state as an image file, as well as

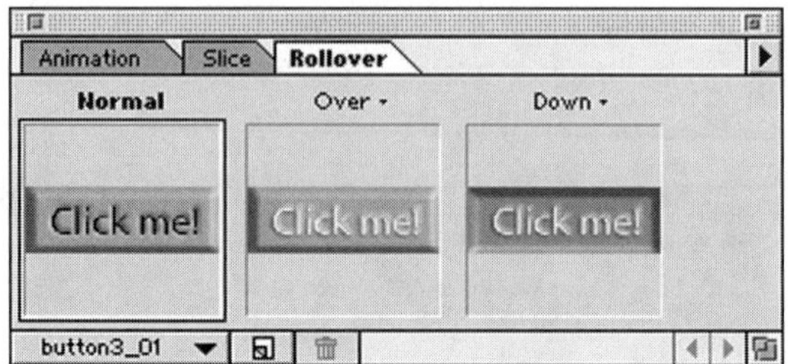

Figure 16.18 To build an interactive button that highlights when pointed to and animates when clicked upon, you'll need to use an image editing application such as Adobe ImageReady.

compiling the necessary JavaScript code to link up the image files and actuate the button animation. You can build a Web page with the normal button image versions, and then copy and paste the interaction code into your Web page to enable the rollover effects. You will find that there are two parts to the button rollover JavaScript code. The first is placed in the <HEAD> section of the HTML page and is used to preload the button animation as well as supply the instructions on how to switch images; the second part is code used in the <BODY> of the HTML page wherever an animated button appears to tell the JavaScript program which image to display and switch out when activated. Only Web browsers that support JavaScript will be able to see the rollover effects.

Link Highlighting

One simple form of special effects you can add to your Web pages is to have text links change color when you point to them (without clicking). This is called a hover effect, and is accomplished with a special capability only found in the latest generation of Web browsers that support text style sheets. Simply place the code in the following figure within the <HEAD> section of your HTML page.

```
<head>

      …

<style>

      …

<!--
A:Hover   { color: #FF6600; }
-->
</style>
</head>
```

Place this code within the <HEAD> section of your HTML page. If your document already has <HEAD> or <STYLE> tags, you don't need to duplicate them.

The A:Hover command with its color parameter is the key to the hovering effect. You can use the #000000 color code to specify any standard Web-safe color that you'd like used when the link's hover is activated by pointing to it.

Adding Embedded Media

Most Web pages only contain text and images, but there are many other types of digital media that can be used in Web pages, with the proper support for them on the viewing computer. Supporting an external media type usually involves a browser plug-in and additional software.

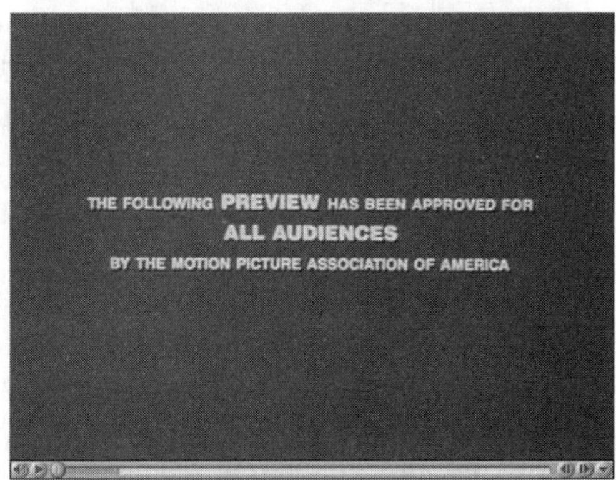

Figure 16.19 This HTML page has an embedded QuickTime movie that is being displayed by the QuickTime browser plug-in.

One of the most common embedded media types is a QuickTime movie, which allows a Web page to present a QuickTime movie within a Web page if QuickTime and its browser plug-in are installed. Other media might include vector animations, 3D object viewing, and audio and video. Let's take a quick look at how you can link up and embed external media into your Web pages.

```
<EMBED SRC="mymovie.mov" WIDTH="480" HEIGHT="376" ALIGN="BOTTOM">
```

> To embed a QuickTime movie or other media file into a Web page, use the <EMBED> tag.

To put an external file into your Web page, you link it in the same way as an image file, but instead of the <IMG> tag, you use the <EMBED> tag. This tag has parameters for the source, width, and height of the media, as well as other common positioning parameters such as align.

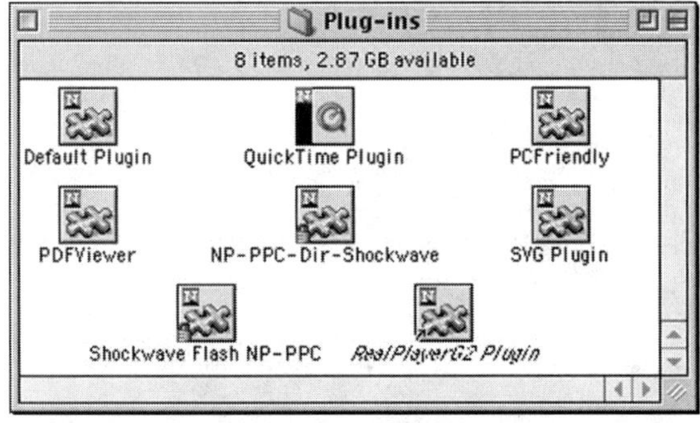

Figure 16.20 Media plug-ins for your Web browser are installed into a Plug-Ins folder, adding support for external and proprietary data files within Web pages.

The file type of the source file will determine automatically how the Web browser will use the media, enabled by either the built-in support (within the browser application) or via a media plug-in. Many software proprietary data formats require a plug-in, and if the media is not recognized by the browser, it will ask you if you want to continue to download the embedded data or get more information on available plug-ins. When you embed special media types into a Web page, you should include a note that a plug-in is required and a link to download it.

Submitting Data via CGI

If you want to use HTML form fields in a Web page and actually retrieve the data that users enter, you will need to set up a server submission interface. This is done by using a CGI (Common Gateway Interface) method for a Web page to interface with a server-side program or script. While this usually involves complex computer programming, many Internet service providers have simple, easy-to-use, preconfigured server programs that you can utilize to retrieve submitted Web page data as an email message and automatically return a confirmation to the user. By getting the data of a form Web page back in email, you can easily import it into a database program or other software to use and analyze.

PERSONALITY

One of the best things you can do to make a Web site appealing is to make sure that it has a personality. People like to read about

continued...

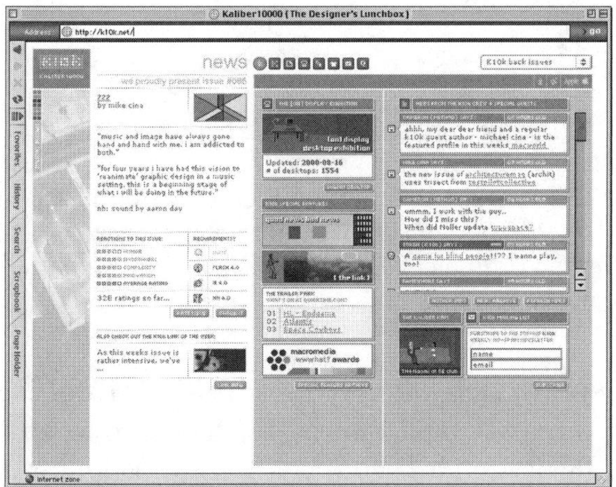

Figure 16.21 A site with personality is the key to holding a user's interest with a fun, intricate, and expressive design. (www.k10k.net)

and interact with people. Anything you can do to add a personal touch—a first person point of view—to make a connection with a reader can have dramatic results on the popularity and usefulness of your site. Active prose can make your Web site come alive.

Adding personal anecdotes, pictures or cartoons, links to associated sites, or simply providing a means for feedback from users are all good ways to add a human touch. Remember that the Internet is a community and that your Web site is part of it. And just like with people, no two Web sites are the same, so enjoy your site's uniqueness and add your own personality to it.

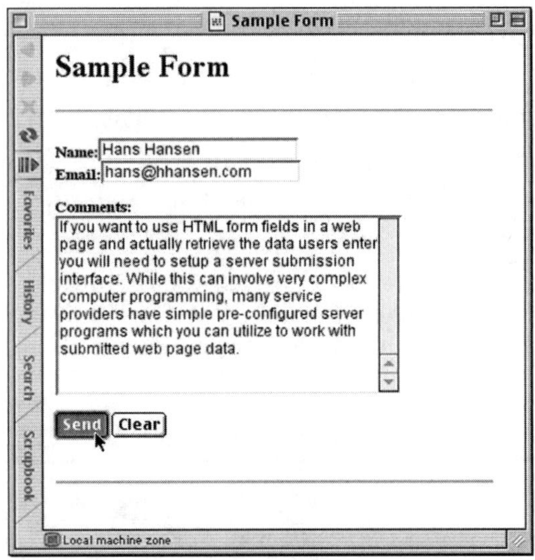

Figure 16.22 Getting data from a Web page form requires using a server-based program established by your service provider. This form is just an example; you can make any form with any number of fields and options.

Every Internet provider will have its own methods of handling data submission from a Web page form; for the purpose of examining this in more detail, we'll use EarthLink for our demonstration. This method only works if you have a service account with EarthLink.

Form into Email

The first thing you need to do to receive the contents of an HTML form is to specify the <FORM> tag's Method parameter as "post" and the Action parameter as the name of the CGI program to submit the data to. In addition, EarthLink has you place two hidden form fields in the HTML page with the Name of "Recipient" and "ThankUR;" the recipient also includes a Value parameter for the email address of the account you want the form data sent to.

```
<!-- begin sample html page -->
<html>
<head>
<title>Sample Form</title>
</head>
<body>
<h1>Sample Form</h1>
<hr>
<form method="post" action="http://home.earthlink.net/cgi-
bin/mailto">
<input type="hidden" name="RECIPIENT" value="user@domain.com">
<input type="hidden" name="THANKURL" value="http://home.earth-
link.net/~username/thankyou.html">
<p>
<b>Name:</b><input type="text" name="name" size="30"><br>
<b>Email:</b><input type="text" name="email" size="30"><p>
<b>Comments:</b><br>
<textarea name="comments" rows="10" cols="50"></textarea>
<p>
<input type="submit" value="Send">
<input type="reset" value="Clear">
</form>
<p>
<hr>
</body>
</html>
<!-- end sample html page -->
```

In the HTML code of the sample HTML Web page form, the highlighted lines of code (bold above) are key to creating a postable submission via EarthLink.

Your HTML form must also include an input button of type="Submit" to initiate posting the data entered by the user, and it should include a Reset button for the convenience of the users to clear any changes they have made in the form.

After a user clicks, submit the data is sent to the server, formatted by the CGI program "mailto" into an email message, sent to the recipient email address, and the URL of a confirmation Web page is sent back to the user's Web browser, which is loaded and displayed. Your Internet service provider may support many other form processing options, as well as CGI programs for other purposes. You can usually find full documentation of CGI support from your provider's Web site.

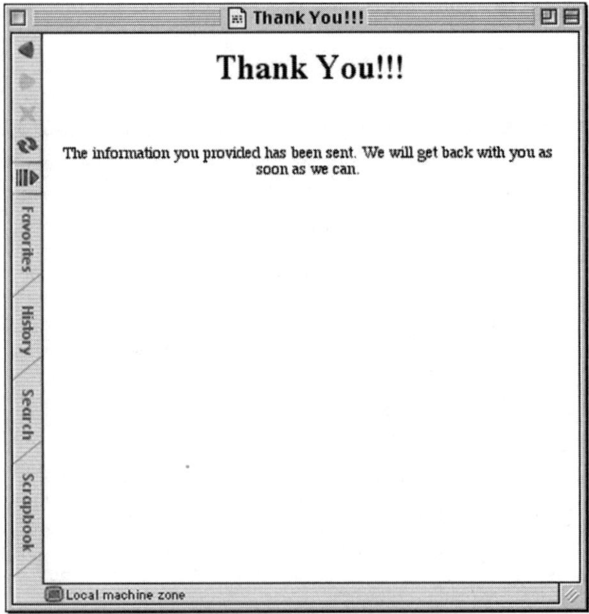

Figure 16.23 It is important to include some kind of confirmation for the users submitting their form data so that they know it has been processed, and are not inclined to repeatedly submit it, waiting for a result.

Personal Web Sharing

Recent versions of the Mac OS include the capability to serve a Web site directly from your iMac with software called Personal Web Sharing. With it you can specify a folder on your hard drive to use as a Web directory and when enabled it will be shared to the Internet at the IP address of your iMac via its Internet connection. Personal Web Sharing is very feature-intensive; with it you can not only serve HTML Web pages, but also retain a detailed log of all page and page item requests, and set up CGI programs to process submitted data and other external interactions.

Figure 16.24 This site, a personal favorite, changes every week and has many digitized old books that you can actively browse through. (www.octavo.com)

> **KEEP IT ACTIVE**
>
> A Web page that changes often will keep people coming back for more every time. It doesn't matter how great your site is—if it never changes or grows, it will be forgotten. You might change a site to organize its content better, feature a different topic for exploration, or to update or change the content entirely. The most elab
>
> *continued…*

orate sites are built using databases that compose their content on the fly, allowing online news sites to update their stories, or information sites to create dynamic reports, searches, and lists.

Another way to make your site seem more active is to literally activate it with interactive elements and animations. Even as simple as making a link highlight when a reader points at it can leave an impression on the reader that the page isn't static and dead.

Set Up Web Serving

To enable Web serving from your iMac, you will need to open the Web Sharing control panel and select a Web folder to share by using the upper Select button. This is the folder where you put all the HTML files and other linked and embedded media, such as images, movies, and sounds. You can also select which of the HTML files is the home page (default is *index.html*), using the lower Select button. This will present you with a list of the HTML files within your Web folder from which to choose.

After you have specified your Web folder and home page, you can enable Web sharing by clicking the Start button. It will take a few seconds for sharing to be established. When it is finished starting

Figure 16.25 Use the Web Sharing control panel to enable personal Web sharing from your iMac.

up, the Start button will change to Stop, and the address of your Web site will appear at the top of the control panel window. You can then give out the address of your site for people to use.

Normally, a Web site is published without access limitations; however, if you want to limit access on your Web site with password protection, you can set up and use the standard File Sharing privileges on the files and folders within your Web folder. Select the Use File Sharing to control user access option in the Web Sharing control panel to enable the use of privileges. Or select Give everyone read-only access to disable privilege limitations.

When your site is sharing, the address for the site will be the IP address of your iMac. If you are using a dial-up account or a DHCP-based connection, this address may change every time you reestablish a connection to your Internet provider. If you have a connection with a fixed IP address, your address is always the same, which gives your Web site more permanence and allows you to register a domain name for your Web site (`yoursite.com`) that points to your IP address.

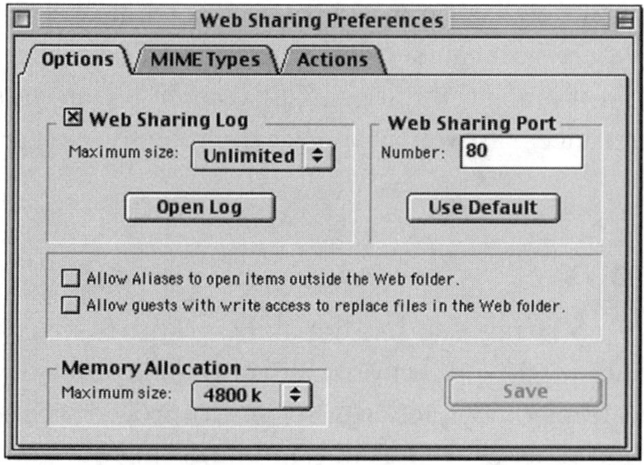

Figure 16.26 Additional Web sharing options are available by choosing Preferences from the Edit menu.

Reading the Logs

As the Web pages you are sharing are accessed, each request for data is logged. The log tracks the IP address the request comes from, the time and date of the request, and the item and method of the request. You can view your log file by choosing Open Web Sharing Log from the top of the File menu or by pressing ⌘O.

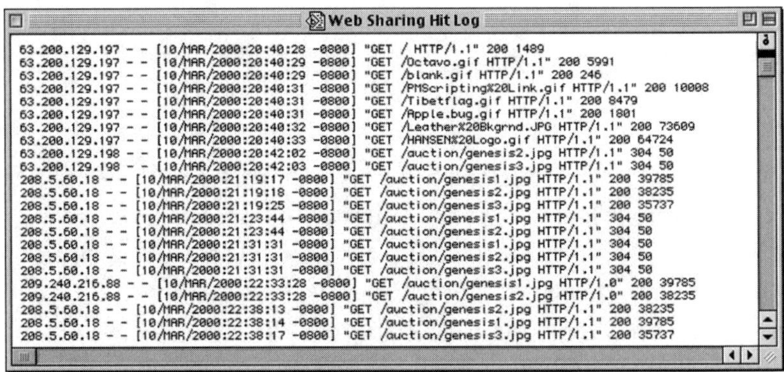

Figure 16.27 A log file created by Person Web Sharing tracks all the requested files from your Web folder.

The log file will need to be opened into a separate text editing application where you can scroll through it and edit it or search it. You can turn on and off the logging of your Web site in the Web Sharing preferences, as well as specify the maximum size for the log file.

Web Actions

Personal Web Sharing also has the ability to process server-side (on your iMac) CGI-type Actions. This capability allows you to assign applications of AppleScript scripts to process requests for certain types of data, as well as to handle posting of data from HTML forms.

To configure your CGI actions, open the Web Sharing Preferences by choosing preferences from the bottom of the Edit menu and selecting the Actions tab at the top of the window. Add an action by clicking the New button and then selecting the type of action from the Action pop-up menu. You can then specify the application or script to use when that type of action occurs.

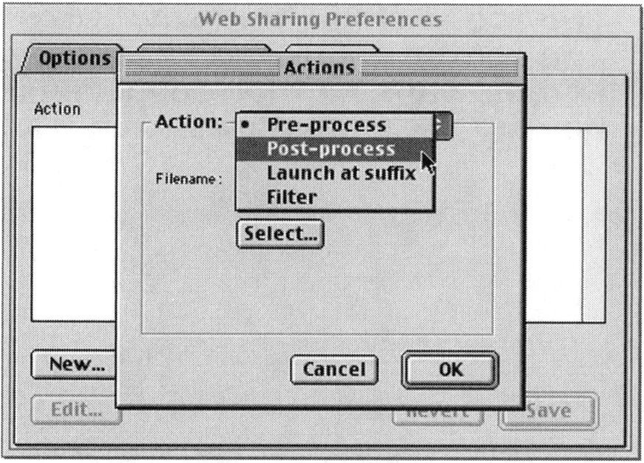

Figure 16.28 Use the Actions section of the Web Sharing Preferences to set up CGI processing.

The steep slope hangs above
The router calm. A digital voyager,
I go by ways neither copper nor glass,
Finding east, west the packets the same.

Wireless Networking

Today, networking computers together is very common. The digital universe, in fact, wouldn't exist if it weren't for sharing data over networks and distributing complex processing tasks. Several years ago local area networking (at home or at work) was different from the networks used for wide area networking (the Internet). Today, the same technologies are being used everywhere, even at home. Anyone who has more than one computer can use a network to share files, printers, Internet access, even to cooperatively run around and defend the digital universe from scary monsters. If, however, you have only one iMac, you probably won't need a network—at least not today.

In this chapter, we are going to look at:

> Building a network of your own

> Learning about the concepts behind networks (the data pathways) of both Ethernet-based wired networking and new wireless AirPort networking

> Organizing and planning an Ethernet network, installing wires, and testing its connections

> Joining your local network to the Internet, sharing Internet access with all your computers

> Installing and configuring a wireless network by using Apple's AirPort technologies

> Setting up and using the Mac OS built-in file sharing to copy data over your network

Data Pathways

A network is all about creating data pathways. Whether you use
wires for Ethernet or go wireless using AirPort, you are enabling
your computers to communicate with each other. A wired network
requires an Ethernet interface, Ethernet cables, an Ethernet hub,
and it uses an Ethernet protocol (either 10Base-T or 100Base-T).
A wireless network requires an installed AirPort Card in your Mac
and an AirPort Base Station (hardware or software), which use a
wireless protocol (IEEE 802.11). While both types of network have
many things in common, let's examine each one separately.

COOL THINGS TO DO WITH YOUR NETWORK

What can you do with a network? We have already looked at how
you can use a network to connect your computers together with a
network-based printer, how to use personal file sharing, and how to
share Internet access over your local network. Other things you
might do are sharing a USB printer, sharing a data storage device,
connecting to computers of other types such as Windows, playing
network games, and controlling other Macs remotely by using program linking.

SHARE PRINTERS

If you have a printer that doesn't support Ethernet or AirPort
networking (e.g., a USB printer), you might think that you can't print
to it from any computer on your network other than the computer to
which it is directly connected. Well, even this is now possible by
using Apple's USB Printer Sharing software. This add-on software is
available for download from the Apple Web site (software updates)
or as an update to your Mac OS system via the Software Updates
control panel. With it installed, you can share a printer with other
machines on your network.

To set up USB Printer Sharing, install it on your iMac and then
open the USB Printer Sharing control panel. Click the Start button
to enable printer sharing. This allows you to share a printer

continued...

connected to your iMac, as well as to connect to shared printers from other computers using printer sharing. Switch to the My Printers tab to specify a printer to share—it must be currently connected and active. Switch to the Network Printers' tab to select shared printers available on the network by using the Add button. You will need the printer driver for the model of printer installed on both computers, and once you have added a shared printer, you will need to select it in the Chooser in order to print to it.

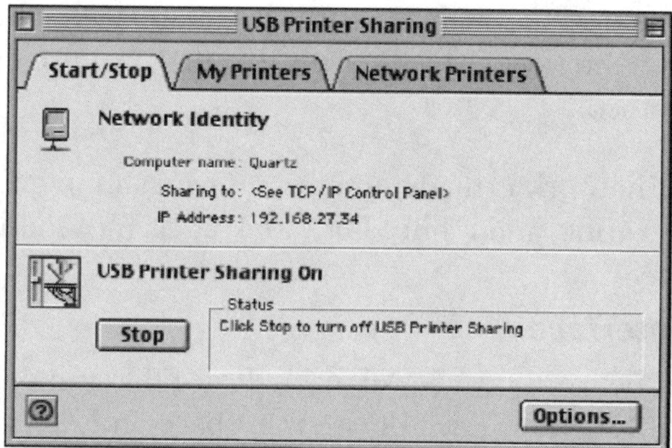

Figure 17.1 The USB Printer Sharing control panel is used to share printers, as well as to access remote printers.

Ethernet Networks

Any network you create that uses wires for your iMac and other devices, such as a printer, will use Ethernet. Ethernet is a wire-based local area network (LAN) technology that transmits information between computers by using phone-like wiring. Ethernet uses a digital protocol, which makes it more efficient and more reliable than an analog modem connection (such as 56 K dial-up); it also means that Ethernet requires special wiring and hardware.

There are several Ethernet standards (definitions), two are most common: 10Base-T and 100Base-T. These standards are capable of moving data at rates up to a maximum of 10 million bits per second (10Mbps) or 100 million bits per second, respectively. Not all devices support the faster 100Base-T standard, and these two standards are not compatible with each other—for example, a device that is set to use 100Base-T cannot directly communicate with one set (or limited) to 10Base-T. 100Base-T is much faster than 10Base-T (10 times!), transferring about 10 megabytes per second, but devices that support it tend to be more expensive, and many don't support it at all (e.g., many Ethernet compatible printers). For most people 10Base-T is simple and very affordable, and 10base-T is still respectably fast, transferring files at about one megabyte per second. Some devices, such as your iMac, come with a built in 10/100Base-T interface, which means that they can use either Ethernet protocol.

An Ethernet network is made up of three parts: an interface on each device, wiring, and a hub. Let's look at each of these parts.

Ethernet Interfaces

An Ethernet network begins with each device that will communicate by using Ethernet. Each device must have an Ethernet interface; this is where the Ethernet wire is plugged in that the device will use to communicate.

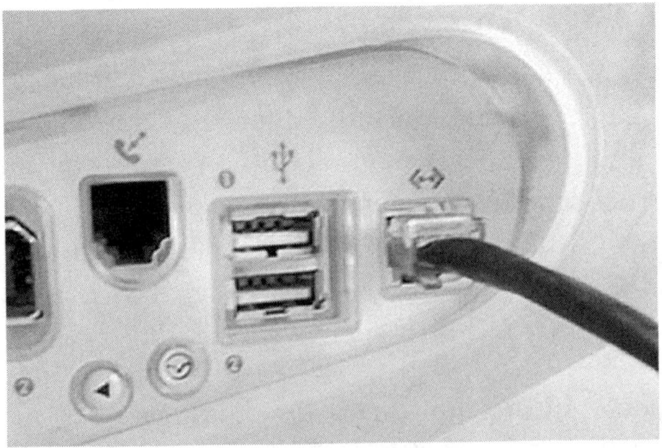

Figure 17.2 Here you see an Ethernet interface on a second-generation iMac with an Ethernet wire patch cable connected.

Some devices come with an interface built in, like your iMac does. Other devices require that an interface card be installed. In addition to the hardware of the interface, the device may require software drivers that tell the device how to use the interface card (on your iMac the Ethernet driver is part of the Mac OS). Each interface will support specific Ethernet protocols, but it may only support the slower 10Base-T, or it may support both, a 10/100Base-T interface.

Ethernet Wiring

It is, of course, the wires that create your network, connecting all your devices. Ethernet wiring is similar looking to phone wiring; it uses RJ-45 connectors, which are slightly wider than standard phone connectors (RJ-11), and contain four wires rather than two. It can be professionally installed in walls, floors, and ceilings, or you can use prefabricated cables (called *Ethernet patch cables*). You should keep in mind that most network problems come from wiring problems, so when using Ethernet cables, there are some things that should be considered. These cables don't like to be bent at sharp angles (like around the corner of a room); instead, cables should comfortably bend in a curve. Cables should be arranged in a way that keeps them from being walked on or pulled, and it's a good idea to use new cables.

The most reliable way to make your own Ethernet network is to use patch cables. These are prefabricated cables that are designed to connect a device to a nearby built-in network—"patching" the device in. Patch cables can be used to directly connect your devices. They come in many lengths and even in a wide variety of colors. You can buy them at most computer stores as well as from network supply companies.

Ethernet networks use special wiring, Unshielded Twisted Pair (UTP), named for how the wiring is made up of multiple pairs of single wires, which are twisted together and are unshielded. The wires are arranged this way to provide a simple form of passive

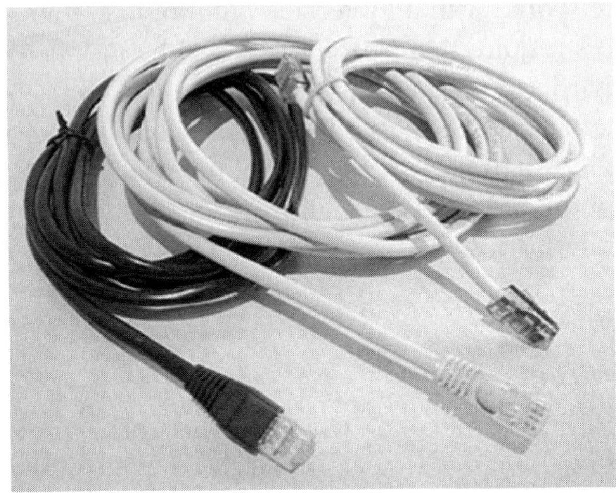

Figure 17.3 These are Ethernet patch cables.

shielding, while also being flexible to install and reasonably inexpensive.

Think of a wire all by itself: wire naturally acts as an antenna, picking up any stray or ambient electrical signals that are near. For a wire carrying network information, this is a bad thing because ambient noise mixes with the data being carried by the wire and causes interference. One method for keeping noise out of network wiring is to shield the wires with a foil or wire braid wrapped around them. This would be just fine except for the fact that intended communication on one wire becomes unwanted noise on the other. So the wires must also be shielded from each other. A better way to shield wires is to twist them around each other, creating a passive filter effect along their length, as well as preventing direct interference. Several pairs of twisted wires can then be grouped together without picking up any electrical noise or causing interference, and additional external shielding is not needed.

In a typical UTP cable, there are four pairs of wires, or eight individual wires. Each pair of wires is twisted together, and a 10Base-T or 100Base-T Ethernet connection requires only two pairs of wires, which means one cable is capable of carrying two Ethernet connections. Of these two pairs of wires, one pair is used for sending data and the other is used for receiving data. When you use a straight-through patch cable to connect your iMac to a hub, the hub connects the send pair coming from your computer to the receive pair of its other ports.

But if you try to connect two computers directly with that same straight-through cable, the pair for sending gets connected to the send pair at the other end, and the connection doesn't work. So if you want to connect only two computers, you can use just one cable, a crossover patch cable.

A crossover patch cable is one that has been wired so that the pair of wires for sending at one end goes to the pair for receiving at the other end. With the wires situated this way, you can connect two computers together directly and not use a hub. Crossover patch cables that you find at the store are usually made with brightly colored cable, often red or orange.

Ethernet Hubs

You can't have a network with just devices, interfaces, and wires—you need something to interconnect them—a hub, which is a box that sits in the middle of your network with each device plugged into one of its ports. It's the job of a hub to accept data in packets addressed to other devices from one port and then broadcast that same data back out to all of the other ports. The device the data is addressed to will use it, while every other networked device just

Figure 17.4 You can see a simple repeating hub with five ports and an uplink port (crossed-over wiring).

ignores the mal-addressed data. So, data goes out from a device's interface, through the wire to the hub, the hub repeats the data to all the other ports, and is heard by all the other devices. This type of broadcasting hub (called a *repeating hub*) is the most basic and least expensive.

A repeating hub works fine until you've got many computers and other devices all trying to communicate at the same time on your network. Then the network slows down from colliding packets of data like a traffic jam. Here is where a different type of hub comes in handy, a switched hub. A switched hub, or simply a switch, behaves much like a repeating hub except that it pays attention to the destination of every packet of data that passes through it and only sends data out of the port to the destination device to which it is connected. This way the noise of the network is kept from computers and devices that don't need to hear it, clearing up traffic jams. But, before you go and just buy a switched hub instead of a repeating hub, you should consider the fact that they often cost much more, and for smaller networks they just are not necessary.

Hubs come in different sizes, with different numbers of ports. For a small network you might only need a hub with four ports that supports up to four devices. However, hubs can have many more

Figure 17.5 This complex Ethernet network has a repeating hub, switched hub, and router all wired together with patch cables.

ports: 6, 8, 10, 12, 18, or 24. Hubs can also be interconnected (using crossover wiring) by joining one port from one hub directly to a port on another hub, thereby expanding your network.

There are several advantages to using hubs for the layout of a network. Because a hub creates a star topology where each arm connects a single device, the network can be more configurable, reliable, and economical (rather than a straight-line bus topology, or an enclosed circular ring topology where each device is connected directly to its neighbors). By separating each device as well as the device's interface and its wires from complicating other device's connections, each device can be set up in a flexible fashion without needing to make considerations for the locations of other devices. Any problems one device has with itself or its wiring won't affect the others. And systematically a star network, while in general using more wire, is less technologically complex and can use less expensive interfaces and components.

When you have only two devices, such as two iMacs (or even two hubs), that you'd like to connect directly together, you don't need a hub; rather, you can use a crossover patch cable. Some hubs will include a special uplink port with reversed wiring so that a normal cable can be used to directly connect another hub or to a router.

When you want to make a connection between an Ethernet network and another network (e.g., the Internet), you need to use a special network device called a router. A router is a device that is sometimes confused with a hub. Routers usually have two ports: one port connects to one network and the other port connects to another network. The router handles directing traffic between the two networks. If you have a wide-bandwidth DSL or Digital Cable connection to the Internet, you may want to share the connection with more than one computer, and you will need a router.

> ### SHARE DATA STORAGE
>
> You can get a simple device called a *Network Attached Storage* file server (NAS server), which you can plug into an Ethernet network designed to share its hard drive(s) with all of the computers on your network. These preconfigured, stand-alone file servers require no setup; just plug them in, and you instantly have a network file server to store data from any computer on your network.
>
> NAS servers cost just a bit more than a hard drive by itself, but they are considerably less than a full computer-based file server. A 10 gig server supporting 10/100Base-T Ethernet can start at about $300, and a 30 gig server averages about $800. However, because of their simplicity, these devices are not very flexible if you want to configure or upgrade them.

AirPort Networks

What could be more ideal than networking computers together wirelessly? Wires are limiting. They tie things down and are inflexible for easy changes and quick getaways. Remove the wires, and you have more than just local mobility, allowing you to take your computer with you (especially if it is a lightweight iBook). You can also take the network with you. You can easily take several computers on the road and have a network anywhere you want: at a convention, in a car, in a park. And while mobility presents an obvious benefit, wireless networking can also be economical and easier to install and configure than Ethernet. This is especially true when you are looking at networking a home or an office with many rooms and may need to drill holes in walls or floors to carefully run network wiring, thus making the slightly higher cost of wireless equipment reasonable.

Using Apple's AirPort networking systems, an AirPort Card for each computer, and an AirPort Base Station, you can quickly set up a network that can run at about the same speed as a 10Base-T Ethernet network (an AirPort can communicate up to 11 megabits per second). Only Mac systems designed specifically for AirPort support can use a wireless network and have an AirPort Card installed in them. This includes the second generation iMacs (except the low-end Indigo model), iBooks, Power Macintosh G4s, and PowerBook G3s with FireWire. An AirPort network also requires a base station in order to establish the network. A base station can either be software installed and running on a computer with an AirPort Card, or you can use a stand-alone hardware device such as Apple's AirPort Base Station.

AirPort uses radio-based digital signals at a frequency of 2.4 gigahertz (similar to some cordless phones), having a range of about 150 feet. Apple's AirPort systems use the IEEE 802.11 DSSS (Direct Sequence Spread Spectrum) industry standard for wireless networking. This allows your AirPort-equipped iMac to interact with 802.11 DSSS wireless equipment made by other companies. Likewise, other computers (even non-Apple) can interact with your AirPort network.

When you have a wireless network, you may be curious about how secure it is—can anyone within 150 feet connect into your network even if you don't want him to? To prevent unwanted intrusion, AirPort software includes some basic protection. When you establish your network from a base station, you can enable a password required for logging in, and that password is used to encrypt the data being transmitted. AirPort uses a simple 40-bit RC5 data encryption method to scramble data, rendering it useless to eavesdroppers, which while reasonably secure can be overcome by people with sufficient technical skill. If you don't enable this encryption, the network will be wide-open for anyone to join in.

AirPort Card (Wireless Network Interface)

An AirPort Card is the interface to an AirPort wireless network. Installed into your iMac (or other Apple computer), it attaches to the computer's logic board as well as to a built-in antenna. Costing about $100, it is all you need to communicate with other AirPort-equipped computers or with a base station.

Figure 17.6 An AirPort Card can be used in almost all current Apple computer models to add wireless networking.

If you own an older computer, you may be able to add a **PCI** card that will give you access to the same 802.11 protocol used by the AirPort Card. There are several companies that make hardware that is designed using the 802.11 DSSS wireless standard. Any hardware that is designed with this technology can be used in your AirPort network.

You can get PCI cards, external antennas and other equipment from Lucent Technologies (WaveLAN or Orinoco), Farallon Communications (SkyLINE/NetLINE), or 3com (AirConnect). These three and many more companies have created a new organization that calls itself Wi-Fi, which is short for wireless fidelity. Their aim is to promote the use of 802.11 DSSS and ensure its interoperability with other wireless technologies. If you're interested in finding out more about all of this, visit `http://www.wi-fi.org`.

AirPort Base Station (Wireless Network Hub and Router)

When using an AirPort network, you can connect two machines together with AirPort Cards by configuring their AirPort software, or one iMac can host up to ten full-speed connections to other AirPort-equipped devices by configuring it as a software base station. (More than 10 devices can be connected but will slow the entire AirPort network.) Running a base station from a computer with an AirPort Card, however, can be precarious. If that machine should be interrupted in any way, the whole network will go down. And, a software base station can be difficult to set up and won't allow you to route AppleTalk connections between Ethernet and AirPort. So in addition to AirPort Cards, Apple also makes a hardware base station, which is easy to set up, and can route AppleTalk and Internet (TCP/IP) traffic.

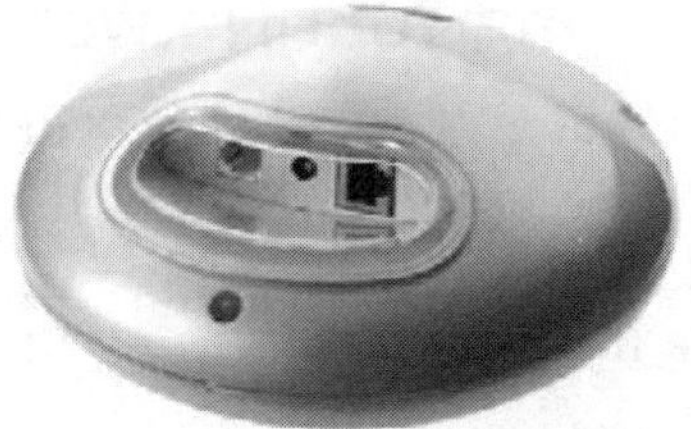

Figure 17.7 The AirPort Base Station is a hub and router for an AirPort wireless network; you can see its modem, power, and Ethernet jacks.

Apple's AirPort Base Station is a small UFO-shaped computer designed to provide a wireless network without using a computer with an AirPort Card to run a software base station. The AirPort Base Station provides a centralized, stand-alone hub and router for your AirPort network. The base station has a built-in 56 K V.90 modem for dial-up Internet access and a 10Base-T Ethernet interface. A single base station can, on average, accommodate 10 simultaneous AirPort users. While it is capable of providing network access to more users, the bandwidth is shared. If you need to provide access for more computers, you can interconnect multiple base stations with Ethernet. If you've already got a connection to the Internet, you can gain access to it through an AirPort Base Station. Just plug in your phone line or Ethernet into the base station and configure it for the connection.

Building an Ethernet Network

If you're ready to build your own Ethernet network, you'll need to follow three general steps: planning, installing, and testing. You need to plan your network because you'll want to have an idea of what equipment you may need to purchase and how you will run your wiring. The installation will be fairly straightforward—just do it. We'll help guide you. And the last step will be testing, which involves some configuration of Mac OS software that uses Ethernet networking. At the end of this topic, we'll also look at routing an Internet connection for all the machines on your network to share.

Planning Your Network

To build an Ethernet network, you'll need to know what devices you'll be networking and where they will be located. You'll want to make a list of the devices. And, for each device, make sure that you have the components needed to form a network: an interface for each device (and know its type—whether it's 10Base-T, or 100Base-T); lengths of wiring to connect to a hub (or if only two devices, a crossover cable); and, of course, you'll need a hub with enough ports of the right type. You may also want to make a rough drawing of your devices and their locations.

If you're going to keep all the networked devices in one room or area, where you can get away with dangling patch cables behind desks and tables while keeping them safely away from trouble, you can easily use prefabricated patch cables to install your network. If your network will need to extend beyond one room, you may decide that it would be better to make your network installation permanent, which involves running wiring through walls and installing outlets. We can't cover all the details of how to permanently install wiring here in this book, so we recommend that you seek professional assistance to install a network in your home or office. However, you can still begin planning your network on your own.

While planning your network, keep in mind any future expansions of your network. Will the network you are planning make it easy to grow? Will there be enough network outlets in enough locations to support your needs? Consider how many devices you currently have to connect to your network as well as what might come in the future. You may also want to provide a few extra network connections in common areas where you might like to have the option of plugging in a PowerBook or a shared iMac. You could even plan to mix your network with wired and wireless access. The printers and desktop computers could have their wires and iBooks and PowerBooks could have their freedom.

You should probably aim as high as you can afford when installing network cabling. One of the main differences between efficient 10Base-T and 100Base-T Ethernet connections is the level of quality of the cables and connections. The main problem when using 100Base-T Ethernet is usually poor network stability, resulting from bad wiring or outlets. And if you think you might like to take advantage of future networking technologies, like Gigabit Ethernet (1000Base-T), you'll need even higher quality wiring and connections.

Figure 17.8 Professionally installed Ethernet wiring in a home or building will have outlets to which you can patch devices (on the right are four Ethernet jacks).

When you are planning your network hardware purchases (a hub, for example), you should keep in mind how they will be used in the future. You can save yourself a great deal of time, effort, and money if you manage to start your network with equipment that scales easily to future needs. For example, you could find a great deal on an inexpensive hub today that in the future may be difficult or impractical to work with. Something of this sort could be a 100Base-T hub that works great for your three iMacs, but later you'll find that you need to connect a 10Base-T device (such as a printer). You would then need to purchase a 10/100Base-T hub to connect everything when you could initially have purchased a 10/100Base-T hub for a bit more money and had its extra flexibility all along.

Some hubs have the capability to use high-speed interconnections that effectively join them into one. This feature is called *stacking*. Some hubs do this by providing custom cables to plug into custom ports, which tends to be unique to a brand. Other hubs provide a linking port to use a standard straight-through patch cable to connect to any other hub. This can be especially useful if you expect to expand your network in the future, but want to avoid the high cost of a single hub with many ports.

> ### Crossing Platforms
>
> You can connect a Windows PC to your Ethernet network simply by patching it in just like any other device. However, in order for the PC and your iMac to communicate, you'll need to use software designed for the task. If your applications use TCP/IP to communicate (e.g., many multiplayer games) or Internet-based software, then you won't need to do anything special. If, however, you'd like to share files between the computers, just as you can with Personal File Sharing, you'll need to install software available from a third party.
>
> One popular AppleShare utility for Windows is PC MACLAN from Miramar Systems available for Windows 3.x/95/98/NT/2000, which costs about $150. With this software installed, you can connect to any AppleShare file server on your network from the PC so
> *continued…*

you can view its directories and copy and move files. You can also use the software to share the PC's files as an AppleShare server, allowing Macs on your network to connect to the PC.

Some software applications that are available for both Mac OS and Windows even use the same file data structure, thereby allowing you to open files created under one system on the other without translation. For files that require translation, the Mac OS will automatically recognize them and use File Exchange to translate them to usable data types

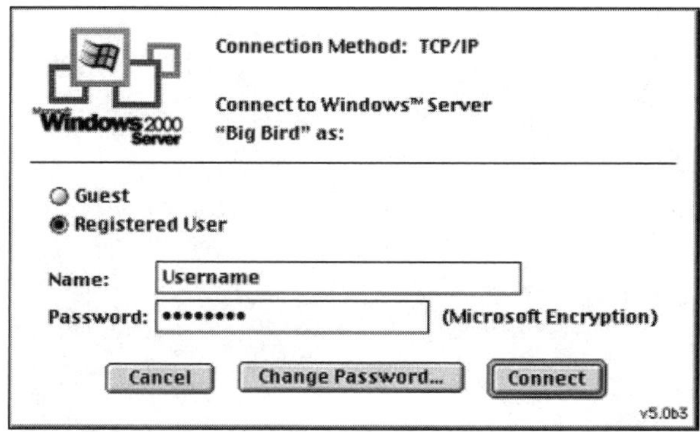

Figure 17.9 Windows NT 4.0 and 2000 are capable of using the Apple File Protocol. They can connect to AppleShare servers, but cannot share volumes as AppleShare servers.

Installing Your Network

Once you've planned your network, installing it should be rather easy. Simply position your devices, run the wires, and connect the wires. If you are networking only two devices, you can simply use an Ethernet crossover patch cable and be done already (of course, you can also use two straight-through patch cables and a hub).

Since your computers and printers are probably already positioned where you want them, begin by positioning your hub in an appropriately central but out-of-the-way location. If you need to install any Ethernet interfaces into any of your devices (such as a printer), you can also get that out of the way at this point.

Next, run your wiring. Let's assume that you are using patch cables or having your network wiring installed professionally. Connect each device one at a time. Connect one end into the interface on a device such as your iMac, run the cable through and around your furniture, and connect the other end to one of the ports on your hub. Do this for each device until they are all connected to your hub. If you already have a device, such as a DSL router or cable modem, connected to one of your computer's Ethernet interfaces, you can simply move its connection to the hub. That computer (only) should be able to find the DSL or cable modem connection via the network.

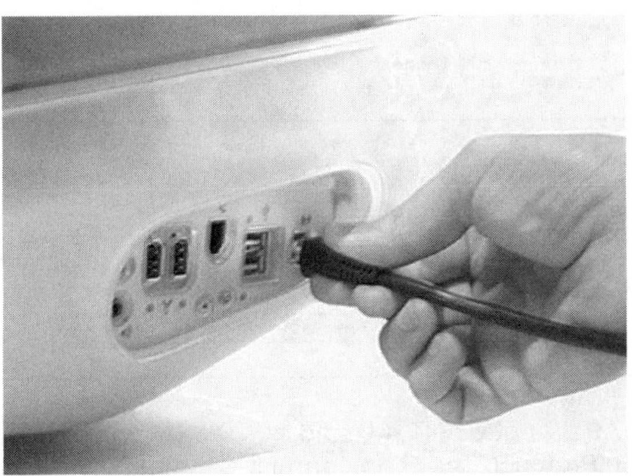

Figure 17.10 Installing your network may be as simple as connecting an Ethernet patch cable to your iMac and the other end to a hub.

If you have permanent wiring installed with outlets on each end, you will use two patch cables to connect a device and then connect to a port on your hub. One patch cable connects the device to the installed wire's outlet, and a second connects the installed wire to your hub.

When you are running your cables, try to be gentle with them. The wires within the cable are quite thin and don't take folding and sharp edges well. Also avoid leaving twisting in the cables when uncoiling them, as this tends to make them bind up and applies extra pressure to the wires.

Testing Your Network

Now that you've installed your network and made all the connections, it's time to make sure it all works and to troubleshoot any inactive connections.

The easiest way to test your connections is to see if each computer can see something else on the network. So if you have a printer connected to your network, verify that the printer is visible to each computer on the network. Or you can use file sharing and the Chooser. First, make sure that file sharing is active on one of the computers on your network by opening the File Sharing control panel, giving the computer a name, and clicking Start. Once one of the computers is sharing, go to another computer, open the Chooser, and click on AppleShare in the area on the left side of the Chooser's window. A list will appear on the right side of the window, which should include the name of the machine on which you've enabled file sharing, as well as any other filesharing devices on your network. If you see any devices, it verifies that the network connection between that computer and the hub is working, as well as between the hub and the other device that you can see. If you can see another device through the hub for each computer on your network, you will be able to establish that they are all connected.

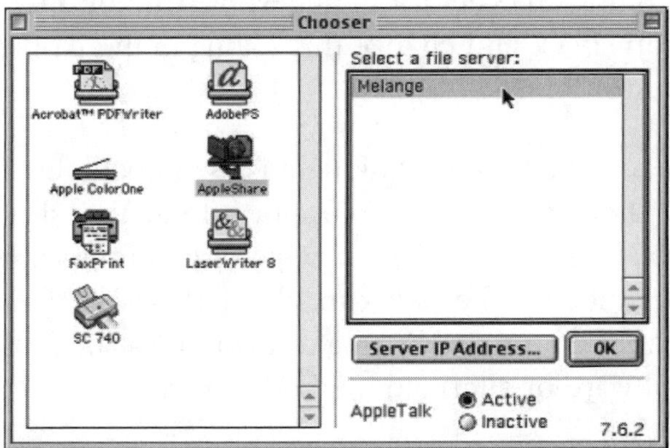

Figure 17.11 The Chooser is an easy way to see if your network is working. Select AppleShare to see if another computer is using File Sharing.

Another test that can be done is to use the lights on an Ethernet hub. Most hubs will have little lights that indicate an Ethernet link. There is one link light per port on a typical hub, and many Ethernet interfaces also have a link light, usually next to the jack where you plug in the Ethernet patch cable (however, there is no link light on an iMac's Ethernet interface). When the link light is on, it means that the electrical connection of the cable's send-and-receive wire pairs is connected properly. You should see the link light turn on immediately after you make a good connection between two devices. By the way, both the device and the hub will need to be powered on to power the link, so make sure your hub is plugged in if it requires external power and that it is switched on.

Occasionally, the link light on a hub will serve a double purpose. It will first turn on for link, and then blink or flicker when there is activity indicating that data is flowing there. If the link light does not turn on, then one or more of three things could be going on: software is not set to use Ethernet, you have a wrong protocol conflict (10Base-T vs. 100Base-T), or bad wiring.

The first and easiest to check is whether or not your computer is set to use any Ethernet for any type of networking protocol (such as either AppleTalk or TCP/IP). You should make sure your computer is set to use Ethernet for either AppleTalk or TCP/IP, or both. You can check and change this setting in the AppleTalk and TCP/IP Control Panels.

The second possibility of no link light is incompatibility between the hub and the device you are plugging into it. You should make sure the hub and the device are capable of communicating. If you plug a printer (likely to be only capable of 10Base-T) into a 100Base-T hub, then it's not going to work, regardless of any change in software or alternate method of wiring.

The third possible reason there is no link is wiring. If your computer is set to use Ethernet, and you've made sure it and the hub can both do the same type of networking, then it must be the wiring between the computer and the hub. Depending on the cables you've used to make the connection, you can test by trying a different cable, by trying different devices (which are working) with that particular cable to test it, or by using special equipment to test and verify that each wire is connected to the right place (useful for complex professionally installed wiring).

Try adjusting these settings and making these changes for any devices that are not connecting, checking their link lights, or looking for them again using the Chooser. At this point your network should be up and running. If you continue to have a problem, you should seek outside advice.

Internet Routing

The last thing you probably want to do when building your own network is to set up access for numerous computers to the Internet, especially if the connection is high-bandwidth DSL or cable modem. These types of Internet services are easily connected to your Ethernet network (or AirPort Base Station); however, the number of computers that they support are usually limited by their providers. In this section we are going to explain this limitation and how you can use a router to overcome it.

Every computer on the Internet must have a unique IP address in order to talk to other computers. Because IP addresses must be unique, they are valuable, and service providers limit them and charge extra for additional addresses. If you have a dial-up account, you probably only have one address. If you have a high-bandwidth Internet connection, it may come with one or more unique IP addresses. These addresses may be fixed, always the same, or dynamic (changing every time the connection is established). In order for each computer on your network to access the Internet, you'll need to have an IP address for each one. You can either pay your Internet provider for more IP addresses, which may be the easiest method, or you can set up a router to create your own Internet-subnet, giving you access to your own set of unique addresses. If you are using an AirPort Base Station, you already have a router that can be configured for a subnet.

To use a router to create your own subnet, allowing all your computers to communicate through your one real address, you use a method called *network address translation,* or NAT. When you use NAT in a router, you are creating a whole subnet of IP addresses for yourself. You'll have as many as 254 IP addresses to use in addressing your computers and devices. However, this subnet will be a deviation from the rest of the Internet. Of all the IP addresses being used in the world right now, there is a small range that has been set aside for private, isolated use. This range includes any IP addresses that begin with 192.168.x.x.

The reason you can use addresses in this range is because of NAT. The router, with NAT turned on, will allow you to communicate with the rest of the Internet through its one real address. To the Internet, every computer on your network will appear to be at one address—the address of the router (which will use the real address supplied by your Internet provider); and, each computer on your network will have full access to the Internet.

Setting Up a Router

First, you'll need to get a router that can do network address translation (NAT) and DHCP (Dynamic Host Configuration Protocol). There are many available, and they can be quite reasonably priced ranging from $100 to $300, money you can easily save back in a year of fees for additional addresses from an Internet service provider.

To install the router, connect it between the external Internet connection (DSL or whatever) and your hub, and then power it. Next, you'll need to configure it.

Some routers use their own software, or you can simply use a Web browser connection to access their settings. Follow the directions that came with the router to set it to the IP address supplied by your Internet provider (or set it to use DHCP to acquire a dynamic address if that is what your provider specifies). Then set up the router to enable NAT and DHCP for your network.

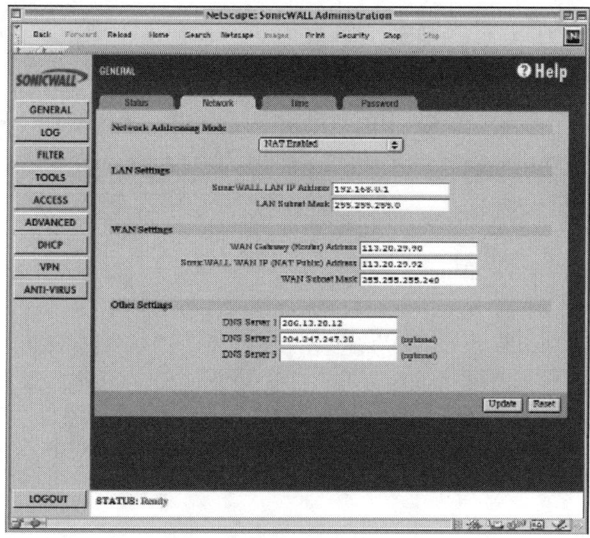

Figure 17.12 Some routers use a Web-based interface for specifying their NAT, DHCP, and other settings.

You now should be able to access the Internet from any machine on your local network. You will need to configure the TCP/IP control panel on each computer for a DHCP connection that will dynamically acquire an IP address from your router. You can begin browsing the Web (a great way to test if everything is working).

Using Wireless Networking

If you have decided to use AirPort networking for your entire network, or use it as just an extension of an Ethernet network, you'll find that it is very easy to set up and configure. AirPort networking can be great at home, at an office, at a school, on a university campus, or as a mobile travelling network.

This section is organized into three parts, each expanding on the former: how to install and use AirPort Cards, how to set up a

Software Base Station using AirPort Cards, and how to install and use a hardware AirPort Base Station to support a network of AirPort Cards.

Using AirPort Cards

An AirPort network begins with the AirPort Card. It is an interface, connecting a computer to the wireless AirPort network. With it you can connect to another computer's AirPort Card or to an AirPort Base Station.

Play Games

Many of the latest computer games include, or are dedicated to, multiplayer network play. Some are competitive, arena type games where you run around trying to shoot each other; others are cooperative, allowing individuals to join together to battle their way through worlds on the same team.

Many of these games also include chatting capabilities so that players can talk to each other while playing, which is useful for strategizing, taunting, and complaining. While most of these are written methods, some games include sound digitizing for verbal communication, or simply have commands for actuating sound effects like "get 'em" and "go to the left."

Figure 17.13 The popular role-playing game Diablo II can be played cooperatively over a network.

Installing an AirPort Card

Only second-generation iMacs and later support an AirPort Card (the low-end iMac models don't). Both have a special connector for the interface on the logic board and a built-in antenna. The card is installed through the door underneath the rear of the iMac, adjacent to where RAM is installed. Follow the installation directions that came with the AirPort Card to connect it.

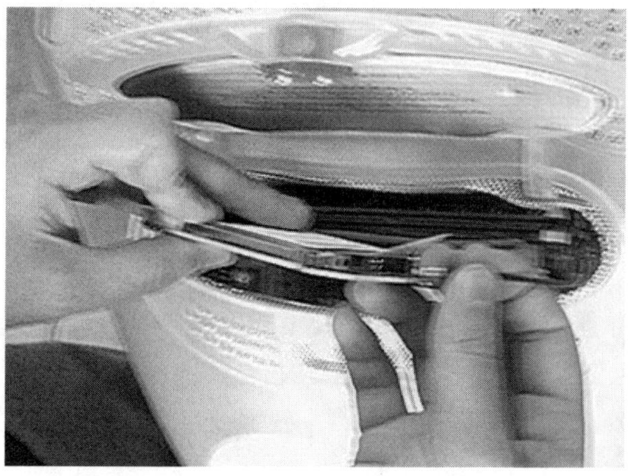

Figure 17.14 To install an AirPort Card in an iMac, you connect it to an internal port next to the RAM and connect the AirPort antenna.

When you run the AirPort Setup Assistant, you'll know immediately if your AirPort Card is installed correctly, as it will run only when an AirPort Card is present in your computer.

Configuring an AirPort Card

The AirPort Card comes with software that you will need to install on your iMac. This software includes System extensions that drive the card, as well as software applications for configuring it: AirPort, AirPort Admin Utility, and AirPort Setup Assistant.

At any time you can use the AirPort Setup Assistant application to help you set up or modify the settings for your AirPort Card. With

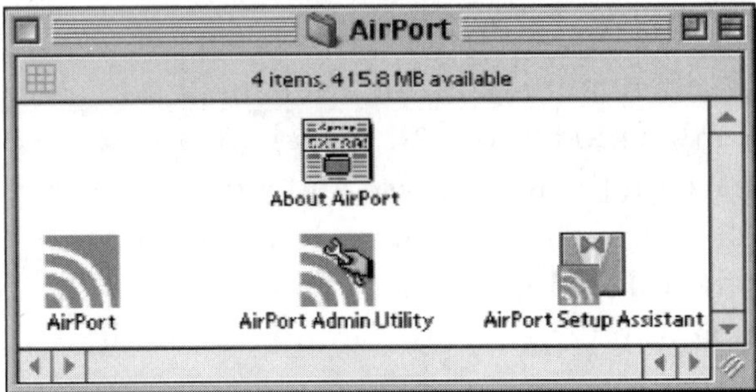

Figure 17.15 Use the AirPort software to configure your wireless network.

the assistant you can set your computer to join an existing AirPort network, configure a hardware AirPort Base Station, or set up your computer to be an AirPort Software Base Station.

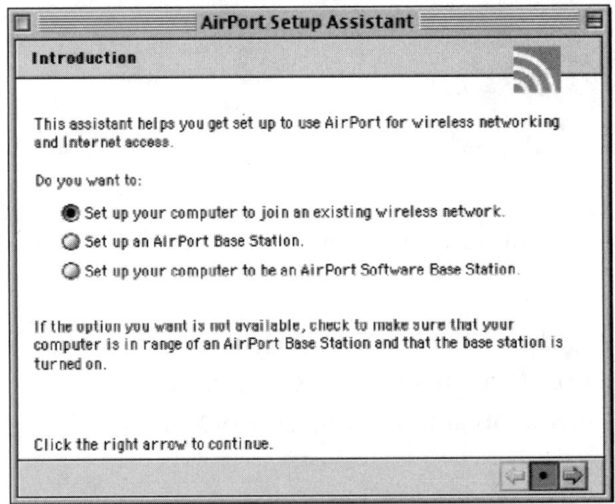

Figure 17.16 Use the AirPort Setup Assistant to set up an AirPort Card, Software Base Station, or hardware AirPort Base Station.

The assistant application also can be used to modify settings you made manually by using the AirPort application. You can see the status of your current connection with the relative signal strength at the top of the AirPort window. In the middle of the window, you'll find the settings for your AirPort Card: its unique ID number, whether to allow logging in to closed networks (by adding another command to type in the name of any invisible networks you may be aware of). This is also where you turn your AirPort Card on and off. At the bottom of the window is a menu for choosing the network you want to connect to, or to connect directly to other computers nearby. At the bottom of the AirPort window is a button to access the setting for establishing an AirPort Software Base Station.

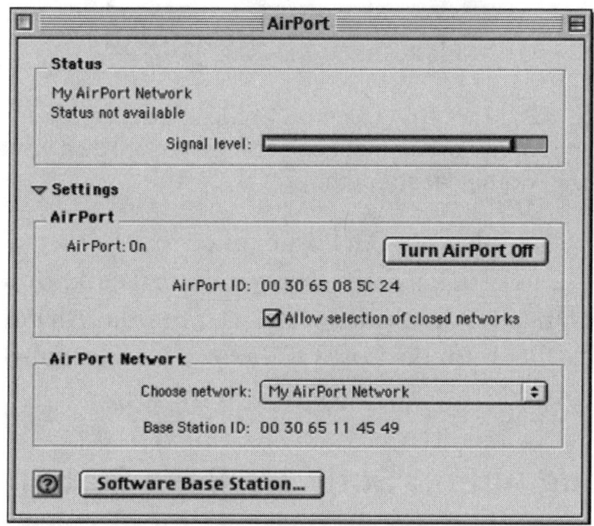

Figure 17.17 The AirPort application displays signal level and allows you to change your network settings.

If you simply want to connect two or more computers together, you can set up a peer-to-peer connection. To do this open the AirPort application and choose Computer-to-Computer from the Choose Network pop-up menu. You don't need to specify which computer, as it will automatically connect to all the computers in the area that are also set to Computer-to-Computer. You won't be able to route Internet access though, for this you'll need to set up either an AirPort Software Base Station or a hardware AirPort Base Station.

You can also control your AirPort connection using the AirPort control strip module. With it you can see the current signal level, select a computer-to-computer network, choose to connect to an active base station, and access the AirPort configuration software.

Figure 17.18 The AirPort control strip module provides easy access to your AirPort connection settings, as well as a visual indicator of AirPort signal strength.

If you want to disable your AirPort connection, to save power in a portable computer such as an iBook or PowerBook, or to prevent radio interference on an airplane, you can use the AirPort application and click the Turn AirPort Off button. You can also disable your AirPort Card from the AirPort control strip.

Configuring AirPort Software Base Station

If you want to share the Internet with several computers using an AirPort network, you can set up one of the computers (presumably with Internet access) to be an AirPort Software Base Station. Use the AirPort Setup Assistant to configure the settings by giving your network a name and a password, and to begin routing. Alternately, you can directly access the AirPort Software Base Station settings from the AirPort application.

Software base stations are handy and inexpensive; however, they aren't as reliable or configurable as Apple's hardware AirPort Base Station. If you want to establish a reliable wireless network for many people to use, you would probably be better off using a hardware base station rather than a software base station.

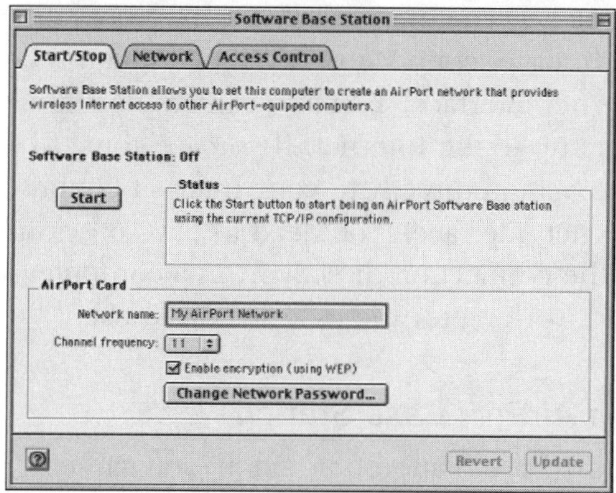

Figure 17.19 The Software Base Station settings are accessible from the AirPort application. Use it to establish a network from a computer with an AirPort Card for other computers to access.

Figure 17.20 When a computer is an active Software Base Station, the AirPort control strip module changes to base station related options.

Using Airport Base Stations

While you can build a very useful and complete AirPort network using just AirPort Cards, you may find that the ease of configuration and the reliability of connections to a hardware AirPort Base Station are worthwhile. This is particularly true if you are establishing a wireless network for a group of people in an office or school.

Installing an AirPort Base Station

Setting up an AirPort Base Station is very easy. Simply plug it in and configure its settings, and then plug it into its power supply.

Connect it to your Ethernet network if you have one, or connect a high-bandwidth Internet connection (DSL or Cable modem perhaps) to its Ethernet interface. You also can connect it directly to a phone line to dial up to the Internet. If you are going to connect the AirPort Base Station directly to your Internet connection (via modem or Ethernet interface), you need to have previously set up and configured the connection directly from a computer so that it will be active and working for the base station to use.

Configuring an AirPort Base Station

With your AirPort Base Station plugged in, you can configure it. Use the AirPort Setup Assistant to specify its network settings, as well as its Internet connection settings and routing options. The AirPort Admin Utility application can also be used to connect to the base station and set it up.

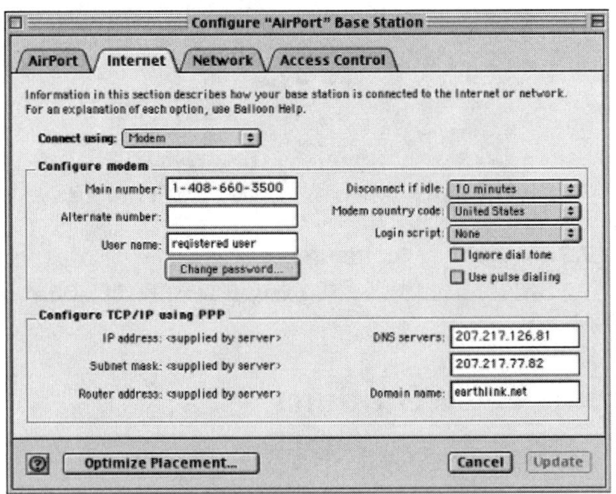

Figure 17.21 Use the AirPort Admin Utility to set up and modify the settings for a hardware AirPort Base Station.

Optimizing Placement

The AirPort Admin Utility has a feature that helps you optimize the placement of your AirPort Base Station so that its signal levels are strongest for everyone using it. Click the button at the bottom of the AirPort Admin Utility window to open the Placement signal-levels window.

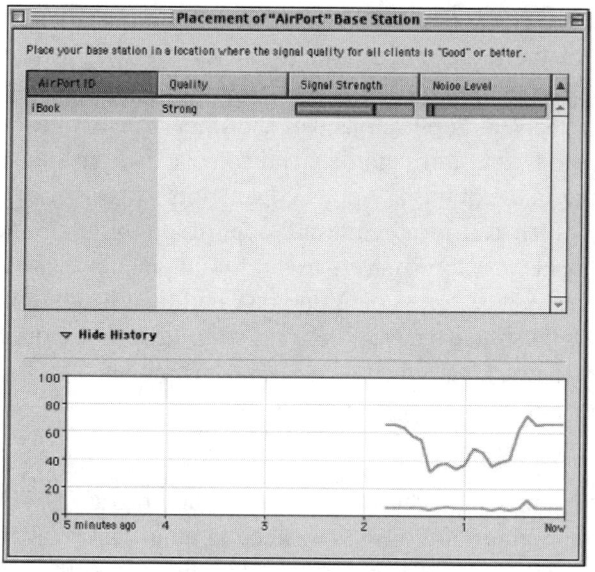

Figure 17.22 Use this window's readouts to optimize the position of your AirPort Base Station for optimal signal strength.

You may find that signals are stronger in unusual locations, which may not be in the middle of your space. Keep in mind that metal materials and other magnetic equipment such as a poorly shielded microwave oven can interfere with radio waves.

Personal File Sharing

One of the most common uses for your own network is sharing files between computers. The Mac OS comes with the software necessary to share files. When file sharing is set up and running on your iMac, every other computer on the network can access the files on its hard drive. Your iMac becomes a server to the other computers on your network. With Mac OS 9 an extra function was added to the file sharing software: using TCP/IP for file sharing, which means that not only can you share to local computers on your network, you can also share to other computers anywhere on the Internet. This is a feature that can be turned on or off, at your choice.

CONTROL OTHER MACS

One of the more unique things you can do with a network is controlling other applications by allowing program linking. With this capability enabled, applications that know how to talk to each other using Apple Events can send data and commands over the network. The best example of this is AppleScript scripts with program linking enabled, which can locate software applications over the network and tell them what to do—very useful for automation that requires multiple computers, one doing one task and then handing it off to another to finish. Or they can be scripted to distribute work among them—each working simultaneously and combining their results when they finish.

To enable program linking, you use the File Sharing control panel and simply click the Start button in the Program Linking section at the bottom of the window. Keep in mind that program linking, while very useful, can be used to tell your software to do

continued…

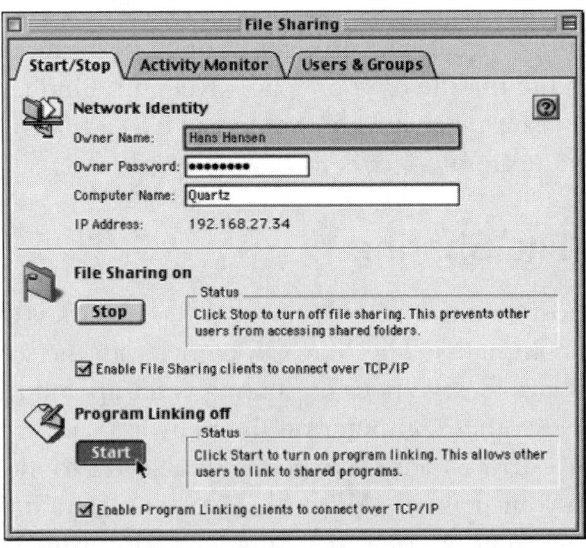

Figure 17.23 Use the File Sharing control panel to enable Program Linking.

anything—and not necessarily by you. Be sure to protect any computers with program linking enabled by specifying a password, and then disable program linking when you aren't using it.

File Sharing Setup

The first thing to do in order to share files is to configure the File Sharing control panel by giving your computer a name and specifying an owner name so that you can tell it who you are when you log in to the computer to mount its hard drive. It is also a good idea to provide an owner password, especially if your computer is on a network where you would like to control access to your computer.

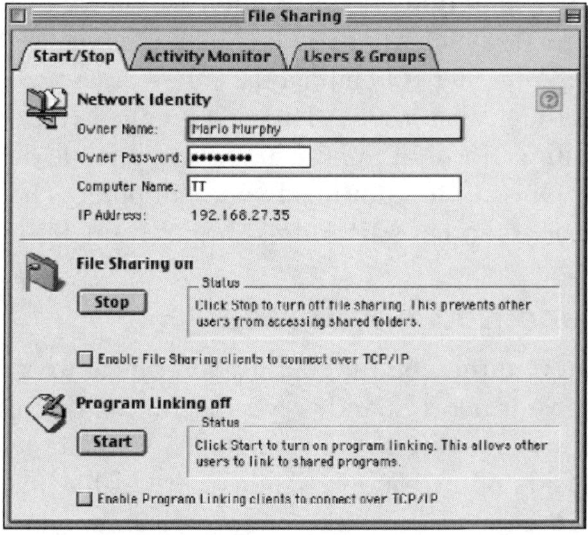

Figure 17.24 The File Sharing window is where you set your computer's identity, start or stop file sharing, or turn on or off file sharing via IP or program linking via IP.

After you've set the owner information and computer name, you can turn on File Sharing. Depending on how much stuff you have on your hard drive, it may take a minute or two for file sharing to start up.

If you want to control your computer from another computer on the network, you can turn on program linking. Program linking allows applications that are running on your computer to be controlled from other computers on the network.

There is an additional option for both file sharing and for program linking that can be turned on allowing sharing and linking to your computer with others out on the Internet rather than just within your network (LAN) by using TCP/IP. If it is file sharing that you'd like to do via TCP/IP, you can use the IP address of your computer to gain access to it. For convenience, the IP address of your computer is displayed in the File Sharing control panel window, between the Network Identity and File Sharing On/Off sections.

One thing to keep in mind if you're going to use TCP/IP to gain access to your computer from another computer via the Internet, is whether your computer is behind a firewall of any sort. If you're using a DSL router that has NAT turned on, then your computer is behind a simple form of firewall and is inaccessible directly from the Internet. One key to knowing if your computer is behind a NAT is if your computer's IP address begins with 192.168.x.x.

Chooser and Network Browser

Now that you've turned on file sharing, you can go to any other computer on your network and access it. You can do this by opening the Chooser and clicking once on the AppleShare icon, which is on the left side of the window. After you've highlighted AppleShare, the right side of the window will show a list of any computers on the network that are sharing. You can then select a computer from the list and log on to it to access its files. You can use the Server IP Address button to specify the address of a computer you want to access via TCP/IP, which could potentially be anywhere on the Internet.

The Chooser is software that has been with the Macintosh for a very long time. And over the years it has been used for several very

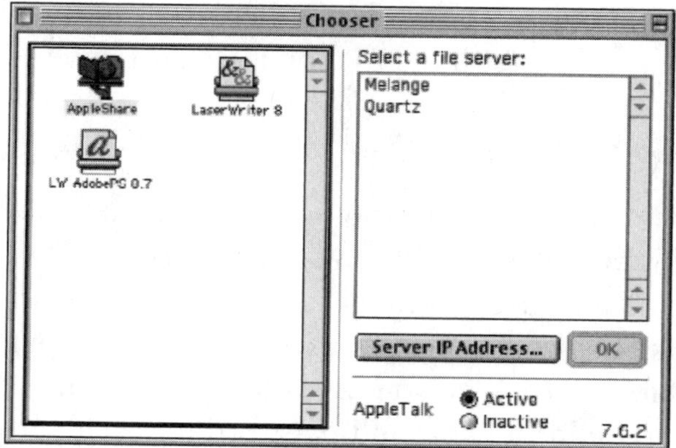

Figure 17.25 Select AppleShare to see which computers on your local network are using file sharing and are available to access.

different actions. It gets the name from its functionality of choosing a printer. But, in its versatility, it can be confusing to use. Another and potentially easier way to view a list of file-sharing computers you can access is with a new piece of software called *Network Browser*. The Network Browser is an application that comes with the Mac OS and is found in the Apple Menu.

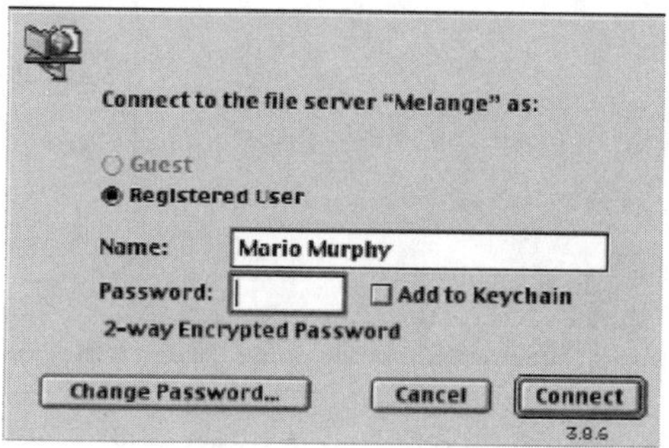

Figure 17.26 The Network Browser can be used to gain access to file sharing computers on your network. To connect to a shared computer, you will need to authenticate yourself.

Using the Network Browser is easy. All you have to do is open it and turn down the triangle for the AppleTalk item. It then will display a list of computers (the same list you'll find in the Chooser) that are sharing on your network. Further, you can double-click on the name of a computer listed to mount its hard drive.

Users and Groups

Not only can you share your whole computer, but you can also share specific volumes or folders at different access levels to multiple individuals and groups of individuals. If there are several people you'd like to give file sharing access on your computer, then you'll need to give each person his or her own account. To do this, you'll have to define a name and password for each person by using the Users & Groups setting under the third tab of the File Sharing control panel.

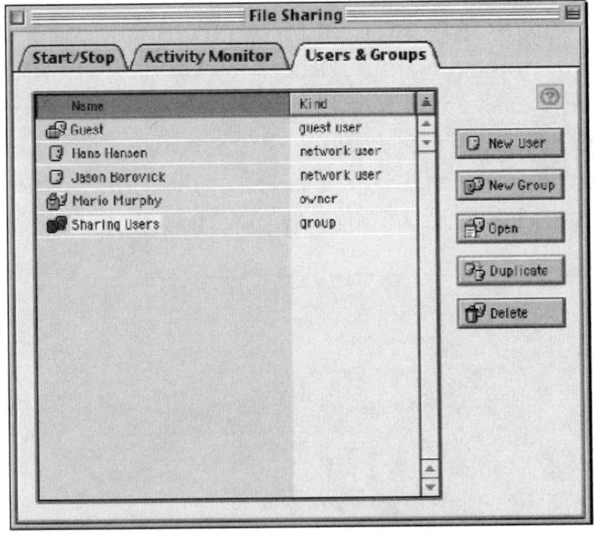

Figure 17.27 This File Sharing window shows the Users and Groups tab. Here you can define user accounts and user groups.

To add a user, click the New User button and edit the name and password for access. To get even more organized about access, you can define groups of people that you want to have specific access. To add users to a group, just drag them either to the icon of the group or the open window of the group.

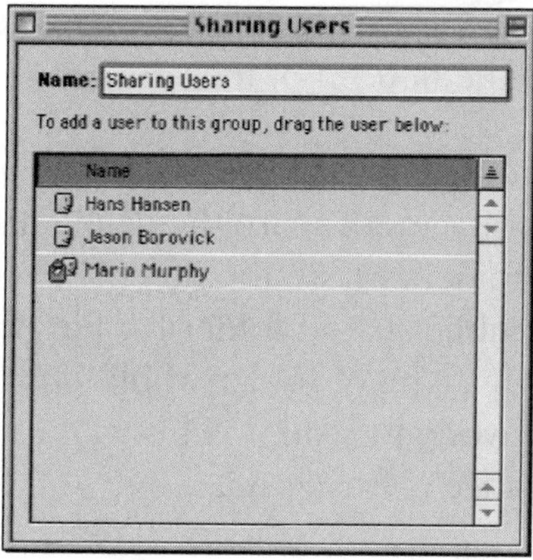

Figure 17.28 Here is a group window showing a list of users.

When you really get into sharing files on your iMac, you'll want to get more specific than just sharing the whole hard disk. This can be done by selecting a volume or folder, getting information on it (type ⌘-I), and then selecting Sharing in the Show pop-up menu at the top of the window. Turn on file sharing for the folder by checking "Share this item and its contents." You can then specify the privileges for accessing that folder. If you want to make sure that

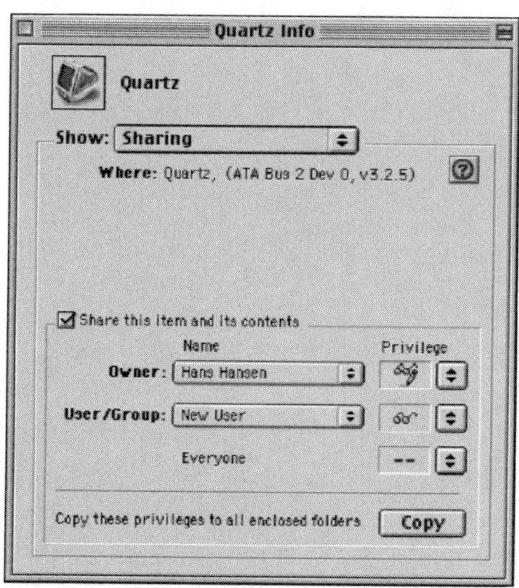

Figure 17.29 The Info window shows sharing settings.

folders within this one are accessible with the same settings, click the Copy button at the bottom of the window.

If you plan on customizing what will be shared on your iMac, you should know that you cannot share the whole disk at the same time as sharing specific folders within the disk. One common form of shared folder is a public shared folder for files from which others may take copies. This type of folder would be set up with its privileges set to allow anyone to read it. This way anyone can copy files from it, but not change or write to it.

Another common shared folder is one for incoming files; it is a folder that people can copy files to but its contents remain unseen. In order to do this, this In Box folder must be inside another folder that is set to allow read access. If you don't do this, no one will be able to mount it with its privileges if it is set to allow write access only.

Only genuine awakening results from tell.
Only fools seek freedom by scripting.
Lifting a hand, the stone object announces
parameters.
Smiling, the application nods its enormous head.

Chapter Eighteen

Automating with AppleScript

Have you ever wanted to make your computer do something auto-matically without guiding it? You can with AppleScript. You can automate repetitive tasks that require a lot of mousing and typing, or you can even use scripts to set your iMac to do things on its own when you're not around. Perhaps you'd like to have it check your email automatically and then carry out special tasks when certain criteria are present in a message. Perhaps you'd like a Web page updated automatically every few minutes based on some changing data on your iMac. Or, perhaps you are working on a project that requires you to click and type the same things repeatedly. You can use AppleScript for all these kinds of tasks and many more.

In this chapter, we are going to look at:

> Learning how AppleScript works

> Discovering how to run scripts

> Creating your own scripts

> Using options to enhance your scripts

How AppleScript Works

AppleScript works by using a special capability called *Apple Events,* which is built in to the Mac OS. Underneath the familiar user interface of menus and windows is a hidden interface used by the system and applications to communicate with each other, in other words to trade bits of data and send requests to execute commands—this is Apple Events. It is invisible, and it is fast, kind of like email. In fact, it is very fast! It can execute thousands of commands and transfer data between applications almost instantly. Think how long it takes you to direct your software applications by using the mouse and keyboard. How many commands can you execute in a minute or in an hour? The power of using Apple Events allows things to move so fast that it must be planned and directed beforehand to "know" what to do. This is where AppleScript comes in.

AppleScript is an integrated software environment designed to organize and execute commands and operations using Apple Events. It is integrated because AppleScript, like Apple Events, is built in to the Mac OS. It is not a stand-alone software application because the Mac OS itself runs the scripts. To create AppleScript scripts, you have to use special script writing and editing software, such as Apple's own application, Script Editor.

SCRIPTING FOR EVERYONE

While most iMac owners may never directly encounter AppleScript, there is a large community of people who use AppleScript every day. This chapter is only a brief introduction to scripting your iMac since there are whole books written on the subject. If you are interested in more information about AppleScript, the best place to go is `http://www.apple.com/apple-script` where you will find the latest information about AppleScript. The AppleScript site includes a complete AppleScript language guide, scripting tutorials and overviews, AppleScript email lists, AppleScript training, other Web sites and resources, and AppleScript related software.

What Are AppleScript Scripts?

AppleScript scripts are text-based instructions that tell software applications what commands to use and how to use them, such as *select the second paragraph of text in the document*, or *check email from this account*, or *apply filter blur to this image*. They can also ask programs questions and get answers, such as *how big is that file* or *what is the first word on the tenth line of the document?* AppleScript scripts can also evaluate data: *if* such and such is true, *then* execute this command (notice that these statements are like logical English sentences). Indeed, AppleScript uses an almost natural prose with nouns and verbs and adjectives, but instead they are objects, commands, and parameters.

```
tell application "Microsoft Word"
    activate
    make new document
    set the text of window 1 to "Hello iMac!"
end tell
```

In this example, AppleScript script directs Microsoft Word to become the front-most application, make a new document, and to set the contents of the front-most window to "Hello iMac!".

While scripts are similar to computer programming, they are different. A program is a set of computer instructions compiled into the codes of a computer's native assembly language, designed to "stand alone" as a software application to accomplish its tasks. A script is a set of instructions that tell one or more other software applications what they should do without doing the task itself. On a more technical level, the actual language in a script is interpreted by the system as it is run, rather than being precomplied into computer assembly code.

Using Script Editor

To compose your scripts, Apple provides a software application called *Script Editor*. It can be found in the AppleScript folder, which is in the Apple Extras folder on your hard drive. With it you can open existing scripts, create new scripts, save scripts as different script types, and run your scripts.

Figure 18.1 Here is the Script Editor application for creating and running AppleScript scripts.

To begin using AppleScript, find and open the Script Editor application. When opening Script Editor itself, it will automatically open a new, empty, untitled script document.

The Script Window

The script-editing window is designed specifically for working with the text of AppleScript scripts. At the top of the window is a text field for a description of your script, which is useful both for keeping track of the script's purpose as well as an explanation of the script for other people. If your script requires certain conditions to run, such as a text document with selected text, it is useful to

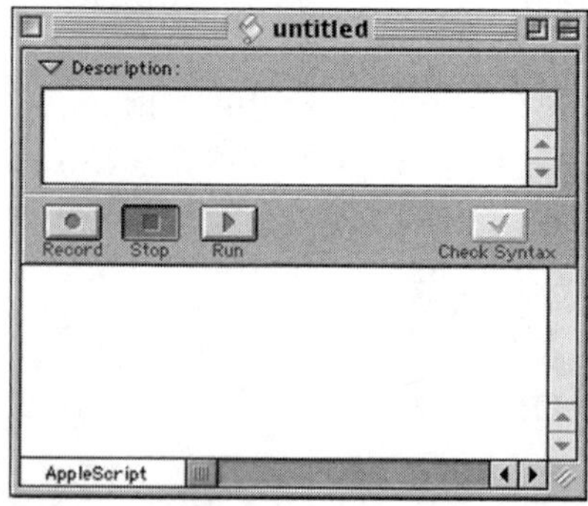

Figure 18.2 Here is a blank window where scripts are written. The upper panel is for writing a general description of the script.

mention such requirements in the description. You can hide the description text field by clicking the small arrow collapsing-control above the field.

Below the script description field are four buttons for working with your script: Record, Stop, Run, and Check Syntax. You can use the Record button to make scripts by setting the Script Editor to record into the script any actions that you want carried out in other applications while the record function is active. Many applications do not support recording, however, and usually the only way to know if they are recordable is simply to try it.

The Stop and Run buttons control the execution of scripts. Clicking the Run button will start the script processing. It will begin at the first line of the script and move down in a line-by-line logical fashion. The Stop button can be used to interrupt a script, but usually your script will have completed its processing before you have a chance to stop it.

The check Syntax button is used to have Script Editor read and check any new lines of text added to your script. Script Editor will look at each element of your script and check to see if it is a recognized AppleScript word and if it makes sense in relation to the words around it. Script Editor also will automatically format the script as it checks its structure, cleans up spacing, and checks capitalization, indentation, and type style—making it consistent and easy to read.

SOUNDS IN SCRIPTS

Adding audio feedback from your scripts can be useful in a number of ways. You can use beep sounds, telling your iMac simply to beep when it finishes a scripting task, to indicate a problem, or to let you know that it has reached a certain point in your script (in other words for debugging purposes). To make a script beep, simply use the command word "beep." Alternately, you can make the Beep command beep several times by adding a number parameter after the command, as in "beep 3," which will beep three times.

continued…

beep 3

In addition to beep, you can also use the Mac OS's built-in speech capabilities to let your iMac speak. By using the Say command along with a string of text, your iMac can talk. Try the following script:

say "Hello, I am your i-Mac."

When writing text to be spoken by your iMac, you might want to adjust your spelling and grammar to affect its pronunciation (iMac is different from i-Mac). You can also specify the voice to use by adding the Using parameter, as in the following example:

say "How are you today?" using "Victoria, high quality"

There are many possibilities for using speech to enhance your scripts as well as to add new functions to your software, such as creating a script to read the subject lines of your incoming email or to announce certain types of events.

Writing a Script

The lower portion of the script document window is where the text of the script is displayed and edited. This is a typical word processing environment where you can type, select with the mouse, and

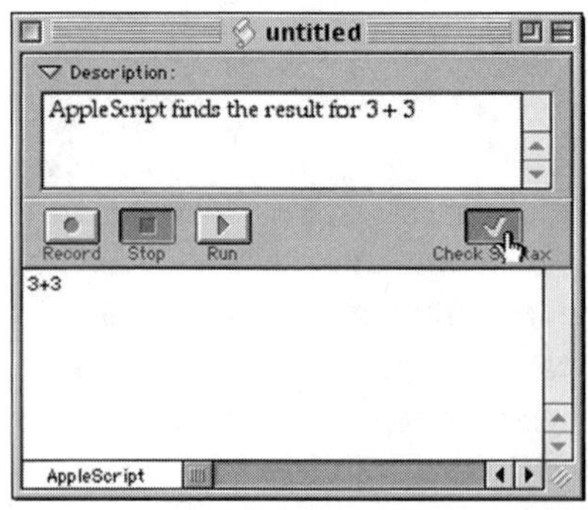
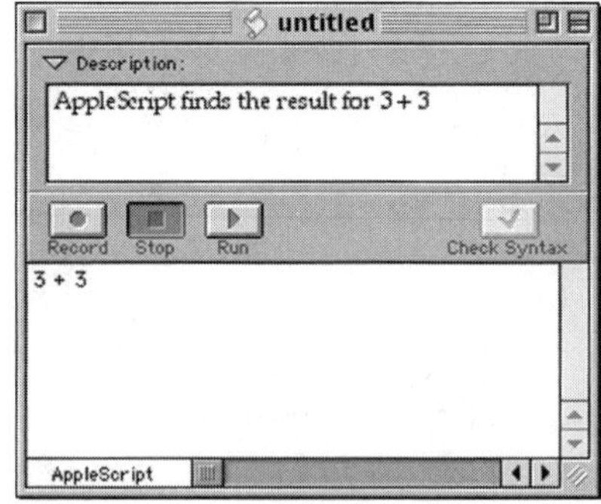

Figure 18.3 Before and after checking the syntax of a script, the formatting (spacing) is automatically corrected as the Script Editor checks the logical structure of the script.

copy and paste. You might notice that it doesn't wrap lines of script text. This is because each line is considered a script statement and is executed all at once. To begin a new line, or statement, press Return.

You'll notice that as you type text into the script document, it is set in a plain typewriter-like font style. When you have finished adding text to a script, you'll want to check its syntax. You can, of course, click the Check Syntax button to do this, but an easier way is simply to press the Return key. The Return key doesn't add anything to your script, such as starting a new line; it simply is the same as clicking the Check Syntax button.

If you'd like to try this, type a simple script such as "3+3." This won't affect any other programs; it simply uses AppleScript's built-in ability to perform logical operations, such as math. After you've typed this example and pressed Return, you'll see that Script Editor reformats it.

Running a Script

After you have a script written and its syntax checked, you can try running it by clicking the Run button. In the case of "3 + 3," Script Editor recognizes that this script produces a result without a desti-

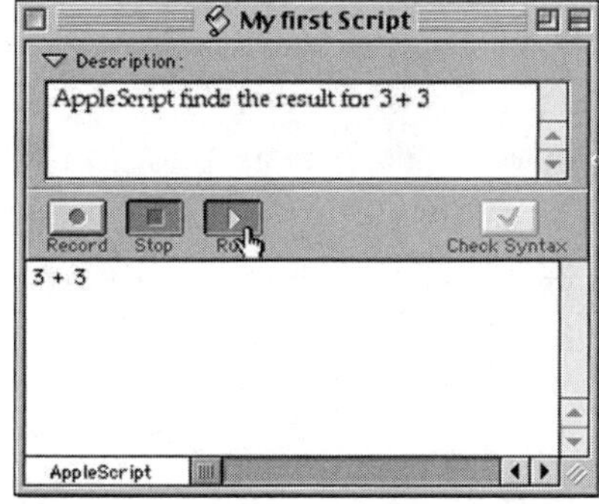

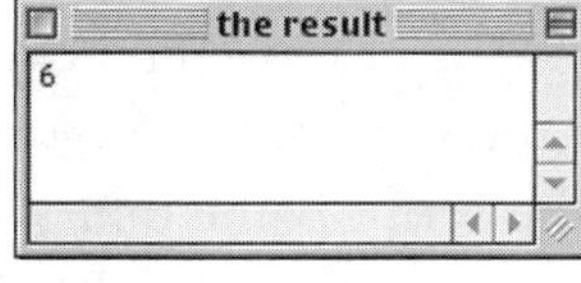

Figure 18.4 Click the run button to execute the script. When needed, the result window will appear to display the results of a script.

nation in which to display it, so it will open its built-in result window to show you that a script of "3 + 3" produces a result of "6."

You should keep a couple things in mind whenever you are ready to run any script for the first time: its scope and expected results. This means that you should recognize what the effect of running the script will be and what you expect the results to be. The scope is important because you need to realize that scripts can do things that cause data loss—just like any human user can delete and move stuff around replacing things. Before you run a script, make backups of any data that could be affected by the script. Knowing the expected result is an important way of recognizing the scope of your script and being able to tell if it is doing what you think it should be doing.

Interrupting a Script

If you write a long script that doesn't seem to be working right, or perhaps the script has some type of looping control in it in which it is caught, you'll want to interrupt the script while it is running. You know that a script is running because the Run button in the script document window will be selected and the cursor (pointer) will usually become a "beach-ball" wait cursor (round with black-and-white quarters). Plus, it will turn and turn and turn until the script is finished.

To interrupt a script, first check to see if you can access the script-document window; then try clicking the Stop button. In most cases this works just as you'd expect. However, if you can't get to the Stop button, or it doesn't seem to actually stop the script, you can use the script panic button: press ⌘-Period. Press ⌘-Period repeatedly or hold the keys down until it successfully interrupts your script.

Script Errors

One part of script writing that is just like traditional programming is dealing with errors and fixing bugs. First, you should recognize that there are different types of errors for different parts of the script writing and running process.

The first errors occur when checking the syntax of a script. When Script Editor finds a problem with the text of a script, it will do its best to point out where the problem is and why it's a problem, usually by explaining what it expected to find but didn't. When you click Cancel to escape the syntax checking function, Script Editor will highlight the text of the script where the problem was found.

Figure 18.5 When checking the syntax of a script fails, an alert such as this one is displayed.

Once a script's syntax is logical to Script Editor, you can run a script, but this doesn't mean it will work. There are many things that Script Editor can't know about the environment and conditions in which you are running your script until it tries to run it. These could be unexpected values of variables or missing handlers for specified operations. When such a problem occurs, the Mac OS, which is the system actually running the script, will notify you of a problem. When this happens you are given two choices: Edit or OK. Click OK if you want to give up and do something else; click Edit if you want to open the script in Script Editor (which

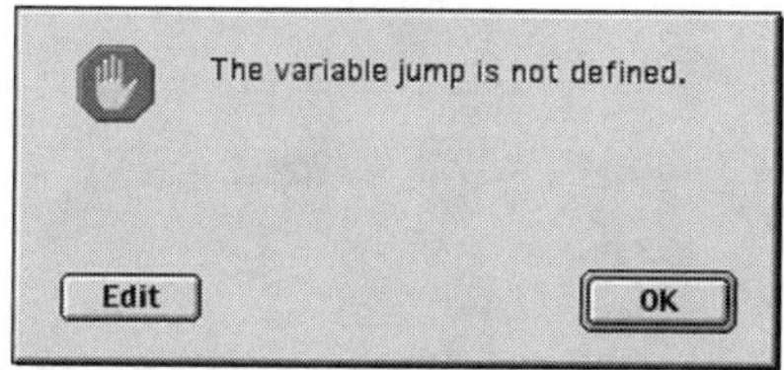

Figure 18.6 When a script's syntax is good, but fails for some reason while running, an alert such as this is displayed, which includes a button to edit the failing part of the script.

might already be open) and try to fix the problem. Just like a syntax error, Script Editor will highlight the problem words in the script.

Sometimes, when you run a script for the first time it will need to locate the software application specified by the script. When this happens the system will display a standard file location dialog box and ask you "Where is" such-and-such application. Simply navigate your hard drive, find the application, and click the Open button.

Figure 18.7 When a software application is specified within a script that cannot be found, an alert such as this is displayed asking you to locate the application.

Saving Your Script

After you have written a script, or even before you have finished creating it, you'll want to save it. There are a few different ways to

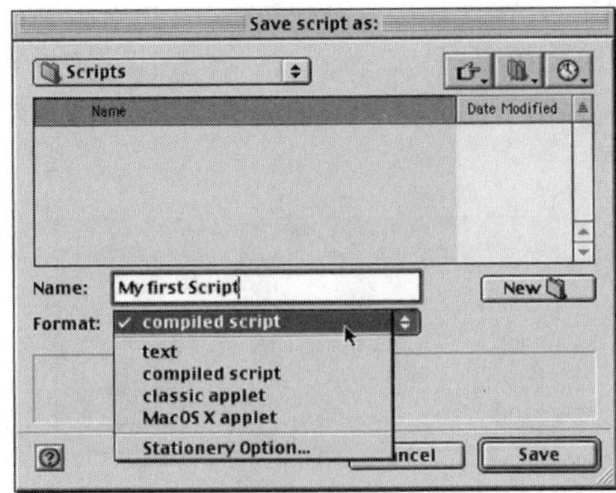

Figure 18.8 Here's how to save a script as a compiled Script Editor document.

save an AppleScript script: as text, as a compiled Script Editor document, or as a stand-alone applet.

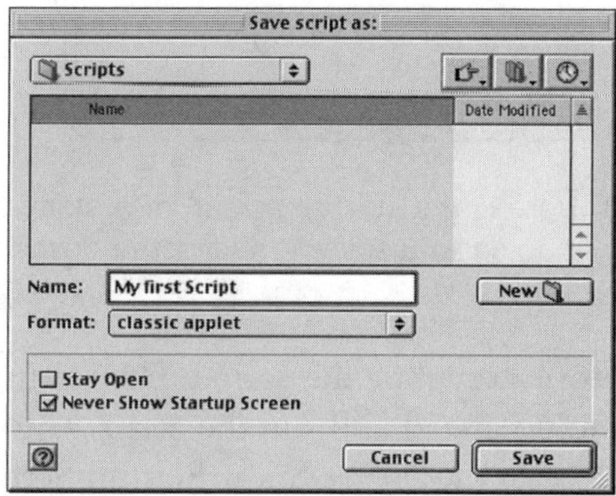

Figure 18.9 Here we are saving a script as a stand-alone executable applet.

The most common types of format in which to save your scripts are
as compiled Script Editor documents. This is simply a script that
has had its syntax checked and is ready to run, but must be opened
by Script Editor in order to run. If a script is still in the process of
being composed and hasn't yet had its syntax checked, or it has
unacceptable text prose, it must be saved as a plain text file.

An alternate way to save your scripts is as stand-alone applets—an
AppleScript script that can run by itself without opening into Script
Editor, much like any software application. To do this, choose
"classic applet" from the Format pop-up menu in the Save Script
file window. You will be presented with two options before saving:
Stay Open and Never Show Startup Screen.

Checking the option for Stay Open will keep the script applet running even after it has finished running, which might be useful for
when the script contains operations that are initiated by other
scripts or application events.

The Never Show Startup Screen option overrides the normal feature of displaying a script's description in a dialog window when

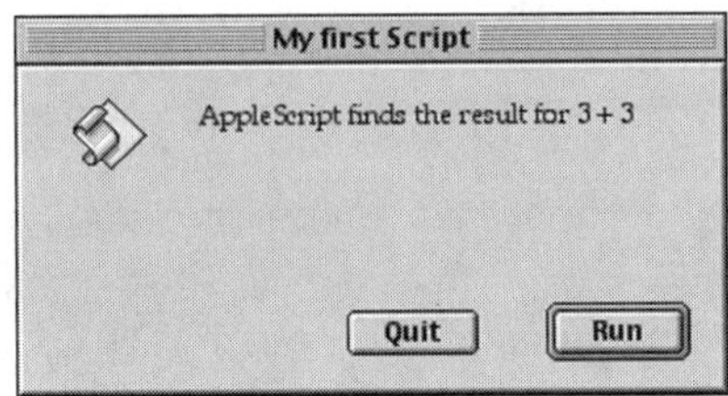

Figure 18.10 Here is the startup screen of a stand-alone script applet; when enabled to display, it shows the description of the script.

launched, but before executing the script. The startup screen also includes buttons to go ahead and run the script or to quit without running the script. Use the Never Show Startup Screen by clicking the Run button option when you want the script to run quickly without interruption.

Writing AppleScripts

So far we've looked at what AppleScript is, how it works, and how to use the Script Editor, so now let's write some scripts. The following topics take you step-by-step through writing and rewriting a series of scripts. These examples are less about what they accomplish, and more about how to emphasize the methods used in forming and refining a script. This is just a quick introduction to script writing, as there are whole books on AppleScript that go into far more detail (such as, *The Tao of AppleScript*).

Before we dive in, let's take a moment to talk about the process of scripting. The first thing to do is to have a goal in mind: what are you trying to accomplish with your script? The second thing to do is to know all the steps involved in accomplishing your script goal: can you perform it manually? If so, do so while taking note of each step. The third thing to do is to begin building the script: writing and testing each step by putting it together one step at a time.

RANDOM NUMBERS

Sometimes, adding a little randomness to a script is fun and useful. For this, AppleScript provides a function called random number, which will generate one on the fly as in the following example:

```
random number from 1 to 100
```

Running this script will produce a result of a random integer between I and I00. Try running it a bunch of times to see different results.

You can also use the Random Number command in more complex scripts. The following example produces six numbers between I and 52—useful for playing the California State lotto:

```
set numberList to {}
set numberCount to 0
repeat until numberCount is 6
    set aNumber to random number from 1 to 52
    if numberList does not contain aNumber then
            set numberList to numberList & aNumber
            set numberCount to numberCount + 1
    end if
end repeat
numberList
```

Again, you can run this script a bunch of times to generate different sets of numbers—if you use it to win the lotto, please remember the authors of this helpful book.

Script Structure

An AppleScript script is written as a series of one-line statements—each statement is executable independent of other statements. Each statement is built from words that have specific functions. Some of these words are commands, while others are references to objects to affect. There are also words for naming variables, defining command parameters, referencing subroutines, using operators, adding comments, and controlling your script with special keywords.

When writing scripts it is important to keep in mind that you are always working with and directing objects. Everything is an object: every file, every folder, every text character, everything. Each and every object is related to other objects; they are either within bigger objects or contain smaller objects. Often, there are many objects together in the same place, each with its own identification.

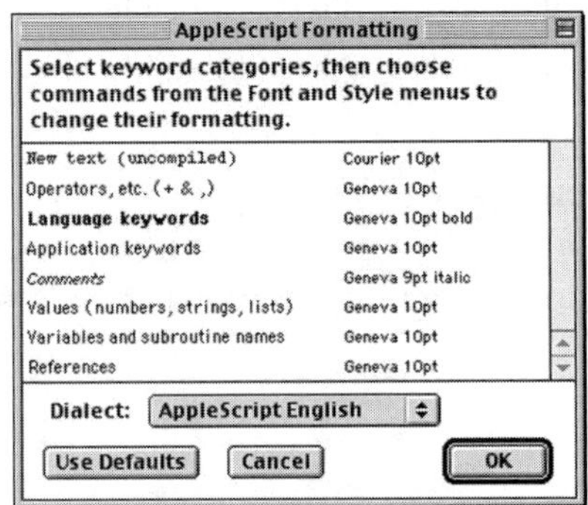

Figure 18.11 The AppleScript Formatting window is used to view and modify the styling of script text.

As you use Script Editor and check the syntax of your scripts, it will automatically recognize the different types of words and format them appropriately. It will also add indentation to statements that are controlled by other statements. You can modify the formatting used by AppleScript by selecting the AppleScript Formatting command at the bottom of Script Editor's Edit menu. This formatting will affect all AppleScript script editor applications.

Do It Manually

The best way to begin scripting is by doing, so let's build some simple scripts. Turn on your iMac and try to follow along. For simplicity we'll focus on scripting stuff in the Finder, manipulating some folders and their properties.

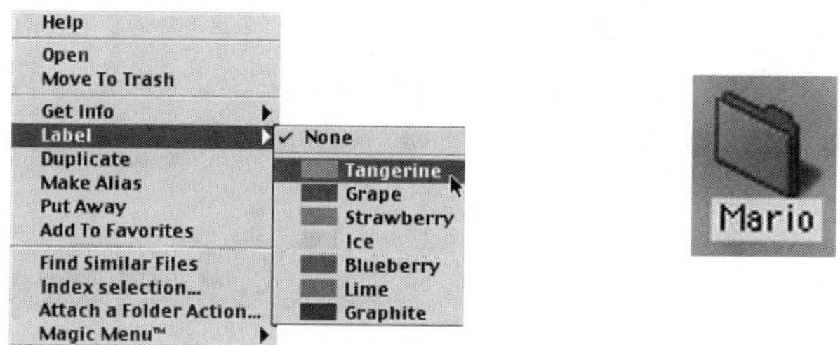

Figure 18.12 Begin a script by performing it manually, in this case applying a label to a folder using a contextual menu.

The first step in writing a script is to know what you want to do and to try doing it manually so that you know all the steps involved. Begin by creating a folder on your Desktop, and name it "Mario." We'll begin our first script by labeling this folder from a script, so try that—apply a label to the "Mario" folder by selecting it, holding down the Control key and clicking on it to reveal the Finder's contextual menu, and selecting the first label from the Label submenu.

Script That Task

Now with the Mario folder created on the Desktop, we have an object to effect with a script. We can set the label property of the Mario folder with the following script:

```
tell the application "Finder" to tell its item named "Mario" to
set its label index to 2
```

Try typing this script into your Script Editor, checking its syntax, and running it. If all is well, the Mario folder on your Desktop will change its color to that of the second label.

This script works by telling the Finder to tell the Mario folder to set its label index property value to 2. In other words, the Finder is the application being told what to do, and what it does is use the Set command on the object named Mario. There are two parts to this script: the *target* object and the *action* to be performed.

The label index is a property that defines the label applied to an object in the Finder, numbers 1 through 7 are the labels in order from first to last, and 0 is the index value for none.

Just as with any language, there are different ways of saying the same things. In AppleScript you can specify the object of a command by first referencing the object it is contained within or by first referencing the object itself. The following variation on the previous script begins by referencing the Mario folder and then the application of which it is a part.

```
tell the item named "Mario" of the application "Finder" to set
its label index to 3
```

This script performs the same function, except its value has been set to the third label.

Script a Different Property of That Object

That's enough scripting of the label property. Another property of the folder Mario that can be set with a script is its position on the Desktop or in a window. The position of an object, such as a file or folder in the Finder, is described as being a number of pixels from the upper-left corner of the screen for the Desktop or the upper-left corner of the area within a window below the title bar for a window. The position is made of two values together, a horizontal distance first, x, and then a vertical distance second, y. These two values are related to a single property and must be formatted as a list in the form: { x, y }. Value lists are always formatted by placing them within braces.

Figure 18.13 The position of objects in the Finder is related to the distance in pixels from the upper-left corner.

Let's set the position of the Mario folder on the Desktop. Try using the following script to move the folder on your Desktop:

```
tell application "Finder" to set the position of the item named
"Mario" to {96, 74}
```

This script tells the Finder to use the position of the Mario folder to the values in the list, {96, 74}. Note that numerical values should not be set in quotation marks. This is so that AppleScript will evaluate them as numbers and not as text.

Move an Object

Now we will move the folder Mario into another folder, in essence moving an object into another object. Before using this script make a new folder on your Desktop named "My Friends" to put the Mario folder into.

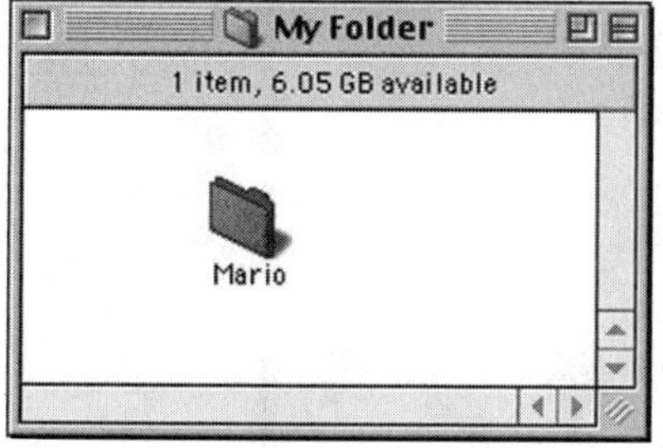

Figure 18.14 Here is an object in which to place other objects.

Type in and run the following script:

```
tell application "Finder" to move the item named "Mario" to the
item named "My Friends"
```

After you have run it, open the folder My Friends and see that it now contains the folder Mario.

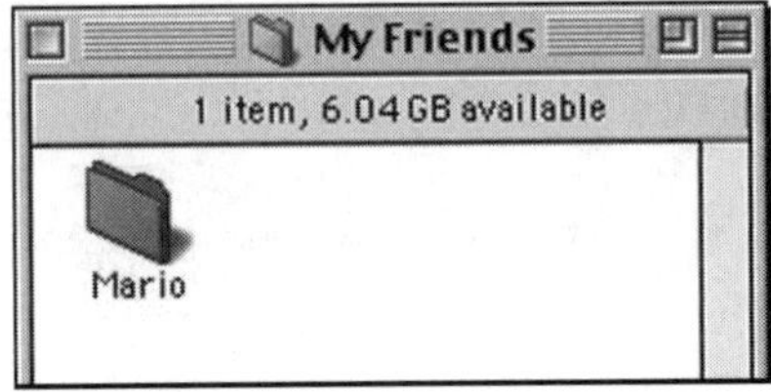

Figure 18.15 The object Mario is now in the object My Friends.

This script uses the Move command to tell the Finder to place the object Mario into the object My Friends.

Specify the Comment Property

Yet another property of an object in the Finder that can be specified with AppleScript is its comment. To view the comments of a file or folder in the Finder, choose General Information from the Get Info submenu in the File menu or select the item and type ⌘-I.

Type in and run the following script to set the comment property of the folder Mario. Note that you now have to specify that it is within the object My Friends.

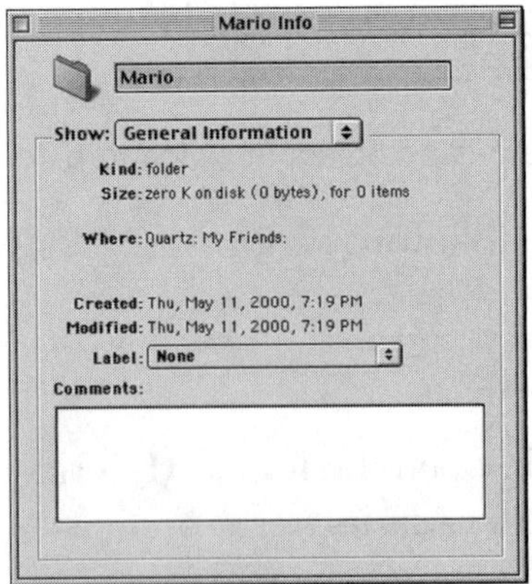

Figure 18.16 The comments property for an item in the Finder is displayed at the bottom of the Get Info window.

```
tell application "Finder" to tell the item named "My Friends" to
tell its item named "Mario" to set its comment to "Hello, my name
is Mario!"
```

This script sets the comment of the object Mario within the object My Friends of the Finder to "Hello, my name is Mario!".

Just as before, you can also specify the objects from most general to most specific or vice versa. The following variation of the previous script begins by specifying the object Mario, then the object My Friends, and then the Finder:

```
tell the item named "Mario" of the item named "My Friends" of
application "Finder" to set its comment to "Hello, my name is
still Mario!!"
```

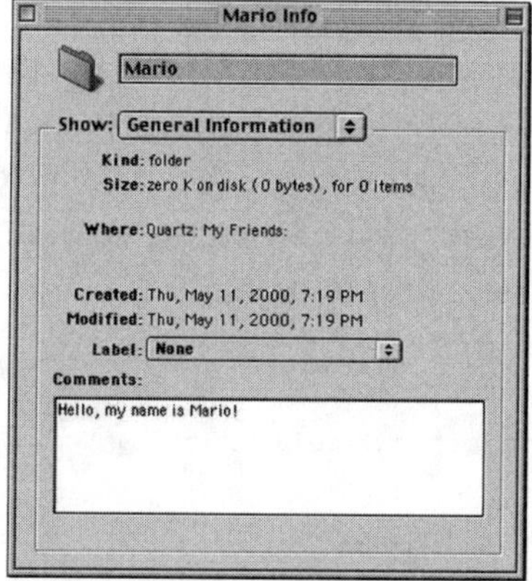

Figure 18.17 After setting the comments property with a script, the comments appear in the field at the bottom of the Get Info window.

In addition to changing the order of the object references in your scripts, you can also leave out some optional words. In this case "the" and "named" have been removed from the previous script:

```
tell item "Mario" of item "My Friends" of application "Finder" to
set its comment to "Hello, my name really  is Mario!!"
```

Even without these words, the script functions in exactly the same way.

Tell Once

So far, in the three examples of setting the properties of the folder Mario, we have used three different scripts, but each can stand and function on its own.

```
tell application "Finder" to tell item named "My Friends" to set
its label index of the item named "Mario" to 4
tell application "Finder" to tell item named "My Friends" to set
its position of the item named "Mario" to {72, 47}
tell application "Finder" to tell item named "My Friends" to tell
item named "Mario" to set its comment to "Hello, my name is
Mario!"
```

However, if you are planning to set all the properties at once, you can combine them together (*nest* them) so that you only need to define the object to act upon once. To do this you can enclose subordinate statements within a Tell control—placing a Tell command before the subordinate statements and an End Tell command after them, as in the following:

```
tell application "Finder" to tell item named "My Friends" to tell
item named "Mario"
        set its label index to 4
        set its position to {72, 120}
        set its comment to "Hello, my name is Mario!"
end tell
```

In this script the object of the three set command statements is defined at the beginning by the Tell command.

Shorter Phrasing within Tell (Dropping "Its")

Once again we can remove unnecessary words, in this case "its." However, this is only because this word becomes obsolete when the target object is defined by a separate Tell command.

```
tell application "Finder" to tell item named "My Friends" to tell
item named "Mario"
        set label index to 4
        set position to {72, 120}
        set comment to "Hello, my name is Mario!"
end tell
```

Adding Comments

As your script begins to grow, you should always add comments
into it to delineate different parts and to explain the purpose of
specified values that might not appear to be obvious. Comments
are an important part of any program writing. They often are
required for a complex project where many people will work with
and extend the function of a body of code.

In AppleScript you can add comments in two ways: enclosed in
brackets "(* *comment* *)" for multiple line comments, and after
double-dashes "--*comment*" for single line comments, as in the following:

```
(* This is the example script that sets three properties of a folder named
   Mario  and created specifically for the purposes of this demonstration. *)
```

```
tell application "Finder" to tell item named "My Friends" to tell
item named "Mario"
        -- change the label color
        set label index to 4
        -- re-position the folder near the top left
        set position to {72, 120}
        -- change the comment
        set comment to "Hello, my name is Mario!"
end tell
```

In this script the two lines at the beginning and the three lines inter-
spersed within the script are completely ignored by AppleScript.

Tell within Tell

You can further break down the objects of the Tell command into
separate Tell commands, each nested within the greater object.

This will allow for more flexibility in your scripts, as you will see in the next topic. The following script separates each object into its own Tell command:

```
tell application "Finder"
      tell item named "My Friends"
            tell item named "Mario"
                  set label index to 4
                  set position to {72, 120}
                  set comment to "Hello, my name is Mario!"
            end tell
      end tell
end tell
```

Each subordinate level of a script is indented within the command that controls its object. Because there are three Tell commands in this script, the lines are indented three levels.

As you become more familiar with AppleScript, you may also find it useful to replace generic terms for specific ones. In the following example we have replaced the generic term *item* with the specific term *folder*.

```
tell application "Finder"
      tell folder named "My Friends"
            tell folder named "Mario"
                  set label index to 4
                  set position to {72, 120}
                  set comment to "Hello, my name is Mario!"
            end tell
      end tell
end tell
```

This script will function in the same way as it did before with the term *item*. However, by being specific, it will now only work with folders, whereas before it would work with any type of object named My Friends or Mario. Being specific can be useful when your script needs to distinguish between different objects with the same identification, but it can be limiting as well.

Multiple Tells within Tell

Okay, it's time to make this script more elaborate—to demonstrate the advantages of using scripts by having more to work with. Let's add two more folders within the My Friends folder for our script: one named "Hans" and the other named "Chris." We'll then add to our script commands label, position, and comment to each of these folders.

When you want to quickly adjust a bunch of objects together, use the combined Tell commands, which allow you to direct different objects within greater objects without having to repeatedly define their relationship. It also creates a better structure for your script with which to easily grow and track what you're working on.

The following script will add separate nested Tell commands for each of the folders in My Friends:

```
tell application "Finder"
      tell folder named "My Friends"
            tell folder named "Mario"
                  set its label index to 1
                  set its position to {36, 36}
                  set its comment to "Hello, my name is
Mario!"
            end tell
            tell folder named "Hans"
                  set its label index to 2
                  set its position to {36, 90}
                  set its comment to "Hello, my name is
Hans!"
            end tell
            tell folder named "Chris"
                  set its label index to 3
                  set its position to {36, 144}
                  set its comment to "Hello, my name is
Chris!"
            end tell
      end tell
end tell
```

If you've typed in and run this script, you'll see that the folders are all lined up, labeled pretty colors, and each has a comment customized with its name.

Although typing in this script has taken a few minutes, and it is very specific to these example folders, which were manually created, look at how fast AppleScript executes these commands. It would take you some time to manually label each folder and go and Get

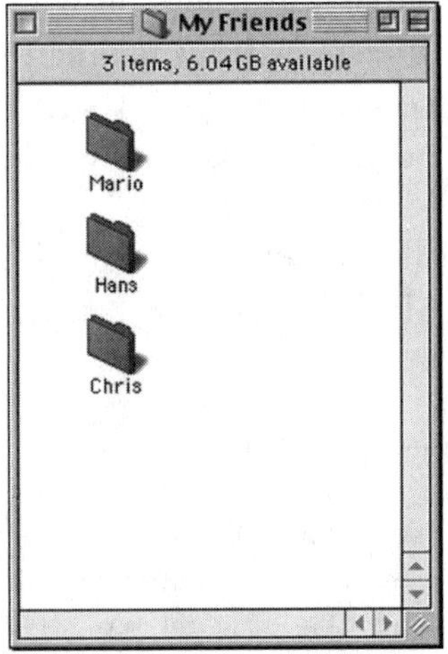

Figure 18.18 The final script cleans up the folders with colorful labels and positions the folders carefully in a column.

Info on each one and type in its comment, and then lining them up so perfectly would have been very difficult—AppleScript can do all this in less than a second.

On Your Own

The examples of scripts we've presented here are only a brief introduction to AppleScript. You can explore lots more. If you feel like you've got enough of an idea to try some things on your own, then you'll want to know about dictionaries. Every application that supports AppleScript has a dictionary you can view to see what commands and objects it has that you can script.

To view an application's dictionary, use the Open Dictionary command in Script Editor's File menu. Select and open the application, and if it supports AppleScript, you'll get a window that will display its commands, objects, and properties.

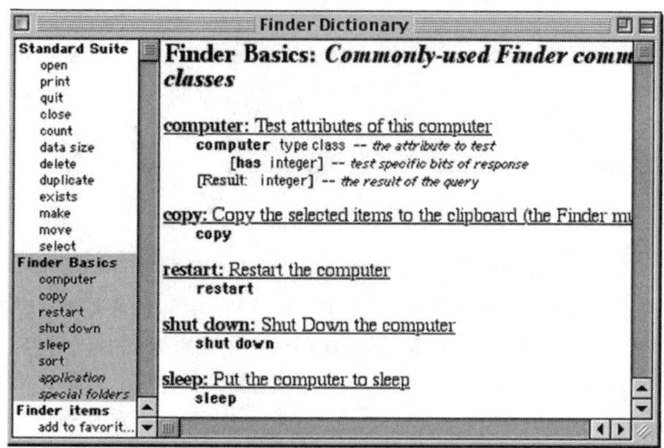

Figure 18.19 Here is the AppleScript dictionary for the Finder.

TELL TIME

You can get and use the current time and date within your AppleScripts by using the Current Date command. Try it by typing this command into a script window and viewing the result:

```
current date
```

The result of this command will be something like: date "Wednesday, May 24, 2000 12:45:19 AM". To use this information in a script, you will most likely want to parse out its elements so that they can be used separately. The following scripts break down the result of the Current Date command to derive a particular element such as the day, the month, the year, or the time, placing them into a variable of the appropriate name:

```
set currDateDay to the first word of ((current date) as
string)
```

```
set currDateMonth to the second word of ((current date) as
string)
```

continued...

```applescript
set currDateDayNum to the third word of ((current date) as
string)

set currDateYear to the fourth word of ((current date) as
string)

set currDateTime to word 5 of ((current date) as string) &
":" & ¬
    word 6 of ((current date) as string) & ":" & ¬
    word 7 of ((current date) as string) & " " & ¬
    word 8 of ((current date) as string)
```

With the results of the current date broken down into these variables, you can then use those elements in your scripts in any pattern you choose, such as in the following example:

```applescript
say "The time is now " & currDateTime & ¬
    ", on " & currDateDay & ", " & ¬
    currDateMonth & " " & ¬
    currDateDayNum & ". " & ¬
    "In the year " & currDateYear & "."
```

This script uses the Say command to speak the current time and date. Give it a try with the lines of script above.

Enhancing Your Scripts

Once you have a grasp of AppleScript, there are many things you can do to enhance your scripts. You can use more advanced programming techniques within your scripts, such as subroutines. You can create script applications that accept items dragged onto them in the Finder on which they can then act upon. You can add functions and features to AppleScript by plugging in third-party scripting additions. There are much more robust script editing applications that include programming features for debugging, such as traceable execution and variable watching. There are developer applications for building complex user interfaces for your scripts, which allow you to develop entire AppleScript-based software applications. And to work with software applications that don't support AppleScript, there are virtual user applications in which you can click and choose commands just as if a person stepped up to your iMac and used the mouse and keyboard.

Subroutines

Sometimes, when you're writing a complex script, you'll find yourself doing something repeatedly, such as using the same lines of scripting code to do the same thing over and over. Wouldn't it be great if you could simply put those lines of your script somewhere and call them into action when you need them by using your own command? You can do just that, and it's called a *subroutine*—programmers use them all the time. Subroutines are a faster, more efficient way to write scripts. They make scripts shorter, thereby reducing redundancy and when you need to change some aspect of your commonly used routine, you only need to change it once, and it will affect all the places in your script that use it.

In addition to conveniently condensing repetitious use of script routines, a subroutine can also be used to evaluate and return values. When a script calls a subroutine into action, it can pass it a value to work with. A subroutine can also be designed to return a value to the script calling it, passing a value back that it has calculated.

To make a subroutine, you need to define it and call it. To define a subroutine, you enclose a script within opening and closing statements:

```
on subroutine()

end subroutine
```

The name of a subroutine always needs to include parentheses. To call this subroutine, you simply use the name of the subroutine in a script as a command:

```
if x = 3 then
    subroutine()
end if
```

This example calls the subroutine whenever x is equal to 3.

Let's look at a subroutine in action. In the following script we have taken our previous example of manipulating folders and condensed the redundant parts together into a subroutine called *friend*. This script is now only three lines, which calls the subroutine and passes it the specific values for each folder. The subroutine is defined below the three lines at the end of the script.

```
friend("Mario", 1, {36, 36})
friend("Hans", 2, {36, 90})
friend("Chris", 3, {36, 144})


on friend(friend_name, friend_label, friend_position)
        tell application "Finder"
                tell folder named "My Friends"
                        tell folder named friend_name
                                set its label index to friend_label
                                set its position to friend_position
                                set its comment to "Hello, my name
is " & friend_name & "!"
                        end tell
                end tell
        end tell
end friend
```

In order to pass values to the subroutine, you place them within the parentheses in the subroutine name. Then in the opening statement of the subroutine, you define variable names for each value that you are passing, which can then be used only within the subroutine.

DISPLAY DIALOGS

Sometimes in a script, you'll need a little bit of interface—perhaps an alert box—that lets users make choices, or to enter bits of information. To do this you can use the Display Dialog command, as in the following example:

```
display dialog "Hello, do you want to continue or stop?" but-
tons {"Cancel", "Continue"} default button 2
```

continued...

This line of script will display a dialog box that is useful when a script reaches a point at which there is no going back, perhaps because the script will alter data or delete something. By placing a description of the action that the script is about to take into a dialog box and then letting the user select Cancel, or Continue, you can add a bit of safeguard against accidents. A feature of the Display Dialog command is that if you choose to name one of the buttons Cancel and the user selects it, it will immediately stop running the script.

You can also use the Display Dialog command to ask for short strings of text from the user by adding the default answer parameter, as in the following:

```
display dialog "Hello, what is your name?" buttons
{"Continue"} default button 1 default answer "your name here"
say "Hello " & text returned of result & "."
```

This script uses the result of the Display Dialog command to speak whatever text is placed in the field.

Drop-Applets

A drop-applet is an AppleScript that is designed specifically to act upon items that are dragged and dropped onto it in the Finder. Drop-applet is short for drag-and-drop application—or shortened

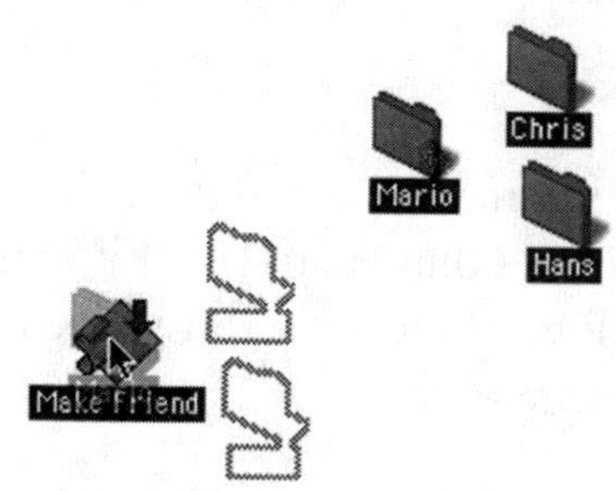

Figure 18.20 An AppleScript drop-applet allows you to apply a script to items in the Finder by dragging and dropping them onto it.

further to drop-let. This could be useful if you have a script that does something to the contents of a folder or to a group of files, because dropping the items on the drop-let simply defines which items to act upon by passing their identity to the script.

To make a script applet into a drop-let, you need to begin your script routine with an *on open* statement with a variable to hold the identity of the items dropped onto it, as in the following example:

```
on open of a_folder_list
        set item_name to ""
        set item_number to 1
        repeat until item_name is "Mario"
                set item_name to the last word of ((item item_num-
ber of a_folder_list) as string)
                set item_number to item_number + 1
                if item_number > (count of a_folder_list) then exit
repeat
        end repeat
        set item_number to item_number - 1
        if item_name is "Mario" then
                tell application "Finder"
                        tell item (item item_number of
a_folder_list)
                                set its label index to 1
                                set its position to {36, 36}
                                set its comment to "Hello, my name
is Mario!"
                        end tell
                end tell
        end if
end open
```

This script captures the names of the items into the variable *a_folder_list* and then evaluates that list to see if it contains an item named Mario. If it does, then the script will set the properties of the folder Mario and be done.

Scripting Additions

AppleScript is an extensible system where commands and functions can be added by "plugging in" features created by Apple and third-party software developers. These extensions are called *Scripting Additions*. To activate a scripting addition, place it into the Scripting Additions folder within the System Folder.

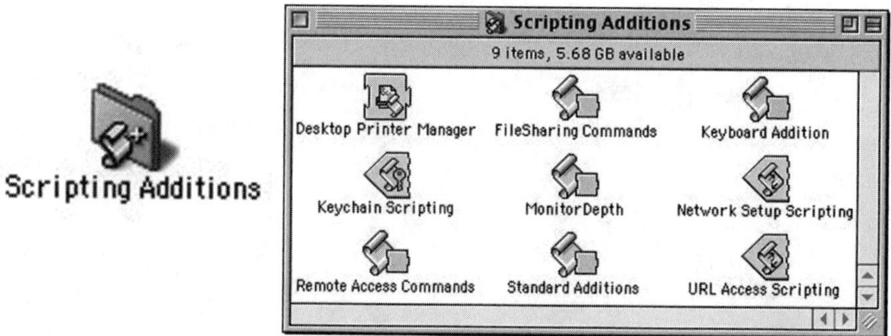

Figure 18.21 You can extend AppleScript features by putting Scripting Additions into the System Folder.

Mac OS 9 includes nine standard scripting additions. To view the features each one adds to AppleScript, open it with the Open Dictionary command in Script Editor.

Other Script Editors

In addition to Apple's Script Editor, there are several other more powerful commercial software applications with which you can compose AppleScript scripts. The biggest advantage that more robust script editing applications provide are their debugging capabilities. This means you can step line-by-line through your scripts while watching the "live" values for variables, as well as set break points to interrupt and pause longer scripts. You'll also find that other script editors also have more advanced text-editing capabilities that include draggable text and language libraries.

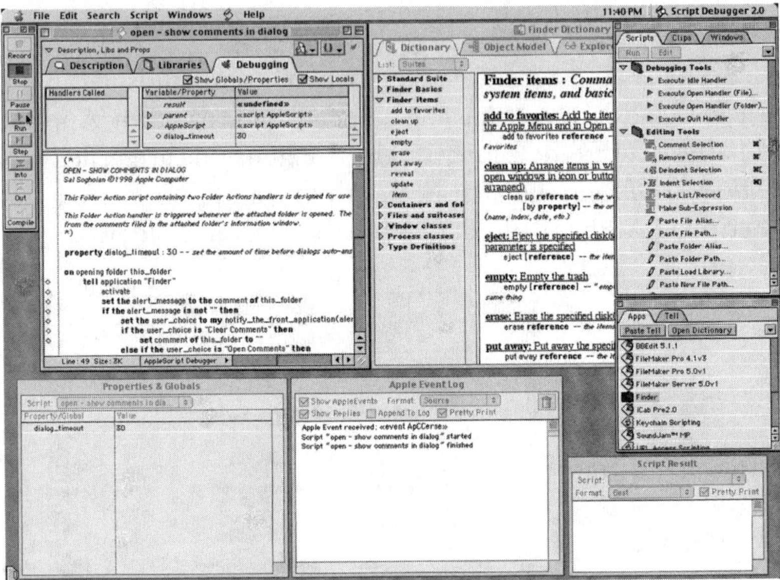

Figure 18.22 Here is a Script Debugger.

Two popular AppleScript script-editing applications are Script Debugger by Late Night Software and Scripter by Main Event Software. Both applications offer very robust scripting tools. Some of these tools include editing with no 32 K limit in the length of scripts, find-and-replace, drag-and-drop, split-pane editing, support for all OSA languages, optional line wrapping, single-step execution, step-into and step-out of handlers, breakpoints, watch points, Apple Event logging, dictionary browsing with views by suite, class, event or object model, expandable suites and classes, ability to create event templates and handler templates, and scripting that is recordable and attachable.

HANDLE ERRORS

One of the more advanced features of AppleScript is its commands for handling errors—errors that occur only under circumstances that you cannot control and that you want your script to ignore or act differently upon. For these situations, you can use the Try and On Error commands. Place the Try command before the

continued…

lines of your script for which you want to handle errors. Then after these lines, use the On Error command to contain a routine for what to do if an error occurs. The following example demonstrates a script that always produces an error, and handles it by simply beeping instead of displaying the usual script error alert dialog box.

```
try
    set variableX to "AppleScript" as number
    on error
beep
end try
```

There are many ways you can use error handling, including doing absolutely nothing—you can leave the On Error command blank to have your script completely ignore any errors.

Virtual Users

When you begin scripting, you'll quickly discover that many applications don't support AppleScript at all. But there is a solution—virtual users, which are software utilities that perform tasks in other applications by using the same controls that a human would use to interact with applications. The software pretends to use the keyboard or mouse to select menu items, initiate commands, or to click on buttons and select objects—just as if it were sitting in front of your iMac. This software is itself scriptable so that you can, in essence, script anything a human can do. It's not as fast or as effective as an application that is scriptable, but it's better than nothing, when the need arises.

Two utilities that provide this sort of functionality are Prefab Player by Prefab Software and QuicKeys by CE Software. Prefab Player is designed specifically for this type of function with AppleScript. QuicKeys is a general macro-automation utility that happens to be scriptable, thus enabling script control of many normally unscriptable situations.

Once the result's found,
Have a good laugh.
Ones and Zeros are faster—
Those useless decimals!

Chapter Nineteen

Ten Quick iMac Tricks

Tricks are what using a computer is all about. In this chapter you'll learn some simple things that you can do to enhance your iMac experience on a daily basis by building some essential skills. All these tricks emphasize doing things in an efficient manner, but they certainly aren't the only way to accomplish these tasks. Perhaps they'll inspire you to discover your own tricks and develop the most effective approach for manipulating data and saving yourself time and trouble. Let the iMac do the work, or at least make it easier for you. When you find yourself clicking repeatedly in the same pattern or typing the same thing over and over and over, find a way for the computer to do it! There is usually an easier, more efficient way. Here are just a few of the "tricks of the trade."

In this chapter, we are going to look at:

➤ Saving time by dragging and dropping

➤ Using contextual menus and the control strip

➤ Launching applications

➤ Taking notes

➤ Searching hard drives and the Internet

➤ Compressing data

➤ Using spell check

➤ Calculating sums of numbers, graphing algebra, and sorting lists

Drag-and-Drop

This first trick is about how to work efficiently with your mouse. When you grab an icon on your desktop with the mouse and drag it to a folder or to the Trash and let go, you are dragging and dropping. Dragging and dropping things has been a Macintosh technique from the beginning, but today you can drag around more things than ever. You can move selections of text from one place in a document to another, you can drag selections onto the desktop to create clipping files, and you can even drag between some applications. (In the past, many of these simple drag-and-drop movements normally required the more laborious cut and paste commands to remove, or duplicate, your data and insert it somewhere else.)

Figure 19.2 Drag and drop a file in the Trash.

When you select and grab something on your iMac, if that object is "draggable," it will come with your mouse as you drag it away. Not everything is "draggable;" obviously, items that cannot be dragged somewhere else simply cannot be picked up at all.

After you have picked up an object, you must have a valid place to drop it. You can recognize a valid dropping location because it will become highlighted in some manner. Perhaps the inside edge of a window will highlight, or an icon will select, or a text insertion point will appear—all under the pointer—as you move the mouse around while dragging an item. When a location isn't a valid place to drop the item you are carrying, the location will not become highlighted or editable.

When you drop an object, it usually will be placed right underneath wherever it is that you end up pointing to. If that location isn't a valid place for the object, it will instead float back to its original location when released.

This technique is something you already should be familiar with by now from moving documents, applications, folders, and disks around in the Finder, but you may not have realized that this technique could be used in other applications. Let's look at a couple places where you can use drag-and-drop shortcuts: places for text, for objects such as pictures, using clipping files, and in unique application-specific places, such as rearranging a list.

THE ULTIMATE TRICK

Before we dive in, here is the ultimate computer trick: save early, save often. Whenever you are working on something—save it! Don't let it get deleted accidentally or let an act of stupidity (like reaching out and unplugging the power from your iMac to plug in your coffee machine while putting the finishing touches on your dissertation) cause you to have to redo all of your work. If you lose your data, nine out of ten times saving it sooner could have prevented it.

Many of the iMac data processing tricks you'll hopefully become accustomed to performing will have data flowing through your fingers and your iMac at speeds you may not imagine today. Training yourself now to save your files, and to keep duplicate backup copies of the files safe, is something you should constantly practice. There is little point in processing words, or crunching numbers, if you lose them along the way.

Text

After you begin using drag-and-drop to edit text, you may never go back to cutting and pasting. Normally, when you want to rearrange words in a word processor, you select them and choose the Cut command (or press ⌘-X). You then move the text insertion point (the blinking vertical line) to the place where you want to place the text with the mouse by clicking or by using the keyboard's arrow keys, and then choosing Paste (or press ⌘-V). Not too laborious, but now compare it to this: select the text, click on and drag the selection, pointing to where you want the text to be inserted, and let go of the mouse button, dropping it into place. This is much more direct.

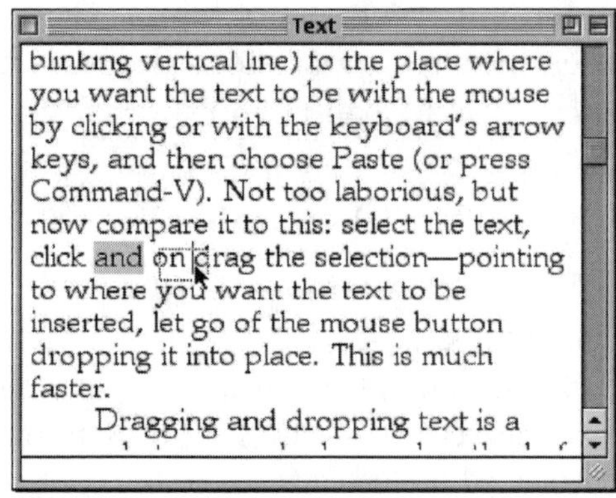

Figure 19.3 Dragging and dropping text is a quick way to rearrange your words.

Dragging and dropping text is a somewhat new and advanced method of editing text on a computer, and while most modern applications support this capability, some do not. If you point to a selection of text in an application and the cursor doesn't change to an arrow pointer from a text selection I-beam cursor, then that application doesn't support dragging text. If you want to see drag-and-drop text in action, you can use SimpleText, which is Apple's simple text-editing application that comes with your system for opening "read me" text files and other small text files. Also, dragging and dropping text isn't a feature of just word processing applications, it often can be used wherever text can be edited.

Objects

Text isn't the only type of data that uses drag-and-drop; many graphics applications also support this capability. Image-editing applications, such as Adobe Photoshop or even SimpleText, support not only the dragging of a selected region of pixels to another place in the same image, but also dragging to other image files and even into other applications that support bitmap image data. You can also drag image selections to the desktop to make clipping files.

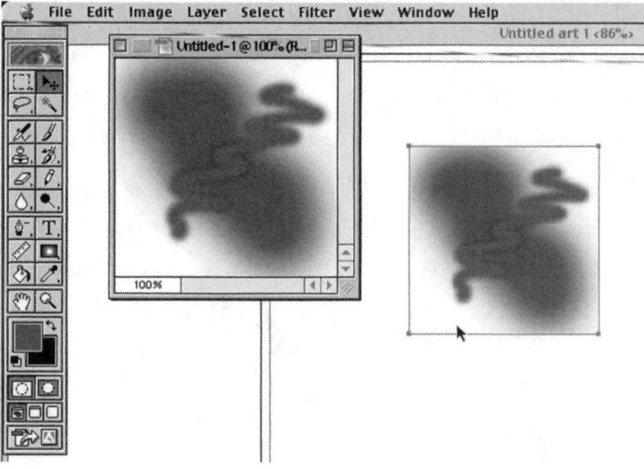

Figure 19.4 Dragging and dropping objects from one application to another is a great way to save a few seconds.

Clippings

Many applications that support dragging and dropping allow you to create clipping files by dragging your text or object selections to the desktop. When you release a compatible selection onto the desktop, it will be stored as a clipping file for later use. This means that

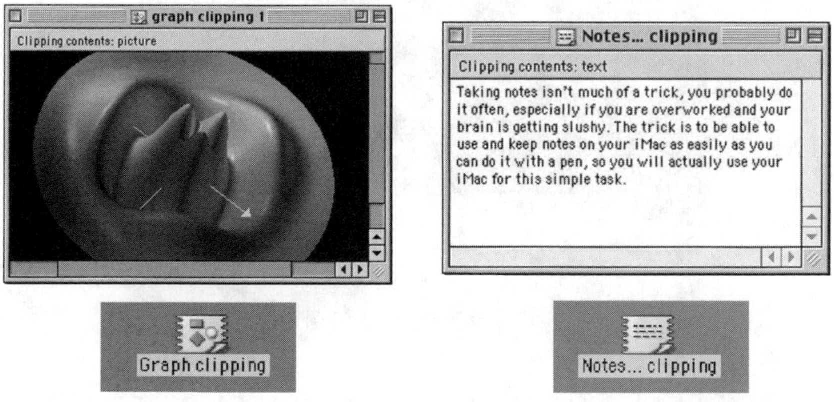

Figure 19.5 Clipping files can be created by dragging anything you can drag and drop between applications to the desktop, such as text from SimpleText or an image from Graphic Calculator.

you can grab a clipping file and drag it into any application that supports its contents, thereby inserting it into your file.

Clippings can be very useful. You can clip text or items that you use frequently; or when the file you want to insert the item into isn't currently active or visible; or, when you want to move several separate items, just as if you were able to copy more than one selection at a time. You can double-click on a clipping file to view the contents in the Finder, as well as name the clipping to remind you of its contents. Clipping files can even be used for a simple form of saving some text or image in such a way that it cannot be modified.

Organizing Lists

Some applications use dragging and dropping in unique ways to facilitate the gathering and ordering of objects—a very natural and intuitive technique. One such application is Apple's iMovie software, which comes with the second-generation iMac DV models; it uses drag-and-drop to accomplish many of its movie editing functions. When you load a bunch of movie clips, either from files on

Figure 19.6 Dragging and dropping is often used to organize lists and objects, such as these clips being organized into a movie timeline in iMovie. (New Year 2000 celebrations in San Francisco.)

your hard drive or right out of a DV camera, iMovie makes each video clip its own object.

You can drag and drop each of the clips together into a timeline to build your movie. You can rearrange the clips simply by picking one up and moving it before, after, or between other clips to reorder them. You can also add transitions between clips by dragging transition objects into the movie timelines as well as adding sounds, music, and titles by dragging and dropping. There is, of course, much more information about using iMovie in Part II, *Digital Video.*

Work in Context

This trick is a shortcut that helps you execute commands without leaving wherever you are to find the command you want in the menus of an application. Many applications provide contextual menus because they are a great timesaver when working with an application's documents and the objects within them. As you work in an application, you can save yourself the time and trouble of going to the menu bar to find and select commands. You can have your iMac pick out those commands that make sense to use on that item and put them in a little menu, right at your mouse cursor, just by holding down the Control key. If you have a third-party mouse with a second button, setting it to reveal contextual menus can be even more convenient.

In the Finder

When you have an item selected in the Finder there are only a few commands, of all the commands that the Finder can do, that can be performed just on that item. Rather than going and searching them out in the menu bar, you can simply hold down the Control key and click on the icon for the item. This will reveal a contextual menu with the commands that you can immediately apply to that item. Very quick, very convenient.

Figure 19.7 When you Control-click on a file in the Finder, you'll get this contextual menu with options that are applicable to the selected file.

Try Control-clicking on the Desktop itself, and you'll even find a few commands that can be applied there. My favorite is the Change Desktop Background command that appears at the bottom of the Desktop's contextual menu. This opens the Appearance control panel directly to the Desktop tab where you can configure the desktop picture or pattern for your iMac.

In Applications

Many modern applications also provide contextual menus. Microsoft Word, for example, has a feature where it underlines in red the words that it doesn't recognize in its spell-checking dictionary; you can Control-click on these "unknown" words to reveal a contextual menu with spelling suggestions and other text-editing commands. Adobe graphics applications, Photoshop and Illustrator, also provide contextual menus for editing selected images and objects. The email application, Outlook Express, supports applying commands to selected email messages from contextual menus such as Mark as Unread, or Replay, and Forward.

Discover for yourself which applications you have that support contextual menus by holding the Control-key and clicking on selected objects or in document windows to see if a menu appears.

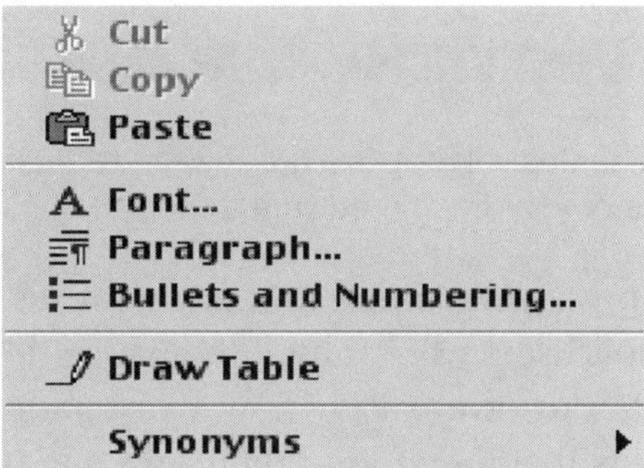

Figure 19.8 Many applications such as Microsoft Word also have contextual menus. In this case Control-clicking on a word in a document reveals a menu with these options.

Adding Features

It is also possible to add third-party features to the contextual menu by installing contextual menu plug-ins. An example of such a plug-in is the Magic Menu plug-in that comes with Aladdin System's StuffIt Deluxe. It adds compression commands for expanding and archiving items simply by revealing the contextual menu when selecting items in the Finder.

There are many third-party plug-ins available for a myriad of editing and control features. To install a plug-in, it must be placed in the Contextual Menu Items folder in the System Folder.

Quick Control

This trick will help you change settings for some types of hardware and software without interrupting your work by opening another application or control panel to fiddle with settings. Near the bottom edge of your screen you probably have a small strip of buttons (or a small tab you can click on to reveal the strip of buttons). This is the Control Strip; it is a system application that provides shortcuts to many of the most commonly adjusted settings for your iMac, such as the display, sound, audio CD, and a variety of network options.

Figure 19.9 The Control Strip is a quick way to adjust settings and configurations of your iMac hardware and software.

The Control Strip was first added to the system several years ago just for PowerBook users who wanted to change their display and sound settings often to save battery power or to adjust for quiet or noisy environments that they found themselves in with their portable Mac. The utility became so popular that it has found its way onto desktop Macs as well.

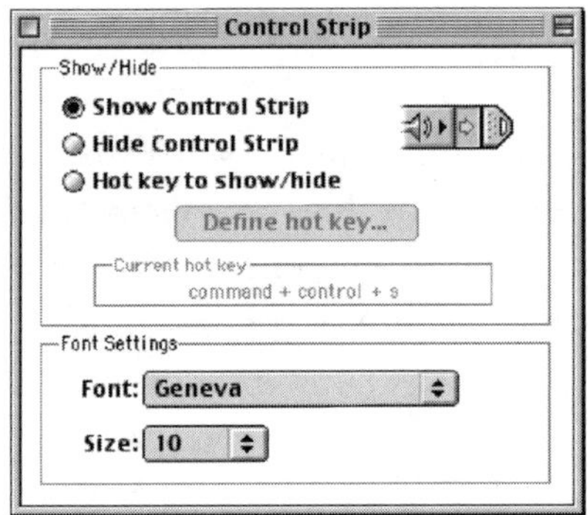

Figure 19.10 The Control Strip control panel has options for displaying and hiding the Control Strip.

If you don't have or see a Control Strip on your screen, it is probably hidden. You can show it (or hide it) by opening the Control Strip control panel. You'll also find options for displaying and hiding it via a command key shortcut, also called a hot key. There are also options for the font and font size used in the Control Strip's pop-up menus.

Use It

To use the controls on the Control Strip you simply click on the button for the feature you want to adjust. For example clicking on the button with the speaker icon is the volume control. It will reveal a level adjustment you can use to turn up or down the sound level of your iMac. As you can imagine, this is much easier than finding and opening the Sound control panel, selecting the appropriate control section, and then adjusting the volume.

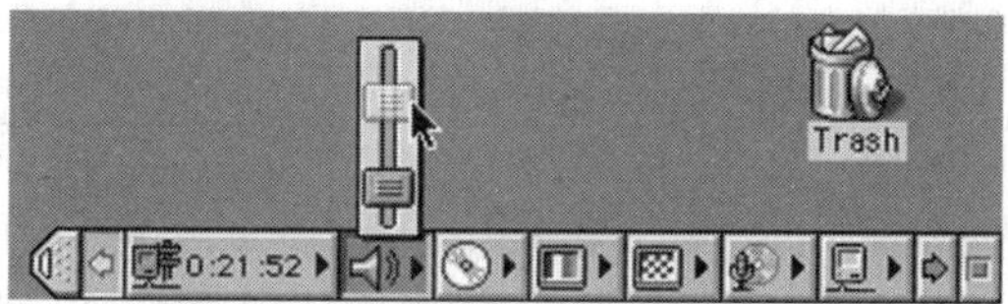

Figure 19.11 Using the Control Strip is as easy as clicking on a button and choosing a setting, as with this control for changing the sound volume.

The Mac OS includes Control Strip modules for many common needs: sound volume, display resolution and color depth, audio CD playback, sound source, remote access connection, AppleTalk settings, file sharing, energy saving, Web sharing, location management, printer selection, and security settings.

Move It

The Control Strip can be moved about and reorganized for your personal needs. It can collapse away to a small tab by clicking at either end of the strip when opened, and it will pop back out when you click on the tab. You can drag the tab out or drag it away to open or close the strip just part of the way. When the strip is only partially open, the arrow buttons at the ends allow you to scroll through the modules. You can also move the whole strip up or down the screen or to the opposite side of the screen simply by holding down the Option key and grabbing the end tab and dragging it.

You can rearrange the order of the modules by grabbing them while holding the Option key down. Simply pick up a module and drag it to a different position on the strip. Some modules also have options for different displays on their buttons such as the Remote Access module that can display the time you have been connected.

Customize It

Any of the control strip modules can be removed or new ones can be added by configuring the contents of the Control Strip Modules folder in the System Folder.

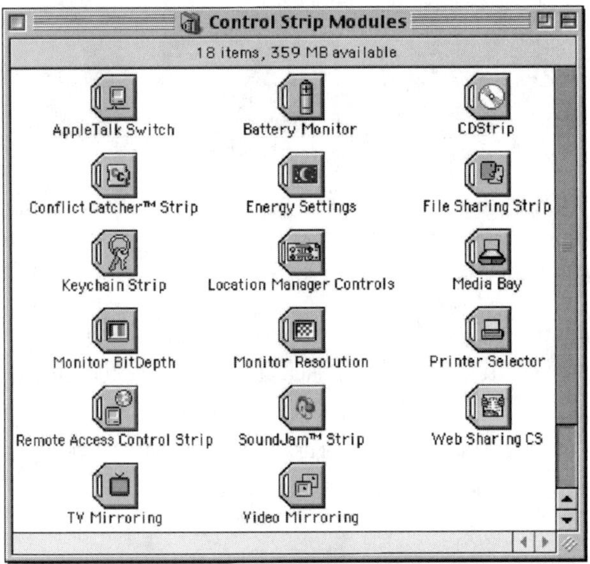

Figure 19.12 Each module in the Control Strip is a component stored and loaded from the Control Strip Modules folder in the System Folder.

If there are modules that you never use that get in your way, you can easily remove them by dragging the appropriate file out of this folder. Some applications come with their own control strip modules (such as SoundJam MP, an MP3 music playing application, for selecting tracks and starting and stopping the music).

Launch Applications

Running software is what you do every time you sit down at your iMac; this trick is about being able to quickly find and launch your software. After all, if you can't open an application such as a spreadsheet faster than you can grab a calculator, you're not likely to use it for simple tasks, *even* if it would work better for them.

The Apple Menu

Adding applications to your Apple menu is easy and offers quick access to them when needed. To add an application so it will appear in the Apple menu, simply put an alias of it in the Apple Menu Items folder inside your System Folder. An easy way to do this is to open the System Folder so that you can see the Apple Menu Items folder.

Locate the application you want to add and, if necessary, reposition the window it is in so that you can see the Apple Menu Items folder at the same time. Then simply drag the icon of the application to the Apple Menu Items folder while holding down the Command and Option keys, dropping an alias of the application into the folder. It is important to hold down those two keys so that you don't move or copy the application itself from wherever it belongs. As soon as the alias is in the Apple Menu Items folder, that item will appear in the Apple menu.

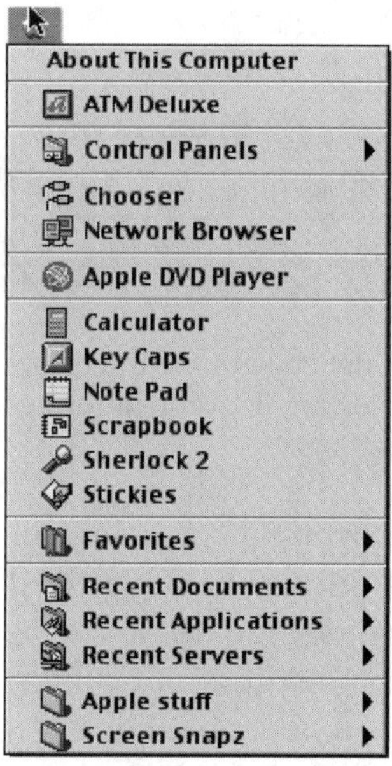

Figure 19.13 The Apple menu is a great place to access commonly used applications.

If you have a lot of stuff in your Apple menu, you may find that a little additional organization would be useful. First, items in the Apple menu are always listed alphabetically, so you can change the names of items to reorder them. Second, if you have Apple Menu Options enabled, you can place folders in the Apple menu and see their contents on hierarchical pop-up menus. This can be a great way to condense your Apple menu and group similar types of applications into categories like applications, utilities, graphics, and games. There are also a variety of freeware and shareware utilities you can install on your iMac to allow for more complex Apple menu organization, such as adding the ability to have numerous separator lines to divide up the contents of the menu into logical groups.

Keyboard Function Keys

Perhaps the best way to launch the applications you use most frequently is to assign them to a function key on your keyboard. Then all you need to do is press a single key to launch the application you want to use.

Figure 19.14 The function keys are the F-keys along the top edge of your keyboard. They are convenient for special functions such as launching applications.

To do this, open the Keyboard control panel and, at the bottom of the window, click the Function keys button. This will open the Hot Function Keys editor where you can assign applications to each of the F1 through F12 function keys along the top row of your keyboard. To assign (or map) a function key to an application, you can use one of two methods: click the F-key button in the Hot Function Keys editor to locate and assign the application you want to open, or simply drag the icon of an application onto the text field, which is adjacent to the F-key button you want to assign. Once assigned, all it takes to launch that application is to press the F-key to which the application was assigned.

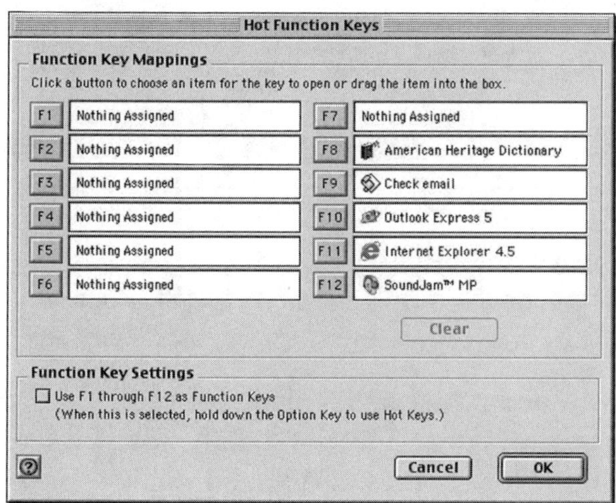

Figure 19.15 Use this interface for specifying which applications to launch from your function keys. Access it from the Keyboard control panel.

At the bottom of the Hot Function Keys editor window is a checkbox option for using the F-keys as normal function keys rather than hot keys for launching applications. When this functionality is enabled, you must hold down the Option key while pressing an F-key to launch an assigned application.

Finder Buttons

Another option for quickly launching applications that you use frequently is to set up a folder with aliases of commonly used applications and view it in button mode. This way you can simply keep this folder handy, perhaps by keeping its window open all the time, or even as a pop-up window at the bottom-edge of your desktop, and then launching any application just by clicking its button.

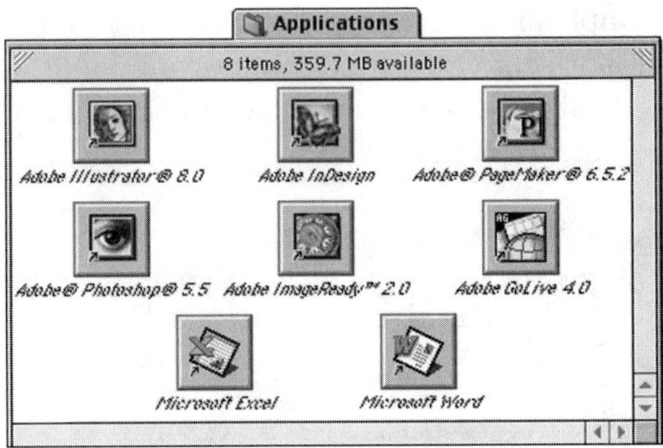

Figure 19.16 Here is one possible way to set up a quick launching pad for your applications. This pop-up window has its view set to Buttons.

To set up this window, first gather aliases of your applications together into a new folder. Why not give the folder a sensible name like "Applications" or "Games?" With the window for this folder open and active, select "as Buttons" from the View menu. If you want to move the buttons around to organize the window, simply click and drag by the name label below the button—clicking on the button itself will, of course, launch that application. You now have a convenient window from which to launch your applications.

At this point, you might want to make this window more convenient still by dragging it down to the button edge of the desktop so that it is always available. Clicking once on its tab will cause this window to pop open like a drawer. You can resize a pop-up window from either of its upper corners, as well as move its tab along the bottom edge of the Desktop by grabbing and dragging it left or right when the window is collapsed. If you have lots of applications, you might even want to divide them into several categorized pop-up windows.

Launcher

Of course, if you would rather not set up and configure a window full of buttons, you can use the Launcher utility instead, which does very much the same thing. Launcher is a utility designed by Apple for assisting novices in finding and running their applications. It functions like a window in the Finder set to button view. To open the Launcher, choose it from the control panels in your Apple menu. The first time you open it, you probably will find two items in it: SimpleText and the AppleScript Script Editor. To add items to the Launcher, simply drag your documents, applications, or folders to it, and they will display as buttons (this won't move the actual applications into Launcher, it will just add buttons for them like an alias). Simply click on a button to open the item. You can remove a button from the Launcher by grabbing its name label and dragging it to the trash; this will only remove the button from the Launcher, it won't delete the original item from your hard disk drive.

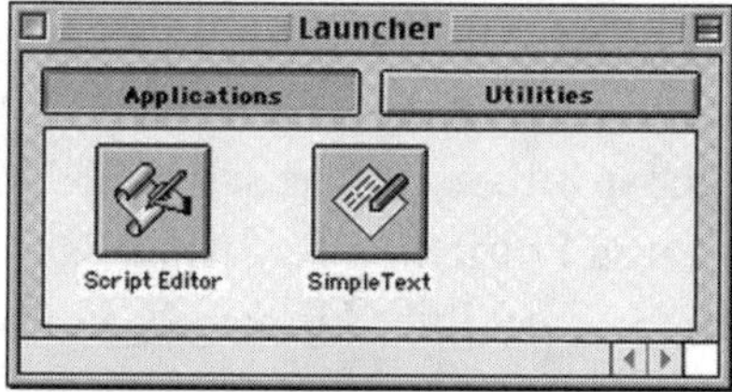

Figure 19.17 The Launcher utility can be accessed from the Control Panels folder. To add items, simply drag the items into the Launcher window or configure the Launcher Items folder within the System Folder.

The items displayed in the Launcher are stored as aliases in the Launcher Items folder within the System Folder. If you want to rename or add and remove items from the Launcher, you can change the contents of the Launcher Items folder. You can also organize the items in the launcher into groups. To do this, place a folder inside the Launcher Items folder and edit its name to begin with a bullet mark by typing Option-8, such as " • Utilities."

DragThing

While there are many ways you can configure your iMac to make launching applications easier, there are also many third-party utilities that have additional features. One very popular and well-designed utility called *DragThing* creates a dock for the icons of your applications.

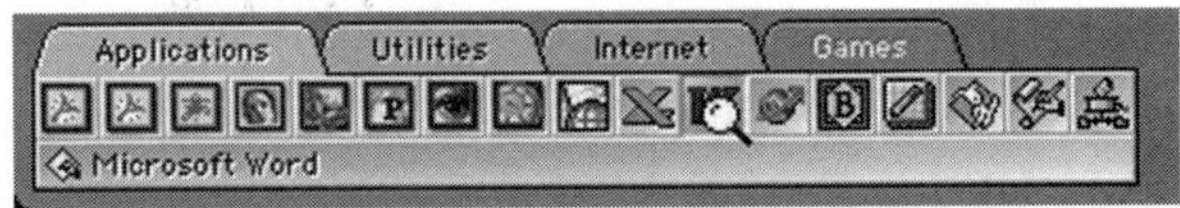

Figure 19.18 DragThing is a great utility for creating docks from which you can launch your applications, as well as keep files, folders, drives, and URLs.

DragThing can be configured in many different ways to suit your needs. For example, you can float the dock in front of the other applications so it is always available, shrinking the dock to a single button when not being used to save screen real estate, or you can have multiple tabbed layers within a dock to keep your applications organized. It also has many visual preferences to fit your aesthetic needs (for example, customized color schemes, button appearances, and layouts). DragThing is a $25 shareware application that you can download from the Hans Hansen's Web site at `http://www.dragthing.com`.

Take Notes

Taking notes is not much of a trick; you probably do it often, especially if you are overworked and your brain is getting slushy. The trick is to be able to use and keep notes on your iMac as easily as you can with a pen, so you will actually use your iMac for this simple task.

It is surprising how many people have a computer at a desk with a phone, but still use a pen and paper (or perhaps a pad of 3M Post-It™ Notes) to jot down a message or otherwise take down a quick note. True, a hand-written note on a tiny slip of sticky paper is very portable compared to a 35-pound iMac that requires a power outlet. But what about all those notes that inevitably get tacked onto the iMac around its screen? With a little forethought and practice, you can take notes on your iMac, and save a small forest of bright yellow sticky trees.

Use the Note Pad

One of the most obvious utilities to take notes with on your iMac is the Note Pad. This simple application provides eight or more small pages for typing out quick notes that can be flipped among by clicking on its dog-eared, lower-left corner. The note pad doesn't support any text styling or formatting; it is just a bare bones, straight forward little application, making it perhaps the most useful utility for jotting down a quick note.

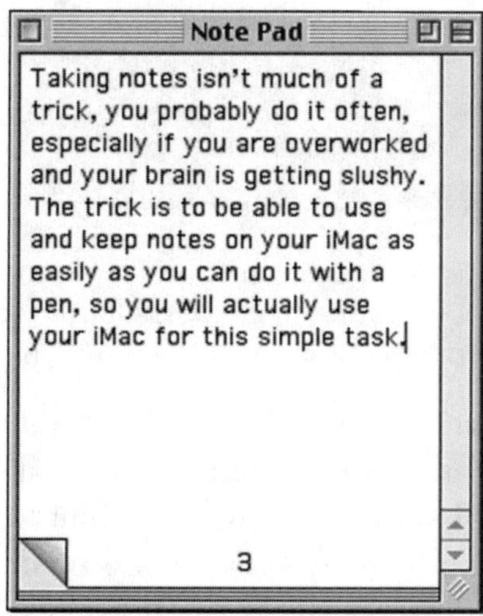

Figure 19.19 The Note Pad is a great utility for taking down notes. If it isn't installed in your Apple menu, search for it on your hard drive with Sherlock. It is probably in your Apple Extras folder.

The Note Pad in years past was installed within the Mac OS as a desk accessory in the Apple menu. Now it is included as an application in the Apple Extras folder. To make the Note Pad more useful, you'll probably want to use one of the application launching tricks from the previous sections to make it more accessible. Try installing it in your Apple Menu Items folder within the System Folder.

Use Stickies

While the Note Pad is a very simplistic utility, there is a more robust application for taking and keeping little quick notes called *Stickies* already installed in the Apple menu on your iMac. This application creates the equivalent of digital Post-It notes for your iMac screen. You can create any number of them, in varying colors, resize them to fit their contents, and even style and format their text.

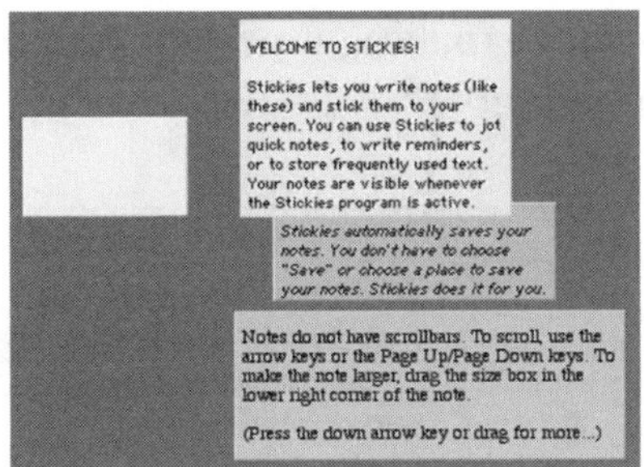

Figure 19.20 Stickies creates small colored windows to function similarly to PostIt notes. You can access it from your Apple menu and set it to open every time you turn on your iMac.

The first time you run the Stickies application it will display some notes, including information about how to use it and its capabilities. Read these notes for some quick tips and hints for using Stickies. Creating a new sticky is a very easy process of simply selecting New from the File menu or pressing ⌘-N. Then just type, paste, or drag whatever text you want to keep track of. You can click on the note to select it and edit its contents, or you can grab its title bars to move it somewhere else on your screen. You can resize it by grabbing its lower right-hand corner, or you can have it automatically shrink to fit its contents by clicking the triangular grow-button at the right-hand end of its title bar. You can change the color of your sticky note by choosing from the Color menu.

Probably the best thing about Stickies is that it can be set to open automatically every time you start your iMac, displaying your little notes and being at hand for you to create more of them—very convenient. To do this, choose Preferences from the bottom of the Edit menu and enable the Launch at system startup option.

Use SimpleText

If the Note Pad utility doesn't provide enough features for text editing, styling, and formatting, you might prefer to just use SimpleText. This straightforward word processing application bundled with the Mac OS is something you are probably already familiar with. Every time you open a read me file or a plain text document it most likely opens into SimpleText. If you keep this application handy, it can be a great utility for taking longer and more complex notes, perhaps for taking the minutes of a meeting or event.

Keeping Notes as Email

Having an application handy that has word processing capabilities is the key to being able to take a quick note. For many people, this may be an email application, simply because it is something that they keep open and running much of the time they're using their computers. You can always just open a new email message and type whatever you want into it without sending it to anyone. Email applications can be particularly useful for keeping random notes because they're designed to store and manage many separate bits of text as messages. And each email message is stamped with a date and time, has a subject field, and in most email applications can be sorted into folders, so keeping a folder of quick notes in your e-mail application can be quite handy—especially if you want to email someone those notes at some point.

Search It Out

This trick is pretty obvious—using your iMac to search through data is easier than doing it yourself. Searching is a task perfectly tailored for a computer, yet many people continue to look things up manually. They might open ten folders on their hard drive looking for a file, or open up ten different documents looking for a bit of text they're sure they have written somewhere. Why not let the iMac do it? And searching for stuff doesn't need to be limited to the contents of the data on your iMac; you can also search the Internet rather than spending hours guessing which Web sites will have that bit of information for which you are looking.

Use Sherlock

For all your searching needs Apple has created Sherlock—a searching utility, which comes with Mac OS 9 and X. Sherlock can search in a variety of modes (the row of icons at the top of its window display, also called channels) from which you can select.

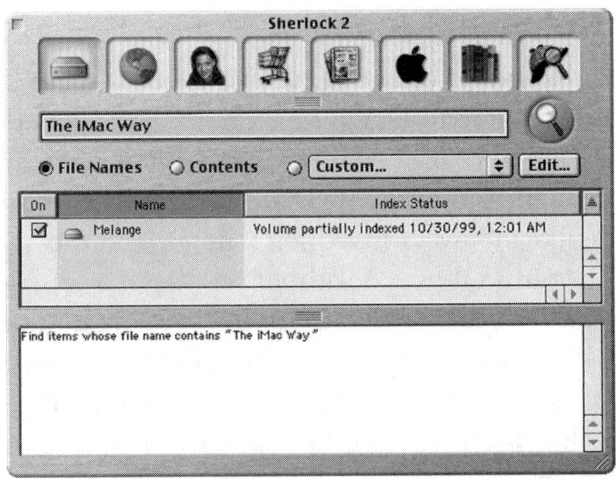

Figure 19.21 Sherlock 2 is included with Mac OS 9 and X. With it, you can search both your local data and remote data on the Internet.

Sherlock can search the names of files on your hard drives or the contents of your documents. It can search on the Internet by searching the World Wide Web for people and email addresses, goods from online stores and auctions, newswire services, Apple's products guides, Tech Info Library, and Web sites. Sherlock also can search online references such as dictionaries and encyclopedias, and it can search even your own custom channels.

518

File Searching

The easiest search you can perform is searching for a file by its name on your hard drive. Open Sherlock by selecting it from your Apple menu or by pressing ⌘-F while you're in the Finder. Sherlock will automatically open in file searching mode, which is indicated by the colored halo around the hard drive icon in the channel selections at the top of the Sherlock window. Your hard drive will be selected with a checkbox in the listing, and if you have any additional storage volumes mounted on your iMac, they will also be displayed. You can check them to add them to your search. Below the channel selection row, you'll see a text field where you can type in your search criteria, i.e., which text you want Sherlock to locate. Right beneath the text field are options for the type of search you want to make. "File Names" will be selected by default; however, you can choose "Contents" or a custom criteria type from the pop-up menu.

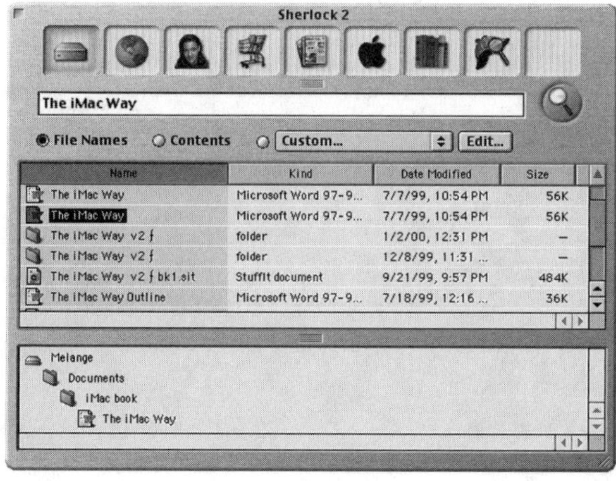

Figure 19.22 Here Sherlock is being used to search for a file on the iMac's hard drive by looking for matches with the name of the file.

To begin a search, simply type the text you want Sherlock to search for and click the Search button (the button to the right with a magnifying glass icon), or press Return. When the search is completed, Sherlock will show you a list of the files, folders, or applications that meet your search criteria. You can click once on any of these items to select them and see where they are located on your hard drive in the bottom section of Sherlock's display. You can double-click any of these items to open them just as you would in the Finder. You can even drag them to new locations in the Finder directly from Sherlock.

File Contents Searching

A far more robust method of searching is to have Sherlock look through the contents of all your files to search within them. To do this, you must first set up and allow Sherlock to index your files, a lengthy process depending on how much data you have on your iMac. The easiest way to get your hard drive indexed is to select Index Volumes from Sherlock's Find menu and schedule the indexing to happen when you won't be needing to use your iMac, perhaps overnight or while you are away during the day.

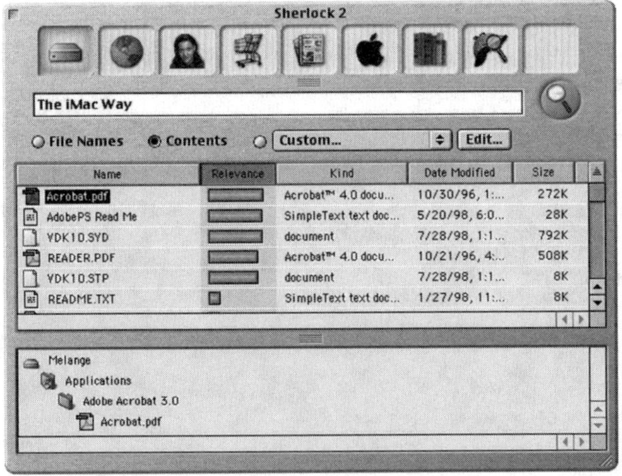

Figure 19.23 Sherlock can also search the contents of files on your hard drive when they are indexed ahead of time.

After your hard drive has been indexed, you can run searches through its contents in the same manner you search file names. Simply type your search text into Sherlock's text field, select Contents from the options, and click the Search button. When the search is completed and a list of files is displayed, you can select any of them from the listing and see a small excerpt of the matched text in the display at the bottom of Sherlock's window.

Internet Searching

In addition to local searches on your own data, you can also use Sherlock for numerous types of Internet searching. You can search Web sites by selecting the second channel with the Earth icon. Sherlock will display a listing of online search engines to use—each selectable with a checkbox. Type a word or phrase to search for and watch it go. (Of course, you must have an Internet connection established for this to work.) When you select Web pages from the found listing, Sherlock will display an excerpt of the page where it found your search criteria.

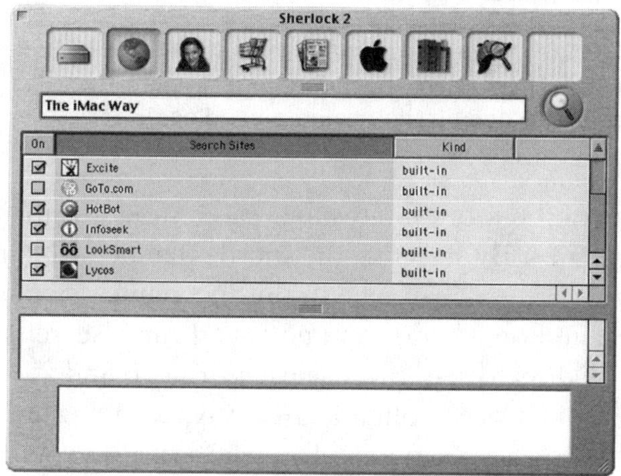

Figure 19.24 When you search the World Wide Web, you first select which Internet search engines from which you'd like to see results.

You can also search for people's email addresses and telephone numbers by selecting the third channel with the icon of a woman's head. In this mode you can type someone's name as a search criteria. Give your own name a try and see if it comes up. The chances of you finding the person you're looking for are usually quite slim, but as more and more personal information gets into the public domain, people get easier to find.

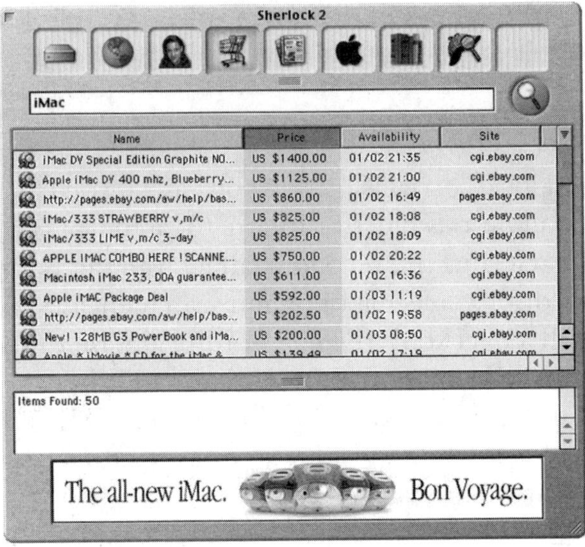

Figure 19.25 When searching for merchandise with Sherlock, it adds special columns for price and availability. Sort these columns by clicking on their column headings.

Perhaps one of the more interesting search modes is the channel for shopping sites. By selecting the fourth channel, which is an icon of a shopping cart, you can type in product names, books, music, or film titles, and other odds and ends and run a search across numerous vendors to see who has what in stock and at what price. Sorting results by price is often a great way of finding good deals. This search mode also can include auction sites so you can see if any private sellers have what you're looking for up for bidding. Found items for auctions include the current bid price and the time left in the auction until the item will be sold.

The remaining channels are fairly straightforward. The fifth channel with the newspaper icon is for searching various newswire and news media services. Typing in a search word or phrase in this mode will retrieve articles and stories that contain a reference to your criteria. The sixth channel with the Apple logo searches Apple's own online resources. This includes detailed product information, extensive technical documentation and troubleshooting

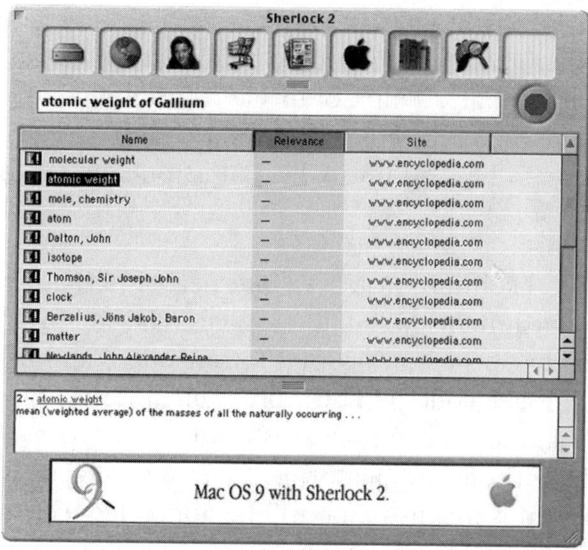

Figure 19.26 You can use Sherlock to search online references for definitions and explanations of terms and ideas.

questions and answers, as well as the rest of Apple's Web site. The seventh channel with the icon of books on a shelf is for searching online reference materials such as dictionaries and encyclopedias. Give this a try by just typing in a single word and asking Sherlock to search for it. When Sherlock displays the items in the found listing, select a listing and see what types of information or definitions Sherlock found.

The last channel is a custom one that is used when you install software that comes with a special Sherlock search plug-in or features. Sherlock is also extensible, meaning that you can add additional channels and search engine plug-ins. For more information about customizing channels and downloading plug-ins, search for *Sherlock* in the Help Center.

Stuff It *and* Unstuff It

While some tricks are about saving yourself some effort, other tricks are about saving some effort for your iMac—or in this case,

probably your iMac's modem. Compressing files is a common
way to make them smaller and more portable while temporarily
sacrificing their usability. Think of this as a form of computer
shorthand where the file needs to be expanded to its spelled-out
normal language to be read normally, but is much faster to write
down initially.

As you download software from the Internet, or perhaps when
receiving file attachments to email messages, you will invariably get
something that has been compressed (or encoded) and needs to be
uncompressed (or decoded). There are quite a variety of compression methods and formats for all sorts of different types of data and
for many different software platforms. One way to recognize that a
file is compressed is that its name will be appended with a three-let-
ter file type following the customary "dot." The most common
compression format on Macintosh computers is *.sit,* for StuffIt. On
Windows PCs, *.zip* is the most common.

For many years on the Mac there has been a software application
that is almost universal for file compression, Aladdin Systems
StuffIt; the complete commercial version is called *StuffIt Deluxe.*
Whether you want to compress multiple files together into a singular archive to send to someone or you have downloaded a software
application from the Internet that is encoded in some manner,
StuffIt is the tool for the job. Your iMac comes with a free version
of StuffIt, which only works for decompressing files called *StuffIt
Expander.* If you want to compress files yourself, there is also a
free version of DropStuff. But DropStuff is only capable of producing a limited set of the file encoding types that are possible. For
this, you will need to purchase StuffIt Deluxe. You can download
any of these versions of the StuffIt software from the Aladdin
Systems Web site at `http://www.aladdinsys.com/`.

Expanding Compressed Archives

Expanding compressed files is a common task for the Internet generation. Your iMac comes with Aladdin System's StuffIt Expander,

a free application exclusively for decompressing and decoding archived files. This utility is included with the preinstalled Internet software on your iMac in a folder called Internet Utilities.

Figure 19.27 There are many variations of StuffIt. For most people, StuffIt Expander is the most commonly used. You can recognize a stuffed archive by its icon and the *.sit* extension to the file's name. Dragging an archive onto StuffIt Expander's icon will immediately begin decompressing it.

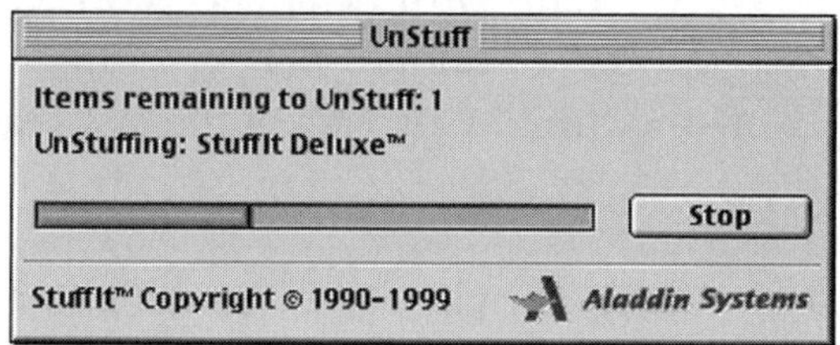

Figure 19.28 It takes some work for your iMac to decompress a file. StuffIt Expander displays its progress with this window.

To unstuff or decode a file, simply drag it onto the StuffIt Expander icon, and it will take care of it. StuffIt is set by default to create a copy of the file or files in the compressed archive as it decodes them, placing them next to the original compressed file. To change this behavior you can hold down the Option key while dropping the archive onto Expander, which brings up a window of file decoding and saving options.

Compressing Files into Archives

These days compressing files just for storage isn't as useful as it once was. Today, we have huge multi-gigabyte hard drives and removable media such as 650-meg CDs and 100-meg floppy disks. But often you'll want to get a whole lot of data into a smaller space—whether to fit it on a removable disk or to send it more quickly over a wire. To do this, you'll need to encode your files into an archive, a single compressed file. The best software for compressing files is StuffIt Deluxe, available for purchase directly from Aladdin Systems on the Internet.

Spell Right

The trick here is to conform. Four hundred years ago there were no English dictionaries, people spelled things haphazardly, and no one was worried about it; the ideas still came across, the words still had meaning—perhaps more so, as dialects more easily represented natural variations of spelling. Today, language is something that everyone considers as uniform and only correct when used in particular ways. Thus, everything must be spelled correctly. Automatic spell checking has become a standard part of writing with a computer—and why not—the Smith-Coronas of the last era could not do this *amazing* task.

The way in which a computer checks the spelling in a document is by comparing each word in your document to a dictionary—if the word doesn't appear in its banks, then it is considered suspect. Of course, this doesn't save you from correctly spelling but misusing a word accidentally. When a suspect word is found, most spell-checkers will offer word suggestions that are similar to the suspect word for you to choose from, which is very helpful.

Different word-processing applications handle spell checking in different ways. In some you run the spell-checker as a review process where you go through your document all at once, while other applications will check as you type, by noting errors whenever you create a new word or type a space or other forms of word separation.

Use AppleWorks

Spell-checking documents with AppleWorks is a review process. To begin a spell check, you choose Check Document Spelling from the Writing Tools menu within the Edit menu. AppleWorks will display a window noting any suspect words and offering suggestions. You can quickly select any of these suggestions by pressing the Command key shortcut adjacent to the item in the listing.

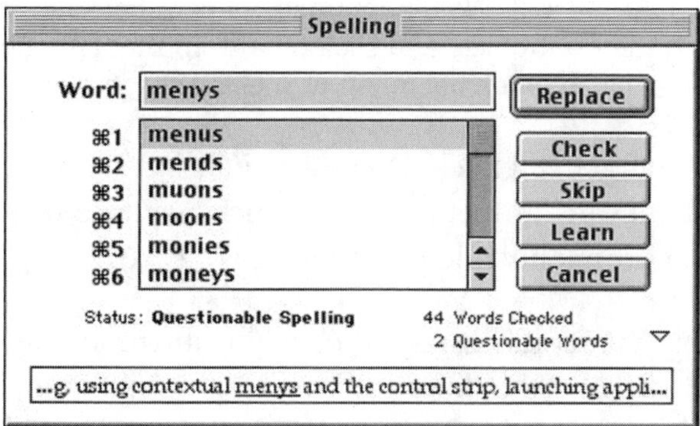

Figure 19.29 To spell check a document in AppleWorks, choose Check Document Spelling from the Writing Tools menu within the Edit menu.

If an application you are using doesn't support spell-checking and you'd like to run a quick review of your writing, copy and paste it into an empty document in AppleWorks, run the check, and then copy and paste (or drag) the text back.

Interactive Spell Checking

Spell checking in Microsoft Word 98 or the email application Outlook Express can be done as an interactive process where suspect words are highlighted while you are composing your document. As you work, these applications consider each word, and as they find "suspects," they underline them in red. You can then either go back and correct the error, or you can Control-click to reveal a contextual menu that will contain spelling suggestions.

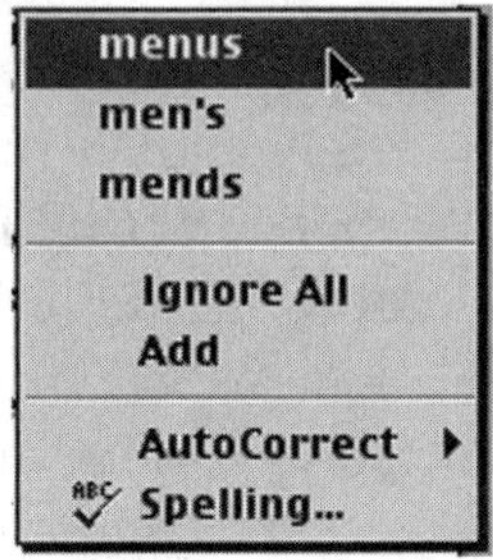

Figure 19.30 To use Word's interactive spell-checking, feature hold down the Control key and click on a word that is underlined in red to reveal a contextual menu of spelling suggestions.

This type of interactive checking can be quite convenient and preferable. Reviewing a document becomes a simple process of looking it over yourself while considering your work.

If you find that you could use spell checking anytime you type stuff on your iMac, there are utilities for you. One popular spell-checking utility is SpellCatcher published by Casady & Greene. This software offers a variety of spell-checking modes and features that can be tailored to fit your needs.

Software Dictionaries

Besides spell checking, many people (even those who can spell) find having a dictionary to look up definitions and usage notes for words to be more useful than simply checking for misspellings. An electronic dictionary has numerous features to offer over its paper-based cousins. For example, in an electronic dictionary you have the ability to find a word quickly, cross-reference to other words almost instantaneously, look up similar sounding and meaning words, as well as advanced features such as anagrams and advanced searches (always useful for solving Scrabble™ problems and crossword puzzles).

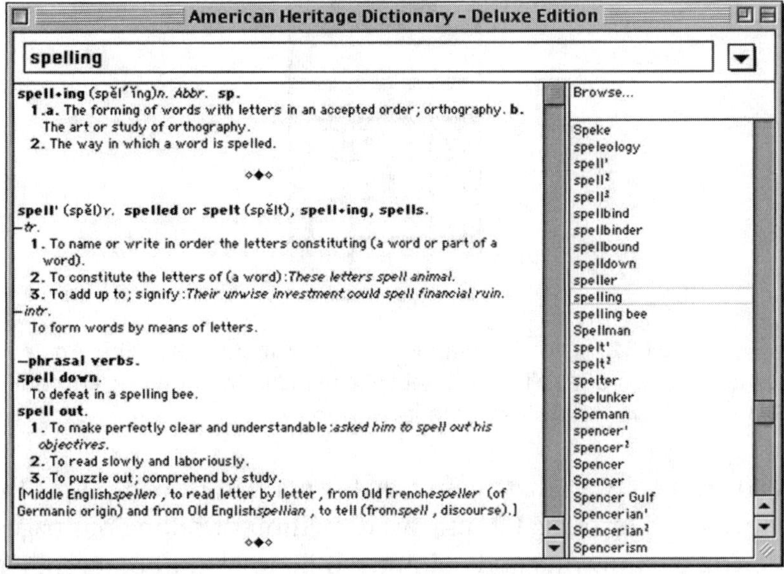

Figure 19.31 An electronic dictionary such as the *American Heritage Dictionary*, Third Edition is a great way to quickly look up word definitions and usage notes.

There are various electronic dictionaries available for your iMac. If your iMac came with the *World Book Encyclopedia* CD-ROM, you already have one. My personal favorite is the *American Heritage Dictionary*. This electronic version is based on the Third Edition of that dictionary and is unabridged. The whole thing fits on your hard drive and is very fast and easy to access.

Calculate on a Spreadsheet

With this trick, you'll find that the power of a spreadsheet can be faster and more effective than a hand calculator, even when the task at hand is very simple. How often do you need to add a list of numbers, say five amounts: $23, $147, $88, $60, and $42? If you had to give me an answer to this question, would you do it in your head? Write it on a piece of paper to figure it? Use a hand calculator similar to the one available in the Apple menu? But, there is a better way!

Figure 19.32 The Calculator accessory installed in the Apple menu is a bit of a relic. If you feel like using it, the numeric keypad on your keyboard will actuate its buttons.

Spreadsheet software has seemingly been a part of computing from the beginning, bringing the practiced method of setting out pages of numerical data in rows and columns to be totaled in different patterns for accounting and analysis. This tedious work is practically why modern computers were invented. While spreadsheet use is as common as word processing in today's world, typically only those people trained in some type of number-crunching field use spreadsheet software, while just about everyone uses a word processor. But everyone can use a spreadsheet; it is incredibly easy and useful for tasks few people realize. Any type of data that can be arranged sensibly into a table can probably benefit from the capabilities of a spreadsheet application to total items, sort items, or compare items in a graph.

Quick Totals

Rather than type a bunch of numbers into a simple calculator, adding each as you go, and watching for human errors, using a spreadsheet to accomplish this task will take less time and be much more reliable and informative.

To try this, open AppleWorks and create a new spreadsheet document. Type a number using the numeric keypad keys on the right side of your keyboard, perhaps 23. Press the Return key, also on the numeric keypad. The number you typed will be entered in the first cell (A1) and the selection will move down to the next cell in the column (A2). If you use the Enter key instead of the Return key, the cell will be entered, but the selection won't move to the next cell down. You can now type another number, perhaps 147, and press Return. Type in another, 88, and press Return. Type in one more, 60, and press Return. And type in the last one, 42, and press Return. You now have five numbers in a column, you can add many more if you want to, all the way down the column.

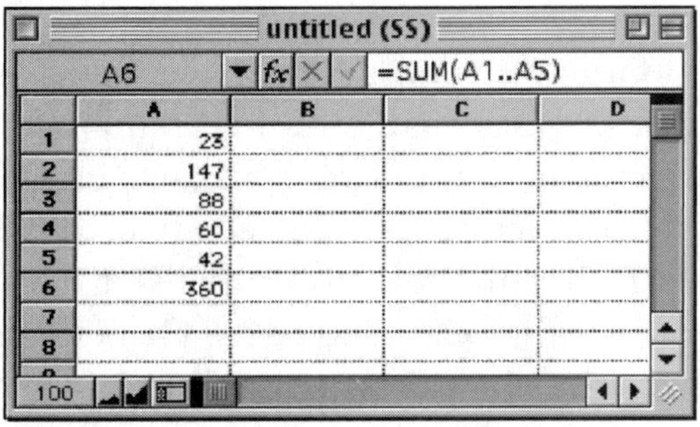

Figure 19.33 Totaling numbers with an AppleWorks spreadsheet document is faster and better than using a hand calculator.

Now let's say that you are typing in all of these numbers so that you can get a total of their value. Simply click in the first cell (A1) to select it and drag down the column, selecting all the numbers you've entered, and then one blank cell at the bottom where AppleWorks will place the total. Now find the Sum button in the button bar at the top (it's the one with the capital Greek letter Sigma (Σ) on it) and click it just once. The total will instantly appear at the bottom of your selected list.

You might notice that the Sum button is a shortcut for entering the formula in the cell at the bottom of the list: *=SUM(A1..A5)*. This is how the spreadsheet actually thinks of the total—the equals sign means that it is a formula and that it should display the results of that formula; the SUM is the method it should use; and the (A1...A5) is the list of cells to apply the formula to. Of course, you don't really need to know this to get the results you're looking for.

While it took a few seconds longer to open AppleWorks and a spreadsheet document than it would to open the Calculator or to grab a hand calculator, You'll find that being able to see the numbers that are being totaled is very useful. You can even go back and change any of those numbers and the total at the bottom will automatically update on the fly. Or you can create subtotals, add more numbers, remove numbers, create labels, format your rows and columns, and even run much more complex calculations. This is where the power of a spreadsheet begins.

If all you ever do with a spreadsheet is total a bunch of numbers, you'll probably be very satisfied, but you can do much more. Perhaps you are creating a list of your bills or purchases and want to label each number so that you can keep track of which number in the list is for which item. Perhaps you'd like to format your numbers as money with dollars and cents. Or perhaps you'd like to add additional columns for different months. All these things are very easy to do and once you discover how, you'll have a hard time going back to using a pad of paper.

	A	January	February	March	Totals
1		January	February	March	Totals
2	Tangerines	$23.00	$54.00	$11.00	**$88.00**
3	Grapes	$147.00	$67.00	$98.00	**$312.00**
4	Limes	$88.00	$284.00	$156.00	**$528.00**
5	Strawberries	$60.00	$32.00	$48.00	**$140.00**
6	Blueberries	$42.00	$12.00	$18.00	**$72.00**
7	totals	**$360.00**	**$449.00**	**$331.00**	*$1140.00*
8					

Figure 19.34 Creating a somewhat more robust spreadsheet only takes a few minutes and can be used over and over, saving you even more time and energy.

For more information on using AppleWorks spreadsheets, choose AppleWorks Help Contents from the Help menu while in AppleWorks and select topics for Spreadsheet Basics.

Graph Equations

Doing algebra at all is a trick. But now you can let your iMac do the hard part, and you can look like an expert mathematician. For example, what are the values of x when it is greater than $y^{3/2}$. Simply see the graph in the figure that my iMac drew.

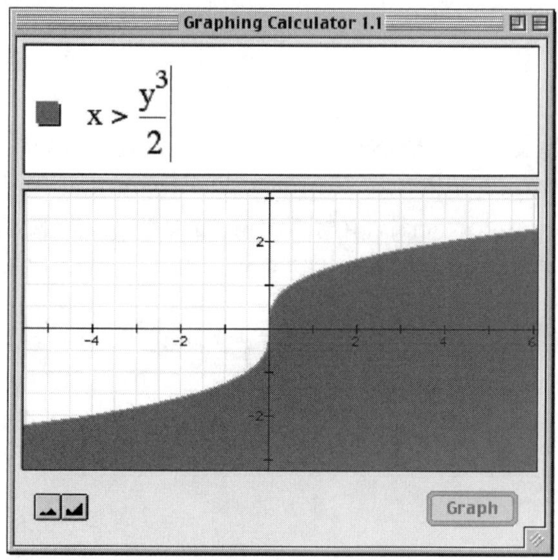

Figure 19.35 Graphic Calculator is a great way to experience algebra! Just type in your equations and let it do all the work.

Most of you who will read this book may no longer be in school, and thus no longer spending much time with algebra problems. Perhaps a few of you use advanced mathematics every day. But there is no doubt that math skills are a part of daily life and if solving and graphing algebra problems can be made easy enough, we'd all use them more. Hang on to your hats, that day has arrived. Well, actually it arrived a couple years ago, but has yet to be discovered by many Macintosh owners—an excellent new piece of software, Graphing Calculator.

Open Graphing Calculator, which you should be able to find either in your Apple menu, or perhaps in the Apple Extras folder.

It came with your iMac, so if you can't easily locate it, use Sherlock to help you find it. After you launch Graphing Calculator, you can quickly get an idea of how to use it and what it can do by choosing a demonstration of its features from the Demo menu. Try choosing Basics or Full demo first, but don't miss viewing the Surfaces demonstration because it is really neat. You can speed your way through the demo by pressing the Tab key, and you can escape the Demo by clicking the Stop button at the bottom of its window.

Quick Algebra

Let's take a quick look at how to use Graphing Calculator. If you've been running a demo, stop it, select the equation by dragging the mouse cursor across its text (or simply press ⌘-A to Select All), and then press Delete to clear it so that you can type your

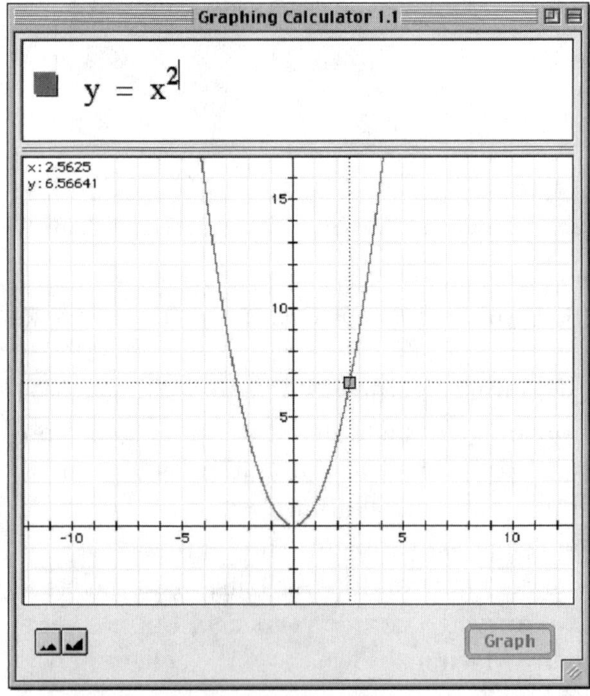

Figure 19.36 Graphing Calculator's interface is very elegant and has many powerful features. Clicking on a solved path will display a specific value for that location.

own equation. Type "y=x^2". The ^ is used to indicate a superior position, and it is typed by pressing Shift-6. When you've typed your equation, simply press Return or Enter, and Graphing Calculator will calculate and draw a graph of the values that solve this equation.

You can move the graph to view more of it by grabbing anywhere on its axis and dragging. You can also zoom in and out with the buttons at the lower left of the graph window. Clicking on the equation's path (the colored line) will display the specific values at that location; you can drag along the path to move this coordinate.

Advanced Explorations

Graphing Calculator is capable of very advanced equation solving, as demonstrated by the routines available in the Demo menu. To enter in more advanced equations, you'll want to show the Keypad palette by choosing Show Keypad from the Equation menu. Clicking the buttons on this palette will enter the particular term into your equation.

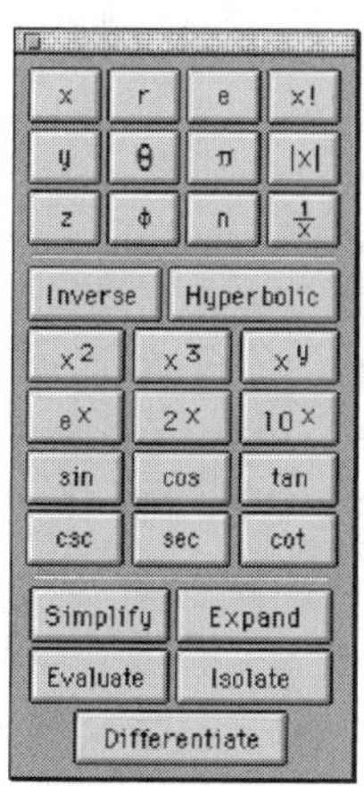

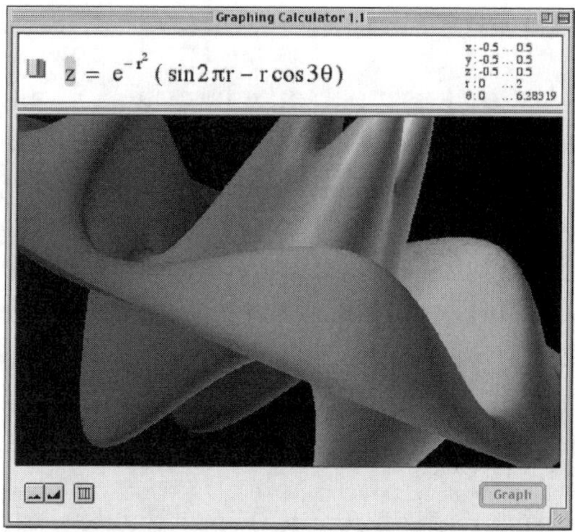

Figure 19.37 Of course, Graphic Calculator can handle much more complex multi-dimensional equations. To enter in special functions, use the Keypad palette available from the Equation menu.

In addition to solving equations by graphing them, Graphing Calculator can also be used to manipulate terms algebraically, letting your iMac do the work of simplifying or reorganizing an equation by dragging the terms. For example, type in the equation y = ax + b; then select the term b and drag it to the left. Graphing calculator will rearrange the equation while keeping the terms expressed properly.

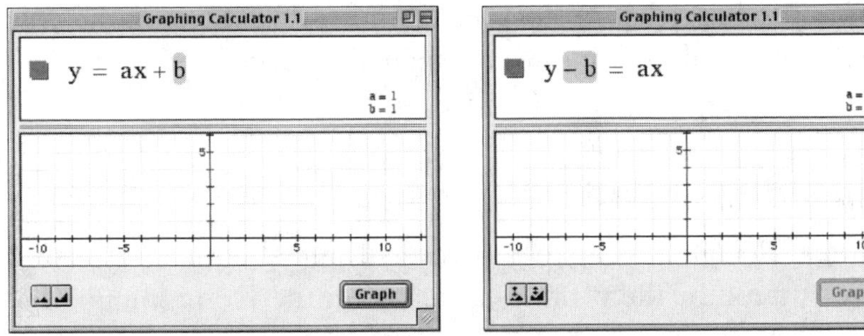

Figure 19.38 Let Graphing Calculator do more than just graphing. It can do algebra just by dragging terms around to rearrange equations.

Sort Lists

This last trick is a personal favorite: sort a long list. Often while using a computer you will work with lists of information, perhaps a long list of names of people you are inviting to a party or a list of items to pick up at a grocery store. The list might not even be something that you create yourself; perhaps it is something you have found on a Web page while surfing the Internet. But, for whatever reason, putting this list in some kind of order, probably alphabetically, would be useful. Rather than do this yourself, let your iMac do it.

This trick uses an AppleWorks database document as the mechanism for sorting; this trick is powerful because it is very easy to move and work with data in a database. Whatever data you choose to sort, it should be words or text of some kind and each item should be on its own line (or paragraph) in a document.

536

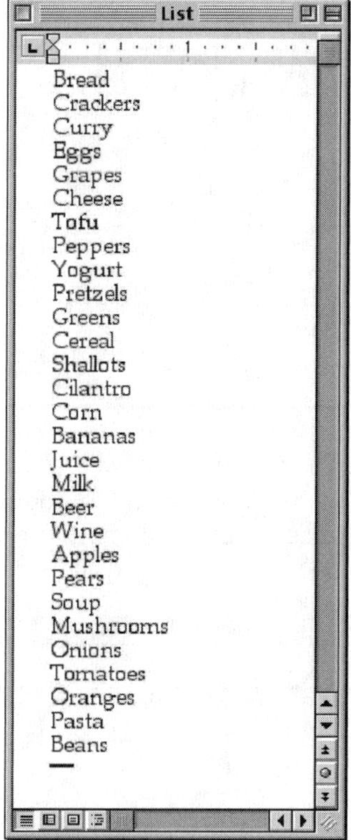

Figure 19.39 Here is an example list for sorting in a word processor.

The first step is to copy your list. Select it within whatever document it is in and use the Copy command in the Edit menu (or press ⌘-C).

Next, open AppleWorks and create a new database document.

When you create a new database document, you will be immediately asked what fields you would like each record to have. Because our list has just a single item per line, you will only need to create one field. You can give this field a name if you want (named "Item" here), or you don't have to name it. Click the Create button to add the field to the database and then click Done to finish creating the new document.

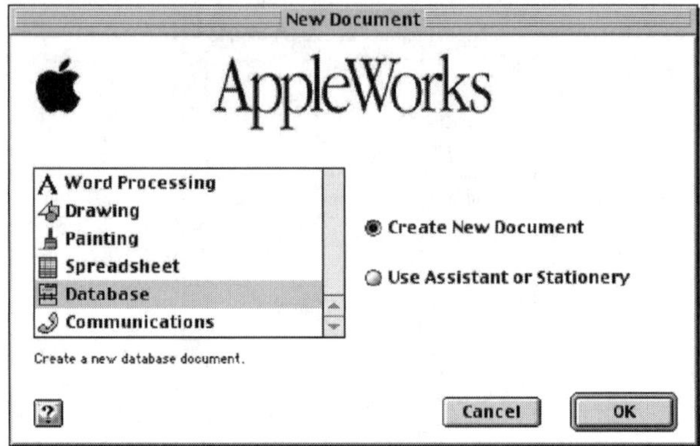

Figure 19.40 Let's create a new Database document in AppleWorks. Save yourself a second by double-clicking on the Database item in the list to quickly create a new document.

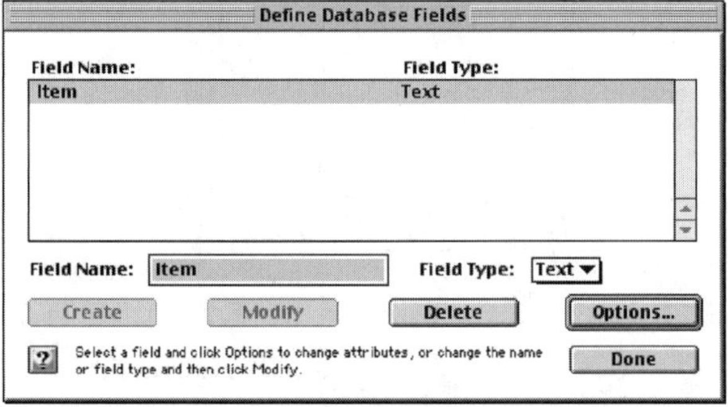

Figure 19.41 Every database document needs to have at least one field for data. Create one by giving it a name and clicking Create; then click Done.

After the document has been created, it will have one empty record and will be waiting for you to type text into the field you defined for the records of the document. Rather than type or paste into this field, instead select the whole record by clicking to the left of the field label. With the whole field selected, you can paste your list, automatically creating a new record for each item by choosing Paste from the Edit menu (or pressing ⌘-V).

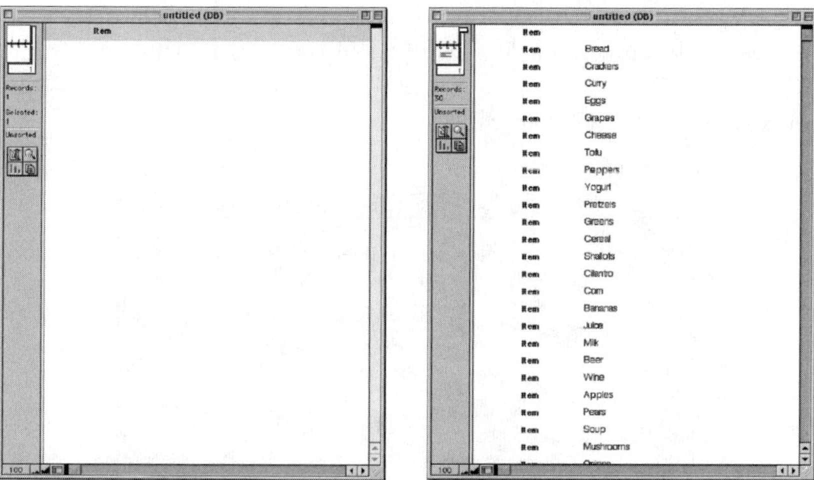

Figure 19.42 Select the whole first record by clicking on the label of the text field. Paste your list into the document, and AppleWorks will automatically create a record for each item.

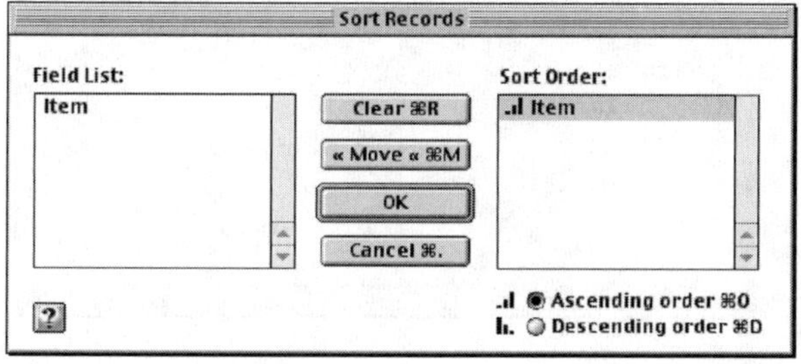

Figure 19.43 Sort the records in the database. Save yourself another bit of time by double-clicking on the field title in the Field List to move it to the Sort Order list. Click OK to run the sort.

You now have all your data in a database document where it can be sorted in a variety of ways. To sort your list, choose Sort records from the Organize menu (⌘-J). In the Sort Records dialog box that will be displayed, select the single field in this database document and then click the move button to add it to the Sort Order listing (or you can simply double-click on the field title to move it). When the field is added, it will be automatically set to sort in ascending order (A to Z); if you want to reverse the sort order (Z to A), you can choose descending at the bottom of the dialog window.

Click OK to sort your list.

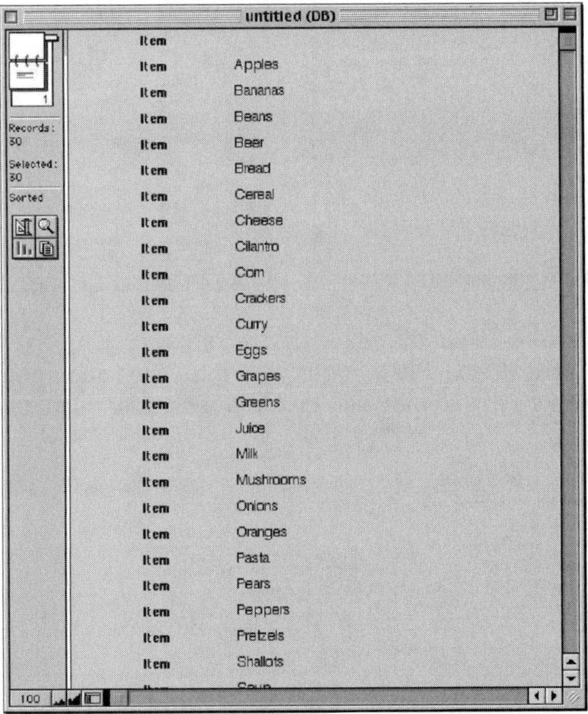

Figure 19.44 Your list is now sorted in this database. You can select all the records and copy them to move your data back to wherever it came from. You can also save this database document for later use.

Your list is now sorted! You can simply use it here in this AppleWorks database and save it for later use, or you can copy your list back to wherever it came from. To copy it, select all the records (⌘-A), copy (⌘-C), and go back to your original document (in this example back to the word processing document my list came from) and paste it.

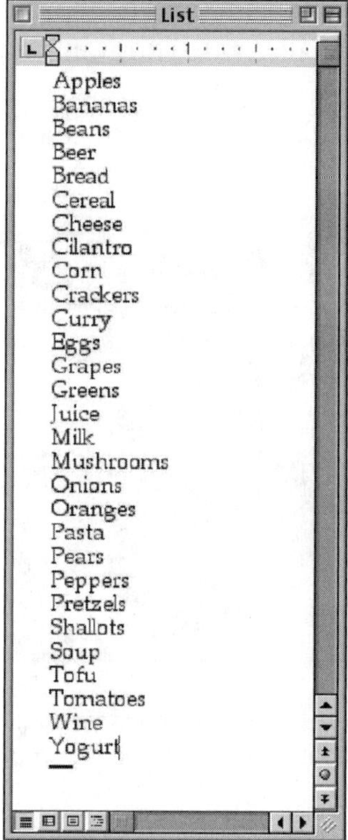

Figure 19.45 Here is the sorted list back in the word processing document from which it originally was copied. After a little practice, this whole process can be accomplished in just a few seconds.

The first time you do this it might take a bit of extra time for experimentation, but once you know how to use a database to sort a list, you will hopefully find that it can be done in just a few seconds.

Keeping a Database

Using a database to quickly sort a list is similar to using a spreadsheet to total a few numbers; there is, of course, much more that can be done with it. If you've never used a database before, you should consider giving it a try. By adding more fields when you create a database document, you can organize lists of data in much more robust ways. You can create fields for first and last names, street addresses, city, state, and zip codes, phone numbers, birthdays, as well as anything else that you want to associate together. Then with all this information you can run sorts, make lists, print labels, using all the standard tools of database software.

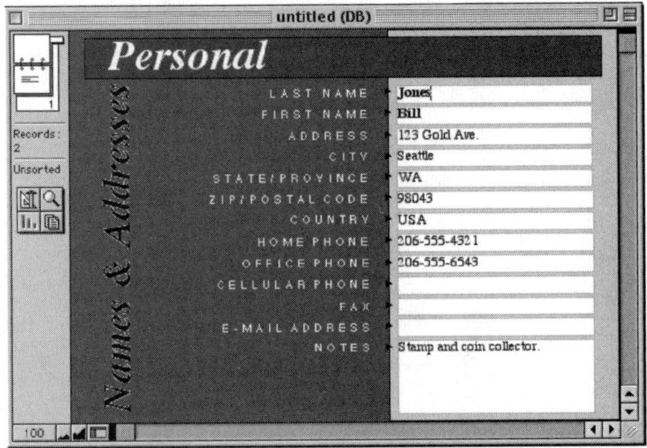

Figure 19.46 Use the assistants within AppleWorks to create a database for personal addresses from a predesigned template.

For more information on using AppleWorks databases, choose AppleWorks Help Contents from the Help menu while in AppleWorks and select topics for Database Basics.

Index

Index continued

Index continued

Index continued

Index continued

Index continued

Index continued

Index continued

Index continued

Index continued

Index continued

Index continued

Index continued

Z